GLOBALIZATION AND BUSINESS

GLOBALIZATION AND BUSINESS

JOHN D. DANIELS

University of Miami

LEE H. RADEBAUGH

Brigham Young University

DANIEL P. SULLIVAN

University of Delaware

Prentice
Hall

Upper Saddle River, New Jersey 07458

Library of Congress Cataloging-in-Publication Data

Daniels, John D.
  Globalization and business / John D. Daniels, Lee H. Radebaugh, Daniel P. Sullivan.—
1st ed.
    p. cm.
  Based on: International business. 9th ed. c2001.
  Includes bibliographical references and index.
  ISBN 0-13-062030-0
  1. International business enterprises.   2. International business
enterprises—Management.   3. Globalization.   I. Radebaugh, Lee H.   II. Sullivan,
Daniel P. III. Daniels, John D. International business.   IV. Title.

HD2755.5 .D346 2002
658. 1′8—dc21

2001036539

Editor-in-Chief: Jeff Shelstad
Executive Editor (Editorial):
  David Shafer
Senior Managing Editor: Jennifer Glennon
Assistant Editor: Melanie Olsen
Marketing Manager: Shannon Moore
Managing Editor (Production): Judy Leale
Production Editor: Keri Jean
Production Assistant: Dianne Falcone
Permissions Coordinator:
  Suzanne Grappi
Associate Director, Manufacturing:
  Vincent Scelta
Production Manager: Arnold Vila

Manaufacturing Buyer: Diane Peirano
Design Manager: Pat Smythe
Art Director: Janet Slowik
Interior Design: Amanda Kavanaugh
Cover Design: Janet Slowik
Cover Photo: Brian Stablyk/
  Tony Stone Images
Illustrator (Interior): ElectraGraphics
Manager, Print Production:
  Christy Mahon
Composition: Rainbow Graphics
Full-Service Project Management:
  Jimmy Sauls
Printer: Phoenix

Credits and acknowledgments borrowed from other sources and reproduced, with
permission, in this textbook appear on appropriate pages within text.

Pearson Education LTD.
Pearson Education Australia PTY, Limited
Pearson Education Singapore, Pte. Ltd
Pearson Education North Asia Ltd
Pearson Education Canada, Ltd.
Pearson Educación de Mexico, S.A. de C.V.
Pearson Education–Japan
Pearson Education Malaysia, Pte. Ltd

Prentice
Hall

10 9 8 7 6 5 4 3 2 1
ISBN 0-13-062030-0

Brief Contents

Contents

Preface

We began writing a survey international business text about thirty years ago, and that text has successfully reached its ninth edition. So, you may ask "Why have you now written a second survey text?" We have two reasons: (1) Student audiences have broadened, creating a need for a shorter text in addition to the traditional longer ones; and (2) Many universities now require that professors use different texts for undergraduate and graduate courses, creating a need for different approaches at the two levels. We'll now elaborate on these two points.

First, when we began writing some thirty years ago, most students taking a survey international business course were upper level undergraduates or MBA students. Although this is still true, student audiences have been expanding both downward and upward. On the downward side, more junior colleges and community colleges have been offering survey international business courses. Many of their students lack the business and economics backgrounds that we assume for students plowing through our ninth edition text of about 800 pages. Further, they frequently lack both the time and background to analyze the short cases we have included at the end of all twenty-one chapters. Clearly, they need a text that is broad enough to cover the issues, but short enough so that they can absorb all the concepts. On the upward side, more business schools have been offering international business or international management courses within executive MBA programs. Professors teaching these courses generally depend more on projects and applications of materials than on lectures and presenting new terms and concepts. They depend on such tools as long comprehensive cases, industry and company analyses, scenario developments, and comparison of countries for business expansion. Given the time demands of working on projects, particularly when students typically work full time, there is little chance for students to cover a long text. Further, executive MBA students find much of the material from longer texts is superfluous because they deal with the issues regularly. Yet, they need shorter readings to synthesize major concepts so that they have a common framework for more orderly class discussions. Fortunately, the same synthesized shorter text version seems to be ideal for both the bottom-end and top-end of course levels. Although this seems incongruous, we have found a similar relationship for texts in other business courses.

Second, universities are increasingly requiring the use of different texts at the undergraduate and graduate levels. The reasoning behind this requirement is understandable, particularly if a school admits most of its MBA students from its own undergraduate business program, because students may otherwise get credit for taking essentially the same course twice. But, many professors teach at both the undergraduate and MBA levels and prefer one set of authors' viewpoints and priority of coverage over others'. This creates a dilemma for them because they may have to use a text by an author whose viewpoints differ from their own. Thus, we have maintained the same viewpoints and essential coverage from our longer text in this shorter text. As a result, we believe that professors can satisfactorily use one of our texts at one level and the other at the other level. They can further differentiate the courses through projects and additional materials.

When we decided to write a shorter text, we were tempted simply to abridge what was in our longer text. That would certainly have saved time, but we feel strongly that a shorter text needs a fresh and very different approach. Although concepts and viewpoints remain essentially the same between the two texts, we have reorganized materials completely. We have gone from 21 to 14 chapters, and we have reduced the length of each chapter by about one-third. Rather than simply eliminating some chapters or combining some of them, we started with a **completely new outline.** In some cases, we have pulled materials from throughout the larger book and put them together in a new format. For example, we did this by pulling almost all strategy material together in Chapter 2 and by pulling issues together on ethical and socially responsible behavior in Chapter 13. Chapter 5, "Links Among Countries," includes discussion of the movement of goods, investment, technology, and people among countries, and Chapter 6, "Stakeholders: Their Concerns and Actions," explains both the issues and how stakeholders press their viewpoints. As far as we know, no other text pulls materials together in this manner. We also put elements of managing the value chain together in Chapters 7, 8, and 9—producing, selling, and collecting.

We have begun each chapter with a short vignette showing a company's situation concerning the issues raised within the chapter. We take the viewpoint throughout that business responds to globalization and further enhances it. We cover this particularly in Chapter 1. We also take both a micro and macro focus throughout, such as covering both business operations and the effects of international business on society. Further, we distinguish the roles of companies and individuals, from such viewpoints as stakeholders, ethics, and careers.

We looked for an attractive visual motif that would be analogous to *Globalization and Business* and one that would express our viewpoint. We decided to use masks. The use of masks is nearly universal (thus the concept of globalization), but every society uses different designs of masks. Likewise, every society conducts business, but how they do business differs because of their unique economic, political, legal, and cultural environments. Thus, both masks and business are more universal on the surface than they are when one examines them closely.

We would like to thank Melanie Hunter for her work on the manuscript.

Supplements to accompany the book:

- *Instructor's Manual and Test Item File.* The Instructor's Manual portion includes chapter objectives, detailed chapter outlines, and lecture support. The Test Item File includes True/False, Multiple Choice, and Essay questions. Together the questions cover the content of each chapter in a variety of ways providing flexibility in testing the students' knowledge of the text.

- *Instructor's Resource CD-ROM.* This Windows based CD-ROM contains the computerized Test Bank, PowerPoint slides, and Instructor's Manual. The PowerPoint transparencies, a comprehensive package of text outlines and figures corresponding to the text, are designed to aid the educator and supplement in-class lectures. Test Manager, containing all of the questions printed in the Test Item File, is a comprehensive suite of tools for testing and assessment. Test Manager allows educators to create and distribute tests for their courses easily, either by printing and distributing through traditional methods or by on-line delivery via a Local Area Network (LAN) server.

- *ON Location! Video.* A collection of end of part video segments is available to qualified adopters. These professionally produced segments feature companies like: *Teva, MTV Europe, Yahoo!* and several others.

- *MyPHLIP Web Site.* The new MyPHLIP provides professors with a customized course Web site including new communication tools, one-click navigation of chapter content, and great PHLIP resources such as Current Events and Internet Exercises.

- *PH Guide to e-Commerce and e-Business for Management.* Free with any PH text, this guide introduces students to many aspects of e-business and the Internet, providing tips on searching out information, looking for jobs, continuing education, and using the Internet in Management courses.

- *GLOBE (Global Landscape of the Business Environment)* By Charles Stanfield and Jerry Westby, this electronic atlas offers political and physical maps to improve students' geography skills. In addition, regional overviews and statistics combine to offer student exercises that illustrate the impact of cultural and economic geography on business decisions. Available at a deep discount when purchased with the text.

GLOBALIZATION AND BUSINESS

Objectives

1. To understand the meaning of globalization and why it has been accelerating

2. To grasp how globalization and business affect each other

3. To realize why countries gain advantages by trading with each other

4. To appreciate the challenges in the trade-offs of positive and negative effects of globalization

5. To discern why international business is different from domestic business

From Exotic to Commonplace *and* Improved

The poinsettia, first introduced into the United States from Mexico in 1828 by Ambassador Joel Poinsett, was once exotic and expensive outside tropical areas. But consumers worldwide now commonly buy potted poinsettias for as little as $2.50 per plant. They buy them mainly in December, when U.S. monthly sales reach about U.S. $300 million. The poinsettia's change from exotic to commonplace has occurred as companies engage in international business to take advantage of technological growth and reduced governmental restriction on the flow of products, technology, capital, and people from one country to another. Today, companies with horticultural research facilities such as Oglevee Ltd., Paul Ecke Ranch, Ball Horticultural (all headquartered in the United States), and Fisher (in Germany) develop new poinsettia breeds—for example, plants that produce flowers in shades of pink, cream, and white in addition to the common red ones. They cultivate small "mother plants," which they send to tropical countries (mainly Mexico and Guatemala), where the plants initially grow faster outdoors than in U.S. and German hothouses. The firms also save on labor costs in these locations. For example, Ball Horticultural sends mother plants to the Mexican flower rancher Floraplant, which grows them outdoors until they reach a critical size. Floraplant pays workers about one-tenth of what U.S. greenhouse employees earn to make small cuttings, quickly cool them, bag them in clear plastic, and surround them in dry ice. Fast and inexpensive transportation systems along with easy clearance at national borders allow the cuttings to arrive at Ball Horticultural's facilities in the United States, the Netherlands, and Canada within the 72 hours that the cuttings can live before U.S., Dutch, and Canadian workers plant them in synthetic rooting soil. (Paul Ecke Ranch relies on Mexican workers who commute daily—under a U.S.–Mexican immigration agreement—to its U.S. facilities near the Mexican border.) Ball Horticultural and Paul Ecke Ranch sell some of the recently planted cuttings to professional growers, whereas they raise others in greenhouses for three or four months before sending them to garden centers and home improvement stores.[1] Professional growers sell to a variety of distributors, such as to florists who fill wholesale and retail orders to mail-order, walk-in, and Internet customers.

The Growth of International Business and Globalization

chapter 1

Painted masks depict fanciful faces on a wooden doorway in Nepal.

Introduction

The poinsettia example illustrates a process that has occurred since the beginning of recorded history. As people have established contacts over a wider geographic area, they have expanded the variety of products available to them. They have altered how they want and expect to live, and they have become more affected (positively and negatively) by conditions outside their immediate domains. We use the term **globalization** to refer to the deepening relationships and broadening interdependence among people from different countries.

We often hear of the globalization of business because business both responds to and expedites globalization. For example, the U.S. poinsettia breeders responded to deepening relationships between Mexico and the United States—governmental agreements and more movement of people, capital, and information between the two countries—when they placed cost-saving operations in Mexico. They could move technologically altered poinsettias between the two countries because governmental agreements and better transportation permitted such movement. At the same time, growers in Mexico broadened their interdependence with companies in North America and Europe because they could unearth and exploit more distant sales and cost-saving opportunities.

Business also expedites globalization. For example, companies aggressively seek out foreign markets for their products and lower-cost locations abroad to produce them. Their competitors and suppliers follow them to these foreign markets and production locations. Further, companies create rippling effects by influencing foreign demand for other products. Companies producing in foreign countries, for instance, may enjoy cost or quality advantages over local companies in those countries. Those local companies may then emulate the production advantages, such as by buying from the same equipment suppliers. Also, when studios distribute movies and television shows abroad, they indirectly influence the sales of products used by the actors—such as jeans. **International business** refers to all business transactions—private and governmental—that involve two or more countries. Private companies undertake such transactions for profit; governments may or may not do the same in their transactions.

Two reasons for studying globalization and international business are:

1. The growth of globalization creates both opportunities and threats for individuals, companies, and countries.

2. The conduct of international business is distinct from that of domestic business because companies must operate in diverse foreign environments and because they must engage in specialized types of transactions, such as exporting and importing and the conversion of currencies.

Why Countries Need International Business

Consumers cannot buy foreign goods and services unless producers in their home country sell enough in foreign countries to pay for them. For example, if U.S. consumers want to buy French products, U.S. producers must earn enough French francs to pay French producers for them, because French producers must pay their employees and suppliers in French francs rather than in U.S. dollars. But why do consumers buy foreign goods and services rather than depending entirely on those that companies can produce within their own countries? There are three primary reasons: availability, cost, and comparative advantage.

Availability

Countries with large landmasses and/or large economies (such as the United States) are more apt to have a wider variety of capabilities within their borders than small countries (such as Belize). These capabilities normally result in a wider variety of domestically produced goods and services. But even large countries lack capabilities for everything. The most obvious example is minerals. The United States must import 100 percent of its supplies of columbium and manganese, which are both essential for the production of steel. It would be hard to imagine the United States doing without steel. Nor can it readily switch to substitutes; other minerals, such as bauxite for aluminum, must also come largely from abroad. And for such tropical agricultural products as coffee and bananas, the United States simply does not have sufficient land in the right climatic zones to satisfy its consumers' desires. Minerals and agricultural products are examples of **natural advantage**—the ability to produce because of readily available resources. But Figure 1.1 shows that agricultural products and mining products together comprise less than a quarter of world trade. Further, their share of world trade has been falling.[2]

Most merchandise trade today is in manufactured products. The initial ability to produce them is an **acquired advantage,** one that is based on research and development. Most new products originate and find their biggest markets in the wealthier countries, where there are more funds to spend in laboratory research and to buy the new products. For these same reasons, most of the leading countries for both exports and imports are the wealthier countries—the United States, Germany, Japan, France, the United Kingdom, and Italy.

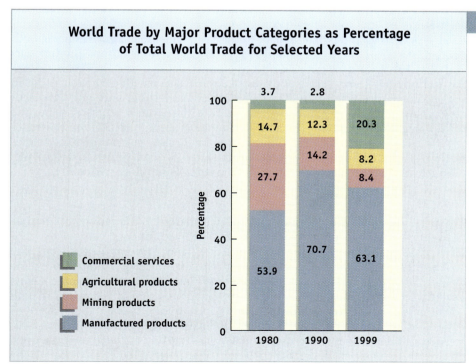

World Trade by Major Product Categories as Percentage of Total World Trade for Selected Years

- Commercial services
- Agricultural products
- Mining products
- Manufactured products

	1980	1990	1999
Commercial services	3.7	2.8	20.3
Agricultural products	14.7	12.3	8.2
Mining products	27.7	14.2	8.4
Manufactured products	53.9	70.7	63.1

Figure 1.1

Manufactured products continue to be the largest category of trade. However, commercial services are the fastest-growing category.

source: World Trade Organization, Annual Report, 2000 (Geneva: World Trade Organization, 2000).

However, invention may come from anywhere, and the country that ultimately accounts for the bulk of production and exports may be different from where the product originated. For example, two of the most significant new products of the 20th century were the birth control pill and the passenger jet aircraft. An Austrian working in Mexico invented the birth control pill, but a U.S. pharmaceutical company, Syntex, pioneered product development. And the U.K. company de Havilland was the first to produce and sell passenger jet aircraft; however, Boeing, a U.S. company, is now the largest producer.

The fastest-growth area in world trade has been in services, which grew from less than 4 percent to more than 20 percent of world trade between 1980 and 1999. This occurred as employment and economic output in the wealthier nations shifted from manufacturing to services. Manufacturing now accounts for less than 20 percent of the economies of the wealthier nations. The growth is due partially to new service products, such as new financial services and cellular communications. It is partially due to rising incomes that allow people to spend more on domestic and foreign services, such as on visits to tourist resorts. Finally, it is due to the globalization process, which causes companies to spend more on international transportation and communications as they move more goods over longer routes. This is especially important as companies save manufacturing costs by shifting more production to poorer countries with lower labor rates while simultaneously spending more on transportation because of greater distances to move output internationally to markets, and as their managers visit foreign facilities to buy, sell, and control operations.

A high and growing portion of both manufacturing and service exports consists of two-way trade in similar products.[3] For example, the United States is both a major exporter and a major importer of tourist services, vehicles, and passenger aircraft because different companies from different countries have developed product variations that appeal to different consumers. For instance, both Boeing from the United States and Airbus Industrie from Europe produce aircraft that will fly people from point A to point B, but U.S. and European airlines buy both Boeing's and Airbus Industrie's aircraft because their models differ in such features as capacity, flying range, fuel consumption, and perceived reliability. Without trade, some airlines in both the United States and Europe would have to forgo buying the aircraft they most want for particular routes. In fact, as people's incomes rise, they buy more and also seek out a greater variation in what they buy. This creates an incentive for companies to create new products and services, which they sell domestically and internationally.

Cost

The production of various goods and services requires different combinations of inputs, such as specialized labor skills, borrowed funds, machinery, equipment, electrical power, minerals, and suitable land. For complex reasons, the cost of these inputs varies from one country to another. For example, the costs of both labor and suitable land contribute to the growing of poinsettia plants used for cuttings in Mexico rather than in the United States. As producers and consumers, it is less important that we understand the reasons for cost differences than that we understand the consequences. Simply stated, input cost differences influence where products and services can be produced most cheaply. Of course, transportation costs must be added to production costs to determine the least-cost place to operate. As consumers, we naturally want the best possible prices, and we try to buy from producers that will get a product to us at the lowest cost. For example, we are likely to buy handmade (knotted) rugs from China, Iran, Pakistan, or Turkey because these countries have skilled workers who knot rugs cheaply. However, we probably buy machine-made rugs (which have slightly different characteristics than the handmade kind) from North America or Europe because producers there have better access to both mechanical rug-making technology and funds for buying expensive rug-making machinery. Further, they can more easily hire skilled workers who can install, work on, and service the machinery.

Governments also influence where products are produced. For economic or political reasons, they support the development, production, and export of certain products. For example, many countries subsidize certain agricultural products, such as sugar, to protect workers in their agricultural sectors. Naturally, consumers seek out products with lower prices, whether the price is due to input costs or to subsidies. Some countries also subsidize manufactured products, sometimes temporarily in their development and early sales stages. Some European governments, for instance, subsidized the development and early sales of Airbus Industrie's passenger aircraft to reduce dependence on a single supplier, Boeing from the United States. This assistance helped Airbus become globally competitive and, eventually, independent of the governmental aid.

Comparative Advantage

When an individual, firm, or country uses its resources to specialize in the production of those goods and services that are most productive and profitable, it is producing according to **comparative advantage.** This implies that the individual, firm, or country may forgo the production of other goods and services even though it is more efficient than others in their production as well. For example, central Florida in the United States can grow oranges at a low enough cost to compete effectively with foreign-grown oranges. Nevertheless, suitable orange grove acreage is rapidly being converted to other uses. One such conversion, Walt Disney Company's purchase of an area about the size of the city of San Francisco, serves to illustrate the comparative advantage concept. Rather than using the land to grow oranges, Disney makes more money by using the land for theme parks, hotels, and office complexes. With less land for growing oranges, the United States imports a growing portion of its orange and juice supplies from Brazil. At the same time, foreigners from all over the world, including Brazil, flock to Florida to visit the Disney attractions. In fact, they spend more than the value of the displaced orange production. To become self-sufficient in oranges, the United States might have to give up the income from foreigners who visit the Disney facilities, and Disney would have to settle for a less ideal location for its eastern theme park. Although the United States could be efficient in either orange production or theme park development, it is better off concentrating on the latter, where its advantage is greater—a so-called comparative advantage.

Another example is Switzerland's lack of a viable personal computer industry. Switzerland certainly has people with the education to successfully acquire and adapt foreign computer technologies for the development of its own industry. However, these people are currently employed in other industries, such as the manufacture of watches and scientific instruments. Thus, Switzerland would have to cut back its development and production operations in these other industries if it were to move into personal computer production.

Comparative advantage implies specialization. Through either planned or fortuitous circumstances, different industries develop more efficiently in some countries than others. This capability tends to perpetuate itself as suppliers and other institutions develop resources to serve those industries. For example, the aerospace industry emerged early on in the United States because the airplane was invented there, the government supported the industry through defense spending, and long distances among U.S. cities made air travel highly demanded. Thereafter, U.S. universities developed programs in aerospace engineering because they foresaw that aerospace companies would hire their graduates, and U.S. parts suppliers invested in research to serve the industry. We find similar examples for other industries in other countries, including French perfume, German printing presses, and Danish furniture. International specialization is akin in many ways to regional specialization within countries. For a variety of reasons, the U.S. automobile industry is heavily concentrated in the Midwest, the textile industry in the Southeast, and the filmmaking industry on the West Coast.

The Growth of Globalization

For most of recorded history, few people knew that certain areas of the world existed. Gradually, groups came into contact and benefited from each other's knowledge, mainly through short migrations from one generation to another. Major explorations, such as by Marco Polo and Christopher Columbus, led to European contacts with people in China and the Americas. Until people established such contact, however, they had no opportunity to gain from each other's discoveries and innovations. For example, humans' domestication of large mammals between 8000 and 2500 B.C. created huge economic advances. But the spread and use of these animals had to await group contact, such as the contact in the 16th century A.D. that brought European horses to the Great Plains and Patagonian Indians in the Americas.[4] It was not until the 17th century, with the European discovery of Australia, that virtually the whole world was known and ready for the contact we now call globalization. This does not imply that we have no more frontiers. Although we have mapped the world geographically, we have penetrated only a small part of its lands with Internet-connected computers, which should bring the world of business even closer together. Projections are that by 2005, less than 5 percent of the world's population will be online.[5] But online percentages are already much higher in the richer countries, and there is concern that we may see a growing "digital divide" between rich and poor countries.[6] Further, we can speculate about intergalactic business only after we map the galaxy and develop efficient means of traveling to it.

Companies' abilities to exchange goods and services internationally, shift their production to other countries, and learn from abroad about more efficient means of operating have been growing because of technological developments, rising incomes, liberalization of cross-border movements, and more cooperative arrangements among countries. Figure 1.2 shows these relationships. These four factors interplay and affect each other. Countries' levels of depen-

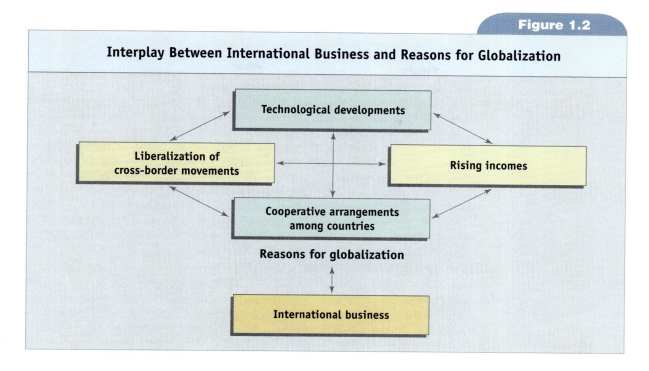

Figure 1.2

Interplay Between International Business and Reasons for Globalization

Technological developments

Liberalization of cross-border movements

Rising incomes

Cooperative arrangements among countries

Reasons for globalization

International business

dence on foreign sales and production have been increasing gradually.[7] But for many firms, each successive move in a geographic operating domain—from local to regional, from regional to national, and from national to international—has come faster than the preceding one.

Unfortunately, we do not have reliable and comparable figures on a long-term historical basis to compare countries' international economic dependence. As borders change, what was once an international transaction becomes a domestic one and vice versa. Further, countries keep records very differently, particularly those dealing with **foreign direct investment (FDI)**—investment that results in the foreign control of a domestic enterprise.[8] Nevertheless, recent figures on trade, FDI, and foreign exchange transactions indicate that the globalization of business has been substantial. (Foreign exchange trading is needed to acquire currencies to buy goods or services from abroad, such as a U.S. importer's exchange of U.S. dollars for Japanese yen to buy Japanese-made automobiles, or a U.S. tourist's purchase of French francs to pay expenses while in Paris. Currencies are also traded in order to make investments abroad.)

Procter & Gamble (P&G), the largest soap company in the United States, manufactures such brands as Camay, Cascade, Ivory, Mr. Clean, Spic & Span, Tide, and Zest. Its experience illustrates how the geographic spread in companies' operations has accelerated. P&G began producing and selling in 1837 in Cincinnati, where it had 16 competitors. Between 1850 and 1890, when U.S. railroad track mileage grew from 10,000 to 160,000, P&G extended its sales throughout the Midwest. By the 1920s, P&G had become a truly national company, having exploited the continued growth in transportation, the development of national radio advertising, and the opportunity to merge and acquire rival firms.

Although P&G expanded somewhat internationally in the 1930s, World War II and pursuant reconstruction interrupted the firm's international growth; consequently, P&G has expanded internationally mainly since the 1960s. P&G and its major rivals (Colgate-Palmolive from the United States, Henkel from Germany, and Unilever from the United Kingdom and the Netherlands) now sell, produce, and compete with each other all over the world.

P&G took more than a century to move gradually into global operations after sequential successes in local, regional, and national markets. But today, many small start-up companies are competing internationally from the outset. This is due partly to the presence of foreign competition within their domestic markets, and partly to their knowledge of and ability to take advantage of opportunities abroad. For example, II, a U.K. software designer, received some of its initial financing from Germany, Austria, and Japan, and its first customers were companies in the United States and Japan.[9] In another case, a U.S. entrepreneur successfully started TelePizza in Spain rather than in the United States because he anticipated a faster growth of pizza delivery in that country.[10]

Technological Developments

More than half the scientists who have ever lived are alive today—on the one hand, because of population growth, and on the other because economic and productivity growth have allowed a larger portion of the population to be involved in developing new products rather than in producing them. Further, as the base of technological development increases, there are more potential applications on which scientists can work, such as improving wheels for new models of automobiles, carts, tractors, airplanes, and earthmoving equipment, rather than just improving wheels per se.

Developments in communications and transportation are at the forefront of technologies that push globalization. Faster and less expensive communications permit information on new products, production capabilities, and the performance of companies' foreign operating facilities to be transmitted instantaneously, almost anywhere in the world, and at a low cost. In contrast, as recently as 1970, use of the fax, videoconferencing, and e-mail was not yet widespread. A telephone call between the United States and the United Kingdom required operator assistance; in many cities, people had to go personally to the telephone company to place a call. Successful connection was highly uncertain even after several hours of trying, and the cost per minute was 10 times that in 2000. Use of fiber-optic bandwidth promises to reduce the price of international communications even more.

Today, technological developments in transportation allow most products to reach almost anywhere at a reasonable cost before they become spoiled or obsolete. For example, this is the first generation in which masses of people in nontropical climates can purchase fresh flowers year-round. Dole Food ships flowers from Mexico, Colombia, and Ecuador so that they arrive in the United States within five hours of being picked. They are then cut, arranged, and put up for sale in supermarkets nationally as early as the next morning; further, these supermarkets can now keep flowers fresh because of innovations in walk-in coolers.[11] In contrast, the exchange of goods by caravan along the Silk Road between China and Europe, which for centuries accounted for an important share of international trade, could carry goods for only about 13 miles per day.

Rising Incomes

The above discussion shows that people and companies are constantly using technology to create, spread word about, and transport new products expeditiously. But these conditions are insufficient to create substantial international business opportunities. People must also have incomes high enough to allow them to buy. In this respect, global discretionary income has risen to the point that there is now widespread demand for products that would have been considered luxuries in the past. The *United Nations Human Development Report* estimates that 1998 global consumption was at twice the level of 1975 and six times that of 1950. However, the same report cautions that consumption is very uneven. For example, the richest 20 percent of the world's population accounts for about 86 percent of private consumption, such as approximately this share of cars purchased.[12]

As disposable incomes have grown, consumers have wanted more, new, better, and differentiated products, thus spurring companies to spend on research and development and to search worldwide—via the Internet, industry journals, trade fairs, and business travel—for innovations and differentiated products. As disposable incomes have grown, a greater variety of goods and services have come to compete with each other. Because of innovations in transportation, more countries compete with each other to supply this greater variety of goods and services.

As incomes grow, so does tax revenue. Much of the revenue goes to programs and projects that enhance the potential of international business. For example, expenditures to improve airport and seaport facilities and to build efficient highways that connect with those in neighboring countries create travel efficiencies that speed and reduce the cost of delivering goods internationally. Further, governments now provide an array of services that help their companies sell more abroad, such as information about foreign markets, contacts with potential buyers abroad, and insurance against nonpayment in the home country's currency.

Liberalization of Cross-Border Movements

Every country restricts the movement across its borders of goods and services as well as of the resources, such as workers and capital, to produce them. Such restrictions make international business cumbersome; further, because the restrictions may change at any time, the ability to sustain international business is always uncertain. However, governments today impose fewer restrictions on cross-border movements than they did a decade or two ago, allowing companies to better take advantage of international opportunities. Governments have decreased restrictions because they believe that (1) so-called *open economies* (having very few international restrictions) will give consumers better access to a greater variety of goods and services at lower prices, (2) producers will become more efficient by competing against foreign companies, and (3) if they reduce their own restrictions, other countries will do the same.

Nevertheless, not everyone is in favor of liberalizing cross-border movements. Many influential critics blame the globalization process for a variety of recent problems, such as the economic crises in Malaysia and Mexico, displaced employees in the United States, and a declining cultural identity in many countries. These same critics have called for more governmental restrictions on international trade and resource movements, and they may become successful in institutionalizing their views.[13] We summarize their views in the later section "Advantages and Challenges of Globalization."

Cooperation Among Countries

Countries cooperate with each other in thousands of ways through international organizations, treaties, and consultations. Such cooperation generally encourages the globalization of business by eliminating restrictions on it and by outlining frameworks that reduce uncertainties about what companies will and will not be allowed to do. Countries cooperate (1) to gain reciprocal advantages, (2) to attack problems they cannot solve alone, and (3) to deal with concerns that lie outside anyone's territory.

Agreements on a variety of commercially related activities, such as transportation and trade, allow nations to gain reciprocal advantages. For instance, groups of countries have agreed to allow foreign airlines to land in and fly over their territories, such as Canada's and Russia's agreements commencing in 2001 to allow polar overflights that will save five hours between New York and Hong Kong.[14] Groups of countries have also agreed to protect the property of foreign-owned companies and to permit foreign-made goods and services to enter their territories with fewer restrictions. In addition, countries cooperate on problems they cannot solve alone, such as by coordinating national economic programs (including interest rates) so that global economic conditions are minimally disrupted, and by restricting imports of certain products to protect endangered species. Finally, countries set agreements on how to commercially exploit areas outside any of their territories. These include outer space (such as on the transmission of television programs), noncoastal areas of oceans and seas (such as on exploitation of minerals), and Antarctica (limits on fishing within its coastal waters, for instance).

An Integrative Example: Cellular Phones

The globalization and interaction of technological developments, rising incomes, liberalization of cross-border movements, and cooperative arrangements all spur international business. Further, international business itself intensifies globalization. For example, Motorola's managers noted that more people needed to communicate while on the move. They developed the cellular phone at U.S. facilities because they had access to technological capabilities there and because they believed that high U.S. incomes would create the best early market for the phones. Thanks to international communications, people learned quickly about the new product worldwide. Because Motorola had already developed global sales and production networks, it quickly took its sales international—especially since governments placed few restrictions on cellular phone imports. (Today's cellular subscribers are almost evenly divided among the Americas, Europe, and Asia.) These sales pushed globalization further because many people without access to conventional telephones (due to the lack of telephone lines) could now communicate via cellular phones. At the same time, news about cellular technology and market growth spread quickly to other companies. The Finnish company Nokia decided in 1992 to develop its own cellular phone. It embraced a newer technology, digital rather than analog, which European governments accepted as a standard—called the

GSM standard. Many countries outside Europe rapidly embraced this standard as well; thus, Nokia reduced its costs per unit because it could sell enough phones to gain global market leadership.[15] The next generation of cellular phones will likely move huge amounts of data very rapidly internationally, thus contributing to even more globalization.

Advantages and Challenges of Globalization

As goods, services, people, and information flow more easily across national borders, events in one country often have effects in other countries as well. This can be either good or bad, depending on what conditions flow into the recipient country and what happens as a result in the outflow country. (Figure 1.3 illustrates this humorously.) As the largest economy in the world, the United States has a profound impact on other nations. It is often said, "When the United States sneezes, the rest of the world catches a cold." Likewise, the United States and companies headquartered therein are vulnerable to events elsewhere. For example, a monetary crisis in Russia caused U.S. stock market prices to fall, and an Asian economic downturn caused Hilton's earnings to fall because fewer Asians visited its U.S. hotels.[16]

Countries face challenges as they try to maximize positive effects from globalization while minimizing negative ones. There are usually trade-offs, such as low consumer prices versus minimal employment disruption. For example, the removal of import restrictions may lower prices while simultaneously causing the layoff of some workers. The possible trade-offs from globalization are almost unlimited; nevertheless, a few examples related to specific societal objectives should illustrate the complexities.

Eugene, who delivers bananas for a large produce company, couldn't sleep at night. He understood why the Europeans, seeking unified financial stability, had gone to the euro. But he also knew that if it disrupted any of the fragile global economies, he could take a big hit on his 401(k).

Figure 1.3

Productivity

Productivity refers to the amount of output relative to the amount of input—how much steel a worker produces per day, for instance; how much wheat a given amount of land yields; or how many shirts a machine (given amount of capital) will produce. Productivity gains usually go to a combination of higher wages for workers, lower prices to consumers, more taxes to government, and increased earnings for shareholders. The combination depends on the countervailing powers of each.

Globalization allows the benefits of productivity developments in one nation to move more quickly to other nations through the transfer of machinery, know-how, and cheaper products. A downside to this transfer is that individuals and companies must adjust to compete. Further, if globalization quickly results in foreign rather than domestic production, domestic workers may not fully see the benefits. For example, U.S. companies have traditionally excelled in developing new technologies that have led to higher U.S. productivity and premium wages for U.S. workers. But as U.S. companies have transferred their technologies abroad faster, they have shortened the amount of time they spend producing in the United States with their U.S.-developed efficiencies. In fact, some companies now transfer new technologies abroad without ever using them at home because they expect cost savings in labor, transportation, land, or taxes; therefore, the U.S. workers may gain less in premium wages than if globalization had occurred more slowly.

Consumers

Consumers benefit from globalization through their ability to choose from a greater variety of products and services—ranging from U.S. imports of automobiles to bottled water—and to buy from cheaper production locations. However, a potential problem for consumers is their weaker control over supplies from foreign countries. Supplies may be erratic for political, economic, or competitive reasons. For example, international limits on exports to Iraq under the Hussein government have created economic hardships for Iraqi consumers. And major oil-exporting countries' limitations on foreign petroleum sales in 1999–2000 resulted almost immediately in substantially increased prices in oil-importing countries. Finally, when Hitachi, the only producer of a key computer chip, sought to bolster its competitive position with major Japanese customers by giving them first access to these scarce chips, Cray Research, the leading U.S. supercomputer producer, could not get enough supplies of them. In any of these circumstances, the foreign customers might have been better off if they had had domestic suppliers. However, countries' attempts to maximize their self-sufficiency have usually resulted in long-term deprivation for their consumers. This occurred for many years after World War II in Albania and is presently occurring in Bhutan.

Employment

Globalization can increase or disrupt employment. Employment may increase because of economic growth as well as the need for specialized international services, such as people to handle documentation of shipments, currency trading, and translation of business communications. Employment may also increase for companies that otherwise could not sell their full capacity within their domestic markets. For example, Boeing's capacity for making passenger aircraft is much larger than the market for passenger aircraft within the United States. Even companies producing abroad to tap foreign markets must usually hire more people at headquarters to oversee the foreign operations. Further, the foreign-owned facilities usually buy components, services, and some products from the headquarters country, thus creating employment for the suppliers.

However, critics of globalization believe that the quality as well as the quantity of jobs should both be considered. They argue that globalization replaces well-paid jobs that enjoy safe working conditions in richer countries with low-paid jobs under adverse working conditions in poorer countries. Advocates of globalization, on the other hand, look to the aggregate change in jobs in both richer and poorer countries, claiming that in aggregate, better jobs are being created in the richer countries, and that workers in poorer countries may otherwise have no jobs at all.

Domestic employment may fluctuate because of volatile foreign economic and political situations that disrupt sales. For example, in the late 1990s, many Asian countries experienced severe economic difficulties, so much so that the loss of export sales to them affected economies in Europe and North America. The effects of political events on employment may be felt even more quickly. For example, the cessation of trade with Iraq after its invasion of Kuwait led to immediate lost markets for exporters to Iraq, including an aggregate loss of over $1 billion a year for U.S. exporters.

The Environment

As economies grow and consumers buy more—positive results of globalization—consumers use more of the earth's resources. Many of these resources are in the poorest areas of the world—such as petroleum in the Niger River delta of Nigeria and rain forests in the Brazilian Amazon—where people can greatly benefit economically from exploiting the resources. On the one hand, many people are concerned about depletion of finite natural resources and about potential climatic changes that could occur following destruction of rain forests. On the other hand, much of the technology that spreads globally is resource-saving technology, such as more efficient gasoline engines, recycling processes, and stronger alloys that use less metal.

Groups throughout the world are becoming more concerned about despoliation of the environment, but countries have been taking diverse approaches to environmental problems. Their actions affect other countries. For example, some countries require their companies to spend heavily on environmentally friendly production methods. Often, these changes result in higher production costs than those incurred by using older, less friendly methods. Yet many other nations, particularly poor ones, have very lax standards, and their

Globalization sometimes results in a mix of traditional and state-of-the-art technologies that bring new or improved products to consumers in remote areas. The photo shows a traveling medical clinic in Somalia that uses a solar energy generator atop a camel's back to refrigerate vaccines.

companies have insufficient funds to change their output processes. With open economies, countries with lax standards may offer enough cost advantages to displace production and workers from nations with more stringent production requirements. Further, some of the adverse environmental effects of their actions—such as depletion of tropical rain forests or dumping of toxic wastes into waterways—may spill over to countries with stringent environmental controls. On the one hand, companies based in countries with stricter requirements may shift production abroad to escape the costly home-country regulations. On the other hand, if they comply with home-country production regulations, they may gain long-term operating advantages by being at the forefront of developing low-cost and environmentally friendly production methods.

Monetary and Fiscal Conditions

An advantage of globalization is that money, if allowed to move freely, should go where it will be most needed and have the highest productivity. However, all countries try to control their money supplies and set taxes to promote various economic objectives, such as price stability, employment, growth, and governmental programs. Maintaining such control has become increasingly more difficult for countries acting alone as capital has become freer to move from one country to another and as companies seek operating locations that will reduce their tax liabilities. The result has been growing cooperation among the richer countries, particularly in coordinating their monetary policies. Monetary, fiscal, and regulatory differences remain, though. For example, the thriving banking operations in the Bahamas, Cayman Islands, and Vanuatu largely result from their secrecy laws and tax regulations. Preferential tax rates have also led many firms to set up insurance operations in Bermuda and shipping headquarters in Liberia. More rapid communications, particularly through the Internet, are increasing firms' abilities to do business from low-tax countries.

Sovereignty

Different nations exist because their people see themselves as different from people elsewhere. In other words, people share essential attributes (such as language, religion, values, and attitudes) with their fellow citizens. These attributes are perpetuated by rites and symbols of nationhood—flags, parades, rallies—and a subjective common perception and maintenance of national history through the preservation of historical sites, documents, monuments, and museums. These shared attributes do not mean that all of a country's citizens are alike. Neither do they suggest that each country is unique in all respects. However, the nation is legitimized by being the mediator of the different interests that lie within its borders.

Globalization may undermine sovereignty in two ways. First, contact with other countries creates more cultural borrowing. Languages add words from other languages, people embrace religions from other countries, and consumers buy foreign products rather than traditional ones. Because of the dominance of the U.S. economy and U.S. companies' operations worldwide, critics of globalization have been particularly concerned about what is sometimes called the "Coca-Colanization" of the world. This has led, for example, to many countries' attempts to prevent foreign inroads into key national areas. Canada, for one, is concerned that U.S. culture will displace Canadian. After all, Canada has only about 10 percent as many people as the United States, and about 90 percent of its population lives within 100 miles of the U.S. border. To help protect its culture, Canada requires that a share of all songs played on radio and television be Canadian, meaning that they must satisfy two of the following conditions: be performed by a Canadian, be written (music or words) by a Canadian, or be performed in Canada.[17] Despite such controls, it is doubtful that a high-income country like Canada can curtail the cultural contact and change resulting from new and better communications and transportation. For example, as of 2000, more than 40 percent of Canada's population had Internet access at home. However, in a poor country like India, where only about 1 percent of homes have Internet access, the government may have more time before cultural inroads decrease the separateness that strengthens sovereignty.[18]

Second, countries are concerned that important decisions may be made abroad that will undermine their national well-being. For this reason, the United States limits foreign ownership in critical defense industries, and Chile limits foreign ownership in its copper industry.

What Makes International Business Different?

International business differs from domestic business by degrees. Although laws, cultures, and economic conditions differ *within* countries, such differences are usually less marked than those *among* countries. Although there are limitations on the movement of goods and services and the resources to produce them within countries, these limitations are usually less pronounced within than among countries. Figure 1.4 illustrates environmental and mobility differences.

Different National Environments

Most countries vary internally, causing companies to alter their business practices from one region to another. Take the United States, where taxes and legal requirements differ among states and municipalities. This is why so many companies place their headquarters in business-friendly Delaware. Certain products also enjoy greater acceptance in some areas than in others, as seen in the higher per capita demand for bottled water in California than in the Midwest. Some tastes differ regionally as well. For instance, people in parts of the Midwest prefer whiter-looking dressed chickens to the yellow-looking ones that people prefer elsewhere. In some areas of the United States, there are non–English-language radio and television programs. Finally, income levels vary, so that purchasing power is higher in some areas than in others.

But some countries have much greater internal variation than do others. Geographic and economic barriers in some countries can inhibit people's movements from one region to another, thus limiting their personal interactions. Decentralized laws and government programs may increase regional separation. Linguistic, religious, and ethnic differences within a country usually preclude the fusing of the population into a homogeneous state, which means that business cannot be conducted in the same way throughout the country. For example, for all the reasons just given, India is a much more diverse country to do business in than is Denmark.

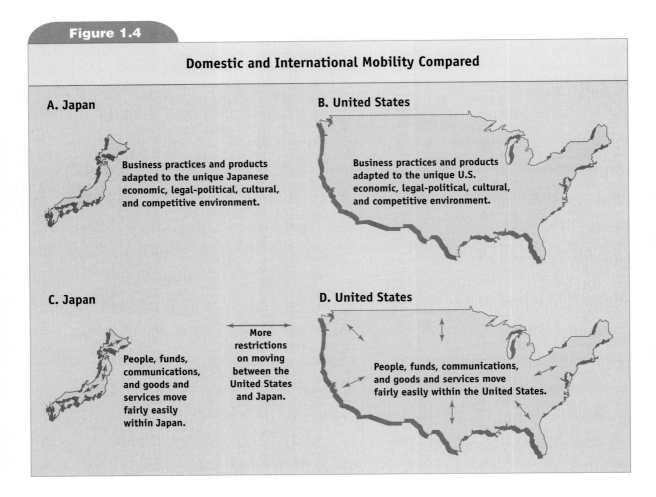

Figure 1.4

Domestic and International Mobility Compared

A. Japan

Business practices and products adapted to the unique Japanese economic, legal-political, cultural, and competitive environment.

B. United States

Business practices and products adapted to the unique U.S. economic, legal-political, cultural, and competitive environment.

C. Japan

People, funds, communications, and goods and services move fairly easily within Japan.

More restrictions on moving between the United States and Japan.

D. United States

People, funds, communications, and goods and services move fairly easily within the United States.

Despite all the differences among regions within countries, this diversity is small when compared to the differences among countries. To conduct business successfully abroad, companies must often adopt practices other than what they are accustomed to domestically. Legal-political, economic, and cultural environmental differences all may necessitate a company's altering every type of business activity, from production and accounting to finance and marketing.

Legal-Political Environment

Despite some differences in regional or municipal laws within a country, overriding national laws link a whole country together. Yes, different countries adhere to various treaties; still, every country in the world is a sovereign entity with its own laws and political systems. These laws dictate what businesses can exist, how they can be organized, their tax liabilities, the minimum wages they must pay to employees, how much they may cooperate with competitors, and how they price their goods and services.

Companies that do business internationally are subject to the laws of each country in which they operate. When laws differ greatly from those at home, a firm may encounter substantial foreign operating problems. For example, Blockbuster Video closed down its German operations because of the strict laws prohibiting retail establishments from being open Saturday afternoons, Sundays, and evenings. These limitations reduced Blockbuster's ability to generate sufficient revenue through impulse rentals from people who do not plan well ahead to view a videotape.[19]

Political relationships between countries also influence what companies can do internationally. For example, China forced Coca-Cola to drop a multi-million-dollar advertising campaign because the ads used the voice of a Taiwanese singer who publicly supports Taiwanese independence.[20]

In some areas of the world, most laws are codified. In others, such as the United Kingdom, there is a common law heritage in which precedents set the rules. In still other countries, like Saudi Arabia, a state religion dictates what is legal. Political systems range across a spectrum from dictatorships to democracies, and democracies vary substantially. For instance, Switzerland and the United States are both frequently held to be models of democracy. In the former, however, the general population votes on most legislation, whereas in the latter, representatives enact legislation. In terms of business operations, companies wishing to have specific legislation enacted may thus lobby public officials in the United States but must influence general public opinion in Switzerland.

Economic Environment

People in rich countries, such as the United States, Canada, and Sweden, earn on average about 100 times more than those in such poor countries as Burkina Faso, Bangladesh, and the Democratic Republic of the Congo. In fact, the average income in most of the world's countries is very low. A number of conditions correlate substantially with countries' economic levels, even though some countries are exceptions.

Generally, poor countries have smaller markets on a per capita basis, less educated populations, higher unemployment or underemployment, poor health conditions, greater supply problems, higher political risk, and more foreign exchange problems. We shall offer just a few examples of how these conditions affect international business.

In terms of market size on a per capita basis, the United States has almost 100 times as many cars as does India, despite India's much larger population. Where much of a nation's population is uneducated (for example, in Bhutan, Chad, and Ethiopia, less than 25 percent of children between the ages of 6 and 17 are enrolled in school), companies often have to respond by providing workers with additional training, using more supervisors, depending more on the transfer of management personnel from abroad, and simplifying work-related duties. They may also have to alter and simplify instructions for the use of products, and they may have very little market for certain types of products, such as books and magazines. Whereas the life expectancy in the richer countries is more than 70 years, that in poorer countries is less than 50 years. Among the reasons for the difference are inadequate access to food, nutritional education, and medical care. The situation in poor countries affects companies' productivity through employee work absences and lack of stamina on the job. Inadequate infrastructure (such as roads, ports, electrical power, and communications facilities) in poor countries causes supply problems. The problems occur because countries sell too little abroad to earn enough to buy all the needed machinery and replacement parts abroad. In turn, companies therein incur added production costs because of production downtime and the longer time required to transport their supplies and finished goods. Because of poverty in poorer countries, there is a greater incidence of civil disorder and a greater tendency for governments to treat foreign firms as scapegoats for the economic ills their citizens face. Finally, poorer countries are more apt than richer countries to depend on primary goods, such as raw materials and agricultural products, to earn income abroad. The prices of these primary products have not risen as rapidly as have prices of services and manufactured products. Further, the prices tend to fluctuate greatly from one year to another because of climatic conditions and business cycles. Exporters to these economies thus face variations from year to year in their ability to sell and receive payment for goods and services.

The Cultural Environment
Culture refers to the specific learned norms of a society based on attitudes, values, beliefs, and frameworks for processing information and tasks. These norms vary from one country to another, and they are reflected in attitudes toward certain products, advertising, work, and relationships among the people of a given society. For example, different countries have different norms regarding the extent of worker participation and decision making within their organizations. Cultural differences are also reflected in the acceptance of certain products. Pork products, for instance, have almost no acceptance in predominantly Muslim societies, nor do meats of any kind in predominantly Hindu societies. Cold cereals are extremely popular in Ireland, but not in Spain.

Mobility

Impediments to the movement of goods and the inputs to produce them are more pronounced among countries than within them. This does not imply that there are no impediments to the movement of some goods and inputs from one area of a country to another. In the United States, for example, some products (such as alcohol and cigarettes) cannot easily pass from state to state because of laws that protect collection of state taxes. Some people are reluctant to move to another state because of having to leave close families and friends or having to be relicensed for certain professions, such as teaching school or practicing law. Still, these impediments are minor compared to international movements.

Countries place substantial restrictions on the international movement of goods. For example, countries trade more than 13,000 different products internationally, and each of them is subject to import restrictions and customs surveillance somewhere. Many products are also subject to export surveillance and restrictions. Many countries also place restrictions on the outflow of funds—unlike the free flow of funds from one region to another within a country. Even when funds can flow from one country to another without restrictions, they almost invariably must be converted at a cost from one country's currency to another. Moreover, the rate at which funds can be converted varies constantly. Companies thus face an element of uncertainty in terms of how much of their own currency they will receive or have to pay in an international transaction. Finally, immigration laws prevent the free movement of people from one country to another, even though job opportunities vary substantially among countries.

Scheme of This Book

Figure 1.5 illustrates the flow of material in this book. You can see that business takes place within a widening process of globalization, which we have just described. You can also note that there are five interconnected areas that we shall discuss in the remaining five sections, comprised of 13 chapters. At the top center is objectives and means of operating internationally; Chapter 2 will emphasize companies' development of international strategies; Chapter 3 will explain the forms of international business operations and the advantages and disadvantages of each. Moving down to the next level and starting on the left, the figure represents Part 3, consisting of Chapters 4, 5, and 6. In these

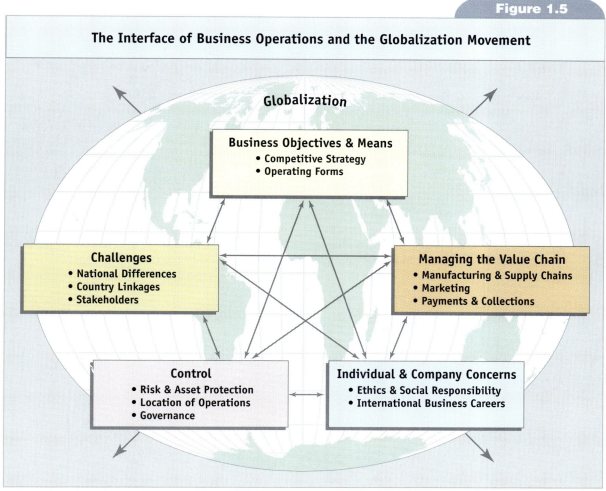

Figure 1.5

The Interface of Business Operations and the Globalization Movement

Globalization

Business Objectives & Means
- Competitive Strategy
- Operating Forms

Challenges
- National Differences
- Country Linkages
- Stakeholders

Managing the Value Chain
- Manufacturing & Supply Chains
- Marketing
- Payments & Collections

Control
- Risk & Asset Protection
- Location of Operations
- Governance

Individual & Company Concerns
- Ethics & Social Responsibility
- International Business Careers

Business throughout the world responds to globalization and intensifies its effects. The arrows flowing outward from the perimeter of the globe show that globalization steadily increases. As entrepreneurs and companies try to prosper within a globalizing environment, they deal with five interdependent areas. These areas, represented by the five interconnected boxes within the circle, define the five principal sections of this text.

chapters, we shall examine challenges to companies' successful operations within the global environment, expanding upon subjects introduced in this introduction—national differences affecting international business, linkages among countries, and the effects of different stakeholder interests on the conduct of international operations. Moving to the right, Part 4 (Chapters 7, 8, and 9) describes the management of companies' international value chain—their strategies for producing, selling, and collecting in international business. Part 5 on the bottom left has three chapters—10, 11, and 12—which deal with aspects of international business control: risk assessment and protection, choosing where to operate, and governing international operations. On the bottom right, Part 6 concludes the book with two chapters—13 and 14—about individual and company concerns: the choice of ethical and socially responsible behavior and careers in international business.

Summary

Globalization—the deepening relationships and broadening interdependence among people from different countries—has accelerated because of technology, rising incomes, and reduced governmental barriers to the movement of trade and production resources. Governments have reduced barriers primarily because consumers want access to a greater variety of products at lower cost. But not everyone benefits from globalization. Thus, countries face challenges as they try to maximize the positive effects of globalization on productivity, consumption, employment, the environment, monetary and fiscal conditions, and sovereignty while minimizing negative effects.

Business responds to and expedites globalization. As companies move internationally, they sometimes face operating environments—legal-political, economic, and cultural—very different from those at home. They also face international impediments to the movement of goods and inputs to produce that are more pronounced than those in their home markets.

endnotes

[1] Joel Millman, "For Poinsettias, Growers Go South of the Border," *Wall Street Journal,* December 17, 1998, p. B1; and Cynthia Crossen, "Holiday's Ubiquitous Houseplant," *Wall Street Journal,* December 19, 2000, p. B1+.

[2] *World Trade Organization Annual Report,* 1997 (Geneva: World Trade Organization, 1997).

[3] These are called Schumpeter goods or S goods. See H. Peter Gray, "Free International Economic Policy in a World of Schumpeter Goods," *International Trade Journal,* Vol. XII, No. 3, 1998, pp. 323–344.

[4] Jared Diamond, "Zebras and the Anna Karenina Principle," *Natural History,* Vol. 103, No. 9, September 1994, pp. 4–10.

[5] Paul Taylor, "How the Internet Will Reshape Worldwide Business," *Financial Times,* April 7, 1999, Information Technology section, p. 1.

[6] Nicholas Timmins, "'Digital Divide' Growing Between Rich and Poor," *Financial Times,* December 20, 2000, p. 8.

[7] Robert A. Lipsey, "Galloping, Creeping, or Receding Internationalization," *The International Trade Journal,* Vol. XII, No. 2, summer 1998, pp. 181–191.

[8] Christian Bellak,"The Measurement of Foreign Direct Investment: A Critical Review," *Foreign Trade Review,* Vol. XII, No. 2, summer 1998, pp. 227–257.

[9] Benjamin M. Oviatt and Patricia Phillips McDougall, "Global Start-Ups: Entrepreneurs in a Worldwide Stage," *Academy of Management Executive,* Vol. 9, No. 2, 1995, pp. 30–44.

[10] Ibid.

[11] Stacy Kravetz, "King of Pineapples Tiptoes to Tulips for Faster Growth," *Wall Street Journal,* July 6, 1998, p. A17+; and Larry Rohter, "Foreign Presence in Colombia's Flower Gardens," *New York Times,* May 8, 1999, p. 1+.

[12] Laura Silber, "UN Report Finds a Richer World with a Lot of Poorer People," *Financial Times,* September 10, 1998, p. 5, referring to the United Nations ninth annual *Human Development Report.*

[13] See, for example, Richard N. Haass and Robert E. Litan, "Globalization and Its Discontents," *Foreign Affairs,* Vol. 77, No. 3, May–June 1998, pp. 2–6; and Jean-Pierre Lehmann, "Who Writes Today's Economic Scripts?" *Financial Times,* March 27, 1998, Mastering Global Business section, pp. 2–4.

[14] Joel Baglole, "Pole Vault: Here Come Shorter Flights to Asia," *Wall Street Journal,* June 8, 2000, p. A19+.

[15] Steven V. Brull, Neil Gross, and Catherine Yang, "Cell Phones: Europe Made the Right Call," *Business Week,* September 7, 1998, pp. 107–110.

[16] Richard Tomkins, "Deere and Hilton Profits Hit as Global Crisis Bites," *Financial Times,* September 15, 1998, p. 21.

[17] Roger Ricklefs, "Canada Fights to Fend Off American Tastes and Tunes," *Wall Street Journal,* September 24, 1998, p. B1.

[18] Nua Internet Surveys, March 2000.

[19] Cacilie Rohwedder, "Blockbuster Hits Eject Button as Stores in Germany See Video-Rental Sales Sag," *Wall Street Journal,* January 16, 1998, p. B9A.

[20] James Kynge and Mure Dickie, "Coca-Cola Ad Touches Raw Nerve in China," *Financial Times,* May 25, 2000, p. 14.

Objectives

1. To understand the meaning of business strategy, especially in an international context

2. To appreciate that well-conceived strategies improve performance

3. To grasp the advantages of international operations that motivate managers to undertake them

4. To discern the advantages of entering international markets via acquisitions versus new venturing

5. To realize how multidomestic, global, and transnational strategies help companies fulfill international objectives

Vision to Reality: Gaining Domestic and International Synergy

Early in McDonald's history, the company stated that its vision "is to be the world's best quick service restaurant experience."[1] If "best" equates with market success, McDonald's vision has materialized. By 2001, the company had about 29,000 restaurants in 120 countries, which made it the largest and best-known food-service retailer in the world. To achieve this growth, McDonald's identified and developed competencies that would be difficult for competitors to emulate, such as brand recognition, signature products (including the Big Mac and Egg McMuffin), value for a low price, and uniformity of product and quality. To help bring about this combination of competencies, McDonald's advertised heavily and opened a high density of restaurants where it advertised. The firm needed a high density of restaurants so that people could obtain what it advertised and so that it could spread the cost of building recognition among many restaurants and customers—thus contributing to a low unit price per meal. Further, McDonald's has set specific objectives and plans that include the development of personnel, innovation (in menu, facilities, marketing, operations, and technology), and managers' openness to share information with each other about the best practices from anywhere in the world.

As its number of domestic restaurants increased, McDonald's became concerned that its outlets were beginning to compete more with each other. (McDonald's has about one restaurant per 21,000 people in the United States.) As a result, in recent years, the company has expanded more rapidly abroad than domestically, has achieved 16 consecutive years of solid international growth, and now depends on its international division for about 55 percent of corporate profits. McDonald's uses the same combination of competencies abroad that it uses for domestic success. For example, it is making its brand name known, actively establishing franchises, and promoting value for price everywhere it operates. However, McDonald's alters its ways of doing business to fit country-specific differences, such as adapting its menus to different countries. In Korea, it sells pork on a bun with a garlicky soy sauce because Koreans are accustomed to the flavor; in India, it sells Vegetable Nuggets because the predominantly Hindu population will not eat meat; and in Indonesia, it has added rice to the menu because of taste preferences and because potatoes (to make fries) are very expensive.

Choosing an International
Competitive Strategy
chapter 2

A Bali mask from Idonesia.

Introduction

As seen in the preceding example, McDonald's has developed and implemented a strategy that includes international sales growth. As companies develop and implement international strategies, countries gain the advantages from international business that we discussed in Chapter 1. But international business will begin only if companies' managers perceive opportunities by engaging in the business. Because companies have limited resources, managers must decide whether to exploit those resources domestically or internationally. Only if they perceive that the international opportunities might be greater than the domestic ones will they divert their resources to sell or produce abroad. Therefore, this chapter focuses on managers' quests to improve their companies' performance by engaging in international business—whether these managers work for large global companies or are entrepreneurial exporters. Figure 2.1 shows how companies' competitive strategies fit within the context of globalization. It also shows that managers

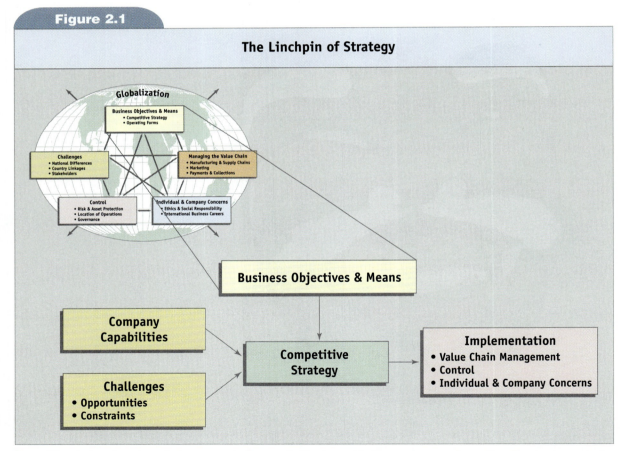

Competitive strategy is an important component of companies' business objectives and means of operating. The development of the strategy takes place within an increasingly globalized economy. In setting its strategy, managers should consider company capabilities and challenges facing them. Once they have set a strategy, they must implement it by managing the value chain, controlling operations, and considering individual and company concerns.

should set strategies based on their companies' capabilities—along with global challenges that include both opportunities and constraints.

Opportunities may include sales to untapped markets or lower production costs. Constraints include competition, national operating environments—legal-political, economic, and cultural—and restrictions to moving goods, services, and assets among countries. Finally, Figure 2.1 also shows that once managers develop a competitive strategy, they must make tactical decisions to implement it. These include how to manage the value chain, how to control operations, and how to account for individual and company concerns. Therefore, companies' strategies are the necessary linchpins to bring about successful business operations in a globalizing economy.

The Concept of International Business Strategy

To determine how a company should best benefit from international operations, it is useful to understand the framework of **strategy,** the specific group of decisions managers take to maximize their companies' performance. There are different levels of such decisions. At the top, a company's founder or senior managers set a **mission**—a guideline stating what the company seeks to do and become over the long term. They may explicitly write this mission, or they may make it implicit by their decisions, directives, and actions. For example, Corning articulates its mission as supplying customers with innovative products using glass technology. A **strategic intent** consists of the goals that stretch the company's performance credibly, so that employees believe that the goals can be reached and will work toward their achievement. For instance, managers may set a strategic intent to become or remain the preeminent supplier or the lowest-cost producer in the industry. To meet their mission and strategic intent, they in turn set **objectives,** which are specific performance targets. Whatever managers do internationally and domestically should be compatible with company strategy so that international and domestic operations complement each other in the improvement of global performance.

Why Study International Business Strategy?

The major reason for studying international business strategy is that some companies consistently perform better than others within their same industries. Performance differences relate largely to the various decisions managers make and their abilities to carry out these decisions. Relatedly, companies with substantial international operations generally outperform those with only domestic operations. This may be explained by the fact that companies have more opportunities in the world as a whole than in any single country. For example, a firm's potential sales in the whole world are certainly larger than those in any single country, and its options for finding the best resources at a reasonable price are certainly greater as well. However, of those companies with substantial international operations, some perform better than others, both overall and abroad.

Further, examining international business strategy is important because managers often suboptimize their companies' international performance for three reasons:

1. Risk-avoidance behavior
2. Choosing locations that do not fit with a well-conceived strategy
3. Failure to know how best to implement decisions in different foreign environments

Risk-Avoidance Behavior

Managers often avoid excessive risk in international operations when they or their companies have little international business experience. Most managers at this point view foreign operations as riskier than domestic ones (and they often are); however, if they have too much intolerance to foreign risk, they may hamper or delay their companies' abilities to avail themselves of better opportunities abroad. As a result, many managers initially undertake international activities reluctantly and follow practices that minimize their risks. They may avoid or delay entry to some countries because they erroneously think all countries in a region are alike. For example, they may avoid operating in any African country because of economic and political problems in some. When the company does enter a country, managers sometimes so limit their commitments there (to minimize losses in case of failure) that the company cannot achieve its objectives. Some U.S. companies in China, for instance, have reported underperformance because managers committed too few resources to their Chinese operations.[2] But as managers learn more about foreign operations and experience success with them, they usually move their companies to deeper foreign commitments that then seem less risky to them. This discussion should not imply that all companies should become highly international, or that all companies eventually becoming highly international should have done so earlier. Rather, managers should make decisions for either domestic or international expansion based on a strategy that examines opportunities and risks realistically.

Nonfit with Strategy

Locating in areas that do not fit with a well-conceived strategy can also adversely affect performance. The lack of fit is sometimes due to a bandwagon mentality—that is, managers decide a company should do something because other companies are doing it, rather than because they have studied their own companies' needs, objectives, and resources. For example, the former vice chairman of Chrysler indicated that when reporters and investment analysts repeatedly ask executives "Why are you so slow on your China strategy?", the executives too often think they are missing something, feel pressured to take action, and end up with disaster.[3] Although the China example is hypothetical, there is truth to it. Foreign companies have recently expanded heavily in China for some very good reasons, such as China's large population, fast growth, and low labor costs. However, many companies have experienced costly failures in China because managers did not analyze adequately whether Chinese marketing and operating realities best fit their companies' particular needs and capabilities. For example, one reality of the Chinese market is that its large size may require foreign companies to reinvest and grow in China for a very long time before they are able to return earnings to their home countries. This is compatible with the needs and capabilities of some companies, but not of others. Managers should thus develop and implement strategy much the way they use a rubber band: stretching expansion enough to take advantage of their firm's underutilized capabilities, but remembering that should they stretch these capabilities too much, they risk incapacitating the company. Figure 2.2 illustrates a managerial decision that will likely be made because of a bandwagon mentality and may stretch the company's resources too much.

Implementation Problems

Finally, even though companies enter the right foreign markets and for the right reasons, they may perform poorly because managers do not know how best to implement strategies in different foreign environments. There is much anecdotal evidence to support this. Again using China as an example, one company described itself in its ads as an "old friend" of China. However, it used the character for *old* that meant "former" instead of "long term." In another case, PepsiCo's managers did not fully understand Chinese tax requirements and left tax handling to its Chinese partner. But the Chinese government's fine for tax evasion hit PepsiCo as well.[4]

Some Related Areas

Core Competencies

Core competencies are those assets that are valuable for improving business, are difficult for competitors to imitate, and can be extended as a value-creating capability for use in other product or geographic markets.[5] They are usually classified into one of three basic groups: (1) superior technological know-how, (2) reliable innovative processes, and (3) close relationships with external parties.[6] Managers should either leverage their companies' existing core competencies by using them to extend operations to another country, or they should extend operations internationally to develop new or improved core competencies. For example, McDonald's leveraged its existing core competencies of gaining brand recognition, developing uniform signature products, and deliv-

Figure 2.2

This manager may attempt to expand internationally for the wrong reasons and without sufficient resources.

"*Miss Davis, bring me everything we've got on turning a two-bit hole-in-the-wall operation into a multinational juggernaut.*"

ering value for a low price when it entered Taiwan. But when Ball
Horticultural entered Mexico (discussed in Chapter 1), it added a core *cost*
competency to combine with its existing core *technological* competency in
production of new poinsettia strains.

Barriers to Entry

Barriers to entry are those conditions that limit easy entry of new competitors
into an industry. Creating entry barriers is obviously advantageous to companies because the higher the barriers are, the higher are the firms' typical profits.
Entry barriers are usually classified into one of four types: (1) brand loyalty,
(2) absolute cost advantage, (3) high capital costs, and (4) government regulations. Although managers may build a combination of barriers to limit competitive entry, most successful companies compete primarily on the basis of one.
Managers may use entry barriers to limit foreign competition in the company's
domestic market or to give their company advantages abroad. But some barriers
more easily affect international competition than others. The following discussion highlights these differences.

Managers may build *brand loyalty* by developing unique products, advertising them effectively, and controlling distribution units in ways that reinforce
and compel customers to buy from them. Coca-Cola, Tredegar Industries, and
Marks & Spencer all compete primarily on the basis of brand loyalty. For example, Coca-Cola managers have created differentiated products, spent heavily on
promoting them, and gained distribution advantages—such as long-term contracts with food franchise operators (for example, McDonald's sells only soft
drinks from Coca-Cola), prime locations for vending machines, and superior
shelf space in supermarkets. Coca-Cola's managers have gained brand loyalty
abroad by using these same methods. Another company, Tredegar Industries,
an industrial supplier of plastic films, sold its products mainly to Procter &
Gamble (P&G) for use in diapers and feminine hygiene products. Tredegar's
managers built brand loyalty with P&G's U.S. purchasing department by delivering reliable products on schedule to P&G's U.S. facilities. When P&G opened
a plant in China, Tredegar had an advantage over potential competitors in selling to that plant. But Marks & Spencer, Britain's largest retailer, has been able to
gain no more than niche markets in such countries as Canada and France
because it entered these countries long after local retailers had gained brand
loyalty, which is difficult to displace.

Companies such as Pohang Iron & Steel from Korea and Southwest Airlines
from the United States compete primarily on *absolute cost advantages*. On the
one hand, Korea's Pohang Iron & Steel has been able to capitalize on its low
labor rates and new, highly productive plants by exporting into world markets.
On the other hand, Southwest Airlines has not been able to capitalize on its
domestic cost advantages by moving internationally. Southwest's chief executive officer saw domestic cost-saving opportunities that managers in other airlines either did not see or could not exploit. These included techniques to minimize aircraft ground time (thus Southwest makes more efficient use of
expensive aircraft), use of less expensive airports (such as Midway instead of
O'Hare in Chicago), and concentration on medium-range route structures (so
that all its aircraft are efficient for that range and can be interchanged easily
from one route to another). Southwest cannot leverage its cost advantage internationally, however, because governments restrict foreign airline operations

worldwide and because few cities abroad have less expensive airport alternatives.

High capital costs result from new-product development or equipment needed in production. For example, the cost of developing a new generation of large long-range aircraft is so high that new companies cannot afford to compete; thus, two companies, Boeing and Airbus Industrie, are virtually the only suppliers worldwide.

Managers also influence governmental authorities to enact *regulations and agreements* that will serve as entry barriers to prevent competition for them. These regulations and agreements usually protect companies only in their domestic markets, such as by preventing foreign-made products or foreign-owned companies from competing there. For example, managers in U.S. companies that make the paperlike cloth used for printing currency have convinced lawmakers to require the U.S. Treasury to buy only such cloth made in the United States by U.S.-owned companies. Therefore, these U.S. suppliers do not have to compete against comparable, and occasionally superior, products from German suppliers. But companies can sometimes gain regulatory advantages in foreign markets. For example, managers in Pilkington from the United Kingdom convinced Chinese governmental authorities to grant them a temporary monopoly on producing plate glass for the Chinese market.

Motives for Foreign Operations

Companies' international operations always involve selling or acquiring in foreign countries. Their motives are to expand their sales, cut their costs, or reduce their operating risks. Although these motives sometimes overlap, we shall examine them separately to explain how they relate to companies' international strategies.

Sales Expansion Motives

Companies' sales depend on two factors: consumers' desires for their products or services and consumers' ability to buy them. Companies expand sales abroad by exporting home-country production to foreign countries and by selling abroad what they produce abroad. In addition to production cost differences, they may produce abroad to save transportation costs, overcome governmental restrictions against foreign-made products, or improve delivery and service.

Managers expand internationally because they assume the expansion will lead to company sales at prices that will earn them profits. Three factors often trigger companies to increase sales through international expansion:

1. Maturity of their domestic markets
2. Slower domestic than foreign growth rates
3. Ability to gain foreign product capabilities

Maturity of Their Domestic Markets
Managers usually decide to develop new company products because they observe a nearby potential market for them. This means that a U.S. company is most apt to develop a new product for the U.S. market, a French company for

the French market, and so on. Once the new product enters the market, it will ordinarily go through a **product life cycle (PLC),** a continuum that consists of roughly four stages: introduction, growth, maturity, and decline. (In Chapter 5, we will discuss how the PLC affects trade, production location, and foreign direct investment.) Figure 2.3 illustrates the stages of the PLC.

In other words, if the product is successful after introduction, sales will grow. However, at some point, sales growth slows—a situation known as a **mature market.** At this point, the market is basically saturated, and sales depend primarily on population growth and a replacement market. For example, washing machines were once a growth product in the United States, but now that most households have washing machines, sales depend on new household construction (because of population growth) and replacement of nonserviceable machines. Managers in such U.S. companies as Whirlpool and General Electric (GE) have had limited success in persuading U.S. households to buy more than one washing machine, even though managers in other companies with mature products, such as automobiles and television sets, have had greater success. Neither have they come up with new features to persuade people to abandon their still-serviceable washing machines as electronics companies did when introducing CD players to replace tape players. Therefore, Whirlpool and GE have recently concentrated on markets such as Korea, where few houses have large appliances such as washing machines and where people's growing incomes are allowing them to make purchases.[7] In effect, Whirlpool and GE are taking advantage of product life cycles for washing machines that commenced at different times in the United States and Korea. Figure 2.4 illustrates time differences in cycles. Similarly, when Ericsson from Sweden and Motorola from the United States faced slower domestic growth for cellular phone sales, they found that some countries were just beginning to see rapid growth of these sales. Foreign-language versions of U.S. television shows, such as *Let's Make a Deal* and *The Price Is Right,* have successfully moved abroad after running their course in the United States.

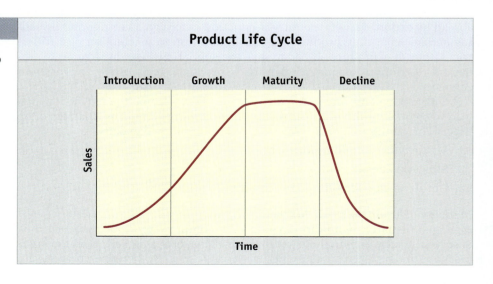

Figure 2.3

Most successful products go through cycles whereby sales grow after introduction but level off as the market becomes saturated. Later, they decline as consumers turn to newer products.

Product Life Cycle

Introduction   Growth   Maturity   Decline

Sales

Time

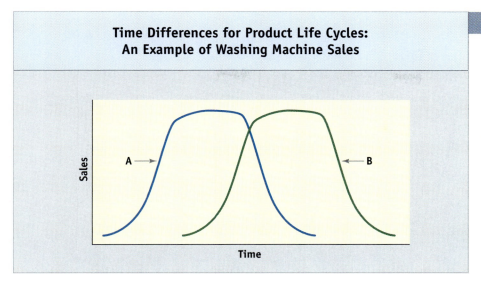

**Time Differences for Product Life Cycles:
An Example of Washing Machine Sales**

Sales

A →

← B

Time

Figure 2.4

The A curve shows the U.S. life cycle for washing machines, and the B curve shows South Koreas. Because of earlier introduction and growth in the United States, that market is now in a mature stage, depending on population growth and a replacement market. The market in South Korea, however, is in a growth stage. A company can sometimes maintain sales growth longer by moving successively to new markets.

Various countries' PLC shapes may also differ. In other words, sales may shoot up very rapidly in one country but slowly in another, and decline may come more quickly in one country than in another. For example, once a product has had success in one market, it may grow more rapidly when a company introduces it to a second market. The company may have already adjusted design characteristics to increase consumers' satisfaction and may have developed production efficiencies to reduce costs when it enters a second market. Further, consumers in the second market may have heard of the product in advance and be predisposed to buy it. Sales of cellular phones, for instance, took longer to grow in some of the initial markets than they did in markets that companies entered later. Part A of Figure 2.5 illustrates this. Further, a company may continue a product's sales longer in one country than in another. For example, Ajax cleanser sustained sales longer in Europe than in the United States because European consumers were less prone to switch to more newly promoted cleansers. Part B of Figure 2.5 illustrates that PLCs may be longer in one country than in another.

Growth Rates

Companies may also encounter differences in potential demand growth because of differences among countries in economic growth. For some time, the rich markets of the United States, Japan, and Western Europe (sometimes called the Triad Market) have accounted for about half the world's total overall consumption, and an even higher portion of consumption for such products as computers, consumer electronics, and machine tools. But some countries, such as China, have recently experienced faster economic growth. For example, according to World Bank forecasts, China will surpass the United States as the world's largest economy by the year 2020. Thus, managers see more possibilities for sales in fast-growth countries than in slow-growth countries, and they put more emphasis on the former. Further, the middle class is growing rapidly in many poorer countries, both in absolute numbers and in percentage of the population. For example, between 1993 and 1998, India's middle class increased by about 110 million

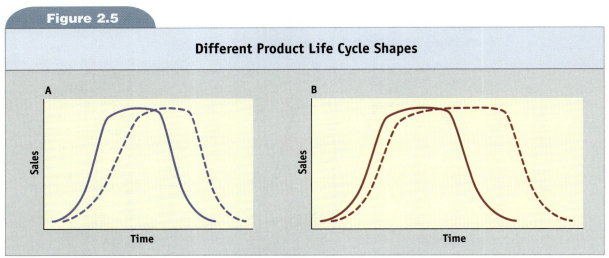

Figure 2.5

Different Product Life Cycle Shapes

A

Sales

Time

B

Sales

Time

In Part A, the product in the country represented by the solid line saw a steeper growth rate than in the country represented by the dotted line, indicating that the market developed very quickly after it was introduced. In Part B, the product stayed at a mature level much longer in the country represented by the dotted line than in the country represented by the solid-line, indicating that the market continued at a healthy level for a longer period of time.

people (approximately the combined population of France and the United Kingdom) and rose from 23.5 percent to 33 percent of the country's population.

New or Differentiated Product Capabilities
Managers not only seek to leverage their companies' core competencies to sell more abroad, but also seek foreign product capabilities for which they can use their core competencies to expand their domestic sales. For example, Pfizer has core competencies in getting new pharmaceuticals approved for sale in the U.S. market and for persuading U.S. physicians to prescribe them. To leverage the value of these competencies, Pfizer maintains a pharmaceutical laboratory in the United Kingdom that has been responsible for many of the new products the company has been able to sell in its home U.S. market. Similarly, DBStar from the United States has technological competency in computer data storage along with close relationships with potential U.S. customers. Although the technology has applications abroad, DBStar would find it difficult to develop the necessary close relationship with customers outside the United States on its own. At the same time, Transtar from France has other computer data storage technology and good relations with French customers, but it lacks customer relations outside France. Consequently, DBStar and Transtar have agreed to share each other's technology and to sell for each other in their domestic markets, where they have marketing competence.[8]

Cost-Reduction Motives
Cost minimization is essential for companies that compete primarily on the basis of price. For other firms, such as those that compete primarily on product differentiation, cost reduction is still important. Companies' international expansion may reduce their costs by spreading their fixed expenses, by

enabling them to produce with cheaper inputs or in cheaper operating locations, and by achieving vertical integration.

Spreading Fixed Costs

The size of a national market does not necessarily correspond with the length of production runs needed to minimize cost. If the optimum production size is larger than the domestic market's size, a company producing therein must either incur excess capacity and high costs or find means of selling abroad. For example, truck manufacturing generally requires large-scale production to be efficient because of the expensive equipment needed in the production process. The Swedish-based truck manufacturer Volvo must therefore export much of its production because of the small size of the Swedish market. Mack Trucks has less need to export from the United States because of the larger U.S. market, although exports are still important for Mack.

The preceding example is based on production technology. In addition, companies frequently have immediate or long-term output capabilities for which there is inadequate domestic demand. This excess capacity may come in the form of known reserves of natural resources or in the form of product-specific human resource capabilities that cannot be diverted easily to the production of other goods. Thus, companies leverage their competencies by using them abroad.

Studies show that in many industries a company can often cut its costs by 20 to 30 percent each time its output doubles, a phenomenon known as the **experience curve.** For instance, with a 20 percent cost reduction and an initial cost of $100 per unit, the second unit produced will cost $80, the fourth $64, and so on. In this example, the average cost per unit goes from $100, to $90, to $81.33, and so on. A reduction may come about because a company spreads fixed costs over more units of output, becomes more efficient as it gains operating experience, and secures quantity discounts on materials and transportation. Therefore, to the extent that the experience curve is applicable, a market leader may garner production cost advantages over its competitors. Of course, a way to increase market is through international sales. However, we caution that the market leader is not always the best performer in an industry; there are simply many other factors to consider. A company can spread some fixed costs, such as those it spends on research and development (R&D), over an infinite number of units sold. Other fixed costs such as plant and equipment, however, can only be spread when it has excess capacity. Figure 2.6 illustrates this by showing that a company can reduce the average cost per unit until it uses all its capacity, after which it needs to increase capacity (such as by building an additional plant). This causes the average fixed cost per unit to go up again with the first unit of production, though not as high as for the first unit in the first plant.

Using Lower-Cost Locations

Companies may produce more cheaply in one country than in another because of differences in input costs and the productivity associated with the inputs. Inputs include labor, land, raw materials, capital, and utilities. Any one of these may be the overriding cost for a specific product (such as labor input in the manufacture of clothing or electricity costs in the fabrication of aluminum). However, the combination of costs determines where a product may be produced most cheaply. If a lower cost for one input, such as labor, is accompanied by a higher cost for another, such as rent, the total cost may be no different than

Figure 2.6

The figure assumes there are $100 of fixed costs to give a capacity of four units; therefore, the fixed cost of production per unit falls for the first four units from $100 to $25. However, it is necessary to add $100 of fixed costs to increase capacity to eight units; thus, the average fixed cost per unit increased to $40 ($200 divided by 5) if five units are produced. The average fixed cost falls again to $25 if eight units are produced.

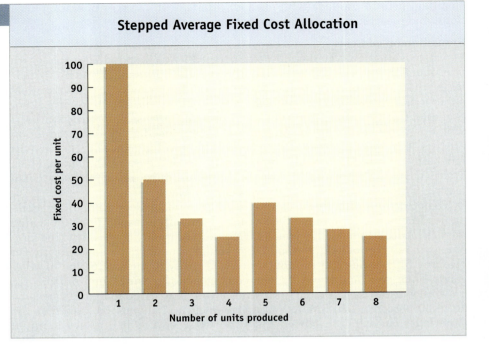

Stepped Average Fixed Cost Allocation

it is where labor costs more and rent costs less. Once a company makes a product, it must transport it to markets, so transport cost is also an important variable in determining the least-cost production location to serve a given market. Further, companies must consider taxes as an additional cost, so a high local tax may undermine cost advantages from using inexpensive labor or raw materials.

We usually associate companies' cost-saving moves abroad with their use of cheap labor. However, moving internationally to obtain any cheaper input is a possibility. For example, LSI Logic Corp., a U.S. manufacturer of custom-made microchips, set up a European company to sell stock at a premium because Europeans had more interest in high-technology firms at the time. The company later borrowed funds in Europe at a lower interest rate than banks were offering in the United States.[9] Relatedly, the large South African mining conglomerate Anglo American moved its headquarters and primary stock exchange listing from Johannesburg to London primarily to raise capital more easily at a reasonable cost. Nevertheless, the company maintains most of its production facilities in South Africa.[10]

Because of cost differences among locations, companies increasingly depend on different countries for their supplies of different components or different products in their lines. (This is known as the global supply chain or **rationalized production**.) Take components. Ford assembled its Escort automobile with radiator hoses from Austria, carburetors from the United Kingdom, seat pads from Belgium, glass from Canada, exhaust flanges from Norway, hardware from the Netherlands, fan belts from Denmark, ignition switches from Germany, cylinder heads from France, wheel nuts from the United States, air filters from Spain, speedometers from Switzerland, hose clamps from Sweden, alternators from Japan, and defroster grills from Italy. Although companies may save costs by using global supplies, they must consider additional hidden costs of managing and moving the complex network of components and inventories through their global supply chains.

Governments also influence the comparative costs of operations via tax rates, operating regulations, and provision of infrastructure and inputs. For example, Liberia's tax advantages for shipping income have led many shipping companies to register their ships there. Bermuda's favorable operating regulations have attracted many insurance companies. A slight difference in corporate income tax may have a significant impact on a company's overall after-tax income and, thus, be important in determining production location.[11] Governments may also offer companies a number of incentives that effectively lower their operating costs. Indirect incentives include general education programs for workers that increase their productivity, provision of a good infrastructure—roads, railroads, and port facilities—that reduces transportation costs, and prevention of crime, which lessens companies' security costs. Governments may also offer specific assistance to specific companies. For instance, the French government extended the Paris railway to Disney's theme park at a cost of almost $350 million, made land on which to build the park available cheaply, and loaned Disney 22 percent of the funds needed for construction at a low interest rate. Government incentives to attract companies to locate within their boundaries are most appealing when they fit closely with companies' corporate strategies.[12] For example, the French government's incentives did not persuade Disney to establish a park outside the United States, or even in Europe; rather, the incentives helped persuade Disney to locate its European park in France, rather than another European country.

Value Chain Integration

A **value chain** is the linked activities that transform inputs into the outputs that eventually reach end customers. For example, to get a cotton shirt to an end customer necessitates links among cotton growers, textile and thread manufacturers, shirt designers, shirt manufacturers, wholesalers, and retailers. Figure 2.7 shows these links. Value chain integration is control of more than one adjacent link in the value chain, whether vertical or horizontal. Companies sometimes control only one link in the value chain. Adding a link away from the final consumer—such as a manufacturer's acquisition of a raw material supplier—is *backward integration.* Adding a link toward the final consumer is *forward integration;* an example is a manufacturer's establishment of retail outlets to sell what it produces. If a company follows an integration strategy, it may need to move internationally because different low-cost opportunities exist in different countries. Further, raw materials, inexpensive production locations, and major markets may be located in different countries. For example, some integrated aluminum companies own bauxite mines in Guinea (because that's where deposits exist), convert the bauxite into aluminum in Canada (because Canada offers inexpensive waterpower for generating electricity), and sell processed aluminum in the United States (because of the large U.S. market). Three possible cost advantages of value chain integration are:

1. Saving transaction costs

2. Building bargaining power with suppliers or customers

3. Minimizing stock-out and overcapacity costs

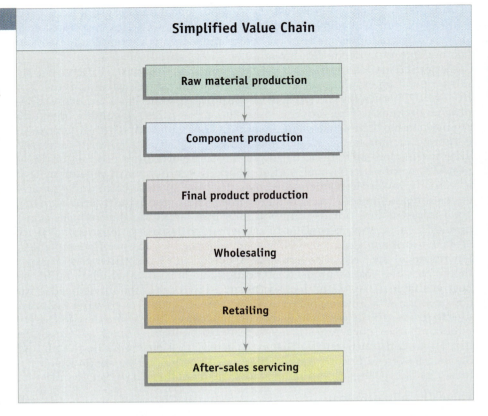

Figure 2.7

This simplified value chain shows the main steps that transform inputs into outputs used by consumers. Additionally, there are services connected with each link, such as transportation, warehousing, promotion, financing, and insurance. Companies decide in which links to operate. They may also handle only a portion of a link, such as making some types of components and buying others.

Simplified Value Chain

- Raw material production
- Component production
- Final product production
- Wholesaling
- Retailing
- After-sales servicing

A company may sometimes integrate activities in a related link of the value chain to save *transaction costs,* including the cost of promoting sales to another company, negotiating a contract with that company, and then monitoring to ensure that the other company adheres to the contract. All these activities are expensive, and companies must weigh them against the costs of self-handling. For example, clothing designer Calvin Klein contracted Warnaco to make and distribute the clothes because Warnaco had expertise and low costs for these functions. However, Calvin Klein later ended the contract because the costs of guaranteeing that Warnaco produced the specified quality and distributed only to agreed-upon retailers were high.[13]

A company may also integrate *some* of the activities of an adjacent link in the value chain to indicate its strategic intent and operational capability and willingness to manage the link. This may coerce the customer or supplier to provide better prices and service. For example, PepsiCo handles some bottling operations itself, which serve as benchmarks for costs and quality. PepsiCo uses these benchmarks to pressure independent bottlers to negotiate contracts that are very favorable to PepsiCo.

Finally, value chain integration provides captive supplies and sales. This is a major factor for most large oil companies. By having captive supplies, they minimize the costs of lost accounts when there are global oil shortages, and also enjoy more assurance that they can sell enough to cover high fixed production costs during periods of excess global oil supplies. For example, Saudi Aramco, the world's largest holder of petroleum reserves, has been acquiring distribution companies to gain captive markets during periods of excess global oil supplies. The captive markets allow Saudi Aramco to maintain its sales during these periods and, thus, allocate its fixed costs more fully than competitors who have excess supplies that they cannot easily sell.

As products and their marketing become more complicated, companies need to combine components that are made in more than one country. They therefore need tight relationships to ensure that production and marketing flow smoothly through the global supply chain.

Risk-Reduction Motives

Most managers believe that international business is riskier than domestic because it requires them to deal with less familiar environments. Nevertheless, international business may reduce companies' business risks by smoothing their sales and profits, spreading their dependence over more suppliers and customers, and preventing their competitors from gaining unobstructed operating advantages from foreign markets.

Smoothing Sales and Profits

Managers may try to avoid wide swings in sales and profits because shareholders value stability, and because it may lower the company's borrowing costs by reducing periods of repayment difficulty. To minimize swings in sales and profits, managers may seek out foreign markets because the timing of business cycles—recessions and expansions—differs among countries.[14] Granted, in theory, the globalization of markets would suggest that different countries follow the same business cycle. In large degree, they do. Still, there are differences in timing because of variations in government policy, consumer sentiments, and economic structures. For example, between 1994 and 1995, Ford sales in the United States and Canada fell, but this was largely offset by gains in Germany and Brazil. Whereas shareholders can easily enjoy product diversification by buying shares of companies in different industries, they cannot easily come by international diversification by buying shares of companies headquartered in different countries. This is because many countries regulate stock purchases by foreigners and because many countries have poorly developed stock markets. Thus, investors value companies that have diversified internationally.

Lessening Dependence on Existing Customers and Suppliers

By increasing its number of suppliers, a company becomes less vulnerable to supply shortages. For example, if it has a single supplier for an essential component, a strike or fire at the supplier's facility may shut down its operations as well. With more than one supplier, however, it can continue receiving some supplies from the company that is still operating. In fact, it may persuade the operating company to work its employees overtime to make up supply shortages. But different suppliers may face production problems simultaneously. For example, major steel producers in the United States all deal with the same union, the United Steel Workers (USW). The USW may coordinate strikes to disrupt total U.S. steel production. Therefore, some major U.S. steel consumers, such as companies in the automobile industry, have sought foreign

Companies engage in international business to gain new markets and obtain products or resources that help them better compete domestically. The photo shows an example of the latter for Levi Strauss, which relies on many foreign locations to make products more cheaply than if they were produced in the United States—mainly because of lower labor rates. The worker in Colombia is inspecting the quality of blue jeans prior to shipping them to the United States.

suppliers to reduce potential disruptions from a domestic strike. In a number of industries, there are very few suppliers, such as for processed aluminum and photographic base paper. The suppliers tend to be from different countries, and industrial customers generally seek to purchase from more than one.

Similarly, a company that is very highly dependent on one industrial customer may be extremely vulnerable to either the fortunes of that customer or the customer's ability to negotiate better terms for itself. Such a situation may dictate diversifying the customer base, and foreign sales expansion offers an alternative for diversifying such a base.

Preventing Competitors' Advantages

Following customers is an important motive for foreign expansion. When a company has a domestic customer that begins to sell abroad, that company may begin to sell abroad indirectly. For example, Bridgestone sold tires to Toyota and Honda, which then began exporting fully assembled cars (including tires), so Bridgestone began to sell abroad indirectly. When Toyota and Honda began assembling cars abroad, they had the alternative of buying tires from local companies. Bridgestone feared not only the loss of the market it had gained indirectly, but also that if Toyota and Honda began buying from other tire companies abroad, those tire companies might even enter the Japanese market to gain the automakers' accounts. Thus, Bridgestone followed Toyota and Honda into Thailand and Indonesia by setting up production facilities within those markets.[15]

Within **oligopolistic** industries (those with few sellers), several investors often establish facilities in a given country within a fairly short time of each other. For example, between 1991 and 1995, 11 different automobile companies received licenses to invest in Vietnam.[16] Although much of this investment concentration was due to Vietnam's recent openness to foreign companies, concentration is often due to companies' decisions to prevent competitors from garnering a larger market, spreading their R&D costs, and making profits that they can reinvest elsewhere. Once one company decides to enter the market, competitors are prone to follow quickly rather than let the first company gain advantages. Thus, companies base their entry decisions not so much on the benefits to be gained as on the greater losses they would sustain if they did not enter the field. In most oligopolistic industries (automobiles, tires, petroleum, and so on), this pattern helps explain the large number of producers relative to the size of the market in some countries. Closely related to this pattern is the decision to enter a foreign competitor's home market to prevent it from using high home-country profits to compete elsewhere.[17]

Acquisitions Versus New Venturing

Successful companies derive new capabilities in terms of products, processes, and markets. These capabilities may enhance their core competencies, allow them to capitalize on already developed competencies, create higher entry barriers for competitors, and inspire new points of strategic intent. The firms may acquire these capabilities from other companies or may develop them on their own. Examples of the former, called **acquisitions,** include buying other companies in whole or in part and buying capabilities from other companies. Examples of the latter, called *new venturing,* include new products or processes from the companies' own R&D, hiring of personnel with expertise to work for them, and building new facilities. There are advantages and disadvantages to either alternative.

Acquisitions

There are many reasons for seeking acquisitions. R&D efforts often yield little in the way of profitable results because companies do not get expected outcomes or because competitors get them first and preempt the market. Through acquisition, on the other hand, a company gets a known product or process, thus reducing the risk from internal development. There may also be cost savings, such as by combining departments and reducing the number of employees necessary when the two companies operated independently of each other. For example, Ford has developed a strategy of having models available in a spectrum of price categories, but one of its gaps was in the category between its Lincoln and Jaguar lines. Rather than spend for risky internal development to fill that gap, Ford sought to acquire a company with models fitting the price gap. There were no possibilities among U.S.-based producers, so Ford acquired the automobile division from Swedish-based Volvo. Since both Ford and Volvo were already well established as international producers and sellers, this acquisition served to enhance Ford's domestic and international presence. Further, Ford obtained the goodwill toward the Volvo name and did not have to break in a new brand name.

An acquisition also brings quicker results because a company avoids the time needed to develop a new product and construct facilities to build it. The company receives an immediate cash flow, rather than tying up funds (sometimes for years) before it develops production and sales. Finally, acquisitions are particularly advantageous when there is excess capacity in an industry. Adding capacity in such a situation risks higher fixed costs per unit for all producers. Further, the situation may lead competitors to engage in price-cutting tactics to try to build market share, which may in turn lead to lower prices and lower profits for all firms in the industry. For example, much of the international expansion by tire companies in the 1990s came through acquisition of other companies because there was excess global capacity for making tires.

New Venturing

Although acquisitions offer advantages, a company may not be able to make them. If its idea for a product or process is new, then no other company will have developed the capabilities that the company hopes to acquire. Even if other companies have capabilities, they may not be willing to sell them at an acceptable price. Or governmental antitrust regulations may prevent acquisitions. Finally, the capabilities a company needs may not exist in the countries in which it wishes to expand.

Even if companies are available to acquire, they may be difficult to manage successfully. Acquired companies might embody substantial problems: Personnel and labor relations may be both poor and difficult to change, ill will rather than goodwill may have accrued to existing brands, or facilities may be inefficient and poorly located in relation to potential future markets. Further, the managers in the acquiring and acquired companies may not work well together. For example, managers in the acquired company may place barriers on ceding their accustomed autonomy. Or companies may have different operating philosophies, such as one company's preference for filling positions by promoting existing employees and the other company's to have existing employees compete against outside applicants.

Implementation Strategies

Regardless of the motive for international expansion, a company must have a strategy for fulfilling its motives. It may use a different implementation strategy for each of its products and for each country in which it operates. Differences may be due to characteristics of specific countries and to the company's international experience. Strategies differ in terms of how much the company alters its operations to fit the needs of specific countries and the degree to which its headquarters controls foreign operating units, as opposed to giving them autonomy. Basically, a company can organize to follow a multidomestic, global, or transnational strategy.[18] In theory, each company can follow any one of these strategies. However, which one a company chooses is ultimately subject to management's sense of its fit with current and planned activities. There is no script that determines the best choice; strategy instead depends on managers' opinions on which one best fits their goals and ambitions.

Multidomestic Strategies

A **multidomestic strategy** is one in which the company allows each of its foreign-country operations to act fairly independently, such as by designing and producing a product or service in France for the French market and in Japan for the Japanese market. The main reason for adopting a multidomestic strategy is that in some cases, cultural, legal-political, and economic conditions may dictate very different optimum operating practices from one country to another. For example, the food industry usually has a high need to adapt to local conditions because taste, competitors, and distributors differ widely at the local level. In such a situation, companies usually make most decisions locally because people who are close to the situation are better able to determine what practices will work best. Although this strategy allows the company to optimize performance for each country in which it operates, it does not allow for much synergy among the different countries, such as by spreading fixed costs via selling uniform products in uniform ways in different countries, or by transferring successful practices from one country to another. Further, firms may sometimes be so overwhelmed by differences—real and imaginary, great and small—among their many operating environments that they believe falsely that each country must have unique practices. This may lead to such extensive decision delegation, or such extensive imitation of proven host-country practices, that the company loses innovative superiority. Furthermore, control may be diminished as managers within each country foster local rather than worldwide objectives.

Global Strategies

Within a **global strategy,** a company integrates its operations that are located in different countries. For example, it might design a product or service with a global market segment in mind. Or it might depend on its operations in different countries to produce the components used in its products and services. In this type of company, managers in the company's home country essentially develop capabilities and make decisions to diffuse them globally. Many organizations and products lend themselves to a global strategy because global performance may be improved by transferring resources internationally and by gaining economies from standardized products and practices. The aircraft engine and industrial chemical industries, for instance, lend themselves to global strategies: Standardization allows companies to gain economies of scale that will greatly reduce unit costs. However, there are dangers in following such a strategy. Corporate management may overlook important local differences or simply assume that they can easily be overcome.

Transnational Strategies

In a **transnational strategy,** a company develops different capabilities and contributions from different countries and shares them in integrated worldwide operations. In essence, this is a hybrid of multidomestic and global strategies in that the company attempts to gain the advantages and benefits of both. In addition, management seeks to develop new knowledge and capabilities not only at headquarters, but also at each subsidiary—both independently and jointly. The company transfers these throughout its worldwide organization. This strategy is ideal for companies that gain a great deal from global integration *and* need a great deal of adaptation to local markets. Such industries as pharmaceuticals and automobiles fall into this category. Despite its potential benefits, however, this strategy is challenging to implement because a company usually must coordinate information and operations among managers from many countries. For example, ABB, the giant Swedish-Swiss heavy equipment manufacturer, has developed a sophisticated information retrieval system that disseminates information about and to the approximately 1,300 operating units in its federation of companies. In addition, it brings together as many as 5,000 managers in meetings. This ensures that upper- and lower-level managers receive the same timely information about the whole organization.[19] Obviously, such a network is costly. Moreover, it is difficult to obtain agreement from such a large and diverse group of managers.

A Mix of Strategies

Although we have categorized strategies, this does not imply that companies should follow one to the exclusion of others. Different products, capabilities, and operating locations dictate a mix of approaches to maximize performance.

Figure 2.8 illustrates examples of some of Avon's international activities. Note that Avon uses such domestically developed core competencies as its ability to manage a huge independent network of salespeople when selling abroad. But Avon has also developed abroad competencies that it brings to its domestic and other foreign operations, such as the Beauty-Centers developed in Argentina, where Avon provides customers with a wide variety of services, including hair-styling and manicures. The company also builds entry barriers through the development of global brand names (such as Rare Gold fragrances and the Avon name on most products) and the printing of about 600 million brochures in 15 languages per year. However, Avon also uses some local brand names—such as Rosa Mosqueta to fit the local language (Spanish) in Chile and the Justine name for products in South Africa—where it wishes to take advantage of goodwill toward a company it acquired. Avon's motive for foreign expansion is mainly its desire to increase sales: Domestic growth has become more diffi-

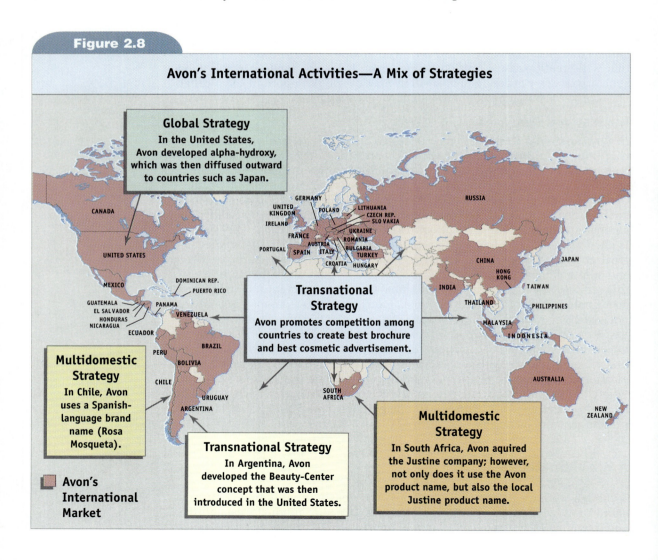

Figure 2.8

Avon's International Activities—A Mix of Strategies

Global Strategy
In the United States, Avon developed alpha-hydroxy, which was then diffused outward to countries such as Japan.

Transnational Strategy
Avon promotes competition among countries to create best brochure and best cosmetic advertisement.

Multidomestic Strategy
In Chile, Avon uses a Spanish-language brand name (Rosa Mosqueta).

Transnational Strategy
In Argentina, Avon developed the Beauty-Center concept that was then introduced in the United States.

Multidomestic Strategy
In South Africa, Avon aquired the Justine company; however, not only does it use the Avon product name, but also the local Justine product name.

Avon's International Market

cult as the U.S. market for cosmetics has matured and as changes in U.S. lifestyles have made door-to-door selling more difficult. However, Avon also goes abroad to find sources of products. For instance, its office in Hong Kong issues about 2,000 supplier contracts for about 600 new products per year from nine Asian countries. In some respects Avon is multidomestic in that each country sets its own prices to reflect local market conditions. In other respects, it is global in that it diffuses its home-country technologies, such as the use of alpha-hydroxy acid, everywhere it operates. And in still other respects, Avon is transnational in that it brings personnel together from different countries to share their experiences and information on their best practices. Avon also promotes competition among countries to create "bests," such as best brochure and best color cosmetic advertisement.

Operational Decisions

The choice of whether to use a multidomestic, global, or transnational strategy interrelates with a number of operational decisions. Throughout subsequent chapters, we shall discuss these decisions and relate them back to implementing strategies. The alternatives that companies face include the following:

- *Location of value-added activities.* This involves choosing where to locate each of the activities that comprise the entire value-added chain, from research to production to after-sales servicing.
- *Location of sales target.* This involves selecting both the country markets in which to conduct business and the level of activity, particularly in terms of market share.
- *Level of involvement.* The choice of operating through wholly owned facilities, partially owned facilities, or contract arrangements, and whether the choice varies among countries.
- *Product and services strategy.* The extent to which a worldwide business offers the same or different products or services in different countries.
- *Marketing.* The extent to which a company uses the same brand names, advertising, and other marketing elements in different countries.
- *Production strategy.* Whether the company uses similar or different equipment, production methods, and materials in all the places it produces.
- *Competitive moves.* The extent to which a company makes competitive moves in individual countries as part of a global strategy.
- *Factor movements and start-up strategy.* Whether and the extent to which production factors are acquired locally or brought in by the company, and whether the operation is made through an acquisition or a start-up.[20]

Summary

As companies successfully pursue international business, countries gain advantages from that business. But international business will begin only if companies' managers perceive opportunities by engaging in the business. And successful international business most likely occurs when companies make international business part of a well-conceived strategy that enables them to take advantage of their underutilized resources or to improve their competencies.

Companies' international operations always involve selling or acquiring in foreign countries. By selling abroad, companies may overcome problems of domestic market maturity and slow growth rates. They may also gain foreign product capabilities that allow them to sell more domestically. Through international operations, companies may spread their fixed costs, find cheaper production locations, and gain cost advantages of value chain integration. They may also reduce operating risks by smoothing sales and profits, lessening their dependence on existing customers and suppliers, and preempting advantages that might otherwise go to their competitors.

Companies may move internationally via acquisitions or new venturing, either of which has advantages and disadvantages. Companies may implement international strategies through multidomestic, global, and transnational operations. They must make tactical decisions concerning where and how to operate.

endnotes

[1] Data on McDonald's were taken from various annual reports and from David Barboza, "Pluralism Under Golden Arches," *New York Times,* February 12, 1999, p. C1+.

[2] Mark Cannice and John D. Daniels, "Operating Modes and Performance," in J. T. Li, Anne Tsui, and Elizabeth Weldon (eds.), *Management and Organization in the Chinese Context* (London: Macmillan and New York: St. Martin's Press, 2000), pp. 157–184.

[3] Bob Lutz, *Lutz' Guts: The Seven Laws of Business That Made Chrysler the World's Hottest Car Company* (New York: John Wiley & Sons, 1998).

[4] Marcus W. Brauchli, "PepsiCo's KFC Venture in China Is Fined for Allegedly False Financial Reporting," *Wall Street Journal,* July 27, 1994, p. A10.

[5] C. K. Prahalad and G. Hamel, "The Core Competencies of Companies," *Harvard Business Review,* May–June 1990, pp. 79–81. The resource-based view of strategy talks about tacit, idio-syncratic, and intangible firm competencies.

[6] Briance Mascarenhas, Alok Daveja, and Mamnoon Jamil, "Dynamics of Core Competencies in Leading Multinational Companies," *California Management Review,* Vol. 40, No. 4, summer 1998, pp. 117–132.

[7] Michael Schuman, "U.S. Companies Crack South Korean Market," *Wall Street Journal,* September 11, 1996, p. A14.

[8] "DBStar and Transtar Sign U.S.-European Cross-Licensing Agreement," *Business Wire*, August 26, 1996.

[9] John D. Daniels and Lee H. Radebaugh, *International Business: Environments and Operations,* 8th ed. (Reading, MA: Addison-Wesley Publishing Co., 1998), p. 825.

[10] "Anglo Goes Global," *Financial Times,* October 16, 1998, p. 21.

[11] James Hines, "Tax Policy and the Activities of Multinational Corporations" (Cambridge, MA: National Bureau of Economic Research Working Paper No. 5589, 1996).

[12] Thomas P. Murtha and Stephanie Ann Lenway, "Country Capabilities and the Strategic State: How National Political Institutions Affect a Multinational Corporation's Strategies," *Strategic Management Journal,* Vol. 15, 1994, pp. 113–129.

[13] Leslie Kaufman, "Calvin Klein Battles Maker of Its Jeans," *New York Times,* June 1, 2000, p. C1+.

[14] Rory F. Knight and Deborah J. Pretty, "The Real Benefits of Corporate Diversification," *Financial Times,* May 9, 2000, Mastering Risk section, pp. 14–15.

[15] "A Come-back After Indy Wins," *Financial Times,* January 29, 1996, p. 14.

[16] Reginald Chua, "Vietnam's Tiny Car Market Draws Crowd," *Wall Street Journal,* January 3, 1996, p. A4.

[17] E. M. Graham, "Exchange of Threat Between Multinational Firms as an Infinitely Repeated Noncooperative Gain," *The International Trade Journal,* Vol. IV, No. 3, spring 1990, pp. 259–277.

[18] For a good overview of these three strategies, see Anne-Wil Harzing, "An Empirical Analysis and Extension of the Bartlett and Ghoshal Typology of Multinational Companies," *Journal of International Business Studies,* Vol. 31, No. 1, first quarter 2000, pp. 101–120.

[19] Christopher A. Bartlett and Sumantra Ghoshal, "Beyond the M-Form: Toward a Managerial Theory of the Firm," *Strategic Management Journal,* Vol. 14, 1993, pp. 23–46.

[20] This list is taken partially from George S. Yip, *Total Global Strategy: Managing for Worldwide Competitive Advantage* (Englewood Cliffs, NJ: Prentice Hall, 1992).

Objectives

1. To appreciate that companies may use various operating forms to sell abroad or to gain foreign resources

2. To understand why trade (exporting and importing) is important for most companies operating internationally

3. To comprehend the reasons why companies depend on production in foreign countries

4. To perceive the advantages of owning foreign production, rather than contracting with another company that owns it

5. To grasp the reasons for and understand the different types of international collaborative arrangements

6. To recognize the problems of international collaborative arrangements and means of addressing the problems

GM Sets Partnership in Russia

General Motors (GM), the world's largest automaker, has expanded heavily in international markets during the past decade. For example, it bought the remaining 50 percent of Saab (Sweden), 20 percent of Fiat (Italy), 20 percent of Subaru (Japan), and an additional 10 percent of Suzuki Motor (Japan). Some of these moves have been to gain models to round out its line of cars, such as the small cars from Fiat. However, much of GM's strategy is to push into markets with high future growth potential, such as China, India, and Russia.

GM began assembling Chevrolet Blazers (from the United States) and Opel Vectras (from its German-owned company) in Russia in 1996; however, a weakened Russian economy put those models and any of GM's other vehicles out of the reach of Russian consumers. In 1999, for example, 85 percent of new cars were sold in Russia for under $5,000. GM's managers reasoned that the company would have to produce a much less expensive car in order to develop sufficient sales in Russia. Shipping from GM's facilities outside Russia would not be feasible because GM (1) had no models in the right price category, (2) could not likely reduce production costs sufficiently, and (3) would have to pay additional transportation costs to get the cars to the market. The only alternative was to produce within Russia.

But how? GM could build a facility in which it would own 100 percent. However, its management reasoned that it would be better off partnering with a company experienced in Russia and in inexpensive car production. In 2001, GM announced a partnership with the Russian company, AvotVAZ. GM's contribution is about $100 million, as well as sales systems, and the distribution of one of the two models—the Lada Niva 2123—in world markets. AvtoVAZ's contribution is tools, engineering expertise, and personnel.[1]

Forms of Operations

chapter 3

Mask from the Indus Valley
in India.

Introduction

GM's entry into Russia illustrates that a company can tap foreign markets in various ways. It might sell domestically produced output abroad, or it might produce abroad what it sells there. If it does produce abroad, it may own the foreign production facility in whole or in part. In addition to GM's options, a company might take no ownership in the foreign production facility, instead transferring its capabilities to another company for a fee. Likewise, a company may acquire foreign resources or capabilities in various ways. It may buy products from a supplier abroad that encompass the resources. It may invest (wholly or partially) in facilities abroad to produce on its own. Or it may secure rights and capabilities from a company abroad to produce the product in its home country. In essence, there are two sides to any international business transaction. Thus, when a company sells abroad, another entity (often another company) buys from it.

Figure 3.1 shows the way international operating forms relate to the conduct of international business. Keep in mind that combinations of external and internal conditions influence managers' selection of international operating forms. But if they have a

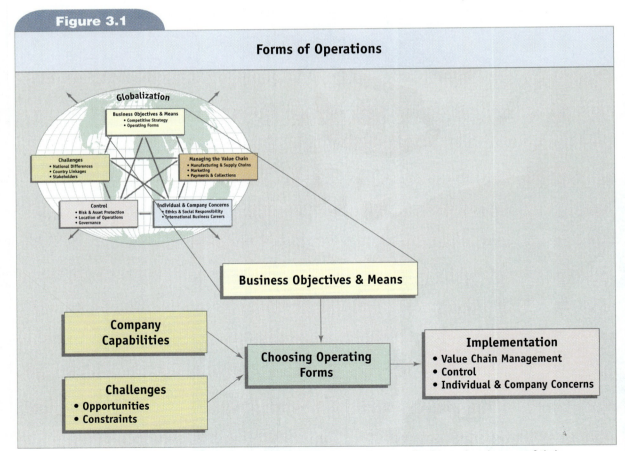

Figure 3.1

Forms of Operations

Operating forms are the means for carrying out business objectives. Companies generally choose them because of their capabilities, international opportunities, and external constraints (such as the environments within countries where they plan to operate). The forms they use affect their abilities to make tactical decisions that will further implement their strategies.

strong preference for using a certain form exclusively, they will be limited in where they go and how much benefit they gain from international operations. For instance, GM could not fully exploit Russian opportunities simply by shipping production from the United States. Generally, managers choose forms initially that require the least amount of financial and managerial commitment to international operations; as they gain experience and success in international operations, they move to forms that require more commitment.

Whether a company produces in its home country or abroad is a convenient way to begin describing operating forms. We'll first discuss the advantages and means (importing and exporting) of moving output from one country to another. Then we'll explain why companies depend on foreign production and the different operating forms the foreign production can take. These forms include foreign equity arrangements—wholly and partially owned foreign direct investment (FDI), joint ventures, and equity alliances. They also include nonequity arrangements—licensing, franchising, management contracts, and turnkey operations. We'll conclude the chapter by discussing the problems of collaborative arrangements, offering suggestions to make them work, and describing how companies' operating forms change over time.

Importing and Exporting

Exports are goods and services sold to residents of a foreign country. **Imports** are purchases from residents of a foreign country. Collectively, exports and imports are known as *trade.* We usually think of exports and imports as sales and purchases of merchandise from one country to another, such as U.S. sales of tractors to Brazil and Brazilian sales of coffee to the United States. These transactions are also called *merchandise trade.* Companies also import and export services, which are known by different names—*service exports and imports, service trade,* and *invisibles.* Service trade is comprised of earnings from and payments to foreign residents for other than merchandise. Some notable areas of service trade are transportation, communications, tourism, financial services, and payments for the use of technology, copyrights, and trademarks.

Trade, especially merchandise trade, is the most important international economic activity for most countries. Generally, larger countries depend less than smaller countries on merchandise imports as a percentage of what their residents consume and less on merchandise exports as a percentage of what their residents produce. This is primarily because larger countries have a greater variety of natural resources and climates and, thus, can produce a greater variety of goods. Some countries, such as the Bahamas, depend primarily on service exports. When non-Bahamians visit the Bahamas, their expenditures there are Bahamian service exports. Likewise, when non-Bahamians pay fees for financial services to the many banks in the Bahamas, these payments are also Bahamian service exports. The United States is the world's largest service trader. Some of the services that the United States sells extensively to foreign residents are education (many foreign students attend U.S. universities) and credit-card systems and collections. However, the United States buys more foreign shipping services than foreigners buy U.S. shipping services. Recall from Chapter 1 that services are the fastest-growing trade sector.

More companies engage in importing and exporting than in any other form of international business. Companies are most apt to export as a means of selling abroad when (1) they are new to international business, (2) their average cost per unit of home-country production declines substantially by increasing output, and (3) they have unique product advantages that competitors cannot rapidly or easily copy.

Companies usually import and export before undertaking other forms of international business. One reason is that importing and exporting require the least commitment of and the least risk to their resources. By importing and exporting, they have little need to transfer capital, personnel, equipment, and production facilities to foreign countries in which they lack operating experience. A second reason is that if companies have excess domestic capacity, they can likely reduce their average cost per unit by increasing home-country production and selling the increase in export markets. But this depends largely on their process technologies. For example, if a company makes a product such as ball bearings, it must use a technology requiring a huge capital investment and a high degree of automation—characteristics that enable the company to reduce costs substantially through economies of scale. This product is an ideal candidate for exporting. However, if a company makes customized metal drums, it must use a labor-intensive technology, which gains little from scale economies; these drums thus are not an ideal candidate for exporting. Further, by using excess domestic capacity to export, companies may better estimate their foreign market potential before they spend on costly foreign production expansions. Finally, companies might export rather than use another operating form because they enjoy advantages in their home-country production—lower cost, higher quality, differentiated or unique products—that competitors cannot easily duplicate by producing in foreign markets.

Once companies establish foreign production, they usually continue to export and import some products and services to some countries. In fact, their foreign operations may distribute products and services abroad for which they still enjoy domestic production advantages. For example, GM exports some of its products, such as Cadillacs, to countries despite producing cars there. Companies may also export components that their foreign facilities assemble.

Finally, as they develop new products or enter new countries, they are apt to start out by exporting. The more companies grow, domestically and internationally, the more likely they are to export.

Importing and exporting do require specialized functions and operations, which we will discuss in detail in Chapter 7. In brief, merchandise trade requires the preparation and delivery of documents, such as those that allow governmental authorities to assess taxes on merchandise and permit it to leave and enter their borders, those that allow transportation companies to ship the merchandise, and those that enable banks to effect payments to sell-

Foreign companies sometimes partner with local companies when they lack experience with local labor practices. This was one factor influencing the U.S. company, General Motors (GM), to partner with the Chinese company, Jinbei Automotive Corp., to produce automobiles in China. The photo shows joint venture workers doing morning exercises, something not customary for GM workers in the United States.

ers in one country by buyers in another. Governments and shipping companies frequently require distinct packing for merchandise trade, and companies need specific expertise and information to clear goods rapidly and cheaply through customs. Frequently, companies use specialized intermediaries that will, for a fee, handle these functions for them. Service trade often requires different operating forms, such as licensing, franchising, management contracts, and turnkey operations. We shall discuss these later in the chapter.

Reasons for Foreign Production

Companies may find advantages of producing in foreign countries. These advantages occur (1) in situations where production abroad is cheaper than at home; (2) when transportation costs to move goods or services internationally are too high; (3) when companies lack domestic capacity; (4) when products and services need to be altered substantially to gain sufficient consumer demand abroad; (5) when governments inhibit the import of foreign products; and (6) when buyers prefer products originating from a particular country.

Cheaper Foreign Production

Competition requires that companies control their costs. For example, U.S., Japanese, and European automakers and their parts suppliers, which compete with each other worldwide, seek to cut costs by placing facilities in lower-cost production locations. Many have thus recently established facilities in Turkey because they can pay skilled labor and sophisticated engineers less than in their home countries. Further, Turks work more days per year and longer hours per day than workers in the companies' home countries; thus, the companies use their equipment more fully and reduce capital costs per unit produced. These companies sell some output in Turkey and some of it in export markets.[2]

Transportation Costs

When companies add the cost of transportation to their production costs, they find that some products become impractical to export. Generally speaking, the farther they must ship products, the higher the transportation costs. Further, the higher the transportation costs relative to production costs, the more difficult it is for companies to develop viable export markets for their products. For example, the international transportation cost for a soft drink is a large percentage of its manufacturing cost, so a sales price that includes both manufacturing and transportation costs would have to be so high that companies would sell little abroad. Thus, firms such as Coca-Cola and PepsiCo have established bottling plants in all the countries where they sell. (Nevertheless, other companies like Perrier and Evian have managed to find niche markets for exported bottled water that sells at high prices relative to production costs.) However, products such as watches have low transportation costs relative to their production costs. Because watch manufacturers lose few sales due to export transportation costs, companies such as Universal Genève and Seiko export watches from Switzerland and Japan, respectively, into the markets where they sell them.

Lack of Domestic Capacity

As long as a company has excess capacity at its home-country facilities, it may be able to compete effectively in export markets despite high transportation costs. In this situation, the company incurs minimal additional production costs by increasing output inasmuch as it does not add any fixed operating expenses (such as the building and equipment) by expanding its sales. In fact, because its average cost of production per unit goes down as foreign sales increase, the company may even be able to build markets by lowering prices. But this strategy may become impractical as foreign sales become so important that the company nears full utilization of its plant capacity. At this point, the company will need to increase capacity, such as by building a second plant. If export sales have grown substantially, the company may opt to build a second plant abroad. This will free domestic capacity for domestic sales and will reduce transportation costs for serving foreign markets.

Need to Alter Products and Services

Companies often need to alter products to gain sufficient sales in a foreign market. This affects their production in two ways. First, the company must make an additional investment, such as an automobile company's adding an assembly line to put steering wheels on the right as well as on the left. As long as the company needs to make an investment to serve the foreign market anyway, its management might consider locating facilities abroad to save transport costs. Second, the company loses certain economies from large-scale production; thus, its least-cost production location to serve given foreign markets may shift from one country to another. The more the company must alter its product for the foreign market, the more likely it will shift production abroad to serve that market. Electrolux, for example—a Swedish producer of major household appliances—first entered Asian markets by exporting. However, it was unable to gain more than minuscule sales with its line of appliances suitable for European and North American markets; so it launched a line of appliances aimed at certain Asian markets that included specially designed hoses to prevent rodents from chewing on them, coatings on circuit boards to discourage ants, heavy zinc coatings to prevent rust, and electrical systems that are more tolerant of erratic electrical current. Given the number of product alterations, Electrolux could gain little from scale economies by producing and exporting to these Asian markets from Sweden. So the company shifted some production to Asia to save transportation costs.[3]

Trade Restrictions

As we discussed in Chapter 1, most countries have been reducing import restrictions; still, every country continues to place some barriers on the import of products and services from abroad. These restrictions sometimes forbid import of a specific product altogether, sometimes allow only certain quantities of imports, and sometimes place a tax on imported products that does not exist on products made domestically. When a company sees a significant market potential that it cannot tap adequately because of trade restrictions, it may decide to produce within the import-restricting country. For example, China places trade restrictions on the importation of elevators. Such firms as United Technologies (Otis Elevators), Schindler Holding, and Mitsubishi now produce elevators within China to tap this growing market.[4]

Country-of-Origin Effects

Factors other than cost affect companies' foreign sales. For example, some customers prefer to purchase locally made goods for nationalistic reasons or because they believe the purchases will employ more of their fellow citizens. In the United States, fiber, textiles, and apparel coalitions have used the motto "Crafted with Pride in the USA" to persuade Americans to buy U.S.-made products. Some industrial consumers additionally fear that they will have difficulty obtaining service and replacement parts for foreign-made goods; they may even be willing to pay higher prices for locally made goods to allay this fear. Such situations may persuade companies to locate some of their production within the countries where they want to sell. Finally, many customers believe that certain products are better from some countries than from others. Companies may thus profit by producing where the image for their products is highly positive.[5]

Foreign Equity Arrangements

A company may or may not take ownership in the foreign facilities that provide products and services to it. Let's say a U.S. company exports to Colombia. It may take no ownership in the Colombian facilities because it sells to an intermediary that warehouses, sells, and services the exported products in that country. Or it might invest in a Colombian facility (company) that handles one or more of these functions. Although a foreign direct investment (FDI), sometimes called simply a **direct investment,** gives the investor a controlling interest in a foreign company, it is difficult to know what percentage of ownership is necessary for control. Governments usually stipulate that ownership of a minimum of 10 or 25 percent of the voting stock in a foreign enterprise is necessary for them to consider the investment as direct for their record keeping and reporting. Generally speaking, the more equity a company has in the foreign operation, the more likely it is to control decisions about that operation. Nevertheless, companies sometimes use administrative devices to gain control even when they have a minority equity interest. These include fragmenting the remaining ownership, stipulating that board decisions require more than a majority (thus giving veto power to minority shareholders), dividing equity into voting and nonvoting stock, and making side agreements on who will control decision making. Figure 3.2 shows the usual relationship between ownership and foreign operating forms.

Likewise, the more equity a company holds in a foreign operation, the higher is its commitment to the particular operation. However, the company may hold a high level of ownership and still minimize its foreign commitment by scaling down the size of that operation. For example, a company may sometimes be able to overcome governmental restrictions on exporting to the country by simply packaging or assembling within the market rather than producing the entire product therein.

By 2000, about 63,000 companies owned about 690,000 FDIs encompassing every type of business function—extracting raw materials from the earth, growing crops, manufacturing products or components, selling output, providing various services, and so on. FDI is not the domain of large companies only.[6]

Figure 3.2

Companies may use
different operating forms to
tap foreign markets. These
forms differ in whether
production is in their home
country or abroad and in
how much ownership they
take when production is
abroad. Companies may use
more than one form
simultaneously. Note that
exporting is the only form
in which production is in
companies' home countries.
Those forms shaded in are
collaborative arrangements.

**Foreign Operating Modes Related
to Ownership and Production Location**

PRODUCTION OWNERSHIP	PRODUCTION LOCATION	
	Home country	Foreign country
Equity arrangements	a. Exporting and importing	a. Wholly owned operations b. Partially owned with remainder widely held c. Joint ventures d. Equity alliances
Nonequity arrangements		a. Licensing b. Franchising c. Management contracts d. Turnkey operations

source: Adapted from *International Business; Environments and Operations, 9/e* by Radebaugh & Daniels © 2001. Reprinted by permission by Pearson Education, Inc., Upper Saddle River, NJ 07458.

Many small companies produce abroad, and many more maintain sales offices abroad to complement their export efforts. However, because large companies tend to have larger foreign facilities and operate in more countries, they own most FDI in terms of value. In terms of output, FDI is now the most important form of international business. For example, although GM is one of the largest exporters from the United States, most of its foreign sales come from production it owns abroad, such as its Opel operation, which designs, produces, and sells automobiles in Germany.

When a company controls a foreign operation rather than collaborating with another company, the situation is often called **internalization.** One reason companies may prefer internalization is that they are reluctant to transfer certain vital resources to another company. These resources may include patents, trademarks, and management know-how that, when transferred, can be used by the receiving company to undermine the competitive position of the original holders. For example, Goodyear collaborated with Bridgestone in Japan by contracting Bridgestone to manufacture tires using Goodyear's technology, a move that gave Goodyear revenue from the Japanese market. However, this technology transfer also enabled Bridgestone to gain and build on capabilities with which it later competed against Goodyear in other markets, including the United States.

Even if a company is willing to transfer its technology, it may have difficulty finding a partner company that can absorb the technology efficiently. In the above example, Bridgestone was already in the tire business, so its personnel could easily learn Goodyear's tire technology. In other cases—say, producing components for computers where there are no existing component manufacturers—the company would probably have to own and manage the facility itself. In so doing, it could transfer its knowledgeable managers and technicians to the facility and minimize the costs of training another company's personnel from scratch.

In addition, companies may decrease operating costs and increase the speed of technological transfer when they self-handle foreign operations for the following reasons:

- Different operating units within the same company are likely to share a common corporate culture, which expedites communications. For example, the merger between Chrysler (United States) and Daimler-Benz (Germany) has resulted in a clash of corporate cultures. The merged company has been plagued by differences between Chrysler and Daimler-Benz in work traditions, governance, and payment of executives.[7]

- The company can use its own managers, who understand and are committed to carrying out its objectives. When General Electric (GE) acquired controlling interest in the Hungarian company Tungsram, for instance, it was able to expedite control and changes because it put GE managers in key positions.[8]

- The company can avoid protracted negotiations with another company on such matters as how income will be divided between them. For example, the U.S. brewer Anheuser-Busch made an investment in the Mexican brewer Grupo Modelo (brewer of Corona). But the companies lost valuable time as they argued over how to calculate Mexican earnings.[9]

- The company can avoid possible problems with enforcing an agreement. For example, Cassini contracted Jovan to promote and extend sales of its fragrances, cosmetics, and beauty supplies to upscale retailers worldwide. But Jovan sold to discount stores. Cassini had to take Jovan to court to win a suit for image injury.[10]

Internalization also allows companies to more easily adopt a global or transnational strategy. For example, if a U.S. company owned 100 percent of its Brazilian operation, it might be able to take actions that, although suboptimizing Brazilian performance, could deal more effectively with actual or potential competitors and customers on a global basis—such as by decreasing prices to an industrial customer in Brazil to gain that customer's business in Germany. But if the company shared ownership in Brazil, the lower prices might be detrimental to the other Brazilian owners. Because most countries have laws to protect minority shareholders' interests, sharing of ownership may restrict a company from implementing a global or transnational strategy.

Motives for Collaborative Arrangements

Despite advantages from controlling foreign operations with wholly owned facilities and self-managing them, companies increasingly collaborate with other companies. Figure 3.3 illustrates these reasons. The following discussion highlights why companies collaborate internationally.

Spread and Reduce Costs

If its volume of business is small, a company may find that contracting certain work to another company, particularly a specialist, is cheaper than doing the

Figure 3.3

The motives for collaborative arrangements on the left may serve companies' goals regardless of whether they operate internationally. The motives on the right are specific to international business.

Motives for Collaborative Arrangements

General
- Spread and reduce costs
- Specialize in competencies
- Competitive factors
- Secure vertical and horizontal links
- Glean knowledge

Specific to International Business
- Gain location-specific assets
- Overcome legal constraints
- Diversify geographically
- Minimize exposure in risky environments

source: Adapted from *International Business; Environments and Operations, 9/e* by Radebaugh & Daniels © 2001. Reprinted by permission by Pearson Education, Inc., Upper Saddle River, NJ 07458.

work itself. Rather than hiring personnel, for instance, an exporter might more cheaply contract specialized companies to handle the packing, transportation, and documentation work because the specialists can spread fixed personnel costs over services to more than one company. If business increases enough, of course, a company buying services may be able to self-handle them more cheaply. Thus, companies should periodically reappraise whether to self-handle operations or have other companies handle them. Such a reappraisal creates a dilemma for companies handling activities for others: The better they do their job to increase sales for the companies that have contracted with them, the more likely those companies will sell enough to justify self-handling, thus possibly dissolving the agreement. However, dissolving an agreement to start one's own venture can be a costly proposition. Abroad, other companies may have excess production or sales capacity. Contracting use of this capacity may be cheaper than self-handling. It may also reduce start-up time and, thus, result in an earlier cash flow.

Specialize in Competencies

The **resource-based view of the firm** holds that each company has a unique combination of competencies. A company may seek to improve its performance by concentrating on those activities that best fit its competencies, thus depending on other firms to supply it with products, services, or support activities in which it has lesser competency. For this reason, large, diversified companies are constantly reevaluating and altering their product lines to put their efforts where their major strengths lie. They may also have products, assets, or technologies that they do not wish to exploit themselves but that may be profitably transferred to other companies. For example, Coca-Cola's logo has value in selling products for which Coca-Cola has no expertise in manufacturing or marketing, so the company sells the right to use this logo on more than 40,000 products in more than 40 countries.[11]

Some firms have a core competency in managing collaborative arrangements. Such companies as Corning Glass conduct most of their business through collaborative arrangements. Further, we see many companies, particularly in the franchising industry, that have expanded domestically through collaboration. It is understandable that these companies use similar operating forms abroad, such as McDonald's use of franchising outside the United States to duplicate its U.S. successes.

Competitive Factors

Sometimes a market is not large enough to justify the entry of as many companies as would like to tap it. Thus, various companies may band together so as not to compete in certain areas. For example, international airlines are entering many alliances, such as the one between Continental Airlines from the United States and Virgin Atlantic from the United Kingdom that jointly operates some of their transatlantic flights. This has led to some customer concerns about what airlines they are really flying.[12] Figure 3.4 illustrates this. Companies may also collaborate to eliminate the need to duplicate investments that might lead to overcapacity. For example, Ford's European plants make cars for Mazda to sell in Europe, and Mazda's Japanese factories make vehicles for Ford to sell in Japan.[13] Or companies may simply collude to raise everyone's prices. Only a few countries, mainly English-speaking ones, make and enforce laws against collusion.[14]

Companies may combine certain resources to combat a market's larger and more powerful competitors. For example, the Swedish-Swiss company Asea Brown Boveri (ABB) is collaborating with the French company Alstom on

Figure 3.4

Alliances sometimes obscure whether companies are competing or colluding.

source: Nick Baker. Reprinted by permission. © Nick Baker.

power-plant equipment to better compete against GE, the global market leader.[15] A group of companies, including AT&T and GTE, is collaborating to compete in the Mexican market against Telmex, the former telecommunications monopoly there.[16]

Secure Vertical and Horizontal Linkages

As we discussed in Chapter 2, companies may gain cost savings and supply assurances from vertical integration; however, some firms lack the competence or resources necessary to own and manage the full value chain of activities. For example, the Tsai family of Taiwan owns manufacturing companies in Taiwan, Hong Kong, China, Indonesia, and Vietnam that turn out about 14 percent of the world's shoes. But the Tsais lack vital distribution skills. To offset this deficiency, they sell output to well-known branded shoe companies.[17]

Horizontal linkage may increase a company's product line, thus giving it economies of scope in distribution, such as by having a full line of products to sell that reduces the cost of sales per visit to potential customers. For example, Avon's representatives in Brazil sell not only cosmetics, but also Crayola products, such as crayons and *Reader's Digest* subscriptions. Grupo Industrial Alfa manufactures and sells a variety of products in the Mexican market on behalf of such foreign companies as Ford from the United States, Yamaha from Japan, AKZO from the Netherlands, and BASF from Germany. This enables Alfa to spread its administrative costs efficiently. A company may also better smooth its earnings by diversifying into more products.

Also, companies might lack the resources to "go it alone"; by pooling their efforts, however, they may be able to undertake activities that otherwise would be beyond their means. This is especially important for small businesses. But big companies team up as well. Volvo and Mitsubishi have teamed up, for instance, to develop trucks to sell in Asian markets.[18] Sometimes a project is too big for one company. For example, groups of firms have developed collaborative arrangements to compete for large contracts in China. One such competition pitted three companies (Siemens and Voith of Germany and GE of the United States) against two companies (the U.K.-French company GEC-Alsthom and the Swedish-Swiss ABB) to supply equipment for a $30-billion dam project in China.[19] One of the fastest-growth areas for collaborative arrangements has been the combination of horizontal and vertical linkage of companies when projects are too large for any single firm to handle, such as new aircraft and communications systems. For example, Boeing estimates that developing the next generation of 747s will cost $7 billion, an amount that strains the capabilities of even a corporation as large as Boeing.[20] From such a project's inception, different firms (sometimes from different countries) agree to take on the high cost and risk of developmental work for the various components needed in the final product; then a lead company buys the components from those firms.

Glean Knowledge

The motive for many companies' entries into collaborative arrangements is to learn: They wish to broaden or deepen their own competencies and become more competitive in the future. For example, China has often insisted on foreign companies' collaboration with Chinese companies as a requisite for the foreign firms' sales in China. This insistence helps Chinese companies gain technologies that better enable them to compete independently in the future. Companies may collaborate abroad to gain industry-specific knowledge, such as technology. Mitsubishi Chemical collaborated with Key Pharmaceuticals in the United States until it gained enough knowledge to return to Japan to compete in that market.[21] In some cases, companies collaborate with a local partner until they have enough experience in the country to feel competent to handle operations independently there. Coca-Cola did this in Norway and Sweden, where it learned from its local distributors.[22] In still other cases, both partners may learn from each other. This has been a driving force for collaboration between U.S. and European wine makers, such as the collaboration between Robert Mondavi from the United States and Baron Philippe de Rothschild from France.[23]

Gain Location-Specific Assets

Cultural, political, competitive, and economic differences among countries create barriers for companies that want to operate abroad. When they feel ill equipped to handle these differences, they may seek collaboration with local companies to help manage the local operations. For example, most foreign operations in Japan involve some type of collaboration with Japanese companies, which can help them secure distribution and a competent workforce—two assets they cannot easily gain on their own in Japan. Access to distribution was the primary reason that Merck entered a joint venture with Chugai in Japan for the development and marketing of over-the-counter drugs.[24] And one reason so many foreign companies have collaborated with Grupo Industrial Alfa in Mexico is that Alfa knows how to deal with Mexican regulations and labor, an ability that would be expensive for them to gain on their own.

Overcome Legal Constraints

Some countries, such as China, India, and South Korea, require foreign companies to collaborate in certain industries if they are to tap those markets. Many other countries limit foreign ownership in sensitive industries. For example, the United States grants U.S.-based airlines the right to carry all passengers between cities in the United States, and it limits foreign ownership in U.S.-based airlines to 25 percent of voting stock and 49 percent of total equity. Thus, non–U.S.-based airlines have developed collaborative arrangements with U.S. airlines to tap potential feeder traffic into their transatlantic and transpacific air routes. One such arrangement involves Delta Airlines and Austrian Airlines, whereby Austrian handles the flight between New York and Vienna on behalf of both airlines, and Delta's vast network of U.S. domestic routes feeds passengers into New York for connections.

Collaboration can also be a means of protecting an asset. This may occur for two reasons. First, many countries provide very little protection for foreign property rights such as trademarks, patents, and copyrights unless authorities are prodded consistently. To prevent piracy of these proprietary assets, companies have sometimes made collaborative agreements with local companies that enjoy good relations with local authorities. These local firms ensure that no one else uses the asset locally. For example, the Business Software Alliance, which represents software companies, estimated that pirated material accounted for 88 percent of the software in use in Egypt. Microsoft announced that it would contract out production of Arabic versions of its programs to Egyptian manufacturers in exchange for their commitment and the Egyptian government's commitment to combat software piracy in Egypt.[25] Second, some countries provide protection only if a company exploits the internationally registered asset locally within a specified period. Otherwise, another company can gain the right to the asset without paying the original owner. Rather than allowing this to occur where they cannot enter a market on their own, companies seek out a local company to pay for the usage.

Diversify Geographically

Not only product diversification, but also geographic diversification among countries, can help a firm smooth its sales and profits. Collaborative arrangements offer faster initial means of entry into multiple markets. As companies depend more on core businesses by divesting noncore ones, geographic diversification may become more important.

Minimize Exposure in Risky Environments

There are many types of risk. However, the possibility that political and economic changes will affect the safety of assets and their earnings is often at the forefront of managers' concerns about foreign operations. One way to minimize loss from foreign political occurrences is to minimize the base of assets located abroad. Doing this may dictate that companies collaborate so that others share in the asset base. Collaboration might also reduce the political risk of expropriation (the government takeover of property) because governments may be less willing to move against a shared operation for fear of encountering adverse publicity from more than one company, especially if they are from different countries. Another way to spread risk is to place operations in a number of different countries, thereby reducing the chance that all foreign assets will be simultaneously subject to such adversity as political unrest or economic crises. As in the case of geographic diversification, a firm's minimization and use of its own assets permits a more rapid dispersion of operations among countries.

Collaborative Forms

Throughout this discussion, keep in mind that there are trade-offs. For example, a company's decision to take no ownership in the foreign production of a product may reduce its exposure to political risk, but the decision could also stymie its ability to learn about that environment, thus delaying (perhaps permanently) its reaping of the full profits from producing and selling the product abroad on its own.

Joint Venture

When two or more companies share ownership of an FDI, the operation is called a **joint venture.** Although companies usually form a joint venture to achieve a limited objective, they may continue to operate it indefinitely as they redefine objectives. Joint ventures are sometimes thought of as 50/50 companies, but often, more than two organizations participate in ownership. Further, one organization frequently controls more than 50 percent of the venture.

When more than two organizations participate, the resulting joint venture is sometimes called a **consortium.**

Almost every conceivable combination of partners may exist in a joint venture, including a partnership of companies from the same country in a foreign market, a partnership of foreign and local companies, a partnership of companies from two or more countries in a third country, and a partnership of private and government-owned companies. The more organizations that are involved, the more complex the ownership arrangement will be. Figure 3.5 shows that as either the number of partners or the sharing of ownership increases, the ease of managing decreases.

Equity Alliances

Equity alliances involve a company's equity position (almost always minority) in the company with which it has a collaborative arrangement. In some cases, each party takes an ownership in the other. The purpose of equity ownership is to solidify a collaborating contract so that it is more difficult to break, particularly if the investing firm's ownership is large enough to secure it a board mem-

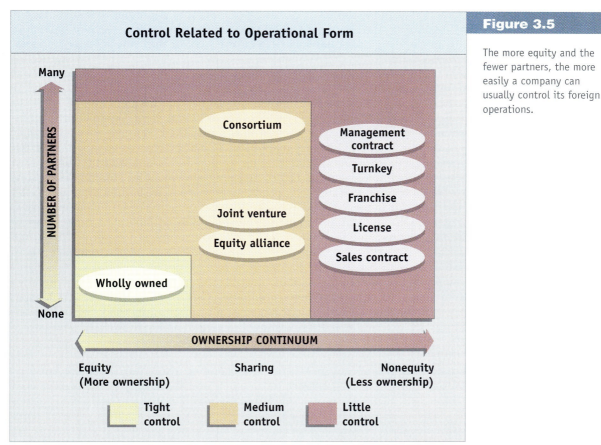

Figure 3.5

The more equity and the fewer partners, the more easily a company can usually control its foreign operations.

source: The figure was adapted from *European Management Journal,* Vol. 12, No. 1, Shaker Zahra and Galal Elhagrasey, "Strategic Management of International Joint Ventures," March 1994, pp. 83–93, with permission from Elsevier Science.

bership. For example, GM (United States) and Fiat (Italy) solidified collaborations in car engine development and marketing (especially in Latin America) through GM's 20 percent ownership of Fiat and Fiat's 5 percent ownership of GM.[26]

Licensing

Under a **licensing agreement,** a company (the licensor) grants rights to intangible property to another company (the licensee) for a specified period; in exchange, the licensee ordinarily pays a royalty to the licensor. The rights may be exclusive (monopoly within a given territory) or nonexclusive. Licensing agreements are most common on the use of patents, trademarks, copyrights, and unpatented technology. The licensor does not have to risk placing tangible assets, such as plant and equipment, abroad. The licensee may find that the cost of the arrangement is less than if it developed the intangible property on its own.

Payments for licensing agreements may be a fixed fee or based on usage, such as a percentage of the sales value or units produced with the license. In either case, the amount paid is negotiated between the licensee and licensor and depends on how valuable the property will be to the licensor. The value to the licensor depends on whether the agreement is exclusive or not, how long it can use the intangible property, and how much of a competitive advantage it will gain from the property. One of the tricky evaluations is technology that is still in the developmental stage, because it may or may not become valuable. Companies negotiate agreements on developmental technology so that licensors in different countries can introduce new products using the technology at about the same time.

For industries in which technological changes are frequent and affect many different products, such as chemicals and electrical goods, companies in various countries often exchange technology rather than compete with each other on every product and in every market. Such an arrangement is known as **cross-licensing.** For example, DBStar from the United States and Transtar from France entered a technology-sharing, cross-licensing agreement for computer data storage. DBStar produces and sells products developed by both companies in the North American market, and Transtar does the same in the European market.[27]

Although we think of licensing agreements as collaborative arrangements among unassociated companies, most licenses are given to companies owned in whole or part by the licensor.[28] A license may be necessary to transfer technology abroad because operations in a foreign country, even if 100 percent owned by the parent, are usually subsidiaries, which are separate companies from a legal standpoint. When a company owns less than 100 percent, a separate licensing agreement may be a means of compensating the licensor for contributions beyond the mere investment of capital and managerial resources.

Franchising

Franchising is a specialized form of licensing in which the franchisor not only sells an independent franchisee the use of a trademark that is an essential asset for the franchisee's business, but also more than nominally assists on a continuing basis in the operation of the business. In many cases, the franchisor also provides supplies. For example, Domino's Pizza grants to start-up franchisees the goodwill of the corporate name and support services, such as appraisal of the proposed restaurant site and cost control systems. As part of the continuing relationship, Domino's offers promotional expertise, new products, and training programs to help ensure the venture's success. It also buys supplies centrally (to save costs and ensure product consistency), such as cheese from New Zealand, that it sells to franchisees. In a sense, a franchisor and a franchisee act almost like a vertically integrated company because the parties are interdependent, and each produces part of the product or service that ultimately reaches the consumer. Franchisors are headquartered in many different countries. Among the many industries that depend heavily on franchising are car and truck dealerships, gasoline service stations, soft drink bottling, hotels, food, and business services.

Franchising success usually depends on uniformity of product and processes and on brand recognition. The former is difficult internationally because operating environments are so different. The franchisor may have to permit country modifications, but if there are too many of these, it will have nothing sufficiently unique to sell prospective franchisees. The latter is difficult as well. Unless the target clientele is internationally mobile, such as business travelers who use hotel franchises, the company may not be known well enough in a foreign country to convince people to invest as franchisees. Further, until there is a critical mass of franchises, neither massive promotion nor headquarters visits to check quality and provide assistance is economical. In entering a new country, franchisors often initially own facilities until they become better known or give rights to a master franchisee to open multiple outlets and subfranchise to others.

Management Contracts

Management contracts are arrangements whereby, for a fee, one company provides personnel to perform general or specialized management functions for another company. Because one of the most important assets a company may have is management talent, management contracts are a means by which a firm may use part of its managerial personnel to assist a foreign company for a specified period. Thus, the company may gain income with little capital outlay. For example, Hilton has management contracts in Egypt, where the government owns hotels. And the British Airport Authority (BAA) manages some airports in the United States, Australia, China, and Italy.[29]

Turnkey Operations

Turnkey operations involve a contract for construction of operating facilities that are transferred for a fee to the owner when they are ready to commence operations. Companies performing turnkey operations are frequently industrial equipment manufacturers that supply some of their own equipment for the project. But most commonly, they are engineering and construction companies. They may also be consulting firms or manufacturers that decide not to make an investment on their own behalf in the country, or are excluded from doing so because the facility will be a government monopoly. There are also turnkey operations for services. For example, International Turnkey Systems (ITS), a Kuwaiti company, sets up information technology operations for companies abroad, such as a software development contract with Siemens in Germany.[30]

What sets turnkey projects apart are that so many are so large—often billions of dollars are involved—and so many are government contracts. The size means that a few very large companies—Bechtel, Fluor, and Kellogg Rust—account for most of the international market. Smaller companies often serve as subcontractors. Government contracts cause companies to hire many former diplomats who have contacts with governmental officials and to time facility inaugurations to coincide with important national days. Further, many projects are in very remote areas; thus, turnkey providers must build entire infrastructures in adverse conditions.

Use of Different Operational Forms

The truly experienced international firm usually uses most of the operational forms available, selecting them according to specific product or foreign operating characteristics. The company may change operating forms as operations expand or contract and as it gains experience. Further, the operating forms may be combined. For example, a company may combine a nonequity form (such as

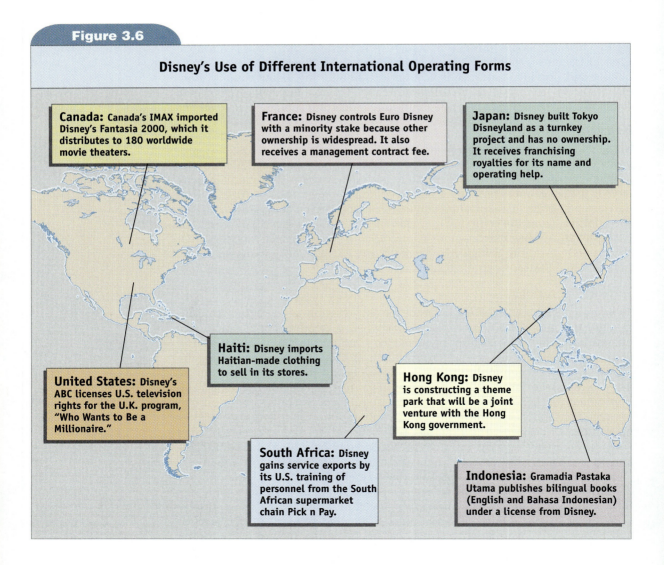

Figure 3.6

Disney's Use of Different International Operating Forms

Canada: Canada's IMAX imported Disney's Fantasia 2000, which it distributes to 180 worldwide movie theaters.

France: Disney controls Euro Disney with a minority stake because other ownership is widespread. It also receives a management contract fee.

Japan: Disney built Tokyo Disneyland as a turnkey project and has no ownership. It receives franchising royalties for its name and operating help.

Haiti: Disney imports Haitian-made clothing to sell in its stores.

United States: Disney's ABC licenses U.S. television rights for the U.K. program, "Who Wants to Be a Millionaire."

Hong Kong: Disney is constructing a theme park that will be a joint venture with the Hong Kong government.

South Africa: Disney gains service exports by its U.S. training of personnel from the South African supermarket chain Pick n Pay.

Indonesia: Gramadia Pastaka Utama publishes bilingual books (English and Bahasa Indonesian) under a license from Disney.

licensing) with an equity form in the same operation. It may also combine output from its production facilities at home with those in a foreign country. Figure 3.6 shows some of Disney's uses of different operating forms internationally.

Managing Operating Forms

Although choosing an appropriate operating form is important, a company must do much more if it is to succeed internationally. If it self-handles international operations, it must staff and control them. If it collaborates, the company must set objectives for the partner and monitor to make sure the partner is performing as intended. There are many examples of licensing, franchising, and joint venture partners that produced poor quality, sold in unapproved outlets, and manufactured in inappropriate ways. The repercussions have had negative global effects on companies' operations. We shall now discuss problems of collaborative agreements, offer suggestions on how to make them work, and show how companies' operating forms evolve.

Problems of Collaborative Arrangements

Although collaborative agreements are widespread and have several advantages, many companies have problems with them that lead to either a renegotiation of working relationships or the breakdown of the agreements. For example, about half of all joint ventures break up because one or all partners are dissatisfied with the venture. In about three-quarters of breakups, one partner buys out the other's interest so that the operation continues as a wholly owned foreign subsidiary.[31] Figure 3.7 shows that joint venture divorce (and divorce in other collaborative arrangements) can follow a number of different patterns.

By mentioning collaborative problems, we do not mean to imply that there are no success stories. There are. Nevertheless, five factors create major strains on collaborative arrangements:

1. *Differing relative importance of the arrangement to the partners.* When, for example, one partner is much larger than the other, a particular collaboration may be given higher priority for decision making in the smaller than in the larger. This can lead to poor relations between the partners.

2. *Differing objectives from the arrangement.* For example, one partner may see the arrangement as potentially competitive with its wholly owned operations and want to minimize growth, whereas the other may see the arrangement as noncompetitive and want it to grow.

3. *Control problems.* For instance, one partner may want to use the operation to fight a competitor globally, whereas the other partner has no global competitors and wants merely to maximize local performance.

4. *Relative contributions and appropriations.* One partner may want all earnings to go to dividends, whereas the other partner may want to reinvest. Or one partner may be making technological breakthroughs that can benefit the collaboration, whereas the other's research and development department has been coming up empty.

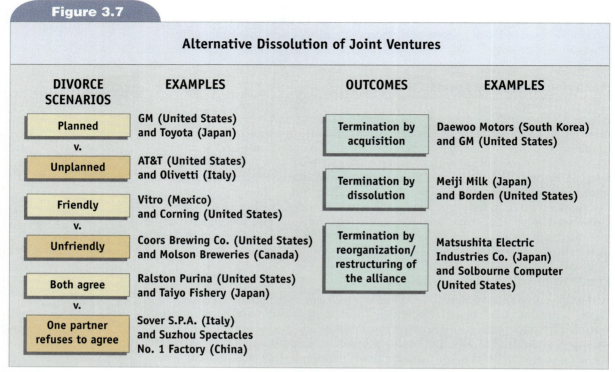

Figure 3.7

Alternative Dissolution of Joint Ventures

DIVORCE SCENARIOS	EXAMPLES	OUTCOMES	EXAMPLES
Planned	GM (United States) and Toyota (Japan)	Termination by acquisition	Daewoo Motors (South Korea) and GM (United States)
v.			
Unplanned	AT&T (United States) and Olivetti (Italy)	Termination by dissolution	Meiji Milk (Japan) and Borden (United States)
Friendly	Vitro (Mexico) and Corning (United States)	Termination by reorganization/ restructuring of the alliance	Matsushita Electric Industries Co. (Japan) and Solbourne Computer (United States)
v.			
Unfriendly	Coors Brewing Co. (United States) and Molson Breweries (Canada)		
Both agree	Ralston Purina (United States) and Taiyo Fishery (Japan)		
v.			
One partner refuses to agree	Sover S.P.A. (Italy) and Suzhou Spectacles No. 1 Factory (China)		

There is considerable variation in both the way that joint ventures dissolve and the outcome of the operation after the dissolution. Any of the scenarios might have any of the outcomes.

source: Adapted from Manuel G. Serapio Jr. and Wayne F. Cascio, "End Games in International Alliances," *Academy of Management Executive,* May 1996, p. 67.

5. *Differences in organizational or national culture.* One company may be accustomed to promoting from within the organization and maintaining a stable workforce. If the partner typically considers outsiders for staff openings and feels that management turnover keeps people productive, the two companies will have difficulty in creating an operation that combines their personnel.

Making Collaborative Arrangements Work

A company can seek out a partner for its foreign operations or it can react to a proposal from another company to collaborate. In either case, a company must evaluate the potential partner not only for the resources it can supply, but also for its motivation and willingness to work cooperatively. A company can identify potential partners by monitoring journals and technical conferences. It can also find partners by networking. For example, after a company makes contact and builds rapport with managers of one local firm, those managers may offer introductions to managers in other firms.[32] Or a company can increase its own visibility by participating in trade fairs, distributing brochures, and nurturing contacts in the locale of potential collaboration—

increasing the probability that other companies will consider it as a partner. The proven ability to handle similar types of collaboration is a key professional qualification. For example, Alfa's track record has made it a candidate for collaboration by companies entering the Mexican market. Because Alfa has this track record, a partner may be able to depend more on trust rather than expensive control mechanisms to ensure that its interests are upheld. Once into the collaboration, partners may also be able to build partner trust through their actions in the collaborative agreement.[33] But every company has to start somewhere. Without a proven track record, a company may have to negotiate harder, make more concessions to a partner, and spell out more in detailed contracts.

Dynamics of Operating Forms

In their early stages of international development, few companies are willing to expend a large portion of their resources on foreign operations; they may not even have sufficient resources for rapid expansion abroad. Consequently, they usually move through stages of increased levels of international involvement. In early stages, they attempt to conserve their own scarce resources and maximize the proportion of the resources that are at home rather than abroad. This leads them to operational forms that transfer the burden of foreign commitment to outsiders. As companies and their foreign activities grow, they tend to self-handle more operations and locate a larger proportion of resources abroad. However, the cost of switching from one form to another—such as from licensing to wholly owned facilities—may be very high because of having to gain expertise from, and possibly pay termination fees to, another company.

Exporting usually precedes foreign production, and contracting with another company to handle foreign business generally precedes handling it internally. A company may be at different stages for different products and for different markets. It also may feel that differences in countries' characteristics necessitate diverse forms of involvement. Because of the multiproduct nature of most companies, varied products sold in the same country also may necessitate different operating forms.

Summary

Companies may serve foreign markets by selling their home-country production abroad (exporting) or by producing abroad what they sell abroad. If they produce abroad, they may own the production facilities in whole or in part, such as by making FDI's, or they may develop collaborative arrangements whereby other companies produce on their behalf, such as through licensing, franchising, management contracts, or turnkey operations. Likewise, companies may gain foreign resources by buying them or by producing them abroad. Their choices should be based on comparative costs, experience, availability of resources, competitive situations, and country conditions. Most companies heavily committed to international operations use a variety of operating forms, varying them by product, by country, and over time.

endnotes

1 David Welch, Christine N. Tierney, and Chester Dawson, "GM Tries to Show Who's Boss," *Business Week,* March 12, 2001, pp. 18–20; Gregory L. White, "GM Board Approves Joint-Venture Plan with Russian Auto Maker AO Avtovaz," *Wall Street Journal,* February 8, 2001, p. A14; "GM's Russian Partner," *Manufacturing Engineering,* February 2001, pp. 20–22; and "General Motors Ponders Russia," *Corporate Location,* third quarter 2000, p. 3.

2 Hugh Pope, "Ford Forges Ahead with Turkey Plans," *Wall Street Journal,* July 24, 2000, p. A17+.

3 Neal McGratt, "New Broom Sweeps into Asia," *Asian Business,* March 1996, p. 22.

4 Joseph Kahn, "Otis Elevator Plans Expansion in China to Defend Market Share," *Asian Wall Street Journal,* May 2, 1995, p. 3.

5 John S. Hulland, "The Effects of Country-of-Brand and Brand Name on Product Evaluation and Consideration: A Cross-Country Comparison," *Consumer Behavior in Asia: Issues and Market Practice,* 1999, pp. 23–39.

6 *World Investment Report 2000* (New York: United Nations Conference on Trade and Development, 2000), p. 1.

7 Tony Jackson, "Culture Crucial to Synergy Equation," *Financial Times,* May 8, 1998, p. 22; and Tim Burt and Nikki Tait, "In Search of More Equal Partnership," *Financial Times,* October 6, 1999, p. 15.

8 Paul Marer and Vincent Mabert, "GE Acquires and Restructures Tungsram: The First Six Years (1990–1995)," *OECD, Trends and Policies in Privatization,* Vol. III, No. 1 (Paris: OECD, 1996), pp. 149–185, and their unpublished 1999 revision, "GE's Acquisition of Hungary's Tungsram."

9 Leslie Crawford, "Anheuser's Cross-Border Marriage on the Rocks," *Financial Times,* March 18, 1998, p. 16.

10 "Cassini Awarded $16 Million in Fragrance Line Squabble," *Wall Street Journal,* June 2, 1988, p. 28.

11 John Willman, "Coca-Cola Aims to Put Fizz into Fashion," *Financial Times,* January 21, 1999, p. 1.

12 Michael Skapinker, "Passengers Not Convinced," *Financial Times,* November 19, 1998, Business Travel section, p. iii.

13 Tim Burt and John Griffiths, "Ford May Use Excess Capacity in Europe to Produce Mazdas," *Financial Times,* March 13, 2000, p. 17.

14 Philip Parker, "How Do Companies Collude?" *Financial Times,* September 28, 1998, Mastering Marketing section, pp. 10–11.

15 Charles Fleming, "ABB, Alstom to Pool European Power Business," *Wall Street Journal,* March 24, 1999, p. A19.

16 Leslie Crawford and Daniel Dombey, "Merger Plan Hits Mexico Telecoms Monopoly," *Financial Times,* April 24, 1996, p. 1+.

17 Jon E. Hilsenrath, "Overseas Suppliers to Brands Thrive," *Wall Street Journal,* March 10, 2000, p. A13.

18 Christopher Brown-Humes and Alexandra Harney, "Volvo Truck Deal Will Relieve Pressure on Mitsubishi," *Financial Times,* October 9–10, 1999, p. 1.

19 James Harding and Peter Marsh, "German-U.S. Consortium Near Three Gorges Order," *Financial Times,* August 16–17, 1997, p. 2.

20 Jeff Cole, "New Boeing 747s Could Cost $7 Billion to Develop," *Wall Street Journal,* November 11, 1996, p. A3.

[21] Jean Hennart, Thomas Roehl, and Dixie S. Zietlow, "'Trojan Horse' or 'Workhorse'? The Evolution of U.S.-Japanese Joint Ventures in the United States," *Strategic Management Journal,* Vol. 20, 1999, pp. 15–29.

[22] Greg McIvor, "Coca-Cola Ends Link with Nordic Producers," *Financial Times,* June 20, 1996, p. 15.

[23] Jason Wilson, "Best of Both Worlds," *Continental,* April 1999, pp. 49–51.

[24] "Merck and Chugai Form OTC Venture," *Financial Times,* September 19, 1996, p. 17.

[25] Mark Huband and Alan Cane, "Microsoft Licensing Deal Wins Egypt Aid on Piracy," *Financial Times,* August 28, 1997, p. 1+.

[26] Paul Betts and Tim Burt, "General Motors and Fiat Close to Signing Strategic Alliance," *Financial Times,* March 13, 2000, p. 1.

[27] "DBStar and Transtar Sign U.S.-European Cross-Licensing Agreement," *Business Wire,* August 26, 1996.

[28] John A. Sondheimer and Sylvia E. Bargas, "U.S. International Sales and Purchases of Private Services," *Survey of Current Business,* September 1994, p. 114.

[29] Bertrand Benoit, "BAA Wins License to Run Chinese Airports," *Financial Times,* August 30, 1999, p. 13.

[30] Essam Mahmoud and Gillian Rice, "Ssaad al Barrak of International Turnkey Systems (ITS), Kuwait," *International Business Review,* Vol. 40, No. 5, September–October 1998, pp. 451–460.

[31] Joel Bleeke and David Ernst, "The Way to Win in Cross-Border Alliances," *Harvard Business Review,* November–December 1991, pp. 127–135.

[32] Anne Smith and Marie-Claude Reney, "The Mating Dance: A Case Study of Local Partnering Processes in Developing Countries," *European Management Journal,* Vol. 15, No. 2, 1997, pp. 174–182.

[33] Sanjiv Kumar and Anju Seth, "The Design of Coordination and Control Mechanisms for Managing Joint Venture–Parent Relationships," *Strategic Management Journal,* Vol. 19, 1998, pp. 579–599; T. K. Das and Bing-Sheng Teng, "Between Trust and Control: Developing Confidence in Partner Cooperation in Alliances," *Academy of Management Journal,* Vol. 23, No. 3, July 1998, pp. 491–512; and Arvind Parkhe, "Building Trust in International Alliances," *Journal of World Business,* Vol. 33, No. 4, 1998, pp. 417–437.

Objectives

1. To appreciate that companies face vastly different operating environments when they operate abroad

2. To realize the importance of analyzing countries' political and economic strategies and performance

3. To sense how different political and economic systems affect the conduct of business

4. To recognize how countries' demographic differences affect business environments

5. To comprehend some of the major cultural differences among countries that impact international business

Gillette: Adapting Practices to Sell Products Worldwide

G illette is one of the world's most international companies. It sells in more than 200 countries and derives more than 60 percent of its revenue from outside its U.S. home market. Virtually all its top managers have had foreign assignments, and many were born outside the United States. Nevertheless, because national operating conditions are so different, the Gillette chief executive officer has said, "Our scarcest resource is globally literate leaders."

Gillette's products—such as razor blades, shampoo, batteries, deodorant, toothbrushes, and ballpoint pens—generally need little or no adaptation to foreign markets. Still, its managers must adapt their strategies and operating methods to differences in countries' environments. For example, when Gillette acquired Parker Pen, it needed to consolidate the operations of the two firms. In most countries, the consolidation moved quickly. The company moved slowly in Singapore, however, because of Asians' respect for age. Gillette's managers took the time to show deference in many subtle ways to Parker's general manager, a Chinese gentleman in his early 60s, who had to report after the consolidation to Gillette's general manger, a Singaporean in his 30s.

Gillette must also consider the legal-political environments in which it operates. For example, when it acquired Wilkinson, another company making razor blades, it had to get approval from authorities in more than 10 countries because of competition issues. The company must also work with governmental authorities to try to stem counterfeiting of its products. For example, it worked with more than 200 governmental agents in China to seize 3 million counterfeit Duracell batteries destined to Russia for packaging and resale to other countries. And like other companies, Gillette must get permission from governmental authorities in most countries to establish operations there. Gillette negotiated with Indian governmental authorities for seven years before being granted permission to produce blades in India, the world's largest market for razor blades. The company finally agreed to own only 24 percent of the operation and not use its own brand name on the blades.

National Differences
Facing Operations

chapter 4

A Japanese mask used in
Bugaku, the world's oldest
traditional performed dance.

Still, differences in economic environments have recently affected Gillette the most. In 1998, Gillette rolled out its new razor, the Mach3, in which it had invested $750 million in research and development (R&D) and $300 million in marketing. The Mach3 razor is more expensive than the model it replaces, and replacement blades will cost 50 percent more. Given the high price, Gillette's managers had to determine where to focus most of their advertising and marketing efforts. They decided to go first to the high-income markets of the United States and Canada, follow a few months later to Europe, and enter lower-income emerging markets the following year. Then the Asian financial crisis hit and affected all emerging-country markets. Gillette could not meet its annual profit growth target.[1] It was also forced to cut 4,700 employees (11 percent of the workforce), close or consolidate some 30 offices worldwide, and close 14 factories. Gillette's stock price plummeted.[2]

Russia is another example of Gillette's emerging-market woes. When it entered Russia, the company reduced the number of blades per package and offered less expensive double-edged blades because of low Russian incomes.[3] But Gillette's Russian sales fell by 80 percent in August 1998 due to political, economic, and currency turmoil. Although consumer demand appeared to be strong, distributors couldn't get foreign currency to pay for the products Gillette produced in other countries, and retailers ran out of inventory. So Gillette had to rescue its distributors financially.

Despite economic problems in emerging economies, Gillette decided to open the Brazilian and Thai markets for sales in 2000. But the company faces continuing uncertainty over whether countries with lower incomes will generate sufficient sales of the more expensive Mach3.

Introduction

Gillette's challenges are the same as those of all companies operating globally. Once a company leaves its home country, it enters a vastly different operating environment. Some countries may be very similar to its home country (say, the United States for Canadian companies), but other countries may be very different (Russia for U.S. companies). Generally, managers operate more easily in countries similar to their homes. This chapter will look at three dimensions of countries' environments: legal-political (the political and regulatory environment), economic (economic systems, basic economic infrastructure, economic levels, and economic stability), and human (the demographic and cultural environment). Figure 4.1 shows how these environmental dimensions relate to companies' international operations.

Politics and Economics

An important aspect of determining where to do business overseas is country analysis. **Country analysis** examines the political and economic strategy and performance of the nation state. It is performed by a variety of interested parties,

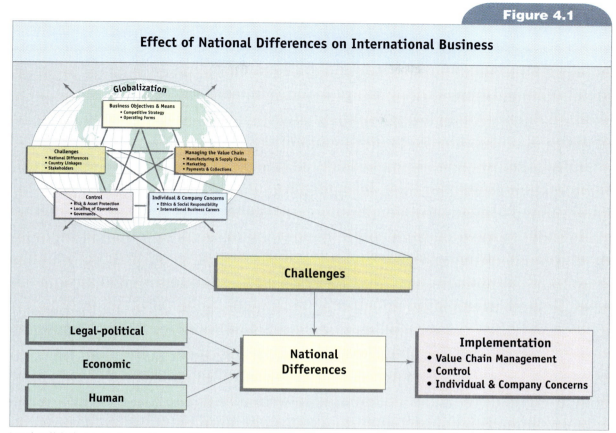

Figure 4.1

Effect of National Differences on International Business

Legal-political, economic, and human (demographic and cultural) differences among countries lead to companies' opportunities and constraints internationally. They especially affect how and whether companies can implement their international strategies.

including foreign investors and bankers. Country analysis involves three steps. Step one is to identify the strategy, context, and performance of the country. Step two is to evaluate performance to explain what is happening in the country at present and why. Step three is to generate scenarios for future performance.[4]

In step one, managers should identify the strategy that the country has pursued to get to where it is right now. That involves looking at goals and policies. Some of the more important policies are foreign and defense policy, fiscal and monetary policy, foreign trade and investment policy, and industrial policy. Each country determines its own goals and policies, and they may be similar to or different from other countries in the region or the world. For example, other countries in Asia have emulated some of the policies developed by Japan and Korea to build industrial competencies. *Context* refers to the political, institutional, ideological, physical, and international environment in which a firm does business. *Performance* refers to indicators of economic activity, which demonstrate how successful the goals and policies of a country are. Performance indicators include things such as gross national product, per capita gross national product, growth in gross national product, domestic and foreign investment, international trade, and income distribution.

In step two, managers evaluate countries' current performance to determine what is happening at present and why. It is important to understand where a country is coming from in order to understand what policies it is currently pursuing. For example, in late 1998, the Brazilian economy was going through a severe crisis. The **International Monetary Fund (IMF)** came to its rescue by promising $41 billion in aid to help the Brazilian government to continue operating without having to default on its foreign loans. In addition, the aid enabled Brazil to avoid depleting its foreign exchange reserves. The policies that Brazil agreed to pursue in order to receive the IMF funding were based on some of the historical problems in its economy. Some examples of these problems were strong state intervention in the economy, government ownership of businesses, a preference for domestic over foreign investment, an import substitution strategy (preventing imports so that Brazilians would have to buy Brazilian products), and hyperinflation. The Brazilian government had to agree to change some of its prior goals and policies in order to solve its problems and move forward. In addition, Brazilians have been going through a political change from military to democratic rule. In the context of this political climate, the IMF felt more comfortable about lending the money to Brazil.

In step three, managers generate scenarios for future country performance. It is not enough to know where a country has come from and what it is doing right now; forecasting where it will head in the future is critical. For example, in 2000, the U.S. economy was growing rapidly with relatively low inflation and low unemployment. Some suggested that the United States was experiencing a new economic situation that could continue forever. Others suggested that inflation would eventually reappear, leading to an increase in interest rates and a slowdown in economic growth. Thus, managers should generate different types of scenarios based on different possible conditions.

Given the preceding discussion of country analysis, it's important to look at two very important dimensions of this analysis: the political environment and the economic environment.

The Political Environment

The political environment can be broken down into three broad areas: the political system, political stability, and the role of government in business. *Political systems* are in turn broadly divided into two categories as illustrated in Figure 4.2: democratic systems and nondemocratic (totalitarian systems). These systems both are important in terms of integrating a society. Societies tend to be relatively heterogeneous, meaning that they are comprised of different types of interest groups. The political system needs to pull together the different demands of these interest groups into one coherent strategy for the future. If it doesn't, then a country may break apart. Even if the breakup occurs peacefully, companies face more fragmented markets, such as occurred with the split of Czechoslovakia into two countries. If the breakup occurs through armed strife, companies additionally face the possibility that their assets will be destroyed, such as occurred with the civil war in Yugoslavia.

Democracy basically involves wide participation by citizens in the decision-making process. Relatively mature democracies, such as those in the United States and United Kingdom, tend to compromise viewpoints when enacting

Figure 4.2

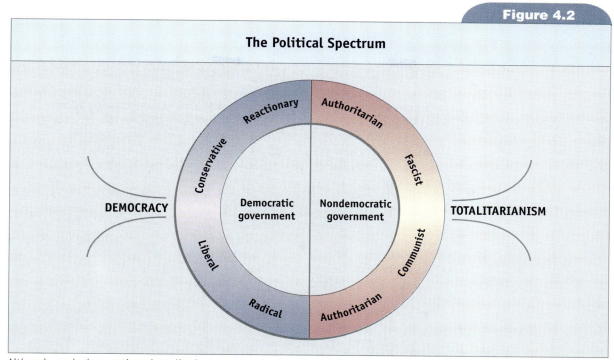

The Political Spectrum

Although purely democratic and totalitarian governments are extremes, there are variations to each approach. For example, democratic governments range from radical on one side (advocates of political reform) to reactionary (advocates of a return to past conditions). The majority of democratic governments, however, lie somewhere in between.
source: Adapted from Manuel G. Serapio, Jr. and Wayne F. Cascio, "End Games in International Alliances," *Acadamy of Management Executive*, May 1996, p. 67.

legislation. They can be liberal or conservative, but they rarely reach the extremes, such as *reactionary* (harking back to the past) or *radical* (calling for significant change). Democracy is typically represented by a high degree of civil liberty, such as freedom of opinion, expression, and the press. Such freedom is necessary to allow individuals to get their opinions out in the open so that those who govern can determine the wishes of the populace.

In a totalitarian state, a single party, individual, or group of individuals monopolizes political power. Decision making is restricted to a few individuals. Some totalitarian regimes are very repressive, others slightly more liberal. Totalitarian states tend to be relatively low in civil liberties and political freedom.

The second important aspect of the political system is *political stability*. Democratic regimes tend to be relatively more stable than totalitarian in that the institutionalization of democracy results in the normal turnover of power from one group or individual to another. However, changes in political philosophies can sometimes result in instability. For example, the government of Austria turned decidedly conservative in 2000 due to the influence of the far-right Freedom Party, called by some a party of intolerance and xenophobia, in a coalition government ruling the nation. Because of sympathetic statements made by its leader about Adolf Hitler and former Austrian SS officers, other European governments suspended bilateral political contacts with Austria.[5]

This created a great deal of instability and uneasiness for business in Europe, especially with respect to Austria.

Another example of political instability is the Russian presidential election in 2000, the first democratic transfer of executive power in Russia's history.[6] However, foreign companies remained hesitant to commit resources to business expansion in Russia because, although statements indicated that the country would continue economic reforms to open the country to more foreign investment, there was uncertainty as to what its exact policies would be. In contrast, the United States also held a presidential election in 2000, but—despite uncertainty over its outcome for many weeks—that election had minimal impact on foreign investment or capital markets, given that U.S. elections result in a relatively stable transition of power that does not veer much from the center between liberal and conservative viewpoints.

The final major dimension of politics is the *role of government in business.* Governments are often looked upon as being individualistic or communitarian. **Individualistic** governments believe in minimal intervention and feel that the purpose and direction of government should be left up to different interest groups. In **communitarian** regimes, on the other hand, there is a focus on prestige, authority, and hierarchy. An example of an individualistic political ideology would be the United States. An example of a communitarian ideology would be Japan or possibly Germany.

Whether a country is communitarian or individualistic, it can try to bring business activity into line with the needs of the community through three principal methods: (1) It can promote marketplace competition, (2) it can regulate the marketplace, and (3) it can establish a partnership with business.[7]

Promoting marketplace competition varies from country to country. In the United States, the market is perceived as being highly competitive, and antitrust policy keeps firms from developing monopolies. The most famous antitrust case brought by the U.S. government against a company in recent years was the Microsoft suit, which alleged that Microsoft had become too big and amassed too much market power and, thus, needed to be broken up into different companies. However, some other countries have an established policy of developing national champions that can compete with global rivals. Some of these national industries are given significant amounts of financial support and are shielded from competition, especially foreign competition.

A second way that the government can bring business activity into line with the needs of the community is through *regulating the marketplace.* This might have to do with whether or not a country allows foreign investment to come in and whether or not it promotes foreign trade on both the import and export sides. As mentioned previously, the Brazilian government formerly used a protectionist policy, which meant that it would not allow certain exports to come into Brazil and challenge Brazilian companies. That allowed Brazilian companies to grow and thrive without having to worry about foreign competition. Antitrust policies are another example of ways that a government can regulate the marketplace.

Third, the government can cooperate through *establishing a partnership with business.* The relationship between government and business in the United States is described as adversarial. However, the relationship between government and business in Japan is considered very cooperative.

Managers develop a strategy for working with the government in their home country, but that strategy might have to change as they move abroad. The relationship between government and business varies around the world, and it's important for managers to understand what that relationship is in each country in which they do business.

The Legal Environment
An important dimension of the political environment is the legal environment. Managers must be aware of the legal systems in the countries in which they operate; the nature of the legal profession, both domestic and international; and the legal relationships that exist among countries. Legal systems differ in terms of their nature—whether **common law** (based on tradition, precedent, and usage), **civil law** (based on a detailed set of written laws), or **theocratic law** (based on religious precepts)—and the degree of independence that the judiciary enjoys from the political process. Some totalitarian regimes that are undergoing a transition to a democracy and to a free market economy do not yet have in place a legal system that deals with business transactions in a global market context. A good example is the problems facing foreign firms doing business in Russia. Russian commercial law is underdeveloped and inconsistent. For instance, the Central Bank of Russia forbids large cash payments, but when the Russian banking system collapsed, companies had no choice but to make large cash payments. As noted by one foreign consultant, most companies, including U.S. firms with offices in Russia, were forced to disobey the law just to survive.[8]

National laws affect business within a country or business among countries. Some national laws that deal with local business activity influence both domestic and foreign companies, especially in the areas of health and safety standards, employment practices, antitrust prohibitions, contractual relationships, environmental practices, and patents and trademarks. For example, the maximum work week in Thailand is 84 hours, and this applies to domestic and foreign firms. Nike subcontracts its shoe manufacturing to a local Thai company. However, because of pressures from labor and consumer groups to follow better employment practices, Nike has established its own maximum of 60 hours, which the local contractor must follow. If Nike wanted to follow the Thai law, it could, but that would be a violation of its own code of conduct.

Laws also exist that govern cross-border activities, such as the investment of capital, the payment of dividends to foreign investors, and customs duties on imports. International laws, such as treaties governing the cross-border movement of hazardous waste, can also determine how a firm operates in transporting shipments internationally.

The Economic Environment

A nation's competitiveness depends on the capacity of its industry to innovate and upgrade.[9] Differences in national values, culture, economic structures, institutions, and histories contribute to competitive success. The *traditional factors of production* are land, labor, capital, and technology. It is important for a country to have an abundance of productive factors for specific industries if they are to develop global competitiveness. Thus, a company doing business overseas must determine the key factors of production in that country and how it can take advantage of them.

Besides factors of production, other conditions shape national economic performance. For instance, if a country has a network of reliable suppliers, it can develop competitive industries that convert those inputs into finished goods. For example, Thailand aspires to develop the leading auto manufacturing industry in Southeast Asia. The Japanese, American, and European companies that opened Thai assembly operations attracted many parts suppliers to service their assembly operations efficiently. It is also important to have a solid strategy, structure, and rivalry in order for firms to create, organize, and manage effectively. Rivals play a vital role by virtue of their persistent stimulus for competitive change. Chapter 5 looks at these issues more closely.

The preceding conditions deal with the so-called supply side of the economy—the factors of production that enable companies to make competitive products. Supply conditions in and of themselves do not fully shape national economic performance. We need to also consider what consumers demand companies to produce. Generally, demand conditions include three dimensions: (1) the nature of buyers' demand in the home country, (2) the size and pattern of growth of home demand, and (3) the internationalization of demand. The composition of demand is known as the quality of demand, and the size is known as the quantity of demand. Size of demand is typically measured in terms of **gross national product (GNP),** the market value of final goods and services newly produced by domestic factors of production.

In the case of the United States, the value of a Ford car manufactured in the United States and the portion of the value of a Ford manufactured in Mexico using U.S. capital and management both count in the GNP of the United States. However, the portion of the value of a Toyota manufactured in the United States using Japanese capital and management would not be counted in the GNP of the United States, but rather in Japanese GNP. An alternative to GNP is **gross domestic product (GDP),** the value of production that takes place within a nation's borders without regard to whether the production is done by domestic or foreign factors. So both a Ford and a Toyota manufactured in the United States would be counted in the GDP of the United States, but a Ford produced in Mexico would not. The absolute size of GNP is important, because it is an indicator of market opportunity. For example, Uruguay and Brazil are neighbors in South America, but Uruguay had a GNP of only $19.5 billion in 1999, whereas Brazil's GNP was $743 billion. For this reason, many foreign companies invested in Brazil and exported to Uruguay instead of also investing in Uruguay.

Another measure of market size is GNP or GDP per capita, specifically GNP or GDP divided by the size of the population. This is an important measure because it gives a better idea of the wealth and potential purchasing power of individuals in a country. Table 4.1 identifies the GNP per capita in 1999 of several regions in the world. The high-income countries include primarily North America, Western Europe, Japan, Australia, and New Zealand. They accounted for 14.9 percent of the world's population in 1999 but 78.4 percent of the world's GNP. The result is that many managers put most of their emphasis on high-income countries because they account for such a disproportionate share of the world's economy. However, if the lower-income countries begin to grow more rapidly, they will offer enormous business opportunities because of their large populations.

Table 4.2 provides another measure of per capita income by dividing the countries of the world into four categories: low, low-middle, upper-middle, and high. The first three categories make up what is known as the **developing countries** or **emerging economies.** They clearly comprise the largest number of economies and population in the world, but not income. Another meaningful way to look at GNP per capita is in terms of its annual growth. For example,

Table 4.1

Relative Number, Wealth, and Population of the World's Economies, 1999				
	Absolute Number of Countries	% of Countries	% of GNP	% of Population
Low	64	31.1	3.4	40.5
Middle	93	45.1	18.2	44.6
High	29	23.8	78.4	14.9
Total	186	100.0	100.0	100.0

source: World Development Indicators Database, World Book, August 2, 2000.

from 1985 to 1995, prior to the Asian crisis, GNP per capita grew at only 1.9 percent per annum in the high-income countries, whereas it grew at 7.2 percent in East Asia and the Pacific. It actually grew at negative 3.5 percent per annum in Eastern Europe and Central Asia. Since the Asian financial crisis, economic growth has slowed dramatically in the developing countries and taken off in some high-income countries, especially the United States. However, economic growth fluctuates in cycles, so it is difficult to predict what will happen in the future. Still, it is interesting to note that when the East Asia and Pacific economies were growing at such a rapid rate prior to 1997, companies from other nations invested heavily in them due to their immense market potential. Once growth slowed, however, investment fell.

Table 4.2

Income and Population by Countries' Economic Levels (1999, values in U.S. dollars)				
Countries by per Capita Income	# of Economies	GNP $ Millions	Population (in millions)	GNP per Capita in $
Low ($755 or less)	64	987,602	2,417	410
Lower-middle ($756 to 2995)	55	2,512,540	2,094	1,200
Upper-middle ($2,996 to 9,265)	38	2,810,650	573	4,900
High ($9,266 or more)	49	22,921,301	891	25,730
World	206	29,232,099	5,975	4,870

source: World Development Indicators Database, World Bank, August 2, 2000.

General Types of National Economies

There are material differences between nations in terms of the ownership and control of production factors, the freedom of price to manage supply and demand, and the purpose of fiscal and monetary policies. Thus, managers must recognize the type of economic systems that make up the world. Wisely positioning your company to address a country's economic context tremendously improves the odds of success. Historically, national economies have been divided into either a market, centrally planned, or mixed economy.

A **market economy** rests on the idea that consumers, by virtue of what they do and do not buy, determine the relationships among price, quantity, supply, and demand. Furthermore, individuals and companies, rather than political officials and government ministries, own productive assets. Therefore, market economies are free from significant government restraints. Importantly, market economies rely on legal and institutional frameworks to safeguard economic freedoms. **Consumer sovereignty,** whereby consumers influence the allocation of resources through their demand for products, is the cornerstone of a market economy.

In a **centrally planned economy,** the government owns and controls all resources. The government sets goals for every business enterprise in the country—how much each must produce, for what consumer segments, and for what price. In this type of economy, the government considers itself a better judge of resource allocation than its businesses or citizens. The prices of goods and services do not often change in a command economy because government officials, not consumers, determine them. Quality, on the other hand, tends to vary dramatically, often getting worse over time because (1) whatever product is made is usually in short supply, (2) consumers typically have no other choices due to bans or high tariffs on imports, and (3) there is not much incentive for companies to innovate and little profits to finance improvements. Historically, centrally planned economies were found in communist countries. These nations simultaneously used the economic and political systems to champion the collective and deemphasize the individual.

In actuality, no economy is purely market or command based, but rather a **mixed economy.** That is, virtually all economies have varying degrees of private and public ownership of production factors. Subject to national political, economic, and cultural ideals, most nations mix free market mechanisms with aspects of centrally planned control. For example, the French government owns significant economic resources, such as oil and automobile companies, but it still permits supply and demand to set prices. Similarly, Sweden is a country that owns few economic resources, but its government levies heavy taxes to fund an aggressive social program. Although the market determines prices, Sweden's fiscal policies control much of its economic activity.

Presently, many centrally planned economies are trying to install a mixed economy. The main stimulus for this change is the failure of centrally planned economies, like Russia, to meet their citizens' needs and wants and the striking success of market-based economies, like the United States. Countries in which the government has been heavily involved in the ownership of resources are rapidly privatizing those assets. Privatization reduces debt by removing the need of the government to subsidize state-owned enterprises. Still, the risk of privatization for many countries is the raw economic reality that only foreign companies have the capital to buy those companies put up for sale. Thus, privatization spurs globalization by letting foreign companies acquire useful assets and gain access to new markets.

Asian Financial Crisis

A good example of the interplay of political and economic forces and their impact on corporate practices is the Asian financial crisis that began in 1997. In 1994, the World Bank predicted that annual real GDP growth would average 7.6 percent in East Asia and 5.3 percent in South Asia from 1994 through 2005. Further, it predicted that the top 10 economies in the world by 2020 would include China (1), Japan

(3), India (4), Indonesia (5), South Korea (7), Thailand (8), and Taiwan (10). There were significant reasons for optimism because these countries had been growing so rapidly and were characterized as having a hardworking, well-educated, highly trained workforce. They also had low inflation, an entrepreneurial class, and relative economic freedom. In 1997, however, the Thai government freed the baht, the currency of Thailand, from its controls and allowed it to fall to its perceived value in the foreign exchange market. It promptly fell by 42.7 percent in relation to the U.S. dollar. Shortly after the currency crisis hit the Thai baht, it spread to South Korea, Malaysia, and Indonesia. In addition to the currency crisis, the stock markets in Asia tumbled in 1997. This was largely a result of the lack of confidence in their economies and the fall of their currencies. The stock market weakness spread to the United States and to Europe.

The Asian crisis resulted in an Asian money shortage (liquidity crisis). Banks and investors had poured billions of dollars into Asian markets. But as the values of Asian currencies dropped, the banks and investors lost confidence and pulled money out—causing currency values to drop even more. This caused interest rates to rise and economic growth to fall. Many companies went bankrupt and closed their factories. Foreign and local companies suspended investment plans. There were political consequences as well. For example, the president of Indonesia was forced to step down because of the economic crisis.

What were some of the major causes of the Asian crisis? There are two theories: Too much government influence and control, and bad private sector decisions. In reality, both factors were contributors. In terms of government influence and control, Asian countries relied very heavily on governmental policies to develop specific industries. They used a variety of fiscal and monetary policies to influence the flow of goods and services across national borders. These policies resulted in governments controlling access to credit, foreign exchange, and imports. Because of close ties among the government, businesses, and banks, politicians tried to rescue politically well-connected firms from insolvency rather than allowing them to go bankrupt. Governments, especially the corrupt

Globalization puts people and products in unusual situations. Here we see disciples of the Muslim faith in Saudi Arabia praying while sharing space with a supremely Western product presented in a thoroughly modern way. Often, people accept these peculiarities as the price of progress. Interestingly, the fact that Muslim teachings and law prohibit the sale of alcoholic beverage has been a boon to soft drink producers.

ones in Asia, were also indecisive and hesitant to make changes. However, bad private sector decisions by both borrowers and lenders were strong contributing factors. Risky projects were undertaken based on the hope that they would bring high profits with little risk. A large proportion of bank loans went to expensive building projects where there was already a glut in the market. Overcapacity caused rents and prices to fall sharply. Because governments were so intertwined with business, banks assumed that projects blessed by the government would always be backed and that bankruptcy would never occur.

Another major contributor was the fact that a lot of countries linked their currencies to the U.S. dollar. During this period, when the U.S. dollar was rising, these countries found it more difficult to export to the rest of the world because their products grew too expensive. The governments of Southeast Asian countries preferred to keep a strong currency instead of solving their internal problems. In addition to dollar-linked exchange rates, a lot of the countries had encouraged significant short-term debt. Much of this debt came due in 1998, and the countries were not generating enough hard (convertible) currency to pay it off. As a result, the crisis spread to the banks very quickly. Another major problem was the lack of financial **transparency** (available financial statements on which lenders could rely). It was often said that the best way to make a loan was to take the borrower to lunch and a round of golf instead of analyzing the financial data. Thus, a tremendous amount of corruption revolved around getting funds.

As the countries in Southeast Asia began to restructure in the mid-1990s, they shifted production to more capital-intensive processes. In order to do this, they had to import capital equipment from the West. At the same time that their imports were increasing, exports were dropping due to their rising prices and competition from other parts of the world, such as China. This combination of rising imports and falling exports resulted in *current-account deficits* (more imports than exports) and a drop in reserve assets.

From a corporate point of view, multinational enterprises that had invested significantly in Asia in expectation of rising local demand for their products were in trouble, because demand fell. This caused their revenues and profits to fall as well. Those companies that invested in the Asian countries to produce for export markets were also in trouble, both because many of them could not import needed parts and equipment and because their prices were rising. Thus, their production fell as well. Foreign companies that were counting on Asian markets as a place to export goods and services were in trouble, too, because purchasing power in those markets declined. Thus, they had to look elsewhere for increased revenues.

Although this general characterization of the Asian crisis shows the interrelationship of politics, economics, and business, the factors in each individual country varied. Nevertheless, one important thing to realize is that an economic crisis can occur quickly and affect companies' operations very negatively. Further, economic conditions in one country can affect economic conditions in others. For example, the U.S. stock market dropped significantly, U.S. exports fell, and U.S. imports increased as a result of the crisis in Asia. U.S. economic growth slowed, and the U.S. government (Federal Reserve Board) had to cut interest rates to stimulate the U.S. economy and thwart a recession. Still, Asian economies—including Thailand, where the crisis began—experienced solid growth in 1999 and 2000. The Asian crisis teaches us that to be successful in this global economy, it is important to understand political and economic forces.

People of the World

Coming to terms with the idea of the world's population can be intellectually and personally remote. Current estimates suggest there are more than 6.5 billion people living in more than 200 different nations. Such a large number of people, like that of national debt levels, makes it hard to grasp the scale and scope of the many people around the world. Also, many of us live in well-defined communities of persons that share many attributes. If inclined, we can overlook the day-to-day circumstances for the many people around the world who live lives in remarkably different ways. Table 4.3 tries to make the idea of the world's population more accessible. These data report the results of collapsing the world's current population, in line with current social ratios, into a

If Earth's population was shrunk into a village of just 100 people, this tiny village would have the following characteristics:	Table 4.3

Gender
52 would be female
48 would be male

Ethnicity
57 would be Asian
21 would be European
14 would be from the Western Hemisphere
8 would be African

Race
70 would be nonwhite
30 would be white

Religion
70 would be non-Christian
30 would be Christian

Income and Lifestyle
6 people would possess 59 percent of the entire wealth of the village and all 6 would be from the United States
5 would own a computer
24 would own a television
48 would own a radio receiver

Health, Housing, and Literacy
80 would live in substandard housing
50 would suffer from malnutrition
70 would be unable to read
1 would be near death
1 would be pregnant
1 would have a college education

source: Compiled from various sources including "The Real World," *San Francisco Chronicle,* August 2, 2000; *The UNESCO Statistical Yearbook,* 1999; and *United Nations Statistical Yearbook,* 1999.

representative village of just 100 people. The following sections elaborate some of these characteristics.

Demographics

As you consider which countries to sell products to or do business in, it is important to understand the basic demographic characteristics of each country. *Demography* is the statistical analysis of the properties of a particular population; important aspects include distribution, density, and trends. Although it is possible to focus on a variety of different demographic characteristics, we will concentrate on population, age distribution, population growth rate, and life expectancy at birth.

From a broader social perspective, the World Bank states that "development is about people and their well being—about people developing their capabilities to provide for their families, to act as stewards of the environment, to form civil societies that are just and orderly. Human capital development—the result of education and improvements in health and nutrition—is both an ends and a means to achieving social progress." The World Bank goes on to describe a variety of factors that are important for understanding the health and well-being of individuals, such as access to health care, percentage of females enrolled in primary education, and literacy levels. These broader issues are crucial if countries are to develop strategies for promoting development, especially in improving the education and well-being of their population as producers and consumers of products.

Population

Population helps define a company's market potential. This does not mean that small countries cannot be good markets for products. Still, larger countries tend to provide greater opportunities for developing strong markets and for finding employees for the production process.

Tables 4.4 and 4.5 help illustrate the difference between population and income potential. Table 4.4 identifies the top 10 countries in the world in terms of population, and also shows the per capita income in each of those countries.

Table 4.4

Top 10 Countries by Population (1999)		
Country	Population in Thousands	Per Capita Income in U.S. Dollars
1. China	1,249,671	780
2. India	997,515	450
3. United States	272,878	30,600
4. Indonesia	207,022	580
5. Brazil	168,066	4,420
6. Russian Federation	146,512	2,270
7. Pakistan	134,790	470
8. Bangladesh	127,669	370
9. Japan	126,570	32,230
10. Nigeria	123,897	310

source: World Development Indicators Database, World Bank, August 2, 2000.

Table 4.5

Top 10 Countries by Per Capita Income (1999)		
Country	Per Capita Income in U.S. Dollars	Population in Thousands
1. Luxembourg	44,640	432
2. Switzerland	38,350	7,120
3. Bermuda	35,590	64
4. Norway	32,880	4,454
5. Japan	32,230	126,570
6. Denmark	32,030	5,317
7. United States	30,600	272,878
8. Singapore	29,610	3,223
9. Iceland	29,280	277
10. Austria	25,970	8,086

source: World Development Indicators Database, World Bank, August 2, 2000. The World Bank estimates that Liechtenstein and the Cayman Islands may be in positions 2 and 10, respectively, but per capita income data are not available.

It is interesting to note that the two largest countries, China and India, have relatively low per capita incomes relative to their population size. Table 4.5 reverses the columns by ranking the top 10 countries in the world in terms of per capita income, then providing the population in the second column. It is interesting here to note that the countries with the largest per capita income are not the countries with the largest populations.

Age Distribution
Another way to examine the population of a country is through its age distribution. This can indicate, for example, the potential market for youth-oriented versus elderly oriented products. It also indicates how many people may be available in the workforce. Figure 4.3 provides some useful information about Germany: The male–female distribution, life expectancy of males and females, and the percentage of the population, both male and female, in each age group. Germany represents a typical high-income industrial country in which there is a relatively low percentage of the under-20 population. The age distribution starts off relatively low in the under-20 age group; expands out a bit until about age 50; then contracts again. This is very common in other high-income countries. In Figure 4.4, you can see the age distribution of Mexico, which has a total population similar to Germany's but a very different age distribution. (In 1999, Mexico had the world's 11th largest population, and Germany the world's 12th largest.) Mexico's age distribution is a pyramid structure, with a larger percentage of the population in the below-20 age group, then gradually tapering off to the upper age groups. It is also interesting to note that Mexico, which is considered a developing country, has a life expectancy a little different from that of Germany. However, this is not true of other developing countries, especially the very low-income countries.

Population Growth Rate
The rapidly aging populations of the high-income countries is further illustrated in population growth statistics. *Population growth* is defined as a percent per year

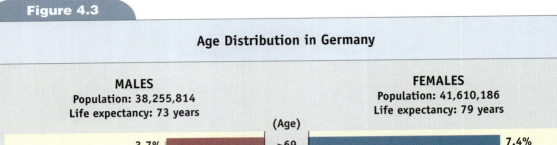

Figure 4.3

Age Distribution in Germany

MALES
Population: 38,255,814
Life expectancy: 73 years

FEMALES
Population: 41,610,186
Life expectancy: 79 years

MALES	(Age)	FEMALES
3.7%	>69	7.4%
3.4%	60–69	5.4%
5.8%	50–59	6.1%
7.4%	40–49	7.2%
6.9%	30–39	6.6%
8.4%	20–29	7.9%
6.9%	10–19	6.5%
5.4%	<10	5.1%

source: Adapted with the permission of The Free Press, a division of Simon & Schuster, Inc., from *The Competitive Advantage of Nations,* by Micheal E. Porter. Copyright © 1990, 1998 by Micheal E. Porter.

of the total population. For high-income countries such as the United States, Germany, France, Italy, and Japan, population growth is less than 1 percent. For example, the growth rate in the United States is 1.0 percent; it is only 0.3 percent in Japan. In the developing countries, however, the population growth rate typically exceeds 1 percent: It is 1.8 percent in Mexico, 1.4 percent in Brazil, 1.3 percent in Brazil, 2.3 percent in Malaysia, 2.2 percent in Vietnam, 1.7 percent in

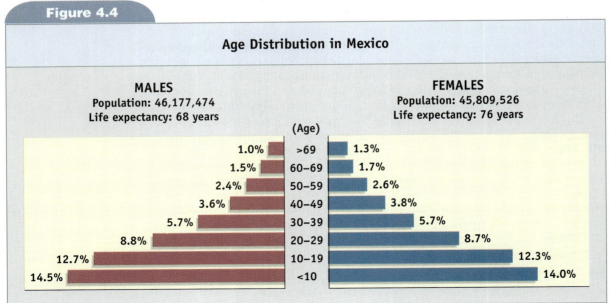

Figure 4.4

Age Distribution in Mexico

MALES
Population: 46,177,474
Life expectancy: 68 years

FEMALES
Population: 45,809,526
Life expectancy: 76 years

MALES	(Age)	FEMALES
1.0%	>69	1.3%
1.5%	60–69	1.7%
2.4%	50–59	2.6%
3.6%	40–49	3.8%
5.7%	30–39	5.7%
8.8%	20–29	8.7%
12.7%	10–19	12.3%
14.5%	<10	14.0%

Indonesia, and above 2 percent in many of the African countries. More rapid population growth along with low life expectancies ensure an age distribution more like Mexico's, whereas a relatively slow population growth along with a high life expectancy ensures an age distribution similar to Germany's.

Indications of Social Health
There are a number of ways to measure the health of a society, which is important in terms of a good workforce as well as a consuming population. The World Bank measures the percentage of the population with access to health care, life expectancy at birth, infant mortality per thousand births, and child malnutrition by the percentage of children underweight. Life expectancy at birth correlates well with the preceding age distribution discussion. As infant mortality rates and child malnutrition drop, and as the percentage of the population with access to health care rises, life expectancy at birth will also rise. Whereas life expectancy at birth exceeds 70 years in the high-income countries and many of the developing countries, especially in Latin America, it is distressingly low in other countries, especially in Africa. For example, the life expectancy at birth is 41 in Rwanda, 37 in Sierra Leone, and 45 in Mozambique. With only a few exceptions, the average life expectancy in Africa is less than 50 years.

The Cultural Environment

The idea of culture is vital for the simple reason that it affects practically every subject we cover in this text. Culture influences where we decide to open operations, how we manage people in the workplace, and the products we sell. Typically, whenever you interact with people from different countries, you encounter differences in culture. For instance, when you travel to another country for the first time, you may experience **culture shock**—the anxiety triggered by the challenge of learning and coping with new cultural cues, expectations, and preferences. Cultural challenges may be as simple as whether and what to tip in a restaurant, figuring out how to hire a taxi to your hotel, or appropriately greeting people. Then again, managers also run into more subtle cultural challenges, such as determining how to negotiate a deal with someone who may not think the same as you, figuring out who is the ultimate decision maker in an organization, or motivating a workforce that has different values about authority and personal initiative. In either case, it helps to identify cultural differences and adjust your personal practices and business methods accordingly.

It is important to note that, as time goes on, cultural differences no longer pop up only when you travel abroad. Chapter 5 reports how the growing links among nations encourages the freer movement of people from country to country. As a result, one increasingly sees people practicing different cultures in one's hometown. Already, we see companies responding to this trend. For example, Sprint, the U.S. telecommunications company, entered into a joint venture with Telemex, a Mexican counterpart, to do business in the United States and Mexico. In the United States, the joint venture started marketing a specialized long-distance service that specifically targeted the 18 million U.S. residents of Mexican descent.[10]

Culture is a notoriously difficult idea to define. Indeed, as far back as 1952, there were more than 160 different definitions of culture.[11] Over time, this list has only grown. The difficulty of defining culture has not discouraged people from trying to make sense of its effects on international business. Generally, people make sense of culture by studying overt and subtle cultural differences between nations. We will now look at each type.

Overt Cultural Differences

Analyses identify many obvious differences between cultures, such as those that deal with things like language, food, etiquette, or appearance. Typically, overt cultural differences are the ones that you immediately notice when you visit a foreign nation or come in contact with a foreign visitor. Not long ago, a manager could get away with being unprepared for overt cultural differences when he or she traveled abroad. The rising importance of globalization in the business world, however, increasingly penalizes those managers that venture aboard without some sense of overt cultural differences. Put simply, poor understanding of a foreign customer's culture can lead to misunderstanding, frustration, and ruined relationships.

For example, consider the act of exchanging business cards. In most countries, this exchange is done automatically, with the giver simply passing his or her card to the recipient who then just puts it away. However, the ordinary act of exchanging business cards is a meaningful ritual in Japan. That is, Japanese businesspersons use the ceremonial exchange of business cards as an indicator of the relative status of an individual as well as his or her sensitivity to Japanese customs.[12] Therefore, as you present your business card (with two hands) to a Japanese businessperson, turn it around so that the person need not flip it over to read it. While a seemingly trivial act, doing so speaks volumes about your sensitivity to Japanese culture. Moreover, when given a business card in return, you must receive it with great care because it symbolizes the reputation of the individual giving it to you. Therefore, you would never casually put someone's business card in your wallet or pocket. Instead, you would carefully inspect the card before placing it in a more formal business card holder. Again, failing to do so would create a culturally awkward moment that could interfere with other issues.

This is just one example of the many kinds of culturally influenced business practices that managers face when doing business in a globalizing market. Readers may wonder how one can find out more about these customs and practices. In general, there are many guidebooks, newsletters, Usenet newsgroups, and Web sites that discuss the basic do's and don'ts of cultural interactions.[13] Table 4.6, for example, lists some Web sites that address overt cultural differences on matters of general attitudes, personal appearance, greetings, gestures, eating, family, and lifestyle. Another terrific source of help is often a phone call or e-mail to people in trade groups, international clubs, companies, or government ministries. For instance, most nations help businesspeople prepare for overseas business culture. One can contact local and overseas embassies to get their advice for a business trip abroad.

Subtle Cultural Differences

There are far more subtle cultural differences that are difficult to identify and cope with when dealing with foreign businesspeople. Examples of these difficulties include the roles and relationships between people in the workplace, the nature of friendship, concepts of time and space, and approaches to problem solving. Some of these differences may not be easy to identify until you have dealt with a culture for quite a while. However, an understanding of subtle cultural differences often determines success or failure in global business matters. A vital problem arises from the difficulty of identifying the subtle cul-

Table 4.6

A Sample of Web Sites on Business Customs, Etiquette, and Cultural Practices Abroad

Web Site	Theme	URL
Web of Culture (Gestures) — Africa and the Middle East	A list of social gestures for 17 African and Middle Eastern countries. Reference links to consulates, embassies, currencies, and cross-cultural resources.	www.webofculture.com/worldsmart/gesture_mid_af.html
Business and Social Etiquette United Kingdom	Business customs, hours and infrastructure, etiquette, travel advisory and visas, citizen services, and holidays.	www.econ.state.or.us/oregontrade/ukbt.htm
Living in Germany for Beginners: A Not Too Serious and Very Much Abridged Primer	Helpful hints on telephone usage, recycling, and punctuality to social events in Germany.	www.usembassy.de/services/e35a.htm
Nonverbal Communication: Chinese Emotion and Gesture	How to communicate Chinese emotions and gestures nonverbally.	www.ling.gu.se/~biljana/gestures2.html
Effective Ways to Embarrass Yourself	A list of things foreigners do to embarrass themselves and others in Japan.	www.japaninfo.org/nonos.html
Indian Etiquette	Information on language, business attires and hours, money, introductions, gifts, postal service, and telecommunications in India.	www2.gol.com/users/coynerhm/india_etiquette.htm
Ten Business Tips of Etiquette to Follow When in Korea	Tips on business etiquette for social, entertainment, and communication relations in Korea.	www.uniconet.com/tip/tip.html
Web of Culture (Gestures) — Asia and the Pacific	Provides links to information on personal and business etiquette for different countries in Asia.	www.webofculture.com/worldsmart/gesture_asia.html
Russia: Some Useful Hints	Links and information on how to behave in public places, drinking water, weather, local traditions, national holidays, and embassy contact information in Russia.	www.moscow-guide.ru/General/Hints.htm
Web of Culture for Central and South America	Social gestures, business, and personal etiquette in Central and South America.	www.webofculture.com/worldsmart/gesture_s_am.html
Ten Mistakes to Avoid in Working with Latin Americans	Ten helpful hints of things to avoid when conducting business in Latin America.	users.erols.com/iauinc/mistakes.htm
Making It in Mexico — Business Customs and Practices	Tips on social customs and business etiquette in Mexico.	www.fas.usda.gov/info/agexporter/1999/makingit.html
Business and Social Etiquette Chile	Information on business customs and infrastructure, travel advisory and visas, and legal holidays.	www.econ.state.or.us/oregontrade/chilebt.htm
Web of Culture (Gestures) — United States and Canada	Social gestures and business and personal etiquette for the United States and Canada.	www.webofculture.com/edu/gesture_n_am.html
Business Culture Worldwide	Links to worldwide business and executive briefings and newsletters, predeparture reports, training and consulting, global business bookstore, corporate intranets, and global management information.	www.businessculture.com
International Business Customs, Protocol, and Practices	Information on international business practices, business protocol, etiquette, cross-cultural communication, negotiating tactics, and country-specific data.	www.worldbiz.com

tural differences and, hence, determining the best way to proceed. That is, businesspeople agree that subtle cultural differences exist. However, they often struggle to define those differences in ways that help prevent cultural oversights from damaging business activities.

A View of Culture

Generally, manager try to make sense of subtle cultural differences from a psychological view. This view assumes that culture is made up of specific learned norms within a community that are themselves based on fundamental, or so-called latent, values. Essentially, culture is sort of a collective mental programming that distinguishes the members of one category of people from another. The collective programming of fundamental values creates a culture that makes intuitive sense to all those in it but appears different to those on the outside.

The psychological view sees culture as a seamless web of deep-seated values that guide a person's everyday activities and long-term leanings. The strength of these values is a function of the way that people acquire them—namely through life-long socialization by other people within the culture. That is, from birth onward, an individual acquires culture from the transfer of values from parent to child, family to sibling, teacher to student, one age peer group to another, and leader to disciple. All along, these transfers help an individual develop and reinforce latent values about forms of personal and group behavior that are culturally appropriate. In effect, culture holds the deep-seated values that directly and indirectly influence an individual's choices and actions in the family, workplace, and society.

Developmental psychologists believe that most children have their basic value systems firmly in place by age 10, after which they do not make changes easily. These fundamental values include such concepts as good versus evil, dirty versus clean, ugly versus beautiful, unnatural versus natural, abnormal versus normal, and paradoxical versus logical.[14] Culture, therefore, has many implications for international business activity. For example, a company's packaging may seem beautiful in one society but ugly in another. Likewise, business negotiations may break down because what seems logical to one negotiator may seem paradoxical to the other. However, individual and societal values and customs may evolve over time, particularly as cultures come into closer contact. Thus, international business activities influence cultural changes. Some governments, however, often limit such business to protect their national cultures.

Finally, understanding a particular culture demands one to understand the values that it endorses. Generally, one can start to understand the fundamental values of another culture by studying its primary language and theology. Language is the key transmitter of culture from one person to another; it is rich in the context of the culture. Similarly, religion is one of the most important developers of culture within an individual.

Principal Types of Cultural Values

Scholars try to explain how the values of a particular culture influence behaviors in the workplace. Over time, these studies have identified seven principal dimensions that shape workplace behavior in a particular nation. These dimensions are (1) power distance, (2) individualism versus collectivism, (3) masculinity versus femininity, (4) uncertainty avoidance, (5) long-term versus short-term orientation, (6) monochronic versus polychronic, and (7) idealistic versus pragmatic.[15]

Power distance describes the relationship between more powerful and less powerful members of a group. Low power distance societies are those with more equality and democracy. High power distance societies are those with high degrees of inequality. For example, Denmark is a country with low power distance; there are considerable consultations between managers and workers. In contrast, Malaysia is a country with high power distance where workers typically prefer autocratic superiors. Other examples of low power distance nations include the United States, Canada, and Britain. Too, other examples of high power distance nations include Mexico, Indonesia, and Korea.

Individualist societies are those in which social ties between individuals are relatively loose. The focus is on "I" instead of "we." People tend to look after themselves. The task to be done is more important than relationships. Collectivist societies are those in which people are integrated into strong, cohesive groups, such as extended families, and exhibit unquestioned loyalty. In a business setting, relationship prevails over task; there is a moral model rather than a legal model of employer–employee relationships; people are known for the groups they belong to; and value standards may differ widely for those in and outside a group. Examples of individualist societies include the United States and Australia. Examples of collectivist societies include most Latin American and Asian nations.

Masculinity and femininity are really misnomers because they don't really have to do with gender but with stereotyped values of gender. **Masculine societies** are those that stress achievement and competition, whereas **feminine societies** stress relationships, intuition, and quality of life. Examples of masculine societies include Italy, Japan, Columbia, and Mexico. Examples of feminine societies include Denmark, Finland, Norway, and Sweden.

Uncertainty avoidance deals with a society's tolerance for uncertainty and ambiguity. It indicates the degree to which individuals feel comfortable or uncomfortable with unstructured situations. Weak-uncertainty-avoidance societies are comfortable with unstructured situations. In the workplace, there is a dislike for rules, formalization, and standardization. Strong-uncertainty-avoidance societies have a high need for both written and unwritten rules, formalization, and standardization. Examples of strong-uncertainty-avoidance countries include Japan, Sweden, and Singapore. Examples of weak-uncertainty-avoidance countries include Peru, France, and Brazil.

A **long-term orientation** values thrift, perseverance, and absolute truth. A **short-term orientation** values virtue regardless of truth, respect for tradition, fulfilling social obligations, and protecting "face." Presently, the cultural value of long-term versus short-term orientation has the least understood effects on the workplace. An example of long-term orientation is Japan, whereas businesses in the United States are seen as having a short-term orientation.

In a **monochronic culture,** people prefer to work sequentially, such as finishing with one customer before dealing with another. Conversely, in a **polychronic culture,** people are more comfortable with working simultaneously on all pending tasks. For example, they feel uncomfortable when not dealing immediately with all customers who need service. Imagine the potential misconceptions that can occur. British businesspeople (a monochronic culture) might believe erroneously that their Italian counterparts are uninterested in doing business with them if they fail to give them their undivided attention.[16]

In an **idealistic society,** such as Argentina, people prefer to determine principles before they try to resolve small issues. In a **pragmatic society,** such as the United States, people focus more on details than principles. For example, labor disputes in the United States tend to center on small and precise issues, such as hourly wages. In Argentina, labor disputes tend to involve less precise demands, depending instead much more on mass actions, such as general strikes or support of a particular political party to publicize principles.

Communications and Language

Perhaps the most challenging aspect of culture originates from the simple act of communication, namely, trying to reach out and connect with someone from another culture. Communication is a key dimension of culture, because it is through communication, especially language, that cultural contact occurs. Communication is the means whereby we express ideas to people, and it is comprised of spoken as well as silent language. The latter includes nonverbal issues such as color associations, cues, tones, symbols, sense of appropriate distance, and gestures that are part of a conversation. As illustrated in the cartoon in Figure 4.5, the challenge is often to find a common language that enables meaningful communication. Some of the most interesting international business blunders are the result of the inappropriate translation of words and ideas from one language to another. For instance, infamous examples of language miscues going from English to another language include Pepsi's "Come Alive," which translates into "bring your ancestors back from the grave" in Chinese, and Ford's brand "Fiesta," which means "Ugly Old Woman" in Spanish. Chapter 8 looks at this issue more closely. Typically, a company dealing with foreign markets faces three primary language challenges: conversation, document translation, and silent languages. We will now look at each challenge.

Conversation

Travelling overseas inevitably creates the need to deal with officials and managers who are not fluent in your native language. Ably managing this challenge leads many to hire an interpreter to ensure the conversations go smoothly. There are many interpreting services abroad that you can use. Many of these services are a part of the global operations of interpreting firms. Another possibility is to heed the recommendations of managers in other countries or the various programs of government officials. For example, the field officers in the different embassies can arrange for interpretation assistance. Similarly, if feasible, you could bring along an interpreter. Finally, you could also learn the local language, although that is impractical unless you plan to spend a lot of time working in one country. Chapter 14 will look at this particular issue more closely.

Conversation challenges are not limited to those who travel abroad. Increasingly, companies must staff their call centers, wherever they happen to be located, with people who can accept calls in any number of languages. For instance, MBNA American, a U.S.-based credit-card company with operations in Canada and Europe, provides around-the-clock telephone support to its worldwide customers. Indeed, whether a calling customer speaks Chinese, Flemish, Gaelic, French, Spanish, or any of more than a hundred other languages, MBNA has linguist specialists ready to go. Operationally, MBNA maintains a foreign-language log that lists specialists across the company who fluently speak a language other than English or Spanish. While a huge effort, communicating with

Figure 4.5

customers across cultures is vital; explained a MBNA manager; "It's critical that we be able to serve our Customers in the language they prefer."[17]

Document Translation

Managing this challenge generally starts with two issues: (1) what types of document services are you likely to need and (2) how do you arrange for the interpreting of documents? Certainly, English is widely used as a business language around the world. Still, it is important to be able to deal in foreign languages in terms of your documents. Some examples of documents that often require translation into the local language are legal documents that relate to agent and distributor relationships, advertising print, brochures, general correspondence, and software code.

Upon identifying those documents that need translation, you then must decide how to do so. Historically, companies out-sourced their document translation jobs to any number of interpreting services. The globalization of business, however, moves more companies to develop in-house translation competencies in order to make sure things go as intended. For example, MBNA Canada goes to great lengths to ensure that the company delivers a message that is consistent with the rest of the MBNA Corporation while meeting the needs of its Canadian customers. Its Director of Marketing explained, "A lot of thought goes into our communications—both written and spoken. We have to be precise and knowledgeable when translating from English to French so that we capture not only MBNA style, but also the nuances of the French-Canadian culture."[18]

Silent Language

The silent language of business includes nonverbal issues such as color associations, sense of appropriate distance, time and status cues, and body language.[19] For example, the color green in Malaysia symbolizes death and disease, whereas the color black has similar connotations in the United States. These colors should probably not be used to advertise certain kinds of products in Malaysia and the United States, respectively. In the United States, the biggest office with the best view on the top floor of an office tower is traditionally given to the most important person in the organization. In Japan, however, it is more common to find supervisors working desk by desk with their employees. Another example of space: North Americans typically stand an arm's length apart, whereas in Latin American cultures, they more commonly stand close together.

The Challenge of Culture

In spite of all the things you can do to prepare for the cultural dimension in doing business overseas, it's impossible to know and prepare for every contingency. As a result, one of the best approaches to managing cultural challenges in global markets is to simply observe what's going on around you, emulate well-regarded people, and respect other cultures. Most individuals in other cultures can sense the sincerity of your interest; they will forgive an oversight when they recognize that it was made out of ignorance, not disdain. Being courteous and respectful of other cultures and other individuals is the best way to adjust to different cultures overseas. Many businesspeople that you deal with abroad have had experience with foreigners and, thus, will be able to adjust to you as well.

Summary

The political, economic, and cultural environments define meaningful parts of the external environment in the business world. As managers and firms try to navigate national and global markets, they must understand how countries differ on these dimensions. Determining where, when, and how to adjust their business practices and operating procedures to meet these challenges, as we saw with Gillette in our opening case, greatly boosts their chances for success. We concede that this is easier said than done. In closing, therefore, we urge you to accept the idea that countries differ on the ideas of the power of the vote, the degree of consumer sovereignty, the makeup of fundamental values, and favored ways of thinking. Accepting, rather than ignoring or worse, condemning, these intrinsic political, economic, and cultural difference moves you down the path of understanding how to prosper and profit from the globalization of business.

endnotes

[1] Mark Maremont, "Gillette Won't Meet Certain Goals While Emerging Markets Face Turmoil," *Wall Street Journal,* September 30, 1998, p. A5; Rosabeth Moss Kanter and Thomas D. Dretler, "'Global Strategy' and Its Impact on Local Operations: Lessons from Gillette Singapore," *Academy of Management Executive,* Vol. 12, No. 4, November 1998, pp. 60–68; Jim Holt, "Gone Global?" *Management Review,* Vol. 89, No. 3, March 2000, p. 13; Jenny McCune, "Exporting Corporate Culture," *Management Review,* Vol. 88, No. 11, December 1999, pp. 52–56; and Dexter Roberts, Frederik Balfour, Paul Magnusson, Pete Engardio, and Jennifer Lee, "China's Pirates," *Business Week,* June 5, 2000, p. 26.

[2] William C. Symonds, "Gillette Takes a Shave and a Big Haircut," *Business Week,* October 12, 1998, p. 44.

[3] Avraham Sharma, "How Have Multinational Corporations Fared in Russia Since Financial Turbulence?" *Journal of Financial Management and Analysis,* Vol. 13, No. 1, January–June 2000, pp. 81–83.

[4] Bruce R. Scott, "Country Analysis," Harvard Business School, Case No. 382-105, March 1984.

[5] "A Conundrum for Austria—and for Europe," *The Economist,* February 5, 2000, p. 45.

[6] Alan Cullison, "Putin Sworn in as Russia's President," *Wall Street Journal,* May 8, 2000, p. A28.

[7] Scott, op. cit.

[8] Mark Whitehouse, "For Business in Today's Disfunctional Russia, Solutions Are Creative, but Not Necessarily Legal," *Wall Street Journal,* June 3, 1999, pp. A19, 21.

[9] Michael E. Porter, "The Competitive Advantage of Nations," *Harvard Business Review,* March–April 1990, p. 73.

[10] Jonathan Friedland, "U.S. Phone Giants Find Telmex Can Be a Bruising Competitor," *Wall Street Journal,* October 23, 1998, p. Al.

[11] A.L. Kroeber and Clyde Kluckhohn, *Culture: A Critical Review of Concepts and Definitions* (New York: Vintage Books, 1952).

[12] Retrieved (October 2000) from the World Wide Web: http://www.arthurandersen.com/BUS-INFO/SERVICES/IES/almanac/japan/jpcult.htm.

[13] A listing of newsgroups can be found at the Usenet Info Center Launch Pad at http://meta lab.unc.edu/usenet-i/.

[14] Harry C. Triandis, "Dimensions of Cultural Variation as Parameters of Organizational Theories," *International Studies of Management and Organization,* winter 1982–1983, pp. 143–144.

[15] Geert Hofstede, *Cultures and Organizations* (London: McGraw-Hill, 1991), p. 8; and Geert Hofstede, "National Cultures in Four Dimensions," *International Studies of Management and Organization,* spring–summer 1983, pp. 54–55.

[16] Marlene Djursaa, "North Europe Business Culture: Britain vs. Denmark and Germany," *European Management Journal,* Vol. 12, No. 2, June 1994, pp. 138–146.

[17] Statement by Mike Gilbert, MBNA Canada's Director of Customer Satisfaction and Telesales, reported in "Breaking the Language Barrier," *MBNA Quarterly,* Vol. 4, No. 1, 2001, pp. 8–9.

[18] Statement by Martin Parizeau, Director of Marketing, MBNA Canada, Ibid.

[19] Edward Hall, "The Silent Language in Overseas Business," *Harvard Business Review,* May–June 1960.

Objectives

1. To understand why nations choose to cooperate with each other

2. To interpret a nation's incentive to trade goods and services with other nations

3. To discern the scale and scope of capital links among nations

4. To realize how the movement of people among nations creates and fortifies links

5. To appreciate the fragility of links among nations and the institutions that monitor them

6. To grasp the idea of the Internet in promoting links among nations

GM in Thailand

I n the mid-1990s the auto markets in Thailand, Indonesia, Malaysia, and the Philippines were booming. Thanks to 8 to 10 percent annual growth in gross national product (GNP), analysts projected that their total car sales would grow from 1.46 million vehicles in 1996 to 2.4 million car sales per year by 2006. In response, carmakers from North America and Europe rushed there.

One way for a foreign carmaker to serve these markets was to make cars in its home nation and then export them. High tariffs on imported cars in these countries made that plan impractical, however—import duties on cars ranged from 20 percent in Indonesia to more than 100 percent in Singapore. Such prohibitive trade barriers make it tough for a foreign company to design, build, and deliver a car via export and still make a profit. Instead, General Motors (GM), Ford, BMW, and other foreign carmakers made foreign direct investments (FDIs) in local manufacturing plants that would build cars for local markets. As part of this investment process, foreign automakers spurred their suppliers to build local plants so that they would not need to import high-priced parts. Eventually, foreign carmakers brought to Thailand, for instance, more than 50 of their key suppliers. Likewise, each company moved managers from its U.S., Asian, and European plants to staff its Thai operations.

In 1997, Asian financial markets collapsed. Carmakers got hit hard given the high cost of their product. In desperation, some planned to export cars made in Thailand to other parts of the world. Fortunately, most carmakers had built a global supply chain that let them move Thai-made cars onto dealers' lots in other countries. Moreover, links between Thai-based managers and their colleagues around the world helped overcome internal obstacles. Finally, extensive links among trade groups and governments had, over time, removed many of the barriers that would have made this option impossible just a few years earlier. By 2000, most foreign auto companies operating in Thailand were exporting a large share of their output to other countries—GM, for instance, anticipated exporting 85 percent of its 2001 output of 40,000 mini-vans to Europe.

Linkages Among Countries

chapter 5

Traditional dancers fill the streets of Chuao, Venezuela, during the Corpus Christi celebration.

The success of GM's export plan was not a sure thing. The biggest problem was the cost of making the mini-van—about $34,000—in Thailand. Fortunately, capital links among the world's financial markets and Thailand gave GM ways to jump this hurdle. During the Asian capital crisis, GM found working capital in other parts of the world at lower rates. These funds let GM continue to make cars in Thailand. Too, the integration of the Thai market into the world capital markets spurred the devaluation of the Thai baht, which lowered the dollar equivalent of local production costs between 15 and 30 percent. This devaluation, combined with the falling wage rates in Thailand, made it economically practical to make cars in Thailand and ship them to other parts of the world.

Introduction

Few can deny that during the last 50 years, the world economy has become much more international. There are many more trades, much higher direct investment flows, and greater numbers of people moving across national borders. Indeed, the case of GM in Thailand illustrates the ardent intent and diligent efforts of companies, governments, people, and financial markets to find ways to move more goods and services around the world. No matter what the unique circumstances of any one situation may be, they share a common denominator: Globalization depends on *cross-national links*. Such a link is, essentially, a convergence of interest or strengthening of relationships that spurs a person, company, or institution in one nation to deal with a person, company, or institution in another. Presently, the network of links among nations lets companies work in targeted nations more efficiently, lets the owners of capital move their funds around the globe more quickly, and permits people to search for prosperity in more nations. A sense of globalization, therefore, depends on grasping the links among nations that allow freer trade, freer capital flows, and freer migration of people. Figure 5.1 shows the relationships among these issues. This chapter looks at each of these ideas.

Trade Links Among Nations

Since 1950, the volume of global trade has grown 16-fold.[1] Significantly, the growth in trade among nations has outpaced the growth rates in national domestic products. It is not a stretch to say that global trade has never been freer than it is today. We start this chapter by reviewing the general performance of and specific explanations for the global trade system. This discussion shows that freer trade promotes deeper relationships and broader interdependencies among the nations of the world.

The General Performance of Trade

Links among nations follow many paths. Generally, they follow the lead of the relationships, arrangements, and channels that move goods and services among nations. Before we begin looking at why and how these links come into play, it helps to get a sense of the scale of trade among nations. In 1999, total worldwide

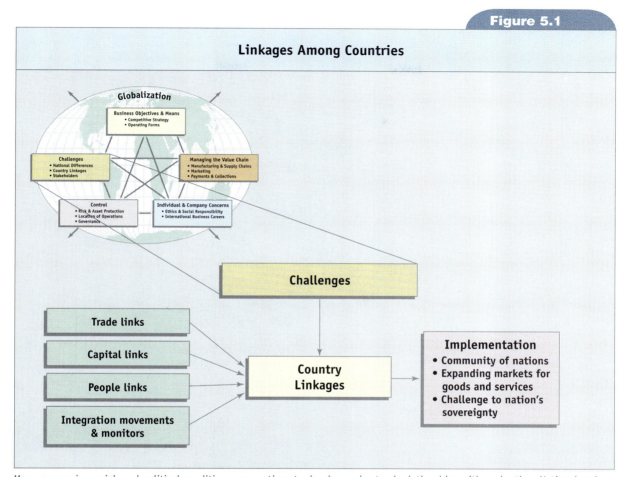

Figure 5.1

Linkages Among Countries

Globalization

Business Objectives & Means
• Competitive Strategy
• Operating Forms

Challenges
• National Differences
• Country Linkages
• Stakeholders

Managing the Value Chain
• Manufacturing & Supply Chains
• Marketing
• Payments & Collections

Control
• Risk & Asset Protection
• Location of Operations
• Governance

Individual & Company Concerns
• Ethics & Social Responsibility
• International Business Careers

Challenges

Trade links

Capital links

People links

Integration movements & monitors

Country Linkages

Implementation
• Community of nations
• Expanding markets for goods and services
• Challenge to nation's sovereignty

Many economic, social, and political conditions spur nations to develop and extend relationships with each other. National and international institutions promote this process. Collectively, these actors and events contribute to the freer movements of products, capital, and people among countries.

cross-border exports exceeded $5,460 billion for physical goods produced in agriculture, mining, and manufacturing and $1,340 billion for services such as transportation, tourism, and entertainment. The rate of growth in goods was about 3.5 percent, whereas for services, it was 1.5 percent. Incidentally, a nation tracks this and related activity in its **balance of payments** (see Figure 5.3).

Historically, worldwide trade in goods has exceeded the trade in services. However, wealthier countries increasingly rely on services to power their international trade. The United States is the premier producer and exporter of services in the world, accounting for about $250 billion of total service exports in 1999, while the next country, the United Kingdom, claimed about $100 billion. U.S. exports of major types of services, as defined in Table 5.1, account for a growing share of its total international trade. This trend will only strengthen. Presently, the service sector is the largest component of the U.S. economy, accounting for about 80 percent of gross domestic product and nearly 85

Figure 5.2

"Derek's sneakers were made in Malaysia. Can
anyone show us where Malaysia is?"

Figure 5.3

The Balance of Payments (BOP)

The BOP is the statistical record of a country's international transactions for a given time period. That is, it systematically measures many of the links among nations by measuring the flow of goods, services, and capital among companies, governments, and individuals across nations. The BOP is divided into the current account and the capital account. The current account measures a country's trade in goods, services, income receipts and payments, and unilateral transfers, whereas the capital account reports transactions in real or financial assets between countries. The most meaningful balance for most countries is the goods balance, which is simply exports less imports—a positive sum is called a surplus, whereas a negative one is a deficit. The goods balance is widely reported in the press and watched as a leading indicator of a nation's trade policy. Overall, the BOP helps forecast a nation's market trade potential and acts as an early indicator of capital trends.

Types of Service Exports: A Look at the Principal Activities of the United States	
Travel and tourism	The largest single category within the U.S. service sector; it includes diverse services in transportation, lodging, food and beverage service, recreation, purchase of incidentals consumed while in transit, and traveling on commercial airlines.
Transportation services	Includes aviation, ocean shipping, inland waterways, railroads, trucking, pipelines, and intermodal services, as well as ancillary and support services in ports, airports, railyards, and truck terminals. Essentially, this category captures the movement of manufactured, mining, and agricultural products to foreign markets, as well as transporting business and leisure travelers around the world on noncommercial airlines such as private jets or group charters.
Education and training services	Includes the management training, technical training, and English-language training done outside the United States. These activities span manufacturing and service industries.
Banking, financial, and insurance services	Includes the activities of U.S. financial institutions' investment banking, account management, credit-card operations, and collection management. Similarly, U.S. insurers underwrite, assess risk, and provide insurance overseas.
Entertainment	U.S. filmed entertainment and recorded music have been very successful in appealing to foreign audiences. U.S. media companies license and sell rights to exhibit films in movie theaters, on television, and on videocassettes, as well as sell music products around the world.
Information services	Includes companies that generate, process, and export electronic commerce activities such as e-mail, funds transfer, and data interchange, as well as data processing and network services, electronic information services, and professional computer services. Increasingly, this category expands to include computer operations, data processing and transmission, online services, computer consulting, and systems integration.
Professional business services	This sector includes the advice and assistance efforts of U.S. companies in areas such as accounting, advertising, legal, and management consulting services. By and large, the international market for these services is expanding at a more rapid rate than the U.S. domestic market.
Architectural, construction, and engineering	Includes the activities of U.S. firms in designing, engineering, constructing, maintaining, and managing foreign-based commercial and residential properties.

Table 5.1

million jobs. Thus, largely powered by Internet and related information technologies, forecasters see U.S. service exports hitting $650 billion by 2010.[2] Still, for most nations, especially the emerging nations, the trade of tangible goods dominates international trade activity.

Reasons to Create Trade Links

Trade in goods and services is perhaps the most visible way that countries create links. The explanation for this is simple: Studies of international trade inevitably show that the gains from free trade are significant, falling somewhere between the view that they are not great enough to be taken very seriously and the view that they are huge and commanding. Despite evidence that freer trade benefits all, national leaders around the world wrestle with the questions of what, how much, and with whom their country should trade. Once they decide, as we will see in Chapter 6, officials set policies to attain their goals. These policies shape the actions of companies because they directly affect which countries are open to imports from foreign suppliers and exports from domestic suppliers. We saw these concerns in play in our opening look at GM and its decision to build cars in Thailand for export to Europe, given that trade linkages between these areas let it do so.

Some countries earnestly manage their export and import policies. Others, however, let market forces determine the type of links that develop with their trade partners. Chapter 6 will look closely at the ways governments try to regulate trade flows. Meanwhile, this chapter looks at the incentives that move nations to trade with other nations—specifically, the ideas of mercantilism, absolute and comparative advantage, strategic trade theory, and national competitive advantage.

Mercantilism

The great trading nations of the 16th through the 19th centuries, such as the United Kingdom, believed a nation was stronger if it exported more than it imported. In this era, a nation accumulated gold bullion through export sales. Therefore, given that gold was the basis of power and prosperity, a country's status depended on how much gold it could earn via trade. Over time, most nations devised policies to ensure that exports grew as fast as possible while imports were restricted or halted. This type of trade strategy, often referred to as **mercantilism,** was the forerunner of the trade strategy pursued by Japan and Korea in the mid- to late 1900s as they sought to develop the strength of their economy and, by extension, their national power.

A mercantilist trade strategy encourages a nation to form links with two sorts of other nations. One set of links is with those markets that are rich in low-cost natural resources (such as cotton or oil), which the nation would then import back to its domestic market in order to convert them into final products (such as clothing or gasoline). The second set of links would follow the effort of the nation to then sell the higher-value finished products to whatever other country could afford them—including back to the nations that originally provided the natural resources. Mercantilism, therefore, encourages one-way rather that truly two-way trade links between nations.

Absolute Advantage

Trade theory shifted from mercantilism to the ideas of **absolute** and **comparative advantage** in the 1700s. Adam Smith's 1776 book, *The Wealth of*

Table 5.2

Leading Exporters and Importers, 1999

Individual Countries' Relative Share of Type of World Trade

Merchandise Trade				Commercial Services			
Exporters		Importers		Exporters		Importers	
Nation	Share	Nation	Share	Nation	Share	Nation	Share
United States	12.4	United States	18.0	United States	18.8	United States	13.7
Germany	9.6	Germany	8.0	United Kingdom	7.6	Germany	9.5
Japan	7.5	United Kingdom	5.5	France	5.9	Japan	8.5
France	5.3	Japan	5.3	Germany	5.7	United Kingdom	6.1
United Kingdom	4.8	France	4.9	Italy	4.8	Italy	4.7
Canada	4.2	Canada	3.7	Japan	4.5	France	4.4
Italy	4.1	Italy	3.7	Spain	4.0	Netherlands	3.5
Netherlands	3.6	Netherlands	3.2	Netherlands	4.0	Canada	2.8
China	3.5	Hong Kong	3.1	Belgium	2.8	Belgium	2.6

source: *World Trade Annual Report,* 2000.

Nations, sparked this radical reinterpretation of the basis for trade. Notably, he reasoned that a country's real wealth was not a function of how much gold it stockpiled, but rather the total amount of goods and services that its citizens could buy in the marketplace. Importantly, in a world with no trade barriers, nations would voluntarily opt to specialize in making those goods that had the greatest value to foreign consumers and import those products that other nations provided at a lower cost than could domestic suppliers. Links among nations, therefore, would follow the direction of the invisible hand of a perfectly competitive market—consumer demand for low-priced products rather than government direction dictates which goods went where.

The key question of absolute advantage is figuring out what products a country should specialize in making for export. Ultimately, Adam Smith pointed out that a country's advantage would be either natural or acquired. A **natural advantage** occurs because of innate features of a nation—such as climate conditions, access to certain natural resources, or availability of certain labor skills. For example, Jamaica's beaches, water, great climate, and hospitality lure tourists from around the world. Therefore, Jamaica's natural advantages spur it to specialize in service exports in the form of tourism. Similarly, China's skilled, low-cost labor pool attracts a lot of foreign investors.

An **acquired advantage** occurs when a nation develops specialized skills and technologies that let it make a high-quality product for a low cost. Originally, acquired advantages were less important than natural advantages. In the 17th and 18th centuries, nations relied on an agrarian economy to convert their natural land, labor, and climate advantages into cost-competitive exports. The industrialization era, beginning in the late 19th century, spotlighted the tremendous competitive power of an acquired advantage over the passive acceptance of existing natural advantages. Over time, as more of the world's trade took place in manufactured products rather than agriculture and mining, more nations tied their export competitiveness to acquired advantages in technology, capital, and ideas.

Countries that export cost-competitive goods and services have, by definition, an acquired advantage in either a product or process technology. An advantage in *product technology* is a country's ability to produce a unique product or one that is easily distinguished from those of competitors, such as Czech crystal or U.S. software. An advantage in *process technology* is a country's ability to make a commodity product (one that is not easily distinguished from that made by competitors, such as steel, gasoline, or rudimentary integrated circuits) more efficiently than its rivals. Always in the background of these situations is the role of technology. Technological change eventually displaces old products with newer, better versions. Such change then alters trading links, such as when Korea, a longtime importer of integrated circuits from Japan, in time became a principal exporter to Japan.

Comparative Advantage

From its inception, pressure grew on the theory of absolute advantage to answer a nagging question: "What happens when one country relative to other countries can produce all products at an absolute advantage?" In 1817, David Ricardo solved this puzzle by extending Adam Smith's theories to develop the theory of comparative advantage. This theory proposed that a country should specialize in making products where it has the greatest comparative advantage, even if it can make all products more efficiently than any other nation, in order to gain the greatest reward for its efforts. For example, if a particular person is the world's fastest typist but also the brightest banker, she should give up typing in favor of the comparatively greater rewards of spending more time doing banking. This theory of trade meant that links among nations should be reciprocal—no single nation tries to make everything and everyone is better off by trading something with someone.

While theoretically straightforward, comparative advantage can mystify national policy makers. Generally, officials are reluctant to believe that their nation should not capitalize on every possible absolute advantage, even though the practice of comparative advantage would result in more goods for lower prices. Consequently, many trade theorists argue that incentives to produce particular goods and services are better decided by the market than some political ministry. Still, Chapter 6 shows that political leaders routinely intervene in international trade flows.

The theory of comparative advantage, like that of absolute advantage, does not automatically tell nations which products they should produce for export and which they should import. Like absolute advantage, the theory of comparative advantage relies on the idea that the invisible hand of the free market makes the best decision. The related theory of **factor proportions** shows how this works. Essentially, this theory proposes that abundant factors of production in a market are almost always cheaper than those factors of production that are scarce. Therefore, in a perfect world, countries ought to focus on developing their comparative advantage by making goods that fit with their particular mix of land, labor, capital, and technology. The essence of absolute and comparative advantage, then, is to make goods and services that use abundant factors of production and import those that use scarce factors of production.

The Theory of National Competitive Advantage

In the early 1990s, a group of scholars under the direction of Michael Porter studied 100 industries in 10 nations in an effort to figure out how a nation achieved international success in a particular industry that would then lead others nations to form links with it.[3] For example, why does Japan do great in the electronics industry, whereas Italy does terrific in fashion design? The results of this study, "The Competitive Advantage of Nations," report four country-specific attributes—factor endowments, demand conditions, related and supporting industries, and firm strategy, structure, and rivalry—that make up the so-called national diamond or **Porter diamond** that shapes the national business environment in which local firms compete (see Figure 5.4). Ultimately, the interaction within the national diamond governs a nation's competitive advantage. For example, favorable **demand conditions** for imaginative software will not lead to a national competitive advantage if the national government has imposed barriers to innovations, such as universal software standards or free access to source code stipulations, that prevent companies from responding to them.

The theory of national competitive advantage holds that the degree to which a country can achieve international success in a certain industry is a function of its national diamond. By extension, this theory holds that the different performances of national diamonds shape the pattern, scale, and scope of links among nations. This view enriches the theories of absolute and comparative advantages by directly considering the role of capital and labor along with technological change, patterns of innovations, and the nature of demand in shaping trade links among nations.

The theory of national competitive advantage points out that two variables—chance and government—can significantly affect the character of a national diamond. Chance events, such as breakthrough ideas, can fan gales of creative destruction that reshape industry structure and provide the opportunity for one nation's firms to gain ground against another's (as we saw in the Finnish company Nokia's rise to global dominance in cellular phones, to the detriment of Motorola in the United States and Ericsson in Sweden). Similarly, a nation's government can adopt policies that bolster or erode its national competitive advantage. For example, some probusiness observers contend that the efforts of the U.S. government to control the market power of Microsoft will facilitate the emergence of foreign rivals with competitive operating systems. Government, as we will see in Chapter 6, influences a home

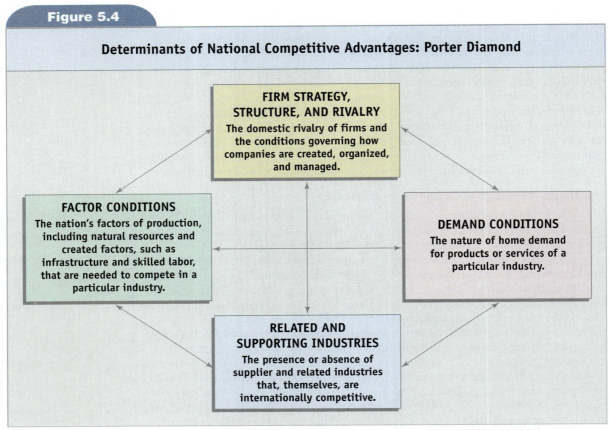

Figure 5.4

Determinants of National Competitive Advantages: Porter Diamond

FIRM STRATEGY, STRUCTURE, AND RIVALRY
The domestic rivalry of firms and the conditions governing how companies are created, organized, and managed.

FACTOR CONDITIONS
The nation's factors of production, including natural resources and created factors, such as infrastructure and skilled labor, that are needed to compete in a particular industry.

DEMAND CONDITIONS
The nature of home demand for products or services of a particular industry.

RELATED AND SUPPORTING INDUSTRIES
The presence or absence of supplier and related industries that, themselves, are internationally competitive.

source: Adapted and reprinted by permission of *Harvard Business Review*. Figure from "The Competitive Advantage of Nations" by Michael E. Porter, March–April, 1990. Copyright © 2001 by Harvard Business School Publishing Corporation.

nation's competitive advantage by manipulating the performance of its national diamond.

Besides the wild-card effects of chance and government policy, the diamond theory of national advantage has exceptions that can blur the appraisal of trade links among nations.[4] First, the existence of a supportive national diamond for, say, a software industry does not guarantee that that particular industry will develop in that country. Successful companies may enjoy favorable national diamonds for many potential business areas but, given resource constraints, choose some to the neglect of others. In fact, the theory of comparative advantage maintains that resource limitations may cause companies in a country not to compete in an industry even though they may command an absolute advantage. For example, Swiss multinational enterprises (MNEs) preferred to protect their global position in high-tech products such as wristwatches and scientific instruments rather than downsizing those industries by moving their highly skilled people into different, yet related, industries like computer chips, personal computers, or cellular phones.

Second, the theory of national competitive advantages only partly explains companies' growing capability, particularly with the aid of the Internet, to gain market information, production factors, and management expertise from foreign sources. Acquiring these foreign-based resources lets an ambitious company break free of its particular national diamond. In other words, the absence or stunted growth of any of the four points of a national diamond does not automatically bar companies and industries in that nation from becoming globally competitive. As a case in point, the globally competitive industries of many Asian countries are shaped not by the character of demand in their domestic markets but rather by their strategic intent to serve targeted export markets.

Strategic Trade Theory

No country in the world permits an unregulated flow of goods and services across its borders. Governments sometimes place restrictions on exports and imports, whereas at other times, they subsidize them. These sorts of trade policies move us from a world of links developed in perfectly competitive markets to a world of links that emerge in managed competition. A leading example of this situation is found in the idea of *strategic trade policy*. Governments around the world apply a strategic trade policy when they use incentives and restrictions to encourage and discourage specific types of exports and imports.

The popularity of this idea largely follows from the suggestion of so-called new theories of trade that governments ought to manage their exports and imports directly rather than placing their faith in the invisible hand of the marketplace. Essentially, new trade theories hold that while traditional trade theories, such as comparative advantage, do explain the flow of goods and services among nations, they tell only part of the story. Fully understanding the network of trade links among nations requires appreciating how governments create market situations that lead to particular patterns of trade.

Strategic trade theory reasons that traditional trade theories do not fully explain how entrepreneurship, innovations, and even blind luck give some countries unique trade advantages that go beyond the justification of their endowment of land, labor, capital, and technology.[5] For example, India has a budding comparative advantage in writing software code—it has many productive, yet inexpensive, code writers. Nonetheless, the United States continues to dominate the global software market by virtue of the strategic advantages that result from Microsoft's early entrance into and ensuing dominance of the computer operating systems industry. Similar situations show up in aircraft manufacturing, liquid crystal displays, computer chips, and capital management. Essentially, strategic trade theory suggests that a country may predominate in the export of a good or service simply because it was fortunate enough to have one or more of its firms among the first to produce it.

This situation changes the pattern of links among nations that otherwise would have emerged under conditions of absolute or comparative advantage. For instance, if you want your personal computer to run the numerous software applications in the market, most likely you will need the Windows operating system. Therefore, whether they want to or not, consumers around the world must look to Microsoft, in particular, and the United States, in general, to provide this product.

These anomalies spur governments to support directly those domestic firms that have potential **first-mover advantages** or compete against firms that continue to dominate vital product markets (such as Microsoft in software, Boeing in aircraft, and Intel in semiconductors). Typically, officials follow one of two paths: They either (1) alter national conditions that affect the economy in general or (2) alter national conditions that will affect a targeted industry. In the first case, the government changes national conditions with the intent of influencing factor proportions, efficiency, and innovation in the overall economy. For example, a country may upgrade production factors by improving human skills through education or by building better infrastructure (transportation, communications, capital markets) so that any and all companies can do business better.

In the second case, political officials target specific industries that they judge to be crucial to the future of the nation—such as health care, electronics, or capital management. Japan, for instance, has gone to great lengths to establish a strategic trade policy by picking national champions. More recently, China has announced a strategic trade policy with the goal of becoming a world-class competitor in such industries as electronics and pharmaceuticals. Often, though, most nations target the same high-tech industries, thereby leading to a lot of tough competition.

Strategic trade theory does not reject outright the theory of comparative advantage. Both theories emphasize the importance of specialization, economies of scale, and efficient use of resources to achieve the productivity needed for competitive exports. However, whereas the theory of comparative advantage relies on the invisible hand of the market to start and regulate things, strategic trade theory puts responsibility for identifying potentially successful industries into the visible hands of political officials. Therefore, a problem with strategic trade theory is that picking potential winners is tough for anyone—whether investors, managers, or political officials. Too, although the marketplace is much more effective, even it often fails—as seen in the unpredictability of companies' performance and equity prices. Also, even if we presume that political officials can pick the winners, it doesn't mean companies in that industry should automatically receive special aid, or that they will be more competitive if they in fact do receive help.

Capital Links Among Nations

From the end of World War II through the early 1970s, the **Bretton Woods Agreement** governed world monetary markets. One of its precepts stipulated fixed exchange values for national currencies. As a result, countries had self-contained financial systems for the simple reason that fixed exchange rates effectively closed national financial systems to each other. Links among nations continue to develop through international trade. In 1973, due to pressure from persistent U.S. trade deficits, emergence of growing stocks of **Eurodollars,** and accelerating inflation, the Bretton Woods system collapsed. Foreign exchange rates began to "float," whereby a nation's currency found its fair value in relation to contemporary economic and political conditions in the nation and the world.

Floating exchange rates let governments, MNEs, entrepreneurs, traders, and people begin building capital links. Governments open their national economies to attract the capital they need to finance growth, fund industrialization, underwrite infrastructure, and pay for development. MNEs shop the world for the lowest-cost capital to fund their operations and expansion. Investors look to other nations' markets for potential investment opportunities. Traders exploit risk-free pricing anomalies between financial instruments in different markets. Finally, travelers visit other countries' markets with less financial anxiety. These links, along with those developed in many similar ways, lead to extraordinary growth and integration in the world's capital markets.

As financial markets grew and matured, they expanded the number and type of capital links among nations. By 2000, we saw an immense global capital market that continued to grow in scope, size, and power. Indeed, the world capital market seemingly exhibits a virtuous cycle, whereby the more that capital flows among nations, the greater the number of financial instruments that emerge to link nations and, thus, the greater the degree to which more nations open their financial markets. And throughout this cycle, capital links forcefully apply the *law of one price*—which states that the price of a product is the same in all markets—to foreign exchange and bonds around the world.

Individually powerful, the cumulative growth and integration of the world's capital market lead some to see it as the "true" engine of globalization. By 2000, many analysts noted that the scale and scope of capital links among virtually all nations give the global capital market the power and instruments to compel the globalization of business. In particular, financial liberalization has tremendous effects in three areas: FDI, the international bond market, and the international equity market. We now look at each.

Foreign Direct Investment

Our earlier look at theories of trade helps explain many of the links among nations. These theories, though, fall short of explaining why a firm, rather than simply exporting from its home base to a foreign market, would opt to build a plant or open an office in that country. Dealing with this question takes us to the matter of FDI. Before turning to the specific features of FDI, we should note that most companies treat exports and FDI as substitutes for each other. When faced with a market opportunity overseas, managers apply the form of international involvement that they believe best fits their global strategy. More specifically, though, managers opt to use FDI when faced with distinct challenges in expanding sales, acquiring resources, minimizing risk, and resolving political objectives (see Table 5.3).

FDI is a form of international involvement that involves a company's significant equity stake in or effective management control of a foreign company. FDI occurs when a firm decides to buy or build part or all of a business operation in a foreign country. In general, such an operation can do any number of things, including functioning as a research and development site, manufacturing facility, supply depot, service network, or administrative office. Importantly, FDI does not require that a company take full control and ownership of its foreign operation. Rather, the U.S. Department of Commerce stipulates that, no matter what form FDI takes, it officially occurs when a U.S. citizen, organization, or affiliated group buys and controls an interest of 10 percent or more in a foreign company. Incidentally, applying this criterion to all businesses around the world in 1999 found that more than 63,600 MNEs have at least a 10 percent ownership interest in more than 690,000 foreign affiliates.[6]

Table 5.3

Motivations for FDI as an Alternative or Supplement to Trade

These Objectives Usually Outweigh the Risks of FDI

Sales Expansion Objectives	Resource Acquisition Objectives	Risk Minimization Objectives	Political Objectives
• Overcome high transport costs • Lack of domestic capacity • Low gains from scale economies • Trade restrictions • Barriers because of country-of-origin effects (nationalism, product image, delivery risk) • Lower production costs abroad	• Savings through vertical integration • Savings through rationalized production • Gain access to cheaper or different resources and knowledge • Need to lower costs as product matures • Gain governmental investment incentives	• Diversification of customer base (same motivation as for sales expansion objectives) • Diversification of supplier base (same motivations as for resource acquisition objectives) • Following customers • Preventing competitors' advantage	• Influence companies, usually through factors under resource acquisition objectives

source: From *International Business: Environments and Operations, 9/E* by Radebaugh and Daniels © 2001. Reprinted with permission of Pearson Education, Inc., Upper Saddle River, NJ 07458.

The growth of FDI over the past 20 years has provoked many explanations. The most compelling one is that, over that time, the business world began globalizing more rapidly through FDI than through international trade. More specifically, the **World Trade Organization (WTO)** reported that total FDI flows increased ninefold between 1982 and 1993 while world trade of merchandise and services doubled in the same period. Tremendous growth in FDI since then has accelerated this trend. Specifically, the **United Nations Conference on Trade and Development (UNCTAD)** reported that total world outflows of FDI came to $648.9 billion in 1998, a year-on-year increase of 36.6 percent, while global FDI inflows rose 38.7 percent to $643.9 billion. More recently, UNCTAD projected that total FDI flows will surge "past $1 trillion U.S." in 2000.[7]

Snowballing FDI flows have both company and country components. Regarding the former, cross-border mergers and acquisitions, particularly by foreign investors buying stakes of newly privatized state-owned enterprises, push FDI flows to record levels. Indeed, the past five years has shown a global market for companies that were bought and sold across borders on an unprecedented scale. From the country view, investment flows to and from industrialized countries still dominate; in particular, Western Europe, North America, and Japan continually rank as major sources of FDI flows. In 1997, these and other wealthier nations claimed $460 billion (71 percent) of total FDI flows. Poorer, developing countries, on the other hand, received $166 billion (25 percent) of total FDI inflows. Finally, with respect to specific countries, in 1999, the five nations with the highest FDI inflows were the United States ($193.4 billion), the United Kingdom ($67.5 billion), China ($43.8 billion), the Netherlands ($33.3 billion), and Brazil ($31.9 billion).

In sum, FDI flows will continue to surge due to national governments' quest to attract more capital flows, processes of privatization that open new markets, and growing networks of links among nations. For instance, from 1991 through 1999, there were approximately 1,035 significant changes by national governments with respect to the laws that regulate FDI; roughly 94 percent of these changes improved the local investment environment for foreign companies.[8]

MNEs prosper in this environment for several reasons: (1) More managers of more firms have gained greater expertise in investing abroad; (2) the more companies invest aboard, the more they then need to in the future in order to meet the burgeoning need to integrate their global manufacturing and supply chain systems; and (3) as we saw in Chapter 1, companies' vision of an integrated worldwide market drives them to make direct investments abroad in order to build a presence in the major region of the world. Finally, fueling this process are the by-products of globalization. Falling trade barriers and investment restriction—along with better capital movement and information access—pave more paths for more FDI.

International Bond Market

The international bond market is made up of all bonds sold by governments, issuing companies, and organizations outside of their home nation. By 1999, this market had grown to more than $1 trillion U.S. in volume, more than doubling the $454 billion volume in 1995. Moreover, the **International Monetary Fund (IMF)** estimates that in 1980, this market had about $20 trillion in total liquid assets; by 2000, it was expected to hit $39 trillion.

Whereas nearly half of all bond transaction volume takes place in Western Europe, every region of the world participates. Strong incentives push nations to reduce barriers to international bond transactions. Fewer barriers mean that local borrowers can negotiate a loan with more nations that may charge lower interest rates or offer more financing flexibility. Similarly, fewer barriers let investors in one country pursue the higher returns on bonds sold in other countries.

The power of the international bond market as a force for the integration of capital markets is admired and feared. Indeed, observers note that the international bond market powers the convergence of economic policy across more and more countries. Those national economies that the international bond market rates as fiscally responsible and politically committed to market-based policies get access to the international debt capital they need to finance growth. Those that are not are forced to redo their fiscal policies if they wish to access foreign capital. Like people who are fiscally responsible, the international market is quick to reward creditworthy nations with more capital at better rates and punish those who fail to do so. For example, in early 1995, Canada and Italy had very high domestic debt due; as a result, their governments had to pay real interest rates 2 to 4 percent higher than the U.S. rates for debt of the same maturity. Over the next two years, the demands of the global capital market plus the severe cost of ignoring them pushed Canada and Italy to revamp their fiscal policies.

International Equity Market

The international equity market is made up of all stocks that are bought and sold outside the home country of the issuing company or government. The inter-

Ultimately, building links between countries requires building the infrastructure to permit the movement of people, products, and ideas. Here we see a worker setting buoys for an undersea fiber-optic cable to improve an individual country's links with the world. The tremendous voice, image, and data transfer capabilities of fiber-optic cables promotes relationships with people, companies, and institutions around the world.

national equity market has grown tremendously over the last 20 years, largely following the abandonment of fixed exchange rates and capital controls in the early 1970s. The IMF estimates that in 1980, this market had about $26 trillion in total liquid assets; by 2000, it was expected to pass $40 trillion.

Although more than half of newly issued equity originates in Western Europe, shares from all parts of the world actively trade on various national exchanges. As in the international bond market, strong incentives push nations to link their equity markets. From the perspective of the exchanges, integration into global equity markets may be the only way to retain their clients. NASDAQ has explored alliances with the London and Frankfurt markets, whereas the New York Stock Exchange has conferred with its counterparts in Paris, Tokyo, Hong Kong, Sydney, Toronto, Mexico City, and São Paulo.[9] Companies spur this process because greater opportunities to issue equities outside their home country give them greater access to deeper pools of lower-cost equity capital. Investors also prosper from globalizing equity markets. Buying shares in companies from different nations creates more investment opportunities and options to reduce the systematic risk in a portfolio.

Expanding links among national equity markets has had some interesting effects. Notably, these links help transfer U.S. ideas about the primacy of shareholder value and market capitalization as the dominant metric for measuring corporate performance to other countries. Increasingly, equity investors around the world are less tolerant of companies that do not deliver strong global growth. While a seemingly obvious thing, this is a dramatic change in investor psychology in countries such as Japan, France, and Germany. By the same token, deeper pools of venture capital give those MNEs that can generate high returns, wherever in the world they reside, easier access to capital. Entrepreneurs and companies that once may have faced daunting capital constraints in their home nation can now access larger supplies of relatively cheap capital.

People Links Among Nations

A vibrant source of links among nations is the many people who leave one country for another. In 2000, there were more than 150 million international migrants worldwide, up nearly 100 percent since 1965. While a large number in absolute terms, we should note that fewer than 3 percent of the world's people have lived outside their home countries for a year or longer. Nonetheless, immigrants now make up almost 10 percent of the total population in Western Europe and North America. In terms of where people move, international migrants travel the world. The largest numbers of international migrants are in Asia, Europe, and North America, followed by Africa, Latin America, and Oceania. In terms of nations, U.S. consulates and embassies registered 3.8 million Americans, not counting military personnel or diplomats, living abroad in 1999.[10] China claims the greatest number of international migrants—estimates are that up to 40 million Chinese live abroad.[11]

By definition, an *international migrant* is a person who takes up residence or who remains for an extended stay in a foreign country. While there is no consistent trigger, people generally cross national boundaries in search of the promise of peace or potential for prosperity. More precisely, international migrants belong to two broad groups—voluntary migrants and forced migrants.

Voluntary migrants include people who move abroad for employment, study, family reunification, enrichment, or other personal reasons. These folks include the tech nomads wandering the globe in search of the latest job slot, executives of MNEs sent overseas for periods ranging from a short time to a lifetime, students attending foreign universities, and artistic cosmopolitans who see themselves as citizens of the world. Forced migrants are those who leave their native countries to escape persecution, natural and human-made disasters, conflict, repression, or other situations that endanger their lives, freedom, or livelihood. These people most commonly include low-skilled workers seeking prosperity and oppressed refugees seeking political asylum.

Whether they are tech nomads or ambitious low-skill workers, immigrants change the social fabric of the places where they settle. They establish businesses; revive industrial, warehouse, and retail districts; invest in housing and other aspects of neighborhoods; celebrate distinct festivals; and bring with them many different cultural practices. These and related actions develop relationships that link nations more tightly together. In some situations, this effect is acutely visible—as we see in the immigrant enclaves of Koreatown in Los Angeles, Chinatown in San Francisco and New York, or Little Havana in Miami. In most situations, though, immigrants diffuse through the community, blending in ways that some say create vibrant "ethnoscapes."[12] The existence of immigrant enclaves produces social networks that sustain and spur international migration flows. This process is greatly helped by the transfer of money—so-called remittances—from immigrants to their families back home.

Sometimes the multiculturalism of international migrants is greeted enthusiastically by host communities. The infusion of polyglot spirit into a uniform group can provoke all sorts of changes. Other times, though, it is met by ambivalence, anxiety, or ill will. Whatever the feelings in the community, the growth of globalization fuels demand for the freer movement of people. And in so doing, the movement of people around the world creates and cements links between communities and countries. Sometimes these links can span so many people across so many different nations that the sense of economic geography can change, as we see in the characterization of Los Angeles as the capital of the Pacific Rim or Miami as the capital of Latin America.

In terms of current trends, we see the wealthier nations continuing to attract and exchange highly skilled labor—the tech nomads of the information age. The developed nations have less and less interest in immigrants with low skill levels. For instance, in the United States between 1900 and 1910, the rate of immigration was 10.4 immigrants for every 1,000 people living in the country. By the late 1990s, this rate had fallen to about 4.0 per 1,000.[13] The fact that the rate has dropped does not indicate a falling number of interested immigrants. Consider the case of the United Kingdom. The number of illegal migrants apprehended at U.K. ports rose from 61 in 1990 to 16,000 in 1999. Also, the number of asylum seekers entering Britain rose from 5,000 in 1985 to 100,000 by 1999.[14] Wherever we look, we see signs of growing pressure for illegal immigration. Wealthy countries react in kind. As of mid-2000, for instance, the U.S. Immigration and Naturalization Service had 8,000 border patrol agents: 300 are on the 4,000-mile Canadian border, while 7,700 are on the 2,000-mile Mexican border.[15]

The root of this predicament is that many poorer countries deal with rapid population growth and low living standards by encouraging emigration of all except the highly skilled. Current estimates hold that between 1995 and 2025, the labor force in low-income countries will grow from 1.4 billion to 2.2 billion people. Neither trade nor FDI at their current levels can create enough jobs in these nations to absorb this looming labor force.[16] In recourse, people in poorer nations seek prosperity in wealthier nations. For instance, as of mid-2000, undocumented Mexicans in the United States earned on average $31 a week in their last Mexican job, compared to $278 a week in the United States; Indonesian laborers earned $0.28 a day in their country versus $2.28 a day in neighboring Malaysia.[17]

International migration sparks strident debate. In broad terms, there are two perspectives. One view champions a univeralist view that claims a moral duty to have a world without borders. This view holds that national borders are arbitrary divisions that should not restrict the movement of anyone, whether managers with MNEs, physicians with Médecins Sans Frontières (Doctors Without Borders), or refugees seeking peace. The other viewpoint endorses the normative ideal of a community of citizens. This view does not automatically dismiss the idea of immigration but does tie it to the immigrant's genuine intent to satisfy citizenship standards that tap the nation's language, historical, civic, and social heritage.

That said, the reality of globalization in business means that few nations can philosophically or practically close their borders to voluntary or forced international immigration. As we saw in Chapter 4, the idea of liberty is the core of a democratic system. Moreover, given that the globalization of business pushes us to rethink our notions of place, community, and locality, it calls us to see the benefit and accept the costs of the freer movement of people across borders.

Regional Integration

The freer movements of products, capital, and people are powerful tools to build links among countries. These types of links, though, happen more by chance than by plan. That is, a company may or may not invest in a foreign

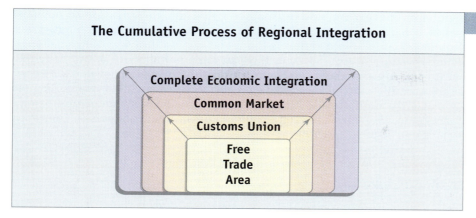

The Cumulative Process of Regional Integration

Figure 5.5

Nations engaged in regional integration typically link together in steps. Initially, nations ally with others to allow free trade with each other. Successful trade performance spurs them to add more links that address, in sequence, trade with non-member nations, freer movement of production factors among member nations, and finally, the adoption of common monetary and fiscal policies among member nations. Therefore, regional integration is a cumulative process. As relationships progress, member nations accept more extensive links with each other. Each additional level of integration expands the scope of its predecessor.

nation or a student may or may not study abroad. Nations are reluctant to let chance singularly shape their integration into the global system. Instead, political leaders, particularly over the past decade or so, manage the creation of links with fellow nations through formal integration programs.

While there are some calls for global economic integration, virtually all the active alliances today are made up of integration agreements among the neighboring countries in a particular region of the world. In general, geographic proximity is a useful way to make sense of the pattern of links among specific nations. At the least, the cost and complexity of moving most goods and services is directly proportional to the distance between two nations. A richer explanation is that neighboring countries are more likely to share a common history and current outlook. These nations will be more willing to link their trade and economic policies. Similarly, companies' practices and consumers' preferences are more likely to overlap among adjacent countries. The **North American Free Trade Agreement (NAFTA), European Union (EU)** in Western Europe, **Andean Pact** in South America, and **Association of South East Asian Nations** in the Far East all showcase the regional orientation of economic integration.

In general, *regional integration* refers to the formal agreement among a set of nations to reduce and eventually eliminate all tariff and nontariff barriers that impede the free flow of goods, services, and factors of production among each other. That said, not all regional integration formats are equal or behave the same. Rather, there are four forms of regional integration, beginning with a free market area, moving on to a customs union, then a common market, and culminating in complete economic integration (see Figure 5.5). Each level of regional integration, from the starting point of a free market to the finish line of complete integration, expands links among the allied nations. These links begin with economic concerns and gradually move on to political, financial, and social matters. As the regional organization builds more links, it becomes significantly easier for products, capital, and people to move among allied nations.

A by-product of initial trade links among neighboring nations is a willingness to consider setting up more links. Therefore, growing trade and capital flows over the past few decades have built links that, over time, spurred people to call for greater integration with other nations. Similarly, the growing intensity of international competition accelerates the number, size, and scope of regional alliances. We saw in Chapter 1 that the globalization of business makes it hard for a national company to hide from strong foreign rivals. Regional economic integration is a popular way to deal with this challenge. Countries can join together and, through the more efficient use of resources within this larger market, help companies within the region develop the necessary competitive capabilities to take on global rivals—in other words, "United we stand, divided we fall." So while 11 new regional economic groups officially came into being between 1980 and 1989, 33 new regional agreements began between 1990 and 1994.

Breaking Links

Links among nations and regions are not easily achieved or sustained. Integration creates enormous economic benefits but can also impose high costs. Nations, when joining a regional bloc or global market, must sacrifice degrees of their national sovereignty and cultural heritage—as expressed in the lament, "Global integration leads to national disintegration." Similarly, whether created by free trade or economic integration, the increased efficiency of the marketplace often destroys careers and companies. These are grave concerns that are hard to reconcile.

In addition to political and cultural concerns, new issues repeatedly arise that threaten to break links among nations. For example, the issue of preserving the environment increasingly motivates some people and **nongovernmental organizations,** such as Greenpeace, to fight a future of extensively networked nations. Specifically, environmental abuse fans tensions among both people and nations over the appropriate mix of economic prosperity and preservation of the environment. Critics of freer trade and capital flows argue that the local economics of globalization extort a high price, essentially costing people control over events inside their own nation.

These concerns press people to question the true benefits of freer trade and tighter links among nations. The concerns erupted in November 1999 at the meeting of the WTO in Seattle, Washington. Thousands of activists took to the streets, effectively turning downtown Seattle into a battle zone, over the issue of what is the "proper" relationship between free trade and prudent use of the environment. So far, there has been little agreement as to the scope of the problem, or even reasonable solutions. As time goes on, we can expect the informal worldwide environmental lobby and sympathetic nongovernmental organizations to oppose freer trade and greater integration.

Protecting Links Among Nations

The globalization of business depends on maintaining and broadening the existing web of links among nations and regions. This realization has spurred governments to invent, in so many words, link masters. That is, just as the web master protects the integrity of a computer network by taking steps to fix fraying links before they snap, so too do link masters monitor the vitality of links among nations.

In general terms, there are many organizations and institutions that try to meet this mission. Most likely, you have read of the activities of the United Nations, World Bank, IMF, and WTO. Although their specific goals differ, each of these organizations helps maintain relationships among nations. For example, the United Nations sees its mission as fostering world peace and social stability, the World Bank has the "dream of a world free from poverty," and the WTO tries to promote freer movement of goods, services, and factors of production around the world. Table 5.4 profiles leading international institutions and their formal missions.

The WTO is notably important to trade and capital links. By design, it is the only organization that deals solely with trade among nations. Thus, most people and nations look to the WTO to make sense of all sorts of trade matters in the areas—to name just a few—of textiles, agriculture, subsidies, competition policy, electronic commerce, antidumping, rules of origin, regionalism, government procurement, trade liberalization, state trading enterprises, trade facilitation, and the trade-off between freer trade and environmental preservation.

In theory, the WTO is well positioned to deal with these challenges. It currently has 136 member nations, with another 30-odd countries, including China and Russia, waiting to join. Importantly, these nations have given the WTO a mandate to protect links in more areas of the global economy. In 1994, the WTO redefined its original mission—to deal with trade in goods—as a new mission to watch over trade in services, investment, intellectual property, and technical barriers to trade, sanitary measures, plant health, agriculture, and textiles. In addition, the WTO set up a powerful new system to deal with trade disputes. Since 1994, the WTO has used its larger membership and broader mission to strike agreements on trade in telecommunications, financial services, and information technology.

Regional organizations complement the efforts of the various global link masters. However, their primary concerns are specialized issues with particular regional significance. Specifically, both the WTO and regional groups primarily try to promote freer flows of goods and services. Regional groups, however, attempt to do this and more. For instance, consider the activities of the European Union (EU). In 1999, the EU launched a common currency, the euro, as a way to liberate the movement of capital within the region. In addition, the EU is steadily increasing the degree of intraregional cooperation in areas such as security and foreign policy—issues presently beyond the formal mission of the WTO. Whereas regional integration deals with the specific problems facing allied nations, the WTO monitors trade links among all countries. Nonetheless, regional economic integration movements might actually help the WTO achieve its objectives by dealing more flexibly with important issues that are beyond the mission of the WTO but that help cement and create more links among more nations.

Currently, NAFTA and the EU are the key regional groups expanding their web of links. In the future, these groups will continue to develop stronger economic, political, and social relationships. Once they do, they will most likely expand to include adjacent nations. The expansion path for the EU is predictable: It will continue to expand eastward until it meets Russia, at which point its expansion will likely halt. The scale and scope of NAFTA largely depend on whether the U.S. Congress ignores domestic calls for trade protec-

Table 5.4

The Missions of Leading Transnational Institutions

Bank for International Settlements (BIS)	Fosters international monetary and financial cooperation and serves as a bank for central banks.
Food and Agriculture Organization (FAO)	Raises levels of nutrition and standards of living to improve agricultural productivity and to improve the conditions of rural populations.
Inter-American Development Bank (IADB)	Helps accelerate economic and social development in Latin America and the Caribbean.
International Labor Organization (ILO)	Seeks the promotion of social justice and internationally recognized human and labor rights around the world.
International Chamber of Commerce (ICC)	Promotes an open international trade and investment system and the market economy. Its conviction that trade is a powerful force for peace and prosperity dates from the organization's origins early in the 19th century.
International Monetary Fund (IMF)	Promotes international monetary cooperation, exchange stability, and orderly exchange arrangements; fosters economic growth and high levels of employment; and provides temporary financial assistance to countries under adequate safeguards to help balance-of-payments adjustment.
Organization for Economic Cooperation and Development (OECD)	Provides governments a setting in which to discuss, develop, and perfect economic and social policy. They compare experiences, seek answers to common problems, and work to coordinate domestic and international policies.
United Nations (UN)	Preserves and promotes peace through international cooperation and collective security by providing a center for harmonizing the actions of nations.
United Nations Children Fund (UNICEF)	Advocates for the protection of children's rights, to help meet their basic needs, and to expand their opportunities to reach their full potential.
United Nations Educational, Scientific and Cultural Organization (UNESCO)	Contributes to peace and security in the world by promoting collaboration among nations through education, science, culture, and communication in order to further universal respect for justice, for the rule of law, and for the human rights and fundamental freedoms that are affirmed for the peoples of the world, without distinction of race, sex, language, or religion, by the Charter of the United Nations.
United Nations Conference on Trade and Development (UNCTAD)	Maximizes the trade, investment, and development opportunities of developing countries, helps them face challenges arising from globalization, and promotes their integration into the world economy on an equitable basis.
World Bank	To fight poverty with passion and professionalism for lasting results. To help people help themselves and their environment by providing resources, sharing knowledge, building capacity, and forging partnerships in the public and private sectors. To be an excellent institution able to attract, excite, and nurture diverse and committed staff with exceptional skills who know how to listen and learn.
World Intellectual Property Organization (WIPO)	Promotes the use and protection of works of the human spirit as expressed in the forms of intellectual property.
World Trade Organization (WTO)	Deals with the global rules of trade between nations. Works to ensure that trade flows as smoothly, predictably, and freely as possible. Its goal is to improve the welfare of the people of the member countries.

tion. Presently, NAFTA is slated to be fully phased in over a 15-year period—by 2009, nearly every tariff should expire. If it can, NAFTA will likely expand to include countries in Central America and South America, notably Chile. If it cannot, then Canada and Mexico will probably sign bilateral agreements with non-NAFTA countries in the region. Regional integration in Africa will likely continue at a slow pace due to political, social, health, and economic challenges. Asian integration will pick up steam as the economies of East and Southeast Asia continue their recovery from the financial turmoil of 1997. Nonetheless, the key to their growth will continue to be their links to Japan and the United States.

Link Making and the Internet

The integrity of the links that support globalization ultimately depends on an informed global society that sees the virtue and accepts the responsibility of the freer movement of products, people, and capital. Thus, the growing worldwide role of the Internet, itself a phenomenon defined by the billions of links among millions of Web sites, foretells a world in which links emerge more easily than ever before. Plainly put, the Internet allows consumers to seek the lowest price from the comfort of their homes and firms to get quotes from more suppliers at a click of a button. Both cases reduce transaction costs and barriers to entry, the forces that slow or stop the creation of links. More practically, the spread of new information and communications technologies will help bankers more efficiently convert capital into bits and bytes of data transmitted from international financial centers, will allow entrepreneurs to conduct trade more easily with improved market information, and will let international migrants more effortlessly keep in touch with events, friends, and families in their homeland. Therefore, we are witnessing the momentous advent of cyberspace as a medium and the Internet as a means for globalization.

In addition, making links through the Internet ultimately will prod us to rethink our idea of links among nations. Right now, we comfortably define links from the point of view of the tangible movement of products, people, or capital across the physical geography of sovereign nations. The Internet, on the other hand, is ushering in an era of intangible cyberlinks among globally dispersed Web sites whose functionality and performance do not fit tidily, if at all, into the discrete slots of sovereign nations. Essentially, the remarkably free flow of information through nationless cyberspace lets more products, people, and capital go where they wish to go rather than where their governments decide they should go. That is, the Internet moves the global market closer to the textbook model of perfect competition, which—besides assuming abundant information, many buyers and sellers, zero transaction costs, and no barriers to entry—presumes that governments are secondary to the market.

If this trend continues, we might soon find ourselves in a radically open global market that makes national policies less relevant. For example, we already can or will soon be able to use a computer and telephone line anywhere in the world to purchase and download a digital packet of music, literature, software, or cinema free from the watchful eyes of national authorities. The resulting changes in the movement of products, people, and capital across nations will consolidate the existing set of links in the physical space, as well as open the potential for links in cyberspace.

Summary

The many links across nations that make up the web of globalization embody the moral of Robinson Crusoe, namely, "No man is an island." From any viewpoint, whether trade, political, financial, economic, or social, links increasingly convert nations into members of the global market. As in all relationships, whether between people or nations, there are natural periods of close involvement and other times when barriers are put up to protect special interests. Importantly, though, few people clamor for a return to independent and isolated markets. Instead, the growing economic, political, and social incentive to exchange goods, services, and ideas is making links among nations more pervasive and much stronger.

endnotes

[1] United Nations and UNCTAD, "World Investment Report: Cross-Border Mergers and Acquisitions and Development, 2000," in *The Global Competitiveness Report 2000* (Oxford University Press, 2000).

[2] "Services May Lead U.S. to Trade Surplus," *Wall Street Journal,* December 4, 2000, p. 1.

[3] Michael E. Porter, "The Competitive Advantage of Nations," *Harvard Business Review,* Vol. 90, No. 2, March–April 1990, p. 78.

[4] Alan M. Rugman, "Diamond in the Rough," *Business Quarterly,* Vol. 55, No. 3, winter 1991, p. 61.

[5] P. R. Krugman, "Is Free Trade Passe?" *Journal of Economic Perspectives,* Vol. 1, 1987.

[6] United Nations and UNCTAD, "World Investment Report."

[7] Ibid.

[8] Ibid., Table 3: National Regulatory Changes, 1991–1999.

[9] Justin Fox, "Why Is It So Hard to Buy Foreign Stocks?" *Fortune,* November 13, 2000, p. 438.

[10] Peter Benesh, "As More Americans Work Abroad, Risks, Rewards for Both Sides Rise," *Investor's Business Daily,* October 4, 2000, p. 10.

[11] International Organization for Migration, *World Migration Report 2000,* www.iom.int.

[12] A. Appadurai, 1990. "Disjuncture and Difference in the Global Cultural Economy," *Public Culture,* Vol. 2, No. 2, 1990, pp. 1–21; and B. Barber, *Jihad vs. McWorld: How Globalism and Tribalism Are Reshaping the World* (New York: Random House, 1995).

[13] Glenda Laws, "Globalization, Immigration, and Changing Social Relations in U.S. Cities," *Annals of the American Academy of Political and Social Science,* Vol. 551, May 1997, p. 89.

[14] "Globalization from Below," *Arena Magazine,* October 2000, p. 45.

[15] Jean-Pierre Garson, "North America: Migration and Economic Integration," *OECD Observer,* No. 214, October–November 1998, p. 18.

[16] Peter Stalker, *Workers Without Frontiers: The Impact of Globalization on International Migration* (International Labour Organization, Lynne Rienner, 2000).

[17] John Salt, "The Future of International Labor Migration," *Migration Review,* Vol. 26, No. 4, winter 1992, p. 1077.

Orange Juice Import Protests: An Unlikely Alliance

B razil, the world's largest orange producer, exports about 99 percent of its orange juice. Much of this goes to the United States, the world's largest consumer. Brazilian juice exports to the United States might be even higher and U.S. juice prices lower if it were not for the U.S. tax (tariff) on imported juice, which adds about 30 cents to the U.S. retail price of Brazilian juice, bringing it up to the price of domestic juice. The U.S. government imposed these taxes because of consolidated pressure from interested groups (stakeholders) in the United States.

First, the Florida Citrus Mutual, which represents 11,500 citrus growers, has supported Florida congressmen and lobbied the International Trade Commission, the U.S. trade regulatory agency, to prevent more juice imports. The Florida Citrus Mutual argued that if more juice imports came in, U.S. growers would lose business. Further, they claimed that they cannot compete because U.S. health and safety standards make U.S. costs higher than Brazilian costs.

Second, the International Brotherhood of Teamsters has used the juice importing issue to strengthen its bargaining position with a processing facility in Florida, whose workers it represents. The Teamsters were unconcerned whether the facility processed U.S. or Brazilian juice until Coca-Cola's Minute Maid sold the plant to Cutrale, Brazil's largest orange juice exporter, which promptly cut 54 of the 280 jobs and scaled back pay and benefits. Cutrale claimed the plant was overstaffed and that its workers were overpaid by industry standards. The Teamsters tried to restore jobs and benefits by complaining to the U.S. National Labor Relations Board and by suing Coca-Cola for giving workers insufficient notice of its sale. Failing in these legal recourses, the Teamsters have since sought to get Cutrale to meet their demands by taking actions that threaten Cutrale's ability to export orange juice from Brazil. The Teamsters reason that Cutrale will give in to their demands for the Florida facility because doing so will likely cost Cutrale less than the loss of export sales would.

The Teamsters' actions also aim at building allies to support juice import restrictions and to boycott Brazilian juice sales. Their main allies have been

Stakeholders: Their Concerns and Actions

chapter 6

Peruvians wearing elaborate wooden masks on a field below dark clouds in Huancayo, Peru.

worldwide groups opposing the use of child labor. To build support, the Teamsters exhibited photos in Washington that showed children picking oranges in Brazil, flew a Brazilian union leader to Florida to make speeches about Brazilian child labor, and organized a rally in front of Coca-Cola's headquarters. The Teamsters used this publicity to influence U.S. customs officials to invoke a 1997 law, the Sanders Amendment, that ends U.S. imports of products made by child laborers confined against their wills. However, the customs officials have not limited Cutrale's orange juice imports from Brazil because of insufficient evidence that children pick a substantial amount of Brazilian oranges, that they pick them involuntarily, or that Cutrale's exports to the United States come from those oranges that are child-picked. Still, the Teamsters contend that underage workers are, by definition, working against their will, and they continue to put pressure on Cutrale. For example, the Teamsters are supporting the establishment of consumer boycotts of Brazilian juice in Australia and Europe. At this writing, Cutrale has not acceded to the Teamsters' demands.[1] However, the future of Brazilian orange juice exports, especially Cutrale's, is far from certain.

Introduction

In the preceding example, U.S. and Brazilian citrus growers, processors, employees, unions, and consumers are stakeholders. **Stakeholders** are individuals and groups that benefit from or are harmed by organizational actions. Stakeholders in business organizations include stockholders, employees, customers, suppliers, and society at large. In the short term, the aims of these groups conflict. Stockholders want additional sales and increased productivity to go to them in the form of higher profits. Employees want additional compensation, better working conditions, and job security. Customers want lower prices. Suppliers want to charge the business higher prices. And societal groups, especially nongovernmental organizations (NGOs) such as Greenpeace and the World Wide Fund for Nature, may want increased corporate taxes and the business's involvement in what they deem socially responsible behavior. In the long term, a company must achieve all of these aims adequately or it will achieve none because each stakeholder group, if powerful enough, could cause its demise. Thus, stakeholders create constraints on companies' actions internationally. Figure 6.1 shows the relationship of these constraints.

The international company must be aware of these various interests but serve them unevenly at any given period. At one time, it may give most gains to consumers; at another, to stockholders. Making necessary trade-offs is difficult in the domestic environment. Abroad, however, corporate managers are usually less familiar with customs and power groups, so they have even more difficulty choosing the best alternative. This is particularly true if stakeholders' powers differ among countries. For example, Cutrale probably underestimated the power of labor unions in the United States because of their weaker positions in Brazil and, therefore, underestimated the amount of agitation U.S. labor unions could cause when it laid off workers.

Companies themselves are stakeholders in society, and they act as pressure groups to governmental and international organizations whose actions can benefit or harm them.

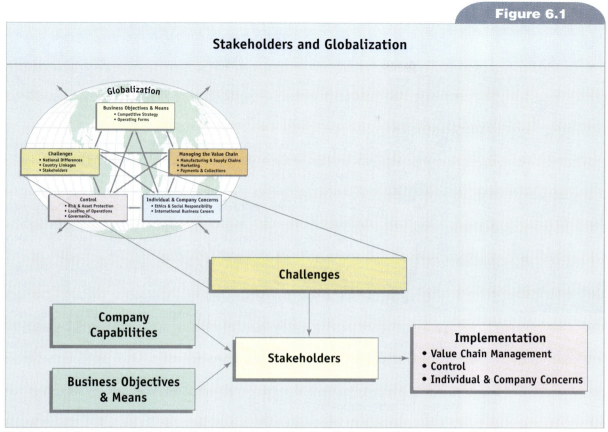

Figure 6.1

Stakeholders and Globalization

Stakeholders influence companies' objectives and strategies, as well as their means of implementing their strategies.

In a sense, they represent the combined interests of their own stakeholders, such as the stockholders, employees, and suppliers whom they represent. Thus, individual companies and coalitions of companies press for laws and regulations that will benefit them. But different companies take different stances on given issues because their competitive situations are different. Likewise, a company's stakeholders may not align with counterpart stakeholders in other companies. For example, employees in one company may feel that freer trade will increase their employer's earnings, thus helping improve their own compensation. However, employees in a second company, perhaps even in the same industry, may fear that freer trade will undermine their job security. In fact, different companies in the same industry commonly take opposing stances on proposed trade restrictions.[2] Thus, the two companies and their employees are apt to take different sides on pending trade legislation and exert opposing pressures on governmental authorities responsible for the legislation.

Similarly, counterpart stakeholders' interests from different countries may conflict. These stakeholders, in seeking to fulfill their own objectives, may undermine companies' abilities to minimize costs and maximize sales on a global basis. For example, avocado processing workers in the United States and Mexico have each wanted a larger share of

Although globalization brings benefits, not everyone shares equally in them. In fact, some people may gain while others lose, and some people may gain more than others. Those who see themselves losing— absolutely or relatively—sometimes become powerful forces that struggle to prevent governments and companies from promoting globalization. The photo shows protesters at an annual meeting of the International Monetary Fund and World Bank in the Czech Republic. The slogans on their banner briefly stating their positions are self-explanatory.

the jobs in the companies that have both U.S. and Mexican facilities. U.S. workers have lobbied for legislation to protect the number of avocado processing jobs within the United States. Mexican workers have influenced the Mexican government to pressure the U.S. government to allow entry of more Mexican-processed avocados. Thus, managers must consider complex effects of their decisions because actions in one country may have repercussions in other countries and because stakeholders in each country try to influence companies' actions.

In a sense, countries are also stakeholders representing the combined interests of their national stakeholders within international forums. At times, their leaders unite with leaders of other countries that share common interests. For example, at the 1999 World Trade Organization (WTO) meeting, poor countries united to oppose demands being made by NGO protestors who favored higher labor and environmental standards in poor countries and higher protection of U.S. workers from foreign competition. The poor countries based their opposition on the belief that they must for the time being compete on low-cost production and export into the U.S. market if they are to get faster-growing economies that will lead to better standards.[3]

Although there are myriad issues that may affect stakeholders, this chapter examines only those that directly influence companies' abilities to transfer goods, services, and production internationally. Specifically, the chapter examines stakeholders' reasons for and methods of restricting and enhancing international trade and foreign direct investment (FDI). The chapter concludes with a discussion of how companies and other stakeholders may influence the policies that enhance and restrict their movements.

Trade Restrictions

Chapter 1 showed that trade increases the variety of products and services available to consumers, allows consumers to buy from lower-cost locations, and increases output by permitting countries to specialize in their comparative advantages. Nevertheless, all countries regulate the flow of goods and services across their borders. They commonly place restrictions on imports and occasionally on exports. They frequently give direct or indirect subsidies to industries that enable them to compete with foreign production either at home or abroad. In general, governments influence trade to satisfy economic, social, or political objectives. (Figure 6.2 shows the rationales for government influence on trade.) They restrict or enhance trade because stakeholders get public opin-

Figure 6.2

Rationales for Governmental Influence on Trade

Economic Rationales
- Full employment
- Maintain balance of payments
- Transform the economy
- Gain access to other markets

Noneconomic Rationales
- National security
- Health and safety
- Pressure other countries

ion and lawmakers on their side. The following discussion highlights the major arguments for governmental intervention in trade.

Employment

Every country has full employment as one of its primary economic and social objectives. At the same time, people who are either unemployed or threatened with unemployment perceive their hardships to be so severe that they become highly vocal about their situations and willingly join groups to protest and present their demands. For example, Korean film industry employees marched through Seoul to support Korean governmental restrictions on screenings of foreign films because they feared additional screenings would jeopardize their jobs.[4] At almost the same time, executives from U.S. steel companies and their union met in the White House with the president, vice president, and top cabinet officials to try to persuade them to restrict steel imports that threatened U.S. steel companies and their U.S. workers' jobs.[5] Although Korean restrictions on imported films and U.S. restrictions on steel imports would likely increase employment in the Korean film industry and in the U.S. steel industry, these restrictions would likely have negative employment repercussions elsewhere in the Korean and the U.S. economies. These repercussions might occur because other countries retaliate, because other domestic industries lose sales through poorer access to foreign supplies, and because foreign consumers have less income to buy Korean and U.S. exports. We'll now examine these repercussions.

A country may retaliate against another's import restrictions by imposing import restrictions of its own. For example, the European Union (EU) restricted imports of U.S. chickens and turkeys valued at about $50 million a year to protect EU jobs. The United States quickly retaliated by saying it would limit wheat imports from the EU valued at about $300 million a year.[6] Thus, the retaliation would cost the EU more jobs than it would gain by limiting imports. As a result, European wheat farmers and exporters quickly opposed protection of the EU poultry industry and succeeded in getting EU officials to remove the protection. The U.S. government then rescinded its threat to limit EU wheat imports. In this situation, the threat of retaliation led to elimination of restrictions. However, retaliation may not work because the targeted industries lack clout with trade policy decision makers. Such was the case with U.S. punitive tariffs against French Roquefort cheese and Danish spareribs and ham, designed to pressure the EU to alter its restrictions on beef and banana imports.[7] In fact, there is a danger of escalating restrictions. For example, the EU might have responded to the U.S. wheat import warning by placing import restrictions on other U.S. products. The United States could have responded with further restrictions, and so on.

Even without retaliation, import restrictions may limit employment in related industries. Take the preceding steel import example. U.S. heavy equipment manufacturers, such as Caterpillar, are among the largest U.S. exporters and largest consumers of steel. If they are forced to use more expensive domestic steel, they may be less competitive in export markets. Further, when a country reduces imports, it reduces foreigners' incomes to buy its exports. In fact, any economic downturn in one country may have repercussions in another country. For example, the Asian economic downturns of the late 1990s adversely affected many companies and employees in the United States.

Import restrictions also cause consumers to pay higher prices and to have less choice, which may also reduce employment because they buy less. For example, higher U.S. tractor prices resulting from Caterpillar's paying more for domestic than foreign steel will mean that U.S. farmers (tractor consumers) have less to spend on other products after buying their tractors. Korean restrictions on foreign films may reduce movie attendance to the point that theaters hire fewer employees. But consumers are usually ill prepared to pressure for reductions in trade restrictions. One reason is that the cost of restrictions to consumers, although high in the aggregate, is so widespread and diffused that individuals perceive they have too little to gain by opposing import restrictions. Thus, U.S. farmers and Korean film viewers are unlikely to mobilize effectively to counter the U.S. steel industry and Korean film employees' protectionist efforts. Further, most members of the general public do not understand the negative consumer effects (choice and cost) and negative employment repercussions of protectionism (export reduction through retaliation, more expensive supplies, and downturns in other economies). For example, a U.S. Harris Poll asked, "Do you think that expanded trade leads to an increase or decrease in the number of U.S. jobs?" Most respondents (56 percent) answered "decrease," whereas only a minority (37 percent) said "increase."[8]

Finally, stakeholders often rely on arguments other than employment, even though their real reason for wanting import restrictions is to protect their jobs. The Teamsters' efforts to protect jobs and compensation at the orange juice processing plant in Florida by eliciting support from groups opposed to Brazilian child labor—described in this chapter's opening—serve as an example.

Balance of Payments

Because the trade account is a major component of the balance of payments for most countries, governments restrict trade to bring imports and exports into balance. Trade restrictions differ from other means of balance-of-payment adjustment (deflation of the economy or currency devaluation) because of their greater selectivity. This may be either an advantage or a disadvantage compared to other adjustment mechanisms. For example, if a country is running a trade deficit, either a devaluation or a deflation can make all domestically produced goods and services less expensive than foreign ones. Thus, the adjustment is widespread and no single industry carries the burden of the adjustment. However, trade restrictions allow a country to choose which products and services to affect, such as by placing restrictions only on the import of luxury products.

Economic Transformation

Certain economic theories promote import restrictions to gain economic growth by developing new industries with growth potential and by diversifying the economy through a broader industrial base. Theorists argue that import protection will entice companies to initiate production within the protected economy. This is known as an **import substitution policy.** If companies establish foreign production to gain a market they might otherwise serve by exporting, the restricting country receives investment inflows that may add to its employment. Such a policy is more likely to work if the potential market is large rather than small. For example, Chinese and Indian automotive import restrictions have enticed substantial inflows of foreign investment to capture sales in China and India's large and rapidly growing markets. However, high import barriers within small countries with small potential markets, such as those in Central America, are apt to do little to entice foreign automotive investment. Rather, the restrictions simply decrease demand and raise prices for the consumers there. Nevertheless, smaller countries have been successful in attracting foreign investment in industries in which fixed capital outlays for production are not as high as for automotive vehicles, such as in the pharmaceutical industry. Pharmaceutical companies need to recoup high research and development (R&D) costs by selling as widely as possible. They can also produce quite widely because production technologies allow for efficient small-scale factories suitable for small markets.

Relatedly, some theorists argue that a government should guarantee an emerging industry a large share of its domestic market until the industry becomes efficient enough to compete against imports. This is known as the **infant industry argument.** Industries may become more efficient as companies gain experience and as they reduce costs through an increased scale of operations. A problem with the infant industry argument is that no one can predict with certainty which industries will reach adulthood and be competitive in international markets. As such, countries' results from infant industry protection have been quite mixed. For instance, governmental protection for automobile production in Brazil and South Korea helped those countries' output become globally competitive, but similar protection in Australia and Malaysia did not. If a government grants infant industry protection to an industry that does not reduce costs sufficiently, its owners, workers, and suppliers will likely constitute a formidable and long-term pressure group to prevent importation of a cheaper competitive product. In fact, the initial protection against import competition may be a disincentive for them to become more efficient. In recent years, most governments (despite much local opposition) have been reducing their industries' import protection so that they are forced to adopt practices that make them more globally competitive.

Most emerging economies depend on commodities—agricultural products and raw materials—for the bulk of their export earnings. For example, Nigeria depends almost entirely on oil for its export earnings, and Ghana on cocoa. Many emerging economies want to broaden their industrial bases so that they are more dependent on manufactured products and less dependent on commodities. Their reasons are threefold: (1) to reverse their deteriorating terms of trade, (2) to avoid severe fluctuations in their export earnings, and (3) to reduce disguised unemployment in their agricultural sectors. We'll now examine these reasons.

The **terms of trade**—the quantity of imports that a given quantity of exports can buy—have been deteriorating for many emerging economies. The deterioration has occurred because most commodity prices over a long-term period have risen more slowly than manufactured products' prices; thus, emerging economies must export more commodities to buy the same quantity of imported manufactured goods. This deterioration is partly due to lagging demand for agricultural products. In other words, people can consume only so much coffee, bananas, or sugar regardless of their incomes, but income alone limits their potential demand for manufactured products. It is also partly due to technology, which affects commodities differently than manufactured products. Technological changes for commodities have generally decreased production costs rather than creating new commodity characteristics. Because commodities are highly homogeneous and because there are many competitors, producers have tried to build market share by passing on much of the savings to intermediate and final consumers. Technological changes for manufactured products, on the other hand, have largely been in the products themselves, such as by improving or adding more features on automobiles. Producers have increased prices of manufactured products with the improved or new features.

Commodity prices fluctuate a great deal because of such uncontrollable factors as weather affecting supply or business cycles abroad affecting demand. These fluctuations can wreak havoc on economies that depend on the export of commodities. It is not uncommon for an emerging economy's export earnings to fluctuate by one-quarter from one year to another because of commodity price changes brought on by climatic conditions that cause supply problems.[9]

Many emerging economies have overpopulated rural areas in which output per person is low. Thus, a protectionist argument is that many people may be able to leave rural areas without greatly affecting agricultural output. If a protected manufacturing sector can employ them, their countries' economies will grow even if the added output is not globally competitive.[10] However, moves from agricultural production to manufacturing production have costs. For instance, massive migration to urban areas often leads to unfulfilled individual expectations because insufficient jobs materialize, income from agricultural production decreases, and demand increases for social and political services. At the same time, taxpayers or consumers will have to spend more if protected local companies manufacture products more expensively than foreign-manufactured products that would otherwise enter the country.

Comparable Access or Fairness

Some companies and industries argue for the same access to foreign markets that their foreign competitors have to their own markets. From an economic standpoint, they argue that, for industries in which increased production will greatly decrease the average production cost per unit, because of either scale economies or experience, producers lacking equal access to a competitor's home market will have a potential cost disadvantage. They have argued this, for example, in the semiconductor, aircraft, and telecommunications industries.[11] Companies also argue in terms of fairness by claiming that the ways products are produced in different countries reflect national differences in social and environmental values rather than in efficiencies. In other words, if a company must adhere to stricter environmental and labor safety standards, its production costs may be higher than those in countries with less strict standards.

There are arguments against the fairness doctrine. First, countries gain advantages from freer trade, even if they impose freer trade unilaterally; thus, restrictions for any reason may deny their own consumers lower prices. Second, implementation of restrictions based on fairness requires that governments negotiate and enforce separate agreements for each of the thousands of products and services that they might import *and* with each country that might export them. This would be overly cumbersome and expensive, especially since companies' costs and countries' social and environmental standards are constantly changing. Third, to restrict imports from countries with lax environmental and labor standards may make those countries poorer, thus provoking them to adopt even lower standards to be competitive.

Noneconomic Objectives

Much governmental trade protection is based not on economics, but rather on political or cultural imperatives. Governments protect essential domestic industries during peacetime, for example, so that they will remain independent of foreign supplies during war. Thus, the U.S. government subsidizes domestic production of silicon so that U.S. manufacturers of computer chips will not have to depend entirely on foreign suppliers. The national security issue has much appeal in rallying support for import barriers. However, in times of real crisis or military emergency, a government could consider almost any product essential. Because of the high cost (to consumers or taxpayers) of protecting a less efficient domestic industry, policy makers should examine how essential the industry really is, how likely the country is able to gain foreign supplies during wartime, and how fast domestic companies can begin producing if foreign supplies cease. However, government policy makers often accept the national security argument on emotional grounds without carefully evaluating the cost, real needs, and alternatives. Once a government grants an industry protection, it cannot easily terminate it. For instance, the U.S. government continued subsidies to angora goat ranchers decades after mohair (which comes from angora goats) was no longer essential for military uniforms. The U.S. government continued the subsidies because the ranchers successfully exerted pressure on their influential congressmen.[12]

Governments sometimes restrict exports, even to friendly countries, so that strategic goods will not fall into the hands of potential enemies. But export restrictions may lead either to retaliation or to the development of alternative supplies abroad. The U.S. government prohibits U.S. companies from exporting powerful encryption technologies, for example, so that potentially unfriendly countries can't get them. However, they often get them anyway from other sources. For example, the U.S. encryption export restriction stimulated the German company Brokat and a handful of other European companies to develop competitive technologies that they are now able to export to markets that U.S. companies cannot serve.[13]

A common sense of identity that sets citizens apart from other nationalities helps hold countries together. To protect this common identity, countries sometimes limit the availability of foreign products and services that might undermine this identity. For instance, Canada limits foreign publishing, cable TV, bookselling, and musical performances.[14] And France protects its movie industry out of fear that the English language and Anglo-Saxon culture will weaken its distinct culture. The French government therefore limits foreign films on French television and gives subsidies to French moviemakers to produce films and dub them into other languages.[15]

Safety is another issue. There is a near consensus that governments should prohibit sales of products—whether foreign or domestically made—that are hazardous to people's health or the environment. On this basis, most countries disallow imports of marijuana and products made from endangered animal species. Some also disallow certain products, such as French bans on chrysotile asbestos, even though the products may not be considered dangerous in other countries.[16] However, there is much evidence that governments sometimes claim they restrict entry because of safety when their real reason is to satisfy stakeholders who want to maintain their jobs and investments. For example, Chile restricted imports of salmon eggs by contending that they might be diseased. The governments of Iceland, Ireland, Norway, the United Kingdom, and the United States all disputed the Chilean contention.[17]

Sanctions

Governments use trade restrictions to coerce other governments to follow certain actions. For example, China threatened long-term trade restrictions against Australia and New Zealand if those countries' leaders were to meet with the Dalai Lama. The United States has placed trade sanctions against many countries to influence them to take actions against terrorism, environmental violations, abuse of workers' rights, regional strife, drug trafficking, human and political rights abuses, and nuclear proliferation.[18] The United States has also placed trading sanctions on countries refusing to support U.S. foreign policy goals in Cuba and Iran, and it has considered placing sanctions against countries not allowing religious freedom.[19] Sanctions have the most impact when large or multiple countries impose them because they more deeply affect a sanctioned country. Nevertheless, sanctions seldom work. For example, longtime U.S. sanctions against Cuba have forced no changes in that country's leadership or policies. Further, companies from countries imposing sanctions lose business, such as U.S. companies' loss of wheat sales to India and Pakistan when the United States imposed sanctions over those countries' nuclear proliferation. Because of business loss, more than 600 U.S. companies joined an organization, U.S.A. Engage, to oppose U.S. trade sanctions. Finally, sanctions tend to hurt innocent people more than the political leaders who are responsible for objectionable practices. For example, multiple country trade restrictions against Iraq created shortages of food and medicines for Iraqi children while leaving the country's leader, Saddam Hussein, unaffected.

Forms of Trade Restrictions

Chapter 5 discussed how countries are working globally through the WTO and regionally through such organizations as the North American Free Trade Association (NAFTA) to remove trade restrictions. Nevertheless, the preceding discussion indicates that pressures for trade restrictions still exist. In essence, these trade restrictions are of four types: tariffs, quotas, bureaucratic practices, and subsidies.

Tariffs

The most common type of trade control is the **tariff,** also known as a **duty,** which is a tax on goods moving internationally. A country may impose a tax or tariff on the percentage of the value of the goods moving internationally, in which case it is an **ad valorem tariff.** A country may also assess on a per-unit basis, in which case it is a **specific tariff.** Or a country may combine the two, which is a **compound tariff.** Historically, many countries imposed transit tariffs on goods passing through their territories as a means of collecting revenues; however, they have nearly abolished transit tariffs through international treaties. Instead, countries sometimes impose tolls on trucks and ships passing through. Export tariffs are also rare because governments fear the tax will raise export prices and limit their companies' ability to sell abroad. Thus, import tariffs are the most common type of tariff.

Import tariffs are protectionist because governments assess the tax only on foreign-made products or services. Hence, the tax raises the price of the imported product, making it less marketable. However, a foreign producer might lower its prices if a government places an import tax on its products. In doing so, it accepts a lower profit margin rather than having its products priced out of the market. This is known as the **optimum tariff** because revenue shifts from the exporting to the importing country through income loss in the exporting country and tax-collection gain in the importing country. There are many examples of companies' not raising prices as much as the amount of the imposed tariff. But governments cannot easily predict if exporters will reduce their profit margins. If they don't, their consumers will face higher prices.

Thus, tariffs also serve as a source of governmental revenue. However, they are of little importance for revenue to large industrial countries. In fact, the EU now spends as much money collecting duties as it actually takes in from them. Nevertheless, import tariffs are an important source of revenue in many emerging economies, particularly those that have difficulty determining incomes and collecting income taxes on them.

Quotas

Quotas are quantitative limits on the maximum amount of product a country will trade in a given year. Governments place quotas most commonly on imports, and they sometimes allocate the overall quota among countries. For example, the United States has import quotas on sugar for about 50 percent of the market and allocates the quota among different countries on a political basis rather than allowing U.S. importers to buy sugar from the countries that might sell most cheaply to them. Import quotas normally raise prices within the importing country by limiting supplies. Further, foreign suppliers have no incentive to lower their prices to compete because the quotas limit how much they can sell anyway. For this reason, U.S. sugar prices are usually about twice the world market price because they reflect the high cost of U.S. production.

Governments usually use export quotas to increase foreign prices or decrease domestic prices. Let's first examine efforts to raise foreign prices. As an example, Saudi Arabia's oil export limits raised foreign petroleum prices in the early 21st century and increased its export earnings. This worked because most other oil-exporting countries also imposed export quotas and because consumers had no short-term means of finding alternative fuels. However, countries cannot easily enforce export controls. If more than one country is a supplier, some country may cheat by exporting more than its allotment. And even if one country has a near monopoly, it must still pay a high cost to curtail contraband exports. Further, a government can raise foreign prices only so much through its export controls. If prices rise too much, foreign consumers may simply buy substitute products, such as tea instead of coffee. Or companies will use their R&D to develop substitutes; historically, for instance, high prices led them to develop synthetics as substitutes for natural rubber and nitrate.

Let's turn to efforts to decrease domestic prices. As an example, Egypt limited cotton exports to lower domestic cotton prices so that its textile manufacturers did not compete with foreign buyers willing to pay higher prices for cotton. But lower domestic prices are a disincentive for domestic producers to expand their output. At the same time, lower supplies abroad create an incentive for foreign producers to expand their output. Further, domestic suppliers may try to smuggle products out of the country so that they receive higher prices.

A specific type of quota that prohibits all trade is an **embargo.** As with quotas, governments place embargoes on either imports or exports, on whole categories of products regardless of origin or destination, on specific products with specific countries, or on all products with a given country. Although governments generally impose embargoes for political purposes, the effects are economic. For example, the United Nations voted an embargo on Haiti in 1993 to weaken its military dictatorship. But the effects on Haiti were economic; the country had difficulty getting supplies, particularly oil, and it could not easily sell its products abroad.

Bureaucratic Practices

Governments establish bureaucratic practices ostensibly for reasons other than protection; however, the practices often restrict imports from foreign countries. For example, governments have testing standards to protect the safety or health of their residents. Companies argue that governments sometimes impose such standards just to protect their domestic producers. The U.S. government requires that U.S. agencies safety-test electric razors imported from Europe even though they have passed rigid EU safety standards, for instance, and the EU retests imported U.S.-made dialysis machines even though U.S. agencies have approved them for U.S. use.[20] In fact, the EU subjects more than half the value of U.S. exports to some form of EU certification, such as costly retesting after the goods arrive in Europe.[21]

Some countries require that potential importers or exporters secure permission from governmental authorities before conducting trade transactions. To gain permission, a potential exporter may have to send samples abroad in advance. Not only may such a requirement restrict imports or exports directly by denial of permission, but it can also result in further deterrence of trade because importers and exporters must incur added costs, time, and uncertainty. Closely akin to this procedure are administrative delays on entry, which create uncertainty and raise the cost of carrying inventory. For example, South Korean customs is slow to clear imported merchandise, thus adding inventory costs to imported products and making some perishable items unsalable.

Governments often subject services to particular regulations that limit the ability of companies to trade them internationally. To begin with, many governments consider some service industries to be essential because they serve strategic purposes or provide social assistance to citizens. These industries may be government owned, domestically subsidized, or not-for-profit. Thus, foreign companies often cannot effectively compete in such sectors as education, health services, transportation, mail, banking, insurance, and communications. Governments also impose standards for licensing service professionals, such as for accountants, actuaries, architects, electricians, engineers, gemologists, hairstylists, lawyers, physicians, real estate brokers, and teachers. Service companies may therefore be restricted from using their home-country professionals, such as lawyers, in a foreign country. Even if they faced no licensing problems, they would still face immigration restrictions when trying to move employees to another country for an assignment.

Subsidies

Government subsidies may be direct or indirect. In either case, a government may reduce its imports by enabling its domestic companies to survive competition or increase its exports by making its companies competitive in foreign markets. For example, if a government compensates a state-owned company directly for its operating losses, the state-owned company will take market share that might otherwise have been imported. Or the government may prefer domestically made products when it makes its purchases. Given that governmental expenditures generally run between 25 and 35 percent of the gross domestic products (GDPs) of most countries, this preference can be substantial. In any case, tax expenditures pay for subsidies, whereas higher consumer prices pay for protection by tariffs or quotas. If a government makes direct payments to domestic companies to compensate them for losses incurred from selling abroad, such as U.S. payments to cotton exporters, it stimulates its exports.[22] However, governments most commonly provide indirect assistance to develop viable domestic production or to make export sales cheaper or more profitable for their companies.

Governments may give indirect subsidies to develop successful industries by altering conditions that will affect industry in general, such as improving education, providing infrastructure (transportation, communications, capital markets, utilities), promoting a highly competitive environment so that companies must make improvements, and inducing consumers to demand an ever-higher quality of products and services.[23] This approach is general in that it creates conditions that may affect a variety of industries. But governmental expenditures are seldom neutral. For example, U.S. governmental support for aviation infrastructure has helped U.S. airlines relative to U.S. railroads and

U.S. international carriers relative to the carriers from many other countries. Thus, a second approach is to target specific production sectors—known as a *strategic trade policy*—so that the country will develop industries that fit its factor endowment and will have future growth potential. However, governments may not easily identify a growth sector in which they can become globally successful.[24] They sometimes pick sectors that do not grow (France's support for supersonic passenger aircraft) or in which they do not become competitive (Thailand's support for a steel industry). Moreover, there has been a tendency for too many countries to identify the same industries, so excessive competition has led to inadequate returns.[25] Nevertheless, there have been some notable government successes. For example, the Indian Ocean country of Mauritius increased its adult literacy rate from 60 percent to 100 percent within three years. It successfully targeted textile manufacturing and a variety of service exports (such as tourism, banking, and phone betting) to transform its dependence on sugar production. Its growth rate in the 1990s was one of the world's highest.[26] Further, there are notable examples of governmental assistance not aimed specifically at developing export capabilities that, nevertheless, had that effect. For example, U.S. governmental efforts to improve agricultural productivity and defense capabilities have undoubtedly helped U.S. exports of farm and aerospace products.

Most governmental help for exporting is general rather than targeted to a specific industry. But it is widespread. For example, more than 20 U.S. federal agencies collect information about foreign markets, which they provide to companies in the National Trade Databank. The U.S. **Export–Import Bank** provides U.S. companies with direct loans and loan guarantees for exporting goods and services. The Market Access Program and the Export Enhancement Program of the U.S. Department of Agriculture partially defray the costs of market research and product promotion for U.S. agricultural products overseas.[27] Although all these programs aim to increase U.S. employment by making U.S. exports more competitive, the results are questionable because other countries provide similar programs. Nevertheless, until all countries implement subsidy reduction simultaneously, no country is apt to eliminate its own subsidies for fear that its companies would face unfair competition.

Influence on Foreign Direct Investment

Globally, there is a love–hate relationship with FDI. Governments want to receive inflows of FDI because of the benefits. However, there are usually costs, so they prohibit foreign investment in some industries and regulate how foreign investors can operate in others. For example, an FDI inflow may contribute positively to a country's objective of full employment; however, foreign investors may make decisions in their home countries to the detriment of stakeholders in countries receiving FDI—say, by deciding to protect the domestic workforce at the expense of a foreign one. There are also differences between short- and long-term economic effects from FDI, such as short-term capital inflows that contribute to growth versus long-term capital outflows as the investor remits dividends and invests elsewhere. FDI may also cause shifts in shares of benefits going to different company stakeholders. For example, a company's move abroad to a lower-cost location might improve efficiencies and make the company more competitive, thus helping most stakeholders, but this may be of little solace to employees in higher-cost locations who lose job security.

Given the costs and benefits of receiving FDI, most countries allow FDI entry (and even promote it). But they regulate FDI to receive the most benefits possible. Some countries regulate FDI in general by placing rules on what foreign investors can and cannot do. Others require foreign investors to negotiate with their governmental agencies to determine whether and on what terms they will allow them to enter. Such negotiations are costly and cumbersome for both the investors and governments. Companies agree to many performance requirements aimed at helping host countries reach economic and noneconomic objectives. Some of the common performance requirements are foreign exchange deposits to cover the cost of imports and foreign exchange payments on loans and dividends, limits on payments to the parent for services it provides to its host-country subsidiary, creation of a certain number of jobs or amount of exports, provisions to reduce the amount of equity held in subsidiaries, price controls, obligatory local inputs in products manufactured, limits on use of expatriate personnel and reconditioned equipment, and ownership sharing.

In recent years, government-to-government capital and technical assistance has been declining. One reason is that, since the end of the Cold War, governments are less interested in giving foreign aid and loans to build political allies. Another reason is that many taxpayers in high-income countries have become disillusioned about the benefits of aid to recipient countries. Regardless of the cause, emerging economies are depending more on multinational enterprises (MNEs) to bring resources they need from abroad when they make foreign direct investments. Figure 6.3 shows these resources. Emerging economies' dependence on foreign investors has recently placed potential investors in a strong position when they negotiate with host-country governments regarding their entry and operating terms. Nevertheless, the love–hate relationship with foreign direct investors continues in both recipient and donor countries. We'll now examine specific issues in this love–hate relationship.

Economic Issues

Recipient Countries

To some extent, almost every country today welcomes inflows of FDI, although some countries welcome them more than others. At one extreme, countries offer a variety of incentives to companies so they will invest there. For example, in 1998, the Czech government announced it would give foreign investors a five-year postponement of corporate taxes followed by tax credits, aid for half the cost of retraining workers, grants for employing workers in depressed regions, free land, infrastructure installation, and duty-free importation of machinery and equipment. But even this generous package was less than what nearby Poland and Hungary were offering.[28] At the other extreme is India, which restricts entry or operating terms for almost all foreign investment. Generally, companies prefer to establish investments in highly developed countries because those countries offer large markets and a high degree of stability. Thus, countries such as the United States, Canada, and Germany receive large amounts of foreign investments without making many concessions to foreign investors.

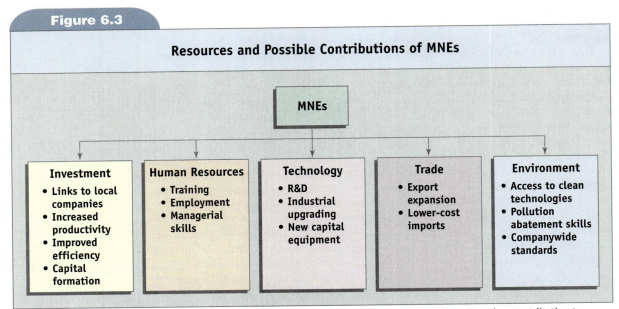

Figure 6.3

Resources and Possible Contributions of MNEs

MNEs

Investment
- Links to local companies
- Increased productivity
- Improved efficiency
- Capital formation

Human Resources
- Training
- Employment
- Managerial skills

Technology
- R&D
- Industrial upgrading
- New capital equipment

Trade
- Export expansion
- Lower-cost imports

Environment
- Access to clean technologies
- Pollution abatement skills
- Companywide standards

MNEs can contribute directly to investment, human resources, technology, trade, and the environment, thus contributing to host-country objectives.

source: Adapted from Transnational Corporations and Management Division, *World Investment Report 1992: Transnational Corporations: Engines of Growth, An Executive Summary* (New York: United Nations, 1992), p. 13. Reprinted by permission.

On the one hand, countries largely want FDI because of the potential positive effects on economic objectives of growth, employment, and balance of payments. They reason that investors may contribute by using the countries' otherwise idle or underemployed resources. For instance, a country such as Nigeria has vast reserves of oil, but it needs foreign companies to locate the oil, supply the capital equipment to bring it to the surface, provide refining technology, and secure distribution. Additionally, foreign investors may upgrade human resources by educating local personnel to utilize equipment, technology, and modern production methods. Further, when foreign companies invest, domestic companies may become more efficient because they have to compete with them.

On the other hand, governments worry that foreign investors merely displace what domestic companies would otherwise have done. Therefore, they sometimes restrict foreign investment that takes over existing companies while welcoming foreign-owned start-up operations. An exception has been privatization; governments have been actively seeking foreign investors to take over poorly performing state-owned enterprises. Some governments also worry that local companies cannot compete with MNEs because of the vast resources MNEs have at their disposal. Their concern is that they will destroy the local entrepreneurial spirit and R&D necessary for future economic development. Thus, governments sometimes restrict foreign investment in sectors in which there are substantial domestic competitors, require foreign companies to transfer technology to local companies, and demand that foreign investors buy from domestic suppliers. Finally, because any investor plans eventually to take out more capital than it brings in, governments worry that the long-term economic effects of FDI will be negative. Thus, some governments limit foreign investors' repatriation of income. They do so by requiring that foreign investors bring in a portion of their capital as loans (which have a fixed remission amount), by mandating remission limits (such as a ceiling on the amount of yearly dividends), and by requiring investors to share ownership locally so that a portion of earnings will presumably stay in the country.

Donor Countries

In the countries in which investors are headquartered, stakeholders have raised concerns about the possible loss of domestic jobs when companies invest abroad and the possible loss of future domestic competitiveness when companies transfer technologies abroad that might make foreign production more competitive in the future. For example, certain stakeholders have criticized U.S. companies for transferring highly advanced technology abroad that they developed partially through U.S. governmental contracts. In fact, some U.S. companies are not only moving their most advanced technologies abroad, but also exploiting these technologies abroad before producing with them in the United States. For example, Boeing transferred advanced aerospace technology to China to produce aircraft parts. According to critics, if Boeing had not transferred the technology, China would have purchased the products in the United States, thus increasing U.S. employment and output. However, China might instead have bought aircraft from Airbus Industrie (a European company) or developed the technology itself had Boeing not transferred its technology.

Closely related to the question of job loss is the question of whether foreign investors' outsourcing of production puts downward pressure on wages in their home countries. On the one hand, there is anecdotal evidence that it does. For example, U.S. companies such as Texas Instruments have made investments in India so that they can hire less expensive programmers than in the United States. (Because of technology, they can send their work by satellite link from India to the United States.) The lower demand for U.S. programmers and the possibility of losing more work to India have caused a recent drag on the real wages of U.S. programmers. On the other hand, when U.S. companies transfer certain low-paying jobs abroad, they increase the number of higher-paid employees in the United States to handle R&D and the global management of production, finance, and sales.[29] Further, companies use income from foreign operations to increase their domestic efficiencies, reduce prices for consumers, and reinvest into other economic activities.

Thus far, critics in donor countries have managed to succeed in getting few outward restrictions on FDI. Their most effective argument has been that capital outflows should be restricted to relieve balance-of-payment deficits. Nevertheless, critics have proposed many limitations, particularly limitations on companies' technological transfers to other countries. Thus, companies always stand the risk that stakeholders within their home countries will diminish their freedom to operate unobstructedly.

Political Issues

The sheer size of many foreign investors concerns stakeholders in the countries in which they do business. For example, the sales of General Motors, Exxon, and

Fear of Foreign
Investment

Many host-country
stakeholders, particularly
in emerging economies,
believe that multinational
enterprises will be used as
political instruments of
their home governments.
Thus, they often put
restrictions on MNEs' entry
and methods of operation.

source: *The Philadelphia Inquirer.* Reprinted with permission of the Universal Press Syndicate. All Rights Reserved.

Mitsubishi exceed the GDP of such medium-sized economies as Argentina, Indonesia, Poland, and South Africa. Critics in recipient countries are most concerned that home-country governments will use MNEs as a foreign policy instrument, such as by making them withhold resources or technologies unless the recipient countries follow certain policies. Figure 6.4 illustrates this concern. Because MNEs' home countries are usually industrial countries, emerging economies are understandably most concerned. But stakeholders in industrial countries worry about foreign policy implications as well. Some other stakeholders worry that an MNE may become so independent of both the home and host countries that stakeholders in neither can take actions in its best interest. For instance, they argue that an MNE can whipsaw labor in each by offering employment only to the group that will produce more output for less compensation. Finally, some stakeholders contend that MNEs might become so dependent on foreign operations that they support host-country policies and practices unpopular in their own countries. For example, they point to lobbying by U.S. MNEs for better U.S. relations with China despite poor Chinese human rights records.

At the heart of the foreign policy issue is the question of **extraterritoriality,** the extension of a country's laws beyond its borders. For example, the United States passed the Helms-Burton Act, which provides for the U.S. government to seize U.S. assets of non-U.S. companies using expropriated property in Cuba that had been owned by U.S. citizens (including Cuban people who were not U.S. citizens at the time). The intent of the act is to weaken the Cuban government by coercing non-U.S. companies to avoid making FDI in Cuba. The act basically says to them, "If you invest in Cuba, you cannot invest in the United States"—of course the U.S. market is much larger than the Cuban market. The legislation has infuriated stakeholders in Canada and Europe. Canadian and European stakeholders have also criticized the U.S. government's extension of U.S. antitrust laws to the foreign operations of U.S. companies.

Host-country stakeholders worry that MNEs will meddle in local politics so that they get regulations favorable to their interests. On the one hand, many critics contend that foreign companies should not participate in local politics at all. On the other hand, a spokesman for Glaxo Wellcome, a U.K.-based pharmaceutical company, said, "We employ 9,000 people in the U.S. We are one of the major taxpayers and have a substantial effect on the economy. And so we make donations [to U.S. political candidates] from that perspective."[30] Host-country stakeholders also fear that home-country governments will put pressure on host-country governments to treat their MNEs favorably. Stakeholders in emerging economies are particularly distrustful because of historical precedents. Throughout the 19th and much of the 20th centuries, home-country governments commonly used military force to protect their foreign investors' interests.

Countries also worry that if foreign ownership dominates key industries, companies in those industries will make decisions abroad that may have adverse effects on local economies. Countries have, therefore, selectively prevented foreign domination of so-called **key industries,** those industries that might affect a very large segment of the economy or population by virtue of their size or influence. Different countries view key industries differently. For example, Canada limits foreign ownership in cultural industries, the United States in the airline and communications industries, and Mexico in the energy and rail industries.

Improving Stakeholder Positions

Some stakeholders take governments' laws, regulations, and decisions as "givens." Others influence governments to make laws, regulations, and decisions that are more favorable to them. Stakeholders also try to directly coerce companies to follow certain practices, such as by influencing customers not to otherwise buy from them. For example, NGOs critical of Shell's environmental practices in Nigeria did two things. They organized a group that included 18 public and private pension funds, five religious institutions, and an academic fund to buy shares in Shell so they could present a shareholder resolution to require the company to give more public accountability of its Nigerian operations. They also organized boycotts in other countries, such as in South Africa.

One method of improving a stakeholder position is to build allies. The most likely allies are other stakeholders whose positions are affected the same way. For example, the largest U.S. direct investors in Brazil joined together under the auspices of the Brazil–U.S. Business Council to try to persuade the U.S. Congress to fully fund the International Monetary Fund (IMF) so that Brazil would be less economically risky to their business interests. The Brazil–U.S. Business Council advertised in major U.S. newspapers to persuade the general public of Brazil's importance to the U.S. economy. By acting collectively, these companies assured that congressional representatives could not disregard consideration of their interests. Further, by informing the public through the advertisements, the companies also helped the representatives justify to

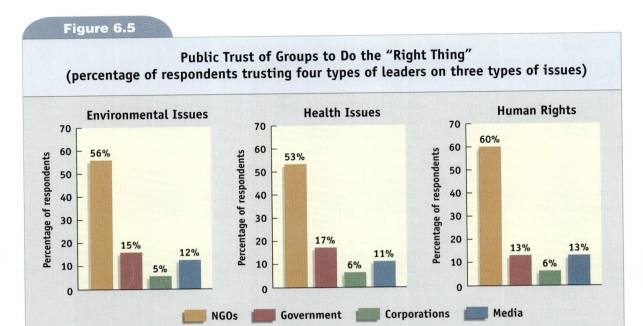

Figure 6.5

Public Trust of Groups to Do the "Right Thing"
(percentage of respondents trusting four types of leaders on three types of issues)

Based on surveys of 600 opinion leaders in the United States, Europe, and Australia in 2000, there is much more trust of NGOs than of other influential groups in society.

source: Figures came from "NGOs Win Big on the International Trust-o-Meter," *PR News,* Vol. 56, No. 50, December 18, 2000. They took information from Edelman Public Relations.

their constituents that IMF support of Brazil was in the public's best interest. Stakeholders may also enlist the support of other groups that have different but complementary stakes in an outcome. For example, recall the International Brotherhood of Teamsters' efforts to persuade Cutrale to reinstate jobs in Florida. The Teamsters allied with NGOs opposed to the use of child labor, which on the surface seems far-fetched, but those groups were willing to confront Cutrale because of their complementary interest. Figure 6.5 shows that people trust NGOs more than they trust governments, corporations, or the media. Therefore, companies may find that allying with NGOs may be a very useful strategy to turn public opinion toward their side.

Companies may lobby governmental decision makers, particularly those within their home countries. For example, Philip Morris, Cray Research, and Motorola took highly visible steps, including participation in press conferences and testimony before the U.S. Congress, to persuade the U.S. government to pressure the Japanese government to reduce its trade barriers.[31] Companies can also develop political action committees to lobby directly with decision makers in the government. For example, Sunkist and Diamond Walnut lobby directly to support funding for the U.S. Department of Agriculture's assistance to U.S. exporters.[32] Political action committees typically present a great deal of information about the importance of legislation for themselves and for economic, social, and political interests of the country as a whole.

Companies may also survey stakeholders to determine opinions that might lead to pressures on managerial decisions. In so doing, they can allay misconceptions and anticipate criticism, thereby heading off potentially more damaging legislation or actions geared specifically at them. Many MNEs use publicity at home and abroad in an aggressive effort to win support for their international activities. Such publicity may take the form of newspapers and magazine ads, reports, and films showing the positive effects that companies' international activities have on home- and host-country societies.

Some companies have fostered local participation in their operations to reduce the image of foreignness and to develop local proponents whose personal objectives may be fulfilled by their continued success. This participation has involved assisting the development of their local suppliers, establishing stock option plans for local employees, and gradually replacing home-country personnel with local nationals. Some companies have additionally taken on social functions to build local support. We shall discuss societal responsibility extensively in Chapter 13. For now, two examples are Dow Chemical's financing of a Chilean kindergarten and Citibank's participation in a Philippine reforestation program. By taking on these societal functions, companies feel they are in a stronger position to propose actions favorable to them and to dispel criticism that may be directed at them.

Summary

Stakeholders—individuals and groups affected by organizational actions—often have conflicting interests in globalization. Thus, they form pressure groups to influence the degree to which companies operate internationally. They often sway governmental decision makers to limit foreign trade by arguing that restrictions will aid national employment, improve the balance of payments, transform the economy, force other countries to open their markets, improve national security, protect the health and safety of consumers, and compel other countries to change undesirable practices. There are controversies surrounding each of these arguments. At the same time, certain stakeholders influence countries to restrict flows of direct investment. Although they present arguments for and against the flows, most of their actions aim to improve the share of benefits accruing to their own countries.

endnotes

[1] Matt Moffett, "Citrus Squeeze," *Wall Street Journal,* September 6, 1998, p. A1+; and Anthony DePalma and Simon Robero, "Orange Juice Tariff Hinders Trade Pact for U.S. and Brazil," *New York Times,* April 24, 2000, p. A1+.

[2] Eugene Salorio, "Trade Barriers and Corporate Strategies: Why Some Firms Oppose Import Protection for Their Own Industry," unpublished DBA dissertation, Harvard University, 1991.

[3] Helene Cooper, "Poorer Countries Are Demonstrators' Strongest Critics," *Wall Street Journal,* December 2, 1999, p. 2.

[4] "Koreans Protest U.S. Call for Open Movie Market," *Richmond Times Dispatch,* December 5, 1998, p. A4.

[5] David E. Sanger, "Clinton Warns U.S. Will Limit Cheap Imports," *New York Times*, November 11, 1998, p. A1+.

[6] Brian Coleman, "Dispute with EU over U.S. Poultry Could Affect $386 Million of Shipments," *Wall Street Journal*, April 2, 1997, p. A4.

[7] Geoff Winestock, "Why U.S. Trade Sanctions Don't Faze Europe," *Wall Street Journal*, September 8, 2000, p. A15+; and Joseph Kahn, "President Delays New Import Duties for European Goods," *New York Times*, September 14, 2000, www.nytimes.com/2000/09/14/business/ 14SANC.html.

[8] Michael M. Knetter, "Free Trade: Why the Public Is Unconvinced," *Financial Times*, April 3, 1998, Mastering Global Business section, p. 12+.

[9] Guy de Jonquières, "Commodity Price Falls Hit Poor Nations," *Financial Times*, September 17, 1998, p. 7.

[10] This argument is most associated with the writings of Raul Prebisch, Hans Singer, and Gunnar Myrdahl in the 1950s and 1960s. For a recent discussion, see John Waterbury, "The Long Gestation and Brief Triumph of Import Substituting Industrialization," *World Development*, Vol. 27, No. 2, February 1999, pp. 323–341.

[11] Laura D'Andrea Tyson, *Who's Bashing Whom?* (Washington: Institute for International Economics, 1993).

[12] "Honey, Wool and Mohair Subsidies Are Cut," *New York Times*, October 3, 1993, p. A12.

[13] Edmund L. Andrews, "U.S. Restrictions on Exports Aid German Software Maker," *New York Times*, April 7, 1997, p. C1.

[14] Rosanna Tanburri, "Canada Considers New Stand Against American Culture," *Wall Street Journal*, February 4, 1998, p. A18; and Roger Ricklefs, "Canada Fights to Fend Off American Taste in Tunes," *Wall Street Journal*, September 24, 1998, p. D1+.

[15] Andrew Jack, "French Films to Get State Funds for Dubbing," *Financial Times*, January 23, 1996, p. 2.

[16] "WTO: French Asbestos Ban Is Legal," *New York Times on the Web*, September 18, 2000.

[17] *Financial Times*, September 1, 2000, p. 5.

[18] Steven Lee Myers, "Converting the Dollar into a Bludgeon," *New York Times*, April 20, 1997, p. 5.

[19] Nancy Dunne, "U.S. May Impose Sanctions Over Religious Freedom," *Financial Times*, May 15, 1998, p. 8; and Robert S. Greenburger, "Hopes Fade for Bill to Limit Sanctions," *Wall Street Journal*, September 9, 1998, p. A2+.

[20] "Standard Fare," *Economist*, May 24, 1997, p. 72.

[21] Erika Morphy, "Gaging Tomorrow's Standards," *Export Today*, August 1995, pp. 48–53.

[22] Ari M. Rubenstein, "Commodities Corner: Subsidize This," *Barron's*, August 23, 1999, p. MW12.

[23] Michael E. Porter, "The Competitive Advantage of Nations," *Harvard Business Review*, Vol. 90, No. 2, March–April 1990, p. 78.

[24] Paul Krugman and Alasdair M. Smith, eds., *Empirical Studies of Strategic Trade Policies* (Chicago: University of Chicago Press, 1993).

[25] Richard Brahm, "National Targeting Policies, High-Technology Industries, and Excessive Competition," *Strategic Management Journal*, Vol. 16, 1995, pp. 71–91.

[26] Helene Cooper, "Trade Wins," *Wall Street Journal*, July 14, 1998, p. A1.

[27] Janice C. Shields, "Export Promotion Programs," *Plan Policy in Focus*, Vol. 2, No. 84, May 1997.

[28] Robert Anderson, "Czechs Feel They Must Run to Catch Foreign Investors," *Financial Times*, April 17, 1998, p. 3.

[29] Robert Fuenstra and Gordon Hanson, *Foreign Investment, Outsourcing, and Relative Wages* (Cambridge, MA: National Bureau of Economic Research Working Paper No. 5121, 1995).

[30] Marcus W. Brauchli, Matthew Rose, and Jonathan Friedland, "Foreign Donors: We Have a Stake in America, Too," *Wall Street Journal,* October 31, 1996, p. A19.

[31] Joseph A. Massey, "Guide to the Art of Lobbying," *Financial Times,* March 27, 1998, Mastering Global Business section, p. 5+.

[32] Shields.

Objectives

1. To understand the conditions that shape how companies set up foreign manufacturing facilities

2. To appreciate the relationship between a company's strategy and the design of its global manufacturing system

3. To grasp the trade-offs that companies face in designing a competitive manufacturing system

4. To understand the idea of global supply chain management

5. To realize how global supply chain management helps companies meet international objectives

6. To appreciate the decisions that companies face in making and moving products around the world

Zara: Making and Moving Clothes

While unknown to most, Zara, a division of the Spanish firm Inditex, is a fast-growing clothing retailer that has built an innovative supply chain to power its global expansion. In doing so, Zara has pioneered a new style of quick, custom-made retailing that transforms it into a global player. Zara opened its first store in 1975 but has since expanded to more than 400 storefronts around the world. In 1999, Zara's total sales of nearly $2 billion put it behind Gap ($11.6 billion) and Swedish clothier H&M (about $3.6 billion). Still, sales increased 26 percent from 1998, whereas profits grew 34 percent, to around $186 million. International sales generated nearly half of total revenue.

Zara uses no advertising or promotion, relying solely on word of mouth to market its products. It bolsters its brand with a direct product and pricing strategy: "Armani at moderate prices," noted a Goldman Sachs analyst. Or as Luis Blanc, a director at Inditex, explained, "We want our clients to enter a beautiful store, where they are offered the latest fashions and good service at low prices. But most important of all, we want our customers to understand that if they like something, they must buy it now, because it won't be in the shops the following week. It is all about creating a climate of scarcity and opportunity." In a nutshell, Zara rejects the idea of spring and autumn clothing collections in favor of "live collections" that can be designed, manufactured, distributed, and sold almost as quickly as their customers' fleeting tastes.

This strategy pushed Zara to use speed, customization, and information technology to build a global supply chain that redefined the idea of infotech and fashion. Essentially, Zara can translate the latest fashion trends into designs that are made in less than 15 days and then delivered to its stores twice a week. Zara drops designs that do not sell well within a week.

Some see Zara as the Dell Computer of the fashion industry, using e-business methods to make and move sophisticated fashion at budget prices. That is, Zara's strategy depends on continuous exchange of data between the links in its global supply chain. Its networked stores continually transfer data on which merchandise is selling along with customer requests to Zara's headquarters and logistics center near La Coruña, a midsized city in northwest Spain. There

Global Manufacturing and Supply Chain Management

chapter 7

People in blank and white masks at a pre-Lent festival in Venice, Italy.

French-, German-, English-, Arabic-, Japanese-, and Spanish-speaking executives are on the phone to store managers across four continents, gathering daily intelligence on what shoppers are buying, what they are asking for, and what they do not like.

Headquarters quickly acts on this information via its extensive e-links with suppliers and manufacturers. Unlike Gap and H&M, which outsource most of these functions, Zara produces more than 60 percent of its merchandise in house. Zara sources fabric from numerous suppliers in Spain, India, Morocco, and the Far East. Linked into Zara's network, they are able to quickly ship their product to Zara's state-of-the-art factory, which then cuts and colors the fabric. Using information gathered daily from stores, production managers decide how many garments to make and which stores will stock them. Zara then sends the fabric to local shops that finish the product—and off it goes. This combination of real-time information sharing and internal production lets Zara work with little inventory and still have new designs in the store twice a week versus the industry standard of six weeks. Also, says José Maria Castellano, Inditex's chief executive, "We have the ability to scrap an entire production line if it is not selling. We can dye collections in new colors, and we can create a new fashion line in days."

Presently, no other company can ship new fashion designs to stores as quickly as Zara. Still, the company has achieved the same profit margins with higher sales per square foot than Gap. Over time, Zara's global supply chain leaves rivals less and less time to integrate design, manufacturing, and distribution systems within their own global supply chains. If they don't, warns Keith Wills, European retail analyst at Goldman Sachs, they "won't be in business in 10 years."[1]

Introduction

Every company, from the smallest to the biggest, eventually faces a moment of truth: Should it move from analyzing the international business environment to entering foreign markets? Deciding that the potential returns exceed the risks of international business, in turn, starts a chain of fundamental decisions. Specifically, managers now must resolve where in the world to put a factory, how in the world to move goods and services from suppliers to factories to customers, and what in the world to do themselves versus outsourcing to someone else. Figure 7.1 shows the relationships among these issues.

Answering these questions is usually a lot harder than even the most confident managers imagine. Complications arise from many multinational enterprises' (MNEs') reaction to tough global competition by rushing overseas to lower manufacturing costs or reach new markets. This tendency, if unchecked, can lead companies to make tactical, stopgap decisions when opening a foreign plant or creating an international supply link that ultimately raises their costs or squanders a market opportunity. For instance, companies often find that their cost savings from foreign manufacturing are initially significant—lower wage rates, favorable exchange rates, and low-cost capital immediately boost profits. Gradually, though, companies discover that local overseas wage rates also rise and, if exchange and interest rates turn against them, the savings of overseas production can quickly disappear. Similarly, in the event that a huge supply of labor keeps wages down, companies may find that their labor savings diminish as they must add more workers to offset lower productivity. Also, the promise of location-specific advantages, such as cheap land or cheap electricity, tends to be short lived. Where one company can relocate for such advantages, globalization pushes others to quickly follow. Finally, companies expanding abroad can underestimate the effects of national barriers on getting things done. Communication difficulties with foreign plants and suppliers make it tough to synchronize engineering changes, process improvements, or product modifications.

In each of these situations, MNEs often capture spectacular short-term benefits by moving production to foreign markets. In the long run, however, the rush to build a plant overseas can also create an inefficient global manufacturing system or weak links in the global supply chain. Entrepreneurs and executives alike, therefore, must avoid these risks and, ideally, gain the competitive edge of shrewdly making and moving products around the world. This chapter reviews these issues by surveying the matters of global manufacturing strategies and global supply chain management.

Figure 7.1

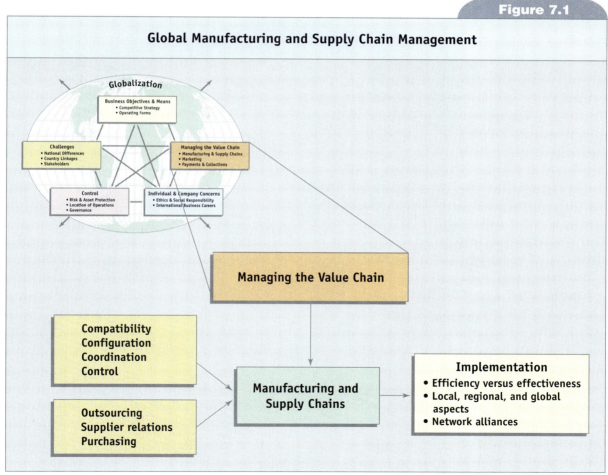

Making and moving products around the world pushes a company to set up the best manufacturing network to supply the affiliates, partners, and customers that make up its supply chain. Throughout these activities, companies balance competing concerns for efficiency versus effectiveness at the local, regional, and global levels.

Global Manufacturing Strategy

We use the generic term *manufacturing* to describe the efforts of industrial and service companies to make products that are sold to foreign markets. Whether a company is making computers or providing consumer credit for the global market, for example, it needs to figure out where it should build a factory or office. Determining the optimum number of plants and selecting the best possible locations compels an MNE to monitor many factors, including but not limited to transportation costs, trade relationships, the need for physical proximity to a market, foreign exchange risk, potential economies of scale in the production process, technological requirements of the manufacturing process, the availability of government incentives, access to transportation hubs, favorable climate, proximity to competitors and suppliers, and national image.[2]

The range of circumstances to study makes it hard to stipulate ironclad rules about devising the best global manufacturing strategy. It is even confusing, for example, to come up with guidelines that reflect the most basic difference among companies—namely, whether they make a good or provide a service. In theory, you would think that making goods (particularly those with razor-thin margins such as personal computers) would spur such companies to maximize cost-sensitive efficiency, whereas those firms providing high-priced services (such as consumer credit cards) would emphasize revenue-sensitive effectiveness. That said, both Dell Computer, the world's leading direct computer seller, and MBNA America, the world leader in affinity credit cards, serve their European operations from "manufacturing" subsidiaries in Ireland. Both companies, for reasons we will discover in this chapter, saw a mix of national factors in Ireland such that it made sense to set up a manufacturing factory or service complex there.

Essentially, then, the idea of a global manufacturing strategy brings into play a mix of economic, competitive, legal, political, and environmental conditions. Fortunately, successful companies such as Dell and MBNA show ways to answer the question, "Where in the world should we build a plant?" Common patterns of decision making among these and other well-run MNEs suggest that the success of a global manufacturing strategy depends on how well managers deal with the 4 Cs: compatibility, configuration, coordination, and control.[3]

The 4 Cs

Compatibility

The degree of consistency between where and how managers set up their foreign manufacturing system and the company's competitive strategy is the first C, *compatability*. Recall from Chapter 2 that a firm has several choices of competitive strategies, such as an international strategy, multidomestic strategy, or transnational strategy. While there are overlaps, each particular competitive strategy leads a firm to treat the same business activities, such as cost management, product diversification, or outsourcing, in different ways. Therefore, designing a resourceful global manufacturing strategy pushes managers to make sure that where and how they manufacture products fits the worldwide goals of the company's competitive strategy.

There are many ways that managers can improve compatibility. Managers can discuss with each other whether their competitive strategy and manufacturing strategy deal with important issues in the same way. In general, impor-

Figure 7.2

"The repairs will take awhile. We need a part from Mexico, a part from Brazil and one from Taiwan."

tant issues include the need for cost-efficient production, quality level of the product, speed of delivery, flexibility of the manufacturing process, and urgency of innovation. For example, if the company's competitive strategy depends on getting the lowest-cost product to the market more quickly than any rival, then managers will need to look for potential factory sites in nations with low-cost labor, cheap land and materials, and a good transportation system. Conversely, if short product life cycles make innovation the key to competitiveness, then potential foreign plants must be put in those nations that support reliable, quick international communications, and provide a highly skilled, agile labor force.

In well-run companies, managers safeguard compatibility by giving greater weight to their forecast of future conditions than they do to current events. That is, managers should refrain from relying on reports of current labor prices or currency rates. Instead, the direction, magnitude, and velocity of strategic trends in vital areas of marketing, product development, and manufacturing anchor a keen analysis of compatibility. In summary, fitting the goals of the company's global competitive strategy with the design of its global manufacturing strategy helps an MNE avoid assembling an assortment of overseas plants that are unduly exposed to wage and currency risks. Instead, smart analysis improves the odds that the company builds integrated manufacturing capabilities that sharpen its long-term competitive edge.

Configuration

Once managers feel comfortable with the compatibility of their competitive strategy and their production goals, they can turn their attention to configuring their international manufacturing facilities. *Configuration* refers to the issue of where the company wants to physically build its factories. One way to think about this decision is to imagine a two-dimensional picture of the world as a playing surface of a board game. An early move crucial to winning the game is figuring out where you want to put your pieces or, in this case, your factories. If you configure the right layout of pieces, subject to your game strategy, then success is much more likely. Back in the business world, managers try to configure the optimum layout of factories subject to three concerns:

1. A company can choose to build a set of *independent plants,* each of which worries only about producing products to supply the local market. This choice makes great sense when there is enough demand in a particular country, such as the large economies of the United States or Japan, to enable a company to gain available economies of scale. Increasingly, this choice is tougher to justify. The freer movement of goods and capital makes it easier to move products among nations, no matter whether a factory happens to operate in a large or small economy.

2. A company can take advantage of regional economic integration to set up a *network of plants* to service a specific region. This option lets the company cherry-pick the best possible sites from a rich set of options. For example, managers designing a manufacturing strategy for the North American markets have the North American Free Trade Agreement to thank for a terrific game board. Depending on their competitive strategy, they have the option of locating a plant in Canada to procure inexpensive raw materials, an assembly plant in Mexico to reach low-cost labor, or a facility in the United States for product distribution, sales support, and warranty service.

3. A company can try to supply the world from a *centralized manufacturing site.* Typically, MNEs that opt for this configuration plan like to locate the factory in their home country. This choice, long popular with MNEs in Far Eastern countries such as Japan and Korea, lets managers avoid the complexities of running factories spread around the world. Instead, they can focus on perfecting the operation of their domestic factory in the effort to translate low production costs into low-priced exports. For example, Zara employs 250 designers, and a further 14,000 at Inditex's centralized manufacturing system around La Coruña. In 1999, they produced 11,000 different designs. The clothes travel on moving hanging rails along 125 miles of underground tracks that link the production sites to the central logistics center. Every garment is electronically tagged so it can be mechanically packed and delivered to the right destination. The successful efforts of "link masters" such as the World Trade Organization (WTO) to promote freer movement of products make this manufacturing strategy increasingly attractive to more companies.

In reality, few companies are able to use just one of these configuration schemes. Companies typically choose a mix of these approaches, depending on their product strategies, political pressure for local manufacturing content, or market trends. Also, companies are often stuck with *legacy manufacturing configurations*—that is, plants that were built a long time ago when trade barriers or market demand in a particular nation was high or because of short-lived advantages in wage rates, currency exchanges, and material costs. No matter what the specifics of a particular configuration happen to be, an MNE always needs to figure out how its configuration of plants can spur developing the unique skills or capabilities that are compatible with its business strategy.

Finally, the matter of configuration is by no means a one-time activity. This chapter shows that manufacturing circumstances continually change in the global market. Prudent MNEs, therefore, continually question the configuration of their game board, seeking ways to improve the positioning of their pieces. For example, in 1998, Johnson & Johnson, a leading pharmaceutical MNE, reconfigured its worldwide network of manufacturing and operating facilities in order to gain efficiencies, increase productivity, and invest in the new opportunities of emerging markets. Johnson & Johnson planned to take 12 to 18 months to reduce the number of manufacturing facilities around the world from 158 to 122, in order to generate after-tax annual savings of nearly $300 million.[4]

Coordination

Opening up foreign plants inevitably compels a company to ask how the different factory pieces on the global game board should work together. That is, once an overseas plant is up and running, managers need to oversee the flow of material, information, and finance among its various customers, suppliers, and distributors. These matters of coordination are especially important because a unified global manufacturing system gives managers the chance to capture synergies available only to MNEs. That is, Chapter 2 showed that the notion of strategy, at its most basic, holds that the whole of the parts is greater than the sum of the parts. Transferring this idea to the global manufacturing strategy means that managers must figure out how to coordinate the activities of each individual plant so little effort is wasted and everything works in sync across the family of factories.

Specifically, managers must coordinate the different activities that go into making and moving a good or service around the world (our later coverage of the global supply chain looks at these activities more closely). For example, Zara's strategy of rapid response to ever-changing fashion trends demands lots of coordination—to get started, Zara must coordinate the efforts of its many salespeople, who act as grassroots market researchers. Operationally, Zara equips all salespeople with wireless handheld organizers that let them punch in trends, customer comments, and orders. Each day, these data are transferred to headquarters, which then uses them to coordinate design, production, and delivery. The resulting task for headquarters is brutal: It must coordinate material flows from its many suppliers and ensure order transmission to its several factories and delivery status to its hundreds of storefronts.

At this point, it is important to note that managers' adept coordination of the overlapping activities among its salespeople or plants achieves all sorts of production efficiencies. For instance, coordinating raw material purchases, service maintenance contracts, or shipping arrangements from a global point of view can translate into volume discounts and more flexible scheduling. Too, well-planned coordination lets factory workers worry less about what is supposed to happen with material transfers and product delivery and worry more about making a high-quality product for the lowest possible price.

Control

Once a company decides where it wants to locate and how it wants to coordinate its manufacturing pieces on the global game board, it then has to come up with a way to control the pieces as planned. For example, tight control over design and production allows Zara to take a fashion trend from a fashion catwalk in Paris to its store shelf in London in as little as two weeks. In comparison, Gap takes about a year, although it is reconfiguring its manufacturing strategy to reduce its time to market to six months. Therefore, a well-designed control system helps everyone in the company carry out their jobs by outlining their roles and stipulating their responsibilities in the company's manufacturing strategy. This boosts the odds that everyone in fact carries out the global manufacturing strategy as planned. Controlling production by specifying everyone's role and duties is a common approach in most MNEs. Our later look at the governance of international operations in Chapter 12 shows that MNEs set up offices, establish procedures, and appoint supervisors to monitor their activities. In general, these explanations of notions of control also broadly apply to global manufacturing. However, there are specific forms of formal and informal control that apply directly to the idea of global manufacturing strategy.

Formal manufacturing controls. Virtually every company relies on controls that are precisely stated in an operating manual. These are typically referred to as *standard operating procedures (SOPs)*. Companies write their SOPs to clearly set out what is supposed to happen in each part of the production process. The last few years have seen more companies organize their formal control efforts in terms of various **International Standards Organization (ISO)** programs (see Table 7.1). ISO standards guide companies' efforts to develop and document the elements of their quality systems. A company earns ISO certification by thoroughly analyzing and extensively documenting its management of the manufacturing process with respect to the precise standards that pertain to different parts of the production process. Getting a company to the point of earning ISO status is tough; keeping it there focuses managers' attention on actively controlling their global manufacturing strategy.

More companies are designing formal manufacturing controls in terms of a control scheme called *six sigma*. In the United States, Motorola and General Electric (GE) blazed the trail. Other MNEs now implementing six-sigma programs are Allied Signal, DuPont, Lockheed Martin, Texas Instruments, and Johnson & Johnson. Technically, six sigma means no more than 3.4 defects per 1 million procedures or products. Companies applying this control system adopt a statistical quality control outlook that breaks a customer's requirements into discrete steps or tasks and then sets the optimum specifications for each part of the process. Managers see the value of six sigma in three areas. First, it gets people away from thinking that 99 percent success is good enough to thinking that 10,000 failures per 1 million activities is not good enough. Second, six sigma makes a company translate its sometimes vague or fuzzy notions of customer requirements into technically measurable standards. Third, six sigma motivates people throughout the company to come up with control systems that improve the quality of the end product, not just the individual piece that they happen to work on. So far, six sigma is changing the idea of formal control in radical ways. For instance, Mr. Jack Welch, formerly of GE, saw GE's six-sigma experience as "the most important initiative this company has ever undertaken. It will fundamentally change our company forever."

Table 7.1

	Selected Types of ISO Certification
ISO 9001	The most comprehensive and detailed standard in the series of ISO standards. It is used when the company has to assure customers of conformance to specific requirements for design, development, production, installation, and servicing.
ISO 9002	Directed to sites not dealing with design and after-market service and, therefore, is intended to assure conformance to specific requirements for production and installation.
ISO 9003	Focuses on final inspection of products or services and testing.
ISO 9004	Describes the philosophy behind the standards by providing guidelines for developing and implementing a quality system. It describes the primary elements of a quality system: product and service requirements, organization and control, customer satisfaction, customer and product responsibility, and system guidance.
ISO 9004-2	Tailors the information contained in ISO 9004 to the service industry.
ISO 9004-3	Describes what a software company must account for in connection with development, supply, and maintenance in order to comply with a quality standard.
ISO 14000	A voluntary standard that deals with a company's environmental management system. The certification process verifies that each manufacturing plant has a formal environmental policy as well as a management system designed to track environmental performance and established mechanism for continuous improvement.

Informal manufacturing controls. Managers also use informal ways to control their global manufacturing strategy. Typically, managers foster a companywide philosophy that encourages workers to voluntarily watch and continuously improve the production process. Often, this control tool is called **total quality management (TQM)** or total quality control. Essentially, these programs assert that managers should develop control systems that make everyone recognize the importance of eliminating mistakes, defects, and poor-quality output. Managers develop this control philosophy by designing a workplace in which employees enthusiastically recommend better ways of doing their job, everyone is open to best practices from other companies, and no one fears getting in trouble for reporting production or quality problems. Often, this control approach leads to using self-managing manufacturing cells of between 5 and 10 workers.

American management scholars came up with TQM in the post–World War II era. At the time, their ideas did not make much sense to U.S. companies. However, Japanese companies quickly adopted the notion of TQM. Eventually, following their terrific manufacturing record, in the 1980s and 1990s, many American companies began to control their manufacturing strategies with TQM programs. Most notably, Ford Motor Company around this time adopted the slogan "Quality Is Job One" as its battle cry.

Primary Moderators of the 4 Cs: Products and Countries

The 4 Cs of the global manufacturing strategy give managers a quick guide to keep sight of fundamental questions. As we have seen in the text so far, though, differences in national markets and cultures regularly push managers to think about related issues that may shape their decisions. The same holds for global manufacturing strategies. Therefore, managers need to look at the possible effects of product and country factors on the 4 Cs.

Product Factors

Value-to-weight ratio. The value-to-weight ratio of a product can make a huge difference in plant configuration decisions. The greater the value of the product to its weight, the less important storage and transportation costs matter. Therefore, those deciding where to manufacture computer chips, software, or aircraft—unlike tractor axles, carpeting, or furniture, for instance—need not pay much attention to the distance between the factory and the consumer.

Purpose of the product. If a particular product serves a universal purpose, as does a telephone or wristwatch, a company can worry less about making it comply with particular national tastes. Other products such as washers and dryers can differ quite a bit from nation to nation. The need to keep touch with local preferences for such goods pushes a company to build separate national factories even if it makes much better economic sense to build a few large regional or global factories.

Complexity of the product. The outright complexity of the product and the corresponding intricacy of the production process shape the direction of a global manufacturing strategy. Furthermore, innovative products are often hard to build in mass quantities. Typically, these products are early in their life cycle. Managers' efforts to perfect them require them to monitor their production closely. This concern typically results in locating the factory near the research and development team so that managers can immediately deal with potential coordination and control problems. Traditionally, MNEs relied on the policy that the more complex the information that must be regularly communicated among groups, the greater the need for closer proximity among the groups. However, the emergence of the Internet and e-mail increasingly relaxes this policy.

Product life cycles. We saw in Chapter 1 that the globalization of business is contracting product life cycles. For example, the expected life of a high-tech product such as a personal computer, digital phone, or data router is now 6 to 12 months. Consequently, companies must devise manufacturing strategies that anticipate the rapid pace of product design, delivery, and obsolescence.

Degree of digitalization. The degree to which a product can be converted into a string of zeros and ones—the process of digitalization—influences several aspects of global manufacturing. Increasingly, products such as software, music, and books can be made virtually anywhere there is a computer and, via communications technologies, can immediately be sent anywhere to any "connected" customer in the world at negligible cost. Too, continuous innovation in information technology makes it easier and cheaper to process large amounts of data, thereby opening up the manufacturing of other products, such as videos, to digitalization.

Country Factors

Coordinating and controlling activities across different plants is a tough thing when they are all located in a single nation. It can be especially difficult when plants are spread around the world. Challenges come from a range of seemingly innocent circumstances. For example, language barriers and time-zone differences can make the routine matter of coordination a never-ending source of friction when it involves plants in different nations. Similarly, Chapter 6 looked at the reasons and methods that nations use to influence trade. A nation's industrialization policy or the goals of its strategic trade policy can create opportunities and threats to a company's configuration scheme.

Challenges can also come from less obvious sources. Typically, a company's global manufacturing strategy needs to prepare for different attitudes and approaches to manufacturing across nations. Indeed, a survey of global manufacturers found that most ran into problems because inconsistent production systems and equipment made it impractical to transfer production from one plant to another.[5] For example, an MNE may have factories in different parts of the world, such as Japan and Mexico, that manufacture the same product but with different production philosophies. The Mexican factory might adopt a traditional assembly-line operation given the local conditions of inexpensive labor, poor transportation infrastructure, and limited exposure to high technology. The company's Japanese factory, on the other hand, might install a "lean production" manufacturing system to take advantage of local labor competency, manufacturing expertise, and efficient transportation systems. The different capital structures and productivity of each type of system complicate managers' process of keeping both plants working in harmony with the other. If ignored, MNEs can suffer production crunches that lead to high overtime costs, reduced quality, disappointed customers, and lost sales.

Finally, the notion of new trade theory that we looked at in Chapter 5 talks about how ostensibly economic decisions are sometimes influenced by good fortune, entrepreneurship, and first-mover advantages. The same holds true for configuring a global manufacturing network. Depending on the particular good or service a company makes, it may have very few choices about where to build a factory. Some nations have what are called *clusters*—groups of world-class companies and suppliers that produce very similar things but that all work within the same city, state, or nation.[6] For instance, an investment bank trying to configure its global office game board will inevitably look at New York City, London, and Tokyo, given that they are the centers of global financial markets. Similarly, Internet software companies almost have to open an office in the United States given its key role in shaping the future of the World Wide Web. In both cases, you can make a good economic argument for putting a plant in many different places around the world. However, adjusting analysis to also look at the state of affairs in a particular nation can inspire different manufacturing strategies.

Global Supply Chain Management

In broad terms, *global supply chain management* describes managers' effort to oversee the flows of raw materials, components, information, and finance through their network of suppliers, assemblers, distributors, and customers located around the world. Raw material and component flows move among many suppliers and customers, such as integrated circuits from Chinese suppliers to Nokia, as well as reverse flows via product returns, servicing, recycling, and disposal, such as from retailers back to distributors and on to Nokia. Inevitably, getting these things done requires sending lots of information among different companies over matters of order status, work-in-process affairs, delivery dates, credit terms, payment schedules, and consignment and title ownership arrangements. Moreover, these information flows are not restricted to a specific part of an MNE. Indeed, the truly complicating part of global supply chain management is the movement of information among many different areas within an MNE, such as manufacturing, marketing, finance, and logistics, as well as among different MNEs. In a moment, we will develop these ideas. Before doing so, we look at the strategic importance and performance implications of global supply chain management.

Traditionally, managers viewed global supply chain management as an important but not especially vital support activity. However, MNEs' reengineering efforts over the past decade have showed that interpreting the global supply chain as part of their competitive strategy significantly boosted profits. Examples like Zara, to say nothing of companies like Dell Computer, Nokia, and GE, increasingly spotlight the potential of well-managed global supply chains to drive business improvement across the entire company.

Specifically, innovative supply chain management creates enormous potential to lower costs and boost earnings. For instance, consider that purchased goods and services can account from 50 to 80 percent of total costs at the typical company; just a 10 percent improvement in better managing various business functions has a dramatic impact on profits (see Figure 7.3). More directly, GE Supply, a $2-billion electrical, voice, and data products distributor based in

Figure 7.3

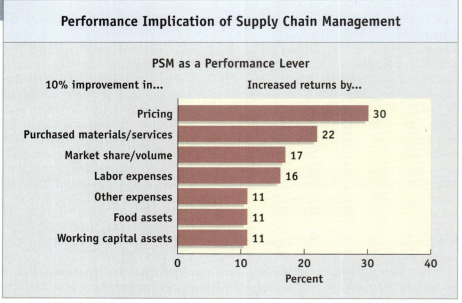

source: Timothy L. Chapman, Jack J. Dempsey, Glenn Ramsdell, and Michael R. Reopel, "Purchasing: No Time for Lone Rangers," *McKinsey Quarterly*, No. 2, 1997, pp. 30–40. Chart is extracted from page 30.

Connecticut holds more than $100 million in inventory and more than 100,000 different products at any given time. It stores these parts in more than 4.5 million square feet of warehouse space, with 150 locations spread around the world. GE Supply relies on a hub-and-spoke information network to connect strategically placed warehouses with thousands of local GE Supply branches, which then let the company fill even the most unusual orders in 24 hours or less. GE Supply's innovative supply chain management skills have led more than 200 other suppliers—some direct product competitors—to hire the company to manage links in their own global supply chains. In return, GE Supply helps its customers increase productivity by integrating the entire supply chain and improving information flow to give the customer better information faster.

Recent trends in technology give managers powerful tools to improve the strategic performance of their global supply chains. At the most basic, firms find it much cheaper to place an order online, and there are likely to be fewer errors in orders and invoicing. For instance, each purchase order at General Motors (GM) that travels through the paper-based order-to-fulfillment process costs the buyer $50 to $55 and the seller $45 to $50. The combined processing cost through the GM e-system is about $10 per order. Similarly, Cisco reports that, at one time, a quarter of its orders had to be reworked because of errors in its phone and fax ordering system. When it switched to online ordering, the error rate fell to 2 percent, saving the company $500 million per year. Moreover, British Telecom claims that buying goods and services online reduces the cost of processing a transaction by 90 percent and cuts the direct costs of the goods and services it buys by 11 percent.

An even greater savings takes place in time, the hidden opportunity cost of a badly managed global supply chain. Better management of the global supply chain lets people shift from spending up to half of each day shuffling paper to performing more value-added activities—sourcing new suppliers, researching consumer preferences, or improving product and service quality. Less directly, studying supply markets helps an MNE figure out how much leverage it has over its suppliers; understanding their operation can help it negotiate better exchange terms for future transactions. In a moment, we will look at these issues more closely. Before doing so, we map out the structure of a global supply chain.

The Basic Configuration of a Global Supply Chain

Typically, when we visualize a supply chain, a step-by-step view of the classic buy-make-move-store-sell cycle comes to mind. For instance, consider the purchase of a wristwatch. The usual image begins with a U.S. buyer of a Seiko wristwatch who connects with a local jeweler or other retailer in his or her hometown, who in turn connects to the wholesaler distribution in Los Angeles, who in turn connects back to the Japanese manufacturer, which connects through many layers back all the way to the worker in Peru operating the heavy equipment to bring bauxite out of the ground to provide the aluminum needed to create the watch case. Although this is a simplified illustration, it still shows how easily a supply chain can stretch around the world. Whether the supply chain is high tech (such as the many computer chips ultimately installed in BMW automobiles) or low tech (the toys distributed with McDonald's Happy Meals), in all likelihood, it has shepherded products through many stops in many countries before they reach their final destination. The potential to wring out dramatic efficiencies and profits, therefore, motivates MNEs to forge strong links among the players in their global supply chain.

Figure 7.4 illustrates the basic configuration of a global supply chain. Suppliers can be part of the manufacturer's organizational structure, as would be the case in a vertically integrated company, or they can be independent of the company. Suppliers can be located in the country where the manufacturing or assembly takes place, or they can be located in one country and ship to the country where the final product is made. Suppliers can also ship their output directly to the factory, an intermediate storage point, a distributor, a wholesaler, or a retailer, or even straight to the end consumer.

Definitions, Distinctions, and Standards of Global Supply Chain Management

Making and moving a product depends on the shipment and transfer of a range of inputs among several factories that are usually spread across several countries. Figure 7.5 gives a sense of this process by showing the number of factories in different nations that supplied parts to make the Ford Escort. Therefore, an important dimension of supply chain management is **logistics,** a practice that is sometimes called **materials management.**

According to the U.S.-based Council of Logistics Management, "Logistics is that part of the supply chain process that plans, implements, and controls the efficient, effective flow and storage of goods, services, and related information from the point of origin to the point of consumption in order to meet customers' requirements."[7] The difference between supply chain management and logistics management is one of degree. Logistics management focuses more on the transportation and storage of materials and final goods. As noted above, supply chain management goes beyond this to include the more complex activities of overseeing the flows of raw materials, components, information, and finance through a network of suppliers, assemblers, distributors, and customers located around the world.

Figure 7.4	

The global supply chain links the suppliers' supplier with the customers' customer, accounting for every step of the process between the raw material and the final consumer of the good or service.

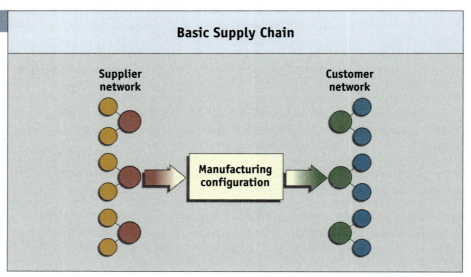

source: From *International Business: Environments and Operations, 9/E* by Radebaugh and Daniels © 2001. Reprinted with permission of Pearson Education, Inc., Upper Saddle River, NJ 07458.

Figure 7.5

The Global Component Network for Ford's European Manufacturing of the Escort

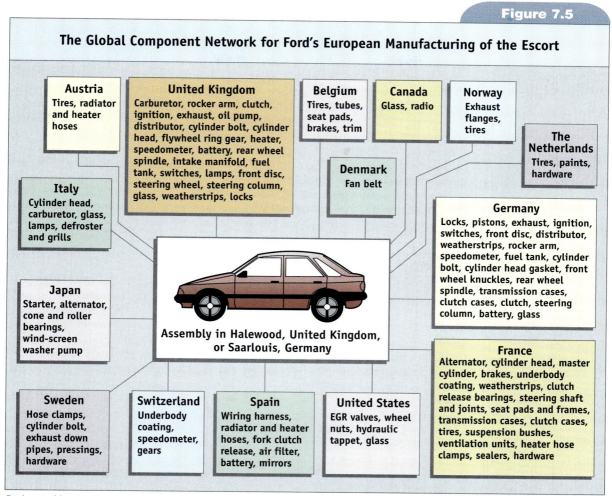

Austria
Tires, radiator and heater hoses

United Kingdom
Carburetor, rocker arm, clutch, ignition, exhaust, oil pump, distributor, cylinder bolt, cylinder head, flywheel ring gear, heater, speedometer, battery, rear wheel spindle, intake manifold, fuel tank, switches, lamps, front disc, steering wheel, steering column, glass, weatherstrips, locks

Belgium
Tires, tubes, seat pads, brakes, trim

Canada
Glass, radio

Norway
Exhaust flanges, tires

The Netherlands
Tires, paints, hardware

Denmark
Fan belt

Italy
Cylinder head, carburetor, glass, lamps, defroster and grills

Germany
Locks, pistons, exhaust, ignition, switches, front disc, distributor, weatherstrips, rocker arm, speedometer, fuel tank, cylinder bolt, cylinder head gasket, front wheel knuckles, rear wheel spindle, transmission cases, clutch cases, clutch, steering column, battery, glass

Japan
Starter, alternator, cone and roller bearings, wind-screen washer pump

Assembly in Halewood, United Kingdom, or Saarlouis, Germany

France
Alternator, cylinder head, master cylinder, brakes, underbody coating, weatherstrips, clutch release bearings, steering shaft and joints, seat pads and frames, transmission cases, clutch cases, tires, suspension bushes, ventilation units, heater hose clamps, sealers, hardware

Sweden
Hose clamps, cylinder bolt, exhaust down pipes, pressings, hardware

Switzerland
Underbody coating, speedometer, gears

Spain
Wiring harness, radiator and heater hoses, fork clutch release, air filter, battery, mirrors

United States
EGR valves, wheel nuts, hydraulic tappet, glass

Ford assembles Escorts in only two facilities in Europe, but parts and components used in the automobiles come from all over the world.

source: From *World Development Report* 1987 by *World Bank,* copyright © 1984 by *The World Bank.* Used by permission of Oxford University Press, Inc.

This distinction gets to the core of global supply chain management by high-lighting the importance of managers' effort to supervise flows—whether these involve products, information, or money—among the links making up the chain.[8] Generally, a firm's global supply chain strategy includes the following elements: (1) customer service requirements, (2) plant and distribution center network design, (3) inventory management, (4) outsourcing and third-party logistics relationships, (5) key customer and supplier relationships, (6) business processes, (7) information systems, (8) organizational design and training requirements, (9) performance metrics, and (10) performance goals.[9]

From a strategic viewpoint, global supply chain management has several goals. We noted above that, at the least, focusing solely on the efficiency of the dealings among the links in the supply chain helps lower a company's cost of doing business. While a terrific benefit, companies now see boosting the efficiency of the supply chain as the low-hanging fruit on a very tall tree. Greater rewards follow from stretching to reach the more difficult rewards of global supply chain management, which promise the greater profits that come from building a stronger competitive position.

Experts point out that these rewards revolve around the standard of customer experience. Again, each step of the buy-make-move-store-sell cycle represents a different buyer or different seller. At the least, globalization makes customers less tolerant of poor customer service. Moreover, customers increasingly want to have a full view into their orders, invoices, and inventory with each of their suppliers; such a view enables a firm to manage the nightmare of forecasting, inventory management, production planning, and after-sales service support for several products stocked in various distribution outlets and sold to different customer segments in multiple countries. Therefore, the goal of supply chain management is moving from the standard of creating more efficient exchanges to that of a full communications network, as seen with our opening look at Zara, among all the links in the chain. In the network model, buyers and sellers in the chain can decide to share long-term forecasting, demand, procurement, logistics, and inventory information. More advanced relationships even let links in the chain work together on product development and business planning.

This change in outlook—from cost-driven supply chain optimization to customer-driven supply chain management—also changes key performance indicators. The traditional metric of successful global supply chain management centered on reducing material and administration costs. Now, however, the operational necessity and strategic value of close relationships with fellow supply chain links makes profitable performance a function of speedy and accurate transactions, real-time data exchange, better inventory control, and enduring alliances. For instance, the Lee Hung Fat Garment Factory of Hong Kong supplies apparel to about 60 companies in Europe. Its use of e-business tools lets it display images and specifications of its entire product line on its Web site. Customers, such as Kingfisher of the United Kingdom, can tinker with these HTML files and transmit their preferred product specs to Hong Kong. Lee Hung Fat can then make exactly what the distributors want. Buyers then rely on their Web access to check on order status, thereby letting them develop better delivery schedules, distribution arrangements, and retail restocks.

The Vital Role of Information

Information technologies, particularly recent trends in the Internet, have given managers many tools to amplify the idea of global supply chain management. The arrival of open, real-time communication among designers, suppliers, subcontractors, manufacturers, distributors, and customers lets managers, whether selling clothes for Zara or transformers for GE, change the supply chain from a simple, linear chain of buyer and seller into a global network of prospective buyers and sellers (see Figure 7.6). Linked through cyberspace, different points in the network can take the lead while interested participants help as they see fit. Collectively, these conditions compel cost effectiveness and customer responsiveness among the various links.

Although a global supply chain network can be quite broad, the coordination of the network takes place through specific interactions between firms in the network. Therefore, the attraction of information technology (including the Internet) in global supply chain management is that it helps automate and

Figure 7.6

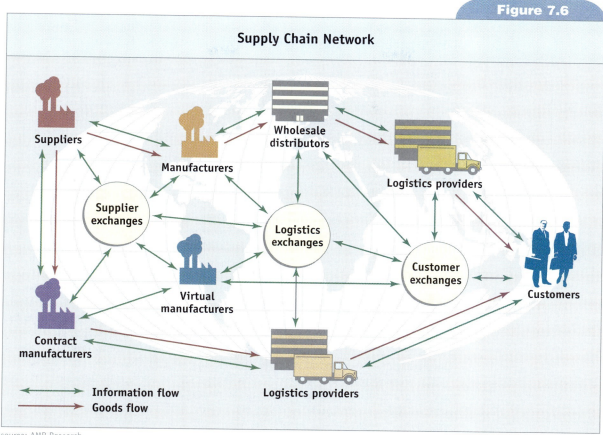

Supply Chain Network

Suppliers
Manufacturers
Wholesale distributors
Logistics providers
Supplier exchanges
Logistics exchanges
Customer exchanges
Customers
Virtual manufacturers
Contract manufacturers
Logistics providers

Information flow
Goods flow

source: AMR Research.

speed up internal processes in a company, as well as spreads efficiency and effectiveness gains to its customers and suppliers. For example, many attribute the growing power of six-sigma control programs to e-business tools; transferring responsibility to, say, complete an online purchase order to the supplier or customer reduces the odds that an employee will enter data incorrectly.

It is important to note that turning the traditional buy-make-move-store-sell cycle into an intricate network requires more than just Internet-enabling existing global supply management systems. Ultimately, information technology is a tool that gives managers the chance to see the company's supply chain in terms of the inner workings of several tiers of suppliers, distributors, and other partners, even when those partners are halfway around the world. For example, Dell Computer has a factory in Ireland that supplies custom-built PCs all over Europe. Customers can transmit orders to Dell via call centers or Dell's Web site. The company relays the demand for components to its suppliers, which Dell dictates must be within a 15-minute drive of its factory. Trucks deliver the components to the factory and haul off the completed computers within a few hours. Dell has established an **extranet** for its suppliers—a linkage to Dell's information system via the Internet—so that they can organize production and delivery of parts to Dell when needed. Dell uses the Internet to plug its suppliers into its customer database so that they can keep track of changes in demand. It also uses the Internet to plug customers into the ordering process and allows them to track the progress of their order from the factory to their doorstep.[10]

Potential Weak Links in the Global Supply Chain

Trying to link all the players in the global supply chain is particularly vulnerable to two types of threats. The first stems from operational problems, the second from strategic issues.

Operational Threats

MNEs often run into problems trying to get the various links of their global supply chains to talk to each other. Communication challenges arise from synchronizing languages across the global supply chain. A flow of parts from the Far East to South America to their ultimate stop in the United States, for instance, creates many possible points of miscommunication. In principle, companies can insist on browser-based communications on the Internet. However, this option still has a way to go before it becomes a reality. European companies, for instance, have widely adopted EDIFACT as the basis of electronic communications interface. In the United States, this interface is largely limited to large manufacturers and their first-tier suppliers—for example, Wal-Mart and Procter & Gamble. Some groups champion the language protocol of the World Wide Web, specifically hypertext markup or XML, as the best global standard. So far, though, there is no agreement on the standards of business exchange. Besides communications, differences in currencies and in measurement systems (metric versus decimal) can create weak links among globally dispersed suppliers.

While these are tough issues, it is unlikely that they will interfere too much for very long with MNEs' supply chains. The rewards of better supply chain management will spur communications and accounting standards, either by a major company with an innovative product (as Microsoft did with Windows) or negotiated by an international institution (as the WTO has done with trade barriers).

Strategic Challenges

Operational threats create tough day-to-day problems. National cultures, technology capabilities, and tax policies pose greater challenges to the strategic performance of global supply chain management.

National Cultures

The globalization of supply chains pushes managers to understand foreign cultures. For example, the performance of even the simplest supply chain depends on each link meeting a specified timetable. Companies in Western countries generally see deadlines as firm promises of delivery. Other cultures, however, see deadlines as guidelines with flexible end dates. Trying to run a global supply chain without preparing for these operational gaps can weaken links among partners and product flows.

National cultures can also impose higher hurdles. For example, different cultures disagree over how much information a company should share with its suppliers. Western cultures typically foster adversarial positions in which the zero-sum relationship between buyer and seller—whether it be GM and the United Auto Workers, or the auto dealership and the prospective car buyer—spurs each to share as little as possible with the other. Companies in other cultures follow different paths. For instance, Toyota requires a broad understanding of a potential supplier's manufacturing capabilities and financial position before it will create a supply link. Toyota says that there is a high degree of risk and high cost of failure if one of its suppliers fails to meet a commitment. Since Toyota retains sole responsibility to the ultimate customer, it believes it must insist on a lot of trust and open communication to ensure quality and reasonable risk with potential suppliers. Generally, this requirement is difficult for non-Japanese companies, which are not used to providing such detailed information to customers and, in some cases, potential competitors.

Technology Capabilities
Presently, the world does not operate on a common technology platform or communications protocol. The gaps show up particularly in the availability of the Internet in different nations of the world (see Figure 7.7). In general, North America is at least five years ahead of some countries in Europe, especially Southern Europe. Many parts of the world, particularly those nations that supply raw materials and inexpensive labor, are far from being wired into the global economy. Therefore, an immense challenge in global supply chain management is dealing with the fact that while some buyer–seller networks can be managed through the Internet, others—especially in emerging markets—cannot because of the lack of technology.

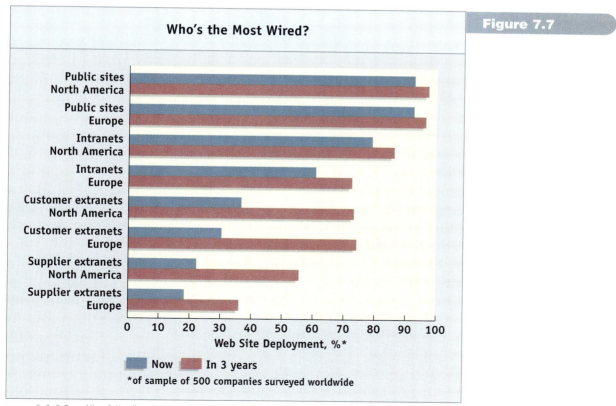

Figure 7.7

Who's the Most Wired?

Web Site Deployment, %*

- Now
- In 3 years

*of sample of 500 companies surveyed worldwide

source: E. J. & Booz Allen & Hamilton.

Although the Internet will ultimately revolutionize communications across all levels of the global supply chain, this will occur at different speeds in different nations and regions. During this transition, MNEs will need to think about how they can leverage e-business initiatives to benefit everyone in the global supply chain no matter where they happen to call home. Presently, MNEs are developing segmentation strategies for supply chain partners that cannot participate in e-business; some are creating several strategies—one for high-tech partners, one for low-tech, and one for no-tech.

Tax Policy

The spread of global supply chains raises significant taxation issues. Each nation has a sovereign right to tax the growth of value that takes place within its borders. Intricately linking supply chains, by giving a company great freedom to configure its employees and facilities, complicates the matters of tax jurisdiction and liability. That is, an MNE must carefully configure its physical operations to create the best possible corporate tax footprint. If it does not, it can inadvertently get hit with an otherwise avoidable high tax payment in a nation with aggressive taxation policies. Making matters worse is figuring out where along the global supply chain an MNE might possibly owe taxes. Some countries declare that taxable value growth occurs where the product is physically made, whereas others say that it occurs where the financing originated or even where the ideas started. Finally, companies that create extensive links with foreign supplies have to avoid unwittingly assuming liability for their partners' tax bills.

The Strategy of Making and Moving Products: Important Moderators

This chapter shows that many issues shape how a company designs a global manufacturing strategy or decides how it wants to manage its global supply chain. Issues such as inventory management, supplier relations, purchasing functions, foreign trade zones, and transportation infrastructures shape managers' decision making. You may want to explore these specialized areas in more detailed sources. To get you started, we will look at outsourcing, sourcing strategy, supplier relations, and purchasing management.

Outsourcing

Throughout the manufacturing and supply chain, managers continually struggle with deciding which activities to perform inside the company and which activities to subcontract to independent companies. This decision is interchangeably referred to as **outsourcing** or "make versus buy." In general, outsourcing decisions boil down to that popular recommendation, "Do what you do best and outsource the rest." Presently, North America leads the world in outsource spending, representing 39 percent of the global total, followed by Asia at 31 percent and Europe at 25 percent.

A company that makes and moves products around the world benefits from outsourcing in several ways. Outsourcing allows both small and large companies to go international by reducing the up-front costs of expansion and speeding the time to foreign markets. Most important, outsourcing encourages a company to work on what it does best. No company, regardless of its size or sophistication, can possibly hope to be the best in the world in every aspect of its operation.

Tough international competition, however, means that none can afford to be anything less then the best in at least one activity. This stark reality leads many MNEs to create for themselves a network of specialized providers that are themselves the best in the world at what they do. Nike, for example, is a world-class design and marketing company with little expertise or interest in actually manufacturing shoes. Nike, therefore, does not own any factories but instead has decided to be a virtual manufacturer and outsource all of its shoe production to those that do the best job for the lowest cost. Similarly, DuPont is a leading maker of chemicals with no particular expertise in

information technology. Therefore, in the late 1990s, DuPont outsourced all of its information technology management to Computer Science Corporation and Arthur Andersen. German automaker Porsche similarly outsourced its entire data management function. As these examples show, the idea of outsourcing echoes the theory of comparative advantage. Different companies in the global supply chain, by the very nature of their business strategy, have developed the people, processes, and technologies to deliver the same- or higher-quality services at comparatively lower costs than any individual customer can on its own.

In deciding whether to outsource, MNEs look at the pieces of their global manufacturing configuration and supply chain to identify those activities that are crucial to the company's strategy and that they have distinctive competency at doing. Managers can then outsource those nonvital activities to suppliers that do them better. Less directly, companies can also use outsourcing as an implied threat to underperforming employees that if they do not improve their productivity, the company will move its business elsewhere.[11] In determining whether to make or buy, the MNE needs to determine the design and manufacturing capabilities of potential suppliers compared to its own capabilities. If the supplier has a clear advantage, management needs to decide what it would cost to catch up to the best supplier and whether it would make sense to do so. Whatever the motivation, the purpose of outsourcing is to leverage a core competency for a sharper competitive edge in global markets.

Sourcing Strategies

Outsourcing activities to fellow supply chain links in the home country enables companies to avoid numerous problems, including those connected with language differences, technology gaps, exchange rate risks, strikes, politics, tariffs, and complex transportation channels. However, many companies cannot find domestic sources that can compete with foreign sources, as exemplified by Nike's reliance on Far Eastern workers to make its shoes. Generally, MNEs in this situation opt for one of three sourcing strategies.

Vertical Integration
In **vertical integration,** the MNE owns most of, if not the entire, global supply chain. ExxonMobil gives a good example of this sourcing strategy. It owns and con-

While the city of Hong Kong slumbers in the distance, it's business as usual at the Hong Kong International Terminal, the world's busiest container port. Ships come and go as stevedores and gantries work around the clock to import and export an endless flow of goods. Notwithstanding companies' strategies and managers' ambitions, the performance of global manufacturing and supply chains depends on these sorts of transportation facilities to move goods from producers to consumers.

trols all oil-related activities in its global supply chain, beginning with ownership of oil fields and finishing up with control of thousands of gas stations around the world. The guiding philosophy of this sourcing strategy is, "We buy what we cannot make." Vertical integration usually results in lower materials costs but higher administrative expenses and less flexibility. More significantly, this sourcing strategy lets a firm closely guard its proprietary product and process technology.

Arm's-Length Purchase

The second sourcing strategy is the arm's-length purchase from outside suppliers. In this situation, the company seeks the best possible deal from independent parties with no formal expectation that the current supply relationship will continue past the present deal. This sourcing strategy is common among entrepreneurs and companies that may need occasional assistance making or moving products internationally. Generally, the parties in an arm's-length transaction do not tell each other more than the other needs to know. Over time, if a continuing relationship develops, this sourcing strategy may progress from simple outsourcing to instituting a formal link in each company's global supply chain.

Some MNEs are moving in this direction already, setting up different classes of suppliers, such as "strategic suppliers" for critical materials, smaller "key suppliers," and a larger number of nonessential suppliers. It is with the strategic suppliers that the company strives to build partnerships that extend beyond delivering high-quality goods or services. It assigns each supplier demanding standards for costs, timing, and quality but, in return, may invite such suppliers along to visit customers to discuss product design, help them fund new technology, and allow them to operate from its own site. In any event, the guiding philosophy of this sourcing strategy is simply, "We make what we cannot buy."

Network Sourcing

The third sourcing strategy is a network in which formally interdependent suppliers work together to manage the flow of goods and services along the entire value-added chain.[12] This sourcing strategy is often modeled after the Japanese **keiretsu** or Korean **chaebol** networks. Both a keiretsu and a chaebol use intricate patterns of minority and majority cross-ownership among crucial links in the global supply chain. The resulting network is then made up of companies that are nominally independent but informally and intentionally interdependent. Keiretsu member companies essentially act as mutual support groups, providing markets and financial support for one another.

There is a growing belief, based on the performance of companies such as Dell, Toyota, and Zara, that this sourcing strategy is a competitive necessity for globally dispersed MNEs. The thinking is that a network sourcing strategy lets a company rely on fewer suppliers. Buying more from fewer companies generally means higher volumes for those suppliers, which ought to encourage them to lower their processing time and prices. For example, Toyota relies on about 150 parts suppliers, versus the 500 to 1,000 suppliers typical for other European automakers, to stock its British auto operations.[13]

Supplier Relations

When Honda redesigned the Accord, it sent its engineers to 33 key subcontractors in Japan and 28 in the United States, which together make parts that represent 60 to 70 percent of the car's value. The purpose of the visits was to reduce manufacturing costs by soliciting suggestions on parts designs. Because of supplier inputs and other efforts at cost control, Honda was able to reduce the cost of components and not increase the price of the new model.[14]

If an MNE decides to outsource or to set up a network of strategic suppliers, a crucial decision is simply how it wants to work with its suppliers. Linking a range of business activities among different companies leaves little margin for error. Managers must actively review their relationships and even offer specialized training and development to each other. Toyota, for instance, set up the Toyota Production System to work with its suppliers. Essentially, Toyota sends a team of manufacturing experts to each of its key suppliers to observe how the supplier organizes its factory, makes its parts, and moves them along the supply chain. The Toyota team then advises the supplier on ways to cut costs and boost quality. For example, Toyota approached Bumper Works, a small 100-person factory in Illinois, and asked its management to design and manufacture an auto bumper that would meet Toyota's rigid manufacturing and delivery specifications. After demonstrating that it could satisfy Toyota, Bumper Works became the sole supplier for that company's U.S. facilities. However, Toyota did not stop there. It told Bumper Works that it expected annual price reductions, higher-quality bumpers, and on-time deliveries or else it would eventually find another supplier. The switching costs of jumping from one supplier to another moved Toyota to further help Bumper Works to meet the rising standards. As an example, Toyota advised Bumper Works on how to install lean production systems so that it could more rapidly change the dies in its metal-stamping process in order to create the production flexibility that Toyota required for different types of bumpers.

It is also common for Toyota to identify two suppliers for each part or service and have the suppliers compete aggressively with each other on Toyota-set standards. The supplier that performs the best gets more business from Toyota, as well as a better competitive position in its industry. However, even the "loser" earns some rewards. The great effort that Toyota expends to set up its global supply chain encourages it to continue its relationship with both suppliers. Moreover, Toyota knows that the winning supplier cannot now rest on its laurels; its competitor is working hard to reclaim the lost business.[15]

The Purchasing Function

The purchasing agent is the link between the company's outsourcing decision and its supplier relationships. Just as companies go through stages of globalization, so too does the purchasing agent's scope of responsibilities evolve over time. Typically, purchasing goes through four phases: (1) domestic purchasing only, (2) foreign buying based on need, (3) foreign buying as part of an international procurement strategy, and (4) integration of the global procurement strategy.[16] Generally, phase 4 occurs when the company realizes the benefits from integration and coordination of purchasing on a global basis and is most applicable to the MNE as opposed to, say, the occasional exporter. When purchasing becomes this global, MNEs often face a dilemma over the right balance of global centralization versus local decentralization. More precisely, MNEs must resolve whether to allow each subsidiary to make all purchasing decisions or to centralize all or some of the such decisions. The primary benefits of local decentralization include increased production facility control over purchases, better responsiveness to facility needs, and more effective use of local suppliers. The primary benefits of global centralization include increased leverage with suppliers, getting better prices, eliminating administrative duplication, allowing purchasers to develop specialized knowledge in purchasing techniques, reducing the number of orders processed, and enabling purchasing to build solid supplier relationships.[17]

There are five major sourcing strategies that companies pursue as they move into phases 3 and 4 mentioned above (foreign buying as part of procurement strategy and integration of global procurement strategy): (1) assign domestic buyer(s) for international purchasing; (2) use foreign subsidiaries or business agents; (3) establish international purchasing offices; (4) assign the responsibility for global sourcing to a specific business unit or units; and (5) integrate and coordinate worldwide sourcing.[18]

These strategies move from the simple to the more complex in much the same way that a company typically internationalizes its activities. Companies start by using a domestic buyer and progress all the way to integrating and coordinating worldwide sourcing into their purchasing decisions so that there is no difference between domestic and foreign sources. Whatever system a company opts to use, the key is for managers to select the best supplier, establish a solid relationship, and continually evaluate the supplier's performance to ensure the best price, quality, and on-time delivery.

Summary

Making and moving products around the world is ground zero of international business operations. It is where the company must transform its global strategic intent into building a production and supply network that can meet its goals. Historically, an MNE aiming to serve foreign markets began by exporting products from its large home-market plants. As the importance of worldwide markets increased, MNEs typically opened manufacturing facilities abroad. Now, however, trends in globalization, technology, and trade have altered this game. MNEs increasingly find that they need to think more innovatively about compatibility, configuration, coordination, and control of their global manufacturing to take advantage of market differences, drive down costs, and build better competitive capabilities.

Besides the heightened risks and returns of the global manufacturing strategy, MNEs realize that this is only half the equation. Success, whether defined narrowly as lower costs or broadly as superior competitive capabilities, depends on innovatively managing global supply chains to offer the right product in the right place at the right time for the right price. Steady improvements in communications technology continue to ease the flow of information worldwide. The increasing use of the Internet to establish extranet connections with suppliers and customers gives aggressive MNEs the flexibility to establish supplier networks that will improve business quality, delivery time, and consumer responsiveness. Companies will be able to choose from a wider array of suppliers, and suppliers can be more responsive to consumers by getting the right product to the right production link at the right time. Said Andy Grove, the chairman of Intel, in 1999, "In five years' time, all companies will be Internet companies, or they won't be companies at all."[19]

As companies study their core competencies, they will have to decide if they want to be in the manufacturing business, like Zara, or outsource their manufacturing, as does Gap. Whichever strategy they adopt, none is excused from designing a stronger global supply chain management system. Efforts under way around the world, from Dell in the United States to Porsche in

Germany, Toyota in Japan, and Zara in Spain, show that companies are findings ways to improve their global supply chain management by rethinking their ideas about outsourcing, sourcing strategies, supplier relations, and purchasing management. Imaginative ideas in these frontiers will give innovators great rewards and, over time, a crowd of emulators.

endnotes

[1] Jane Folpe, "Zara Has a Made-to-Order Plan for Success," *Fortune,* September 4, 2000, p. 80, www.inditex.com; Leslie Crawford, "Inside Track: Putting on the Style with Rapid Response," *Financial Times Limited,* September 26, 2000, p. 17; and William Echikson, "The Mark of Zara," *Business Week,* May 29, 2000, p. 98.

[2] Paul M. Swamidass, "A Comparison of the Plant Location Strategies of Foreign and Domestic Manufacturers in the U.S.," *Journal of International Business Studies,* second quarter 1990, p. 302.

[3] Stanley E. Fawcett and Anthony S. Roath, "The Viability of Mexican Production Sharing: Assessing the Four Cs of Strategic Fit," *Urbana,* Vol. 3, No. 1, 1996, p. 29.

[4] "Johnson & Johnson to Realign Its Global Manufacturing Network and Take After Tax Charge of $800 Million Against Fourth Quarter Earnings," www.johnsonandjohnson.com/news_finance/41.htm, retrieved April 1, 2001.

[5] Forrester Research survey of 50 global manufacturing executives, reported in Navi Radjou, "Deconstruction of the Supply Chain," *Supply Chain Management Review,* November–December 2000.

[6] To help make sense of the cluster notion, think of structural aspects of the U.S. economy. Prominent economic clusters include Silicon Valley for high technology, New York for financial services, and Los Angeles for entertainment. Less visible clusters include furniture in North Carolina, pharmaceuticals in New Jersey, and aircraft design for Seattle.

[7] Council of Logistics Management, clm1.org, retrieved August 27, 2000.

[8] "Energizing the Supply Chain," *The Review,* Deloitte & Touche, January 17, 2000, p. 1.

[9] Ibid.

[10] Ibid., p. 11.

[11] John McMillan, "Managing Suppliers: Incentive Systems in Japanese and U.S. Industry," *California Management Review,* summer 1990, p. 38.

[12] Russell Johnston and Paul R. Lawrence, "Beyond Vertical Integration—The Rise of the Value-Adding Partnership," *Harvard Business Review,* July–August 1988, p. 98.

[13] Ibid.

[14] Karen Lowry Miller, Larry Armstrong, and David Woodruff, "A Car Is Born," *Business Week,* September 13, 1993, p. 68.

[15] Joseph B. White, "Japanese Auto Makers Help Parts Suppliers Become More Efficient," *Wall Street Journal,* September 10, 1991, p. 1.

[16] Robert M. Monczka and Robert J. Trent, "Worldwide Sourcing: Assessment and Execution," *International Journal of Purchasing and Materials Management,* fall 1992, pp. 4–5.

[17] Stanley E. Fawcett, "The Globalization of the Supply Environment," *The Supply Environment,* Vol. 2 (Tempe, AZ: NAPM, 2000); Frank Dubois, Brian Toyne, and Michael D. Oliff, "International Manufacturing Strategies of U.S. Multinationals," *Journal of International Business Studies,* Vol. 24, No. 2, 1993, pp. 313–314.

[18] Monczka and Trent, pp. 17–18.

[19] "The Net Imperative," in "Business and the Internet: A Survey," *Economist,* June 26, 1999.

Objectives

1. To understand how companies develop unifying product policies to serve foreign markets

2. To realize the contingencies that complicate implementing a consistent pricing policy for international markets

3. To recognize the conditions that challenge promoting a product in foreign markets

4. To understand the idea of brand management in foreign markets

5. To appreciate how companies develop the competencies to distribute products to customers spread around the world

Wal-Mart Climbs Walls Overseas

Begun in 1962 in Rogers, Arkansas, Wal-Mart had grown into a nearly $200-billion-a-year retail empire by 2000. Many linked Wal-Mart's success to its terrific execution of some straightforward ideas about distribution, pricing, product availability, and merchandising in honoring its promise to sell things for less at everyday low prices (the so-called EDLP strategy). Wal-Mart's growth has taken it far from Rogers. By 2000, the company served more than 100 million customers weekly in all 50 United States along with Puerto Rico, Canada, China, Mexico, Brazil, Germany, the United Kingdom, Argentina, and South Korea. Overall, Wal-Mart has done well abroad. However, like most companies, it has faced challenges to marketing its vision of "Wal-Mart Discount City: We sell for Less" around the world.

For instance, Wal-Mart entered Argentina and Brazil in late 1995. At that time, Wal-Mart planned to give consumers in these countries the benefits of quality goods for lower prices with American-style service and convenience. Upon the announcement of South American expansion, the company's then chief executive officer said that this decision "reflects our belief that consumers throughout Argentina and Brazil are like consumers everywhere in their desire for high value and wide assortment. We look forward to a long and growing relationship." Still, Wal-Mart's marketing message of "Hometown USA" triggered local resentment. In Argentina, customers questioned Wal-Mart's decision to overlook local norms and customs; for example, Wal-Mart chose not to change the format of its hypermarkets to fit local preferences for the comfort of smaller *tiendas*.

Wal-Mart ran into different challenges in Germany. In 1998, it bought Wertkauf-Mann, a $1.4-billion-a-year retailer in Germany. This acquisition made Wal-Mart a leading hypermarket operator in the country. Wal-Mart immediately began installing the unique mix of marketing practices that defined its tried-and-true low-cost strategy. These practices, particularly the EDLP tactic, sparked marketing controversies. Notably, in mid-1999, Wal-Mart triggered a price war that quickly drew in the German-based store operators Aldi and Lidl.

International Marketing

chapter **8**

Spaniards wear silk hoods
during a Semana Santa
Procession in Cordoba, Spain.

German officials, under pressure from other retailers, intervened. In late 2000, the German Cartel Office said the price war threatened the survival of smaller stores, adding that a policy of regularly selling basic foodstuffs for less than cost could force smaller rivals out of business and pave the way for higher prices in the future. The Cartel Office stated that "the material benefit to consumers is marginal and temporary, but the restriction of competition by placing unfair obstacles before medium-sized retailers is clear and lasting." Wal-Mart conceded that it would change its prices to comply with German law. Wal-Mart's German headquarters stated, "We understand and recognize the decision taken by the Cartel Office today and will orient our pricing in line with these recommendations." Still, Wal-Mart noted that it remained "committed to lowering the cost of living in Germany by offering our customers the best quality products at the lowest possible prices."[1]

Introduction

This chapter looks at the topic of international marketing. Generally, similar marketing principles are in play in domestic and foreign markets. However, environmental differences often prod managers to carry out these principles differently abroad. Therefore, in this chapter, we will examine how managers analyze national markets around the world and apply international product, pricing, promotion, and distribution strategies—the so-called marketing mix—in foreign markets. Figure 8.1 spotlights these issues and their key relationships.

Product Policy

General marketing texts propose a range of product policies. By default, however, these texts tend toward analyzing product policies within the setting of a single national market. The play of international business, on the other hand, complicates many of these issues. Table 8.1 gives a sense of these issues in listing some of the questions that marketers must ask prior to launching a product internationally. This section of the chapter studies these questions and highlights the international application of common product policies in the form of a production, sales, customer, strategic marketing, or societal marketing orientation.

Production Orientation

Companies that focus primarily on aspects of their production process, such as efficiency or high quality, usually do not develop elaborate international marketing programs. Typically, a production orientation leads to a slight analysis of the needs of foreign consumers. Rather, companies applying this policy assume customers simply want lower prices or higher quality in the belief that if you build a cheaper or better mousetrap, people will beat a path to your door. Often, companies following this product policy carry out "marketing" efforts in the following ways:

Figure 8.1

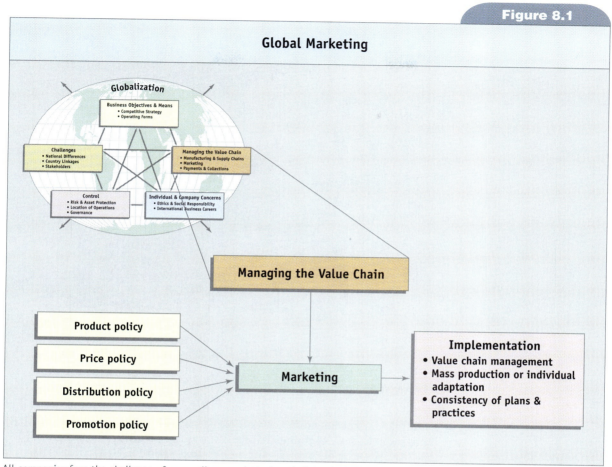

Global Marketing

All companies face the challenge of persuading people to buy their product. International business greatly complicates this challenge. Companies adapt their marketing plans for differences in consumer preferences, market situations, and legal conditions around the world.

- **Commodity Sales.** Companies typically sell raw materials (like oil) and agricultural commodities (such as sugar) based on price, under the doctrine that many consumers believe that oil is oil and sugar is sugar. The fact that there is universal demand for such products reduces the incentive to try to differentiate them with elaborate customary marketing tools. Instead, commodity producers tend to invest in business-to-business marketing by providing innovative financing and guaranteeing timely delivery of high-quality supplies.

- **Passive Exports.** Some companies view export as a nonstrategic dimension of their firm. Foreign sales are seen as a way to reduce excess inventory or stabilize production scheduling—or as something to do when there is free time to worry about it. Companies following this policy are called passive exporters. They see little value in modifying their established production scheme to adapt their products to foreign consumers' preferences.

Figure 8.2

"It's a whole different world over here, isn't it?"

source: © The New Yorker Collection 2000, Jack Ziegler from cartoonbank.com. All Rights Reserved.

■ **Parallel Market Segments.** A company may develop a product aimed at large segments of its domestic market and then find there are smaller market segments abroad willing to buy that product. Sometimes the product may have universal appeal, such as French champagne. At other times, a company may target a mass market at home and niche markets abroad; a leading example is U.S. bourbon producers, which sell to a large domestic market but small niche markets elsewhere in the world.

Table 8.1

International Product Policy: Issues to Consider

- What foreign markets use the same or a similar product?
- What foreign needs can the product satisfy?
- Should we modify the domestic version of the product for overseas markets?
- Should we develop a new product for overseas markets?
- What specific product features, such as design, size, color, packaging, brand name, and warranty, should we give the product?
- Do we have the necessary service and repair capability?

Sales Orientation

This product policy works in the company that tries to sell abroad the same product it sells in the home market. A sale orientation, therefore, takes for granted that consumers at home and abroad share overlapping product preferences. Although similar, this orientation does differ from a production orientation, principally in that it endorses an active approach to finding international sales but does not spur a firm to modify its established production scheme. A company with a sales orientation usually asks questions such as: "Should we send some exports abroad?" and "Where can we sell more of product X?" In effect, the product and manufacturing process are held constant while the sales location is allowed to change.

Overall, this product policy has a spotty performance record. There are successful examples of companies transferring products abroad, such as the Pokémon product line, with little or no research on the wants of foreign consumers. Experience shows that this approach is particularly successful when companies target image-conscious consumers. On the other hand, companies suffer product failures overseas when foreign buyers do not behave like domestic buyers or simply turn a deaf ear to heavy sales efforts telling them they ought to use this product.

Customer Orientation

A customer orientation poses a direct question: What product can we sell to consumers in country X? Unlike the production- and sales-oriented product policies, a customer orientation reasons that the product design and manufacturing process can be set up to make the distinct products that customers in a foreign market will buy. This product policy, as odd as it may sound, follows managers' intent to work in those foreign countries that have a particular mix of customer preferences and market conditions. As with the production orientation, a company using a customer orientation may deal with foreign markets passively by simply serving consumers who behave like its traditional customers. Or, a company can actively seek potential overseas customers who likely will parallel the purchasing preferences of its customary domestic customers.

Increasingly, companies urge their purchasing agents to set product specifications and then solicit the expertise of a foreign manufacturer. For example, the Hong Kong company S. T. King makes clothing to the exact specifications of companies such as Calvin Klein. In responding to foreign product requests, a company may make a product that differs markedly from what it sells domestically. In such cases, the supplier depends on the buyer to determine precisely what the ultimate customers are willing to buy and to bear the risk if they in fact do not do so. The supplier is concerned only with making and shipping what other companies believe they can sell in other nations.

Strategic Marketing Orientation

Companies committed to consistent foreign sales often adopt a strategy that coherently combines aspects of the production, sales, and consumer orientations. These companies see international business as a vital part of their current growth and long-term profitability. Managers, therefore, work hard to figure out how to adapt their current product policy for overseas markets in ways that directly build on the company's distinctive capabilities and are compatible with its current marketing mix. For example, breweries such as Heineken, Stroh, Bass, and Lion, facing alcohol prohibition in Saudi Arabia, turned to making nonalcoholic beer and marketing it as a malt beverage in this market.[2] While officially a new product, the malt beverage did not require these companies to extensively change their production processes. Furthermore, this product policy let them tap into their strategic intent to sell products internationally, as well as to respond directly to the particular needs of a foreign customer segment.

Societal Marketing Orientation

Companies implementing a societal marketing orientation act on the belief that meaningful international marketing requires prudent consideration of potential environmental, health, social, and work-related problems that may arise when selling a product abroad. The growing global consciousness of groups such as consumer associations, political parties, labor unions, environmental activists, and nongovernmental organizations has led them to express aggressively their opinion of companies' product policies. They contend that companies have a moral obligation to deal with the social consequence of how consumers purchase and dispose of their products. If these practices are socially destructive, then companies should figure out socially desirable options.

For example, about one-third of the world's population—or approximately 2 billion people—have no electricity in their homes. The biggest challenge is the high cost of constructing major power plants near their homes. Moreover, environmental groups question whether there will be adequate future supplies of fossil fuels and argue that burning fossil fuels to generate electricity simply creates too much pollution. These concerns have sparked investments in solar power research that has yielded marketable products to fill electricity gaps in developing countries. These products include small-scale solar panels to provide electricity to homes in Brazil, herders' tents in Tibet, and mobile refrigeration units atop camels in the deserts of Somalia.

Reasons for Product Alteration

In theory, every company has the option to follow its preferred product policy. In reality, though, its choice may be either a terrific idea or utterly impossible. Legal, cultural, and economic conditions in a particular nation can force a company to alter its products in ways that it never intended or even imagined.

Legal Reasons

Legal requirements may obligate companies to modify products for foreign markets. Legal stipulations vary widely by country, but most are meant to protect consumers and the environment. Regarding consumers, almost all governments regulate pharmaceuticals and food products in terms of purity, testing, and labeling. Some consumer protections are

Marketing takes many forms around the world, from famed shopping zones, like the Ginza in Tokyo and Rodeo Drive in Los Angeles, to open-air market stalls in Puno, Peru. The photo of the latter shows vendors who have tailored the presentation of single items and mix of indigenous and foreign products to fit the circumstances of their local market.

country specific. Automobiles sold in the United States, for instance, must meet safety and pollution standards not found in many other countries. Similarly, environmental regulation is growing. Presently, many nations focus on commanding companies to adjust their packaging to formats that do not harm the environment. Some countries prohibit certain types of containers, such as Denmark's ban on aluminum cans. Other countries restrict the volume of packaging materials to save resources and decrease trash. For instance, exporters of Scotch whiskey to Germany must remove the bottles from the cardboard box before shipment. There also are differences in national requirements as to whether containers must be reusable and whether companies must use packaging materials that can be recycled, incinerated, or composted.

In the event that legal requirements in foreign markets are less stringent than domestic ones, a company may not be legally obligated to alter its products for foreign sale. Nonetheless, the company in this situation must still weigh whether the cost of complying with its domestic standards in overseas markets is more or less than the cost of possible domestic or foreign backlash. Some multinational enterprises (MNEs) have run into domestic criticism for selling products in foreign markets, such as toys, automobiles, contraceptives, and pharmaceuticals, that did not meet home-country safety or quality standards.

Legal reasons for product modification are a recurring point of controversy. The basis of law in a nation's normative values paves the way for widely different views of the right thing to do. A popular solution, from the perspective of business, is to develop international product standards that take precedence over national legal requirements. Although countries have reached agreement on some products (such as technical standards for mobile phones and bar codes to identify products), standards for other products (railroad gauges, power supplies, and shapes of electrical sockets) still vary.

Economic Reasons

The world, despite efforts to promote prosperity for all, has an unbalanced distribution of income and wealth. Thus, to make the obvious point, if foreign consumers lack sufficient income, then they are usually unable to buy many products that are routinely sold in wealthier nations. An MNE, if it intends to reach these large market segments, must design less expensive versions or develop alternative products that satisfy the same need for a lower price. Regarding the former, Mattel has been unable to sell enough Holiday Barbie dolls in some foreign countries because its prices are too high. In recourse, Mattel is developing lower-priced dolls for those markets. Similarly, consumers in many markets can afford to buy personal items only in small quantities, such as one aspirin, one piece of chewing gum, or one cigarette at a time. Companies have the option—or, some might argue, the moral obligation—to design new types of packaging that deal with such circumstances.

Even if a market segment has sufficient income to purchase the same product that the company sells in its home market, differences caused by the local infrastructure may demand product alterations. Emerging economies generally have poorer transportation and storage systems. Consequently, companies may gain advantages by selling products that can withstand rough terrain or power outages. In contrast, economic reasons can indirectly lead to product modifications in nations that have a great deal of wealth. Too few parking spaces, congested roadways, and high gas prices are enduring features of the Japanese infrastructure for automobiles. Hence, Japanese consumers prefer to buy small, maneuverable, fuel-efficient cars that cost less than big cars, SUVs, or pickup trucks.

Cultural Reasons

The buying behavior of consumers, whether they live in your hometown or in foreign markets, is complex. Far more often than not, marketing managers have a tough time understanding how the local culture shapes foreign consumers' interest in and willingness to buy different products. For example, Rubbermaid has found that most Americans like housewares in neutral blues or almond colors. The Dutch, though, like them in white, whereas Southern Europeans prefer them in red. Americans favor open-top wastebaskets, yet Europeans fancy tight lids. To be competitive, Rubbermaid has had to alter colors and lids from one national market to the next. Progress in understanding the attitudes and attributes of national culture, as we saw in Chapter 4, helps managers sort out these vexing product issues. Still, no matter how much we think we "know" about a foreign culture, it is an enduring wild card in devising the best product policy.

The Costs of Product Alteration

Some product alterations are a bargain to make yet greatly boost consumer demand in foreign markets. Most commonly, these changes involve product packaging. For example, in Panama, Aunt Jemima Pancake Mix and Ritz Crackers are sold in cans rather than boxes because of the high humidity—a low-cost change that has a high payoff. Before making a decision, marketing managers should always compare the cost of an alteration to the cost of lost sales from no alteration. For complicated industrial products, MNEs often try to balance pressures for global uniformity with those for local alteration by standardizing crucial components yet still tailoring some product features to local needs. Whirlpool, for example, captures production economies of scale by using the same basic compressor, casing, evaporator, and sealant system in refrigerators that it makes around the world. However, the company meets local needs for alterations through cost-effective modifications such as adapting doors and interior shelves to different national preferences.

Extent and Mix of the Product Line

Most companies produce a bundle of different products. However, it is highly unusual for each product in a multiproduct family to generate enough sales in a given foreign market to justify the cost of penetrating that market. Even if it possibly could, a company might offer only a limited portion of its product line, perhaps as an entry strategy. Therefore, making product-line decisions calls upon marketing managers to look at the possible effects on sales and the cost of having one successful product versus a family of moderately successful products. Finally, in the odd situation, a company may find it must produce and sell some low-margin products if it is to sell its more lucrative ones, such as sherry glasses to match crystal wine and water glasses.

If the foreign market is small compared to the domestic market, selling costs per unit may be excessive because of high fixed costs. In this situation, the company may try to reduce per-unit selling costs by broadening the scope of its product line, either by consolidating the product lines of several manufacturers or by developing new products for the local market that the same salesperson can haul. For example, Avon sells products in some countries that it does not offer in the United States to increase the average order per household, such as Crayola products in Brazil, Disney products in Mexico, and the *Reader's Digest* in Canada, Brazil, Australia, France, and New Zealand.

Pricing Policy

The question of the best price policy question traps an MNE on the horns of a dilemma. On the one hand, the price must be low enough to get people to buy the product; on the other, it must be high enough to generate the profits needed to pay for the expense of doing business along with a good rate of return. In theory, the "proper" price will not only assure short-term profits, but will also give the company the resources necessary to achieve long-term strategic goals. Pricing raises complex questions in foreign markets due to the influence of market conditions, political policies, environmental changes, and relationships among parts of the global supply chain. Table 8.2 identifies important issues to consider when devising a promotion policy for international markets. In the following pages, we will look at these and related issues.

Governmental Intervention

Every country has laws that affect the prices of consumer goods. At the most basic, governmental price controls can set either the maximum or minimum price for a product. Governments often design price regulations to prevent competitors from unfairly lowering their prices in an effort to bankrupt local rivals. As we saw in our opening discussion of Wal-Mart, Germany is particularly aggressive in policing MNEs' pricing policies. Besides monitoring the list price, the German government prohibits giveaways and discounts through coupon and box-top specials by a company unless these price promotions are a standard feature of the company's regular price policy. Also, to maintain an

---

Table 8.2

International Price Policy: Issues to Consider

- What is the "right" price to charge for our product in foreign markets?
- What type of pricing structure fits with our desired product position strategy—skimming, penetration, or cost-plus?
- Is our price competitive with the price of competing products in the foreign market?
- Should we offer foreign customers discounts (i.e., trade, cash, quantity) and allowances (advertising, trade-offs)?
- How should the firm price a product to make sure it fits with the price strategy of the total product line?
- Do foreign countries impose price regulations?
- Can we control potential price escalation in the export channel?
- Should we use different prices to reach different market segments?
- Do we have any pricing options in the event our costs unexpectedly change?
- Will foreign governments see the price of our products as fair or exploitative?

orderly market, Germany permits retailers to have sales only twice a year, once in summer and once in winter. By no means is Germany the exception. Japan, for example, prohibits retailers from offering large discounts, as well as bypassing sales tax—two conditions that especially challenge the price strategies of business-to-consumer companies on the Internet. A company accustomed to relying on particular types of pricing policies, therefore, must develop new methods when facing these and similar restrictions.

On the flip side, governments may set maximum prices for numerous products in order to give local consumers access to cheaper products. This policy can often backfire. Rather than lower its prices, an MNE may decide not to operate in that country. Over time, though, companies develop ways to escape the burden of price controls. An MNE can take direct steps, such as lowering the quality or reducing the size of the product but continuing to charge the same price. In this situation, a company will sometimes change the brand name of the modified product. Then, if price controls are eventually lifted, it can reintroduce the higher-quality, higher-priced product that consumers had associated with the original brand name.

Faced with MNEs they suspect of unfair price manipulation, governments can ask the World Trade Organization (WTO) to sanction trade regulations to halt these abuses. So far, the WTO has consistently ruled that nations have the inalienable right to restrict any import that comes in at a declared price below that charged to consumers in the exporting country. Although countries typically refrain from imposing onerous price restrictions, their ultimate power to do so is often enough of a threat to deter companies from distorting their prices. In many situations, companies hold the upper hand in setting prices because of the intrinsic flexibility of their operations. That is, access to more than one national market gives an MNE a lot of agility to search for the right price mix for a particular product. A company can often justifiably charge different prices in different countries because of competitive and demand factors. For instance, Levi sells its trademark denim jeans in Europe for more than twice the U.S. price due to different demand factors in the two markets.[3]

Greater Market Diversity

Companies often divide a single domestic market into different segments and then charge different prices for products sold within each segment. Country-to-country variations create even greater opportunities to tailor prices to fit distinct consumer segments. For example, companies can sell few sea urchins or tuna eyeballs in the United States at any price. However, they can easily export them to Japan, where they are high-priced delicacies. More commonly, MNEs often find themselves setting their price policies in markets in which they have either little or a lot of flexibility. In the case of the former, a company has to compete against many, well-managed rivals. Therefore, it has little freedom to set its preferred price but rather has to deal with the price range determined by the market. Other situations in some countries give the MNE a lot of price flexibility. Specifically, an MNE may derive pricing power from the particular stage of the product's life cycle, government-granted manufacturing rights not held by competitors, or proprietary brand image or product technology. Typically, MNEs in these situations apply one of the following price strategies:

- A *skimming price strategy* whereby the company charges a high price for a new product by aiming first at consumers eager for the product at any price. As sales slow in these segments, the MNE progressively lowers the price to generate demand in other consumer segments.

- A *penetration price strategy* whereby the company brings a product to the market with a remarkably low price in order to offer such an outstanding value that even an indifferent consumer will think about buying it. This strategy is especially popular in product markets in which the cost of the product is substantial and consumers are reluctant to switch to a new, unknown supplier. Thus, for example, Lexus's entry into the luxury car segment, Komatsu's entry into the global earthmoving equipment industry, and Dell's entry into the personal computer market saw each company charge penetration prices to take on the respective markets' leaders, Mercedes, Caterpillar, and Compaq.

- A *cost-plus price strategy* whereby a company sets its product pricing in terms of its particular financial goal. If, for instance, a company decides it must earn a return on investment of 10 percent, it would tally up its total investment, figure out what price yielded a 10 percent return, and then charge that price.

Price Escalation in Exporting

A major reason why pricing is more difficult internationally is inescapable price escalation through the global supply chain. Under any conditions, markups in the price of a product occur within distribution channels—because each seller along the supply chain wants to earn a fair return. Consequently, it will price its efforts into the product. Additional or inefficient links in a global supply chain, therefore, add expenses that increase the price to the final consumer.

Table 8.3 shows that international business is especially prone to this problem. Global supply chains usually span greater distances over many nations, and, if unchecked, include many links. Besides the costs of supply chain inefficiencies, price escalation can happen simply from the tariffs imposed by the various nations whose market the product passes through. The consequences of price escalation are straightforward. Presumably exportable products may turn out to be noncompetitive in overseas markets if companies use cost-plus pricing—which many do.[4] To become competitive in exporting, a company may have to sell its product to intermediaries at lower prices to reduce price run-ups. This situation, however, is gradually improving. Chapter 7 showed that global supply chains are becoming more efficient. Exporters' access to more complete supply information should improve their ability to manage their preferred price policy as their products head toward the consumer.

Currency Values and Price Changes

A recurring headache in managing pricing policy in foreign markets is floating exchange rates. No matter how well managers forecast market and currency trends, sudden changes or just making the wrong estimate can wreck a company's price strategy. For instance, the surprisingly steady decline of the euro, relative to the U.S. dollar, from its inception in 1999 through 2001 jumbled the pricing plans of many MNEs, including Gillette, Coca-Cola, Matsushita, and

Table 8.3

Sample Cost-Plus Calculation of Domestic vs. International Product Cost

		Domestic Sale	Export Sale
Factory price		10.00	10.00
Domestic freight		1.00	1.00
	Subtotal	11.00	11.00
Export documentation			.60
	Subtotal		11.60
Ocean freight and insurance			1.50
	Subtotal		13.10
Import duty (10% of landed cost)			1.31
	Subtotal		14.42
Wholesaler markup (20%)		2.20	2.82
	Subtotal	13.20	17.30
Importer markup (10%)			1.73
	Subtotal		19.03
Retail markup (50%)		6.60	9.51
Final consumer price		19.80	28.54

Sony. In any event, it is the job of marketing managers to devise pricing plans that assure the company of enough funds to replenish its inventory and still make a profit—even in the face of fluctuating currencies. If not, the company may end up making a "paper profit" while inadvertently liquidating itself. That is, what shows on paper as a profit may result from the company's failure to adjust its prices for declines in the value of the local currency while its products are traveling through its supply chain. For example, Peruvian inflation in the late 1980s forced Procter & Gamble (P&G) to raise its detergent prices 20 to 30 percent every two weeks. P&G also eliminated its 60-day free credit to retailers and began charging interest on 15- to 30-day payments.[5]

Companies have devised many ways to minimize the exposure of their price strategy to currency changes. Depending on competitive factors and governmental regulations, a company can stipulate in its sales contracts the price as an equivalency of a **hard currency.** For example, a U.S. manufacturer's sale of equipment to a company in Uruguay may specify that payment be made in dollars or in pesos at an equivalent price, in terms of dollars, at the time payment is made. Despite their best intentions, however, marketing managers face persistent pricing problems. For instance, frequent price increases to counteract currency fluctuations make it difficult for a company to quote prices in letters, brochures, or catalogs. Frequent price increases can also alter the company's preferred distribution outlet. For example, it is frequently difficult to make price increases in vending machine sales because of the need to reset machines and to come up with coins or tokens that correspond to the targeted increase in price.

Fixed Versus Variable Pricing

The extent to which manufacturers can or must fix their prices at the retail level varies substantially by country. Some countries try to impose price stability by limiting MNEs' ability to change their prices quickly—known as **fixed pricing.** For instance, Indian law, requires that soft drink bottlers print the product prices on the bottle or container rather than attach an easily changed price tag.[6] **Variable pricing** refers to situations whereby the price of the product is negotiated at the point of sale. There is substantial variation across nations in whether, where, and for what products consumers will bargain. For instance, in most mature industrial markets, consumers commonly bargain for automobiles, real estate, and large orders of industrial supplies, but not for everyday items such as goods bought at the grocery store. In contrast, consumers in other countries, such as Guatemala, ardently bargain over the price of food in traditional markets but accept at face value the fixed price of an automobile. Bargaining is much more prevalent in purchases from street vendors in India than in Singapore, whereas bargaining in high-priced specialty stores is more frequent in Singapore than in India. As such, laws and customs significantly shape companies' flexibility to set their preferred price policy.

The gap between fixed and variable pricing is changing as the Internet redefines price policies. At the least, the Internet provides extensive information on the prices of products from manufacturers. More significantly, a host of Web-based intermediaries independently track prices for virtually every product category. Too, shopping "bots" scour the World Wide Web for products and prices at your command. Finally, companies are setting up business-to-business net-based markets whereby they abandon fixed prices in favor of prices set through auctions. So far, the Internet has begun to change price policies in just a few nations. However, we can see these trends spreading as entrepreneurs and MNEs transfer these price tools to their management of global supply chains.

Retailers' Strength with Suppliers

In principle, dominant retailers can use their market power to exhort suppliers to offer them lower prices. This, in turn, lets them challenge each other for the rewarding status of being the lowest-cost retailer. In practice, though, retailers have struggled to transfer this domestic power to foreign markets. For example, Wal-Mart, Marks & Spencer, and Carrefour have tremendous influence in their domestic U.S., U.K., and French markets, respectively. However, each has been hard pressed to gain the same advantage when entering the other's dominant market.

We saw in our opening case, however, that Wal-Mart fights on. It is steadily transferring its U.S. clout around the world in the belief that its promise of "everyday low prices" is a message clearly understood in any language. Wal-Mart began its international expansion in 1991 when a Sam's Club opened near Mexico City. Two years later, Wal-Mart International was set up to oversee growing worldwide opportunities. This division currently employs more than

255,000 associates to staff over 1,000 stores in Argentina, Brazil, Canada, China, Germany, Korea, Mexico, Puerto Rico, and the United Kingdom. Its scale of international expansion, when combined with its immense U.S. retail base, is gradually positioning Wal-Mart to leverage its buying power around the world.

Promotion Policy

Promotion is the presentation of messages intended to help sell a good or service. The types of messages and the method of presentation may vary widely, depending on the company, product, and country of operation. Generally, MNEs manage this variety by coming up with the best possible solution to the questions of (1) the push versus pull mix, (2) standardization of advertising programs, (3) product branding, (4) language factors, and (5) brand acquisitions. Table 8.4 identifies important issues to consider when devising a promotion policy for international markets. We now review these issues.

The Push–Pull Mix

MNEs can use different forms of promotion to try to create demand for their products. In general, promotion is categorized as **push,** which uses direct selling techniques, or **pull,** which relies on mass media. For instance, companies applying a push marketing campaign adopt door-to-door selling, such as Avon or Amway do to market their products. On the other hand, an example of pull marketing is Philip Morris's use of magazine advertisements, billboards, and event sponsorship to fan demand for its cigarettes. Most companies use combinations of push and pull strategies. Managers look at several issues to figure out the best mix of push and pull promotion strategies for a particular nation.

Type of Distribution System

Some distribution systems are tightly controlled by competitors (notably in Japan), government regulated (as in many developing countries), or highly fragmented among many small outlets (common in Europe). MNEs that enter these markets will likely adopt aggressive pull promotions in the hope that creating

Table 8.4

International Promotion Policy: Issues to Consider

- Can we use our current labels and brand name? If required, can we produce our labels in the official or local dialects?
- Are the colors used on our label and packaging attractive to foreign buyers? Perhaps more important, are these colors offensive to foreign buyers?
- Do international or foreign brand names help or hinder the local image of the product?
- Do local laws require that labels provide information on product content, product risks, or country of origin?
- Do we need to use different standards to state weights and measures?
- Do we need to modify our advertising images to reflect local needs, wants, and dreams?
- Must each product be individually labeled and packaged?
- Do the local laws protect our trademark or prevent direct imitation of our brand?

consumer demand with a flood of mass media will lead buyers to demand distributors stock the product.

Cost and Availability of Media to Reach Target Markets

More than half the population in rural India is illiterate, and just over one-third of households have televisions. Colgate-Palmolive reaches potential consumers in this market by promoting the merits of its toothpaste with half-hour infomercials that are "narrowcast" from colorful video vans that travel the Indian countryside.[7] In many countries, government regulations pose an even greater barrier to the use of mass media channels. For example, Scandinavian television has long refused to broadcast commercials.

Consumer Attitudes Toward Sources of Information

Generally, people can choose from a rich menu for their preferred source of product information, such as company Web sites, product testing organizations, consumer advocacy groups, product point-of-sale displays, personal recommendations, salespeople, and so forth. Thus, nations that rely heavily on self-service situations, for instance, in which there are no salespeople to whom customers can turn for opinions on products, compel a company to select a pull strategy that uses mass media or at-the-point-of-sale advertising.

Price of the Product Compared to Local Incomes

Generally, consumers around the world behave differently when they buy something. Studies show that the amount of consumer involvement in making a purchase decision varies by country because of income levels. When a product's price compared to consumer income is high, consumers usually want more time and information before making what is a relatively big decision. Information about high-cost items is best conveyed in a personal selling situation because it provides the means for immediate and direct communication. Thus, MNEs usually rely on push strategies in emerging markets because incomes are commonly low relative to the price of the product.

Standardization of Advertising Programs

Where possible, MNEs standardize their advertising programs. In the perfect scenario, an MNE would use the same advertising promotion the same way in every nation in order to leverage its idea and investment. A popular example of a standardized campaign was Coca-Cola's "I'd Like to Buy the World a Coke" ads showing people singing in 12 different languages; at the final count, this ad reached 3.8 billion viewers in 131 countries.[8] However, our earlier look at cross-national cultural differences suggests that this option is often impractical. Instead, MNEs develop standardized advertising programs that are similar from market to market rather than a universal campaign that is identical in each and every country. This constraint leads managers to pinpoint consumer segments in countries that share similar attributes and, hence, would perceive the intended message in the company's advertising promotion.

The motivation for advertising standardization is straightforward: The cost savings of an advertising promotion are directly proportional to how many markets the company can use it in. Whereas the economies of scale of a standardized advertising program are less than those for product standardization, they nevertheless are a meaningful source of competitive advantage for a company. In addition to reducing costs, advertising standardization has other benefits. A universal advertising message and promotional campaign often exhibits better quality than one created in local markets, given that local agencies may lack the necessary expertise. Too, standardization prevents internationally mobile consumers from seeing confusing or contradictory images for the same product. Finally, a standardized message speeds the entry of products into different countries.

Standardized advertising is not cost free. The effort to maximize efficiency can lead to greater concern for cost conditions at the risk of ineffective promotions. Also, trying to stretch a promotional budget over many brands raises the odds that the promotion for each is not as effective as it might have otherwise been, given that managers likely underinvested in favor of building fewer, more powerful brands. Over time, MNEs address these problems by tweaking their promotion policies to deal with the recurring snags of translation gaps, legality issues, and message needs.

Translation Gaps

When a particular media channel reaches audiences in multiple countries, such as MTV programs aired in Europe, ads cannot be translated because viewers from any number of countries watch the same broadcast. However, when a company plans to advertise in a country with a different language, translation is usually necessary. For example, Wal-Mart encountered problems when it sent English-language circulars to Quebec instead of translating some into French or some combination of the two languages. The most audible problem in commercial translation is dubbing, because words on an added soundtrack never quite correspond to lip movements. Marketing managers can avoid dubbing problems by creating commercials in which actors do not speak, along with a voice or print overlay in the appropriate language. Pillsbury does this in India, where its Doughboy ads are shown in six languages. Marketing managers may use voice and print overlays for ads in different countries with the same language to accommodate different spellings and accents.

You would think that translating a message would be easy—indeed, it is increasingly possible to use software programs to translate and back-translate any individual word into any language. However, problems often arise when trying to translate a message that plays on words or relies on nuances to convey a subtle message. A number of simple but costly translation mistakes illustrate this challenge. For example, General Motors thought its Nova model could easily be called by the same name in Latin America, since the name means "star" in Spanish. However, people started pronouncing it "no va," which is Spanish for "it does not go." General Motors soon changed the brand name to Caribe. Furthermore, sometimes what is an acceptable word or direct translation in one place is obscene, misleading, or meaningless in another. For example, the Milk Board's ad "Got Milk?" comes out as "Are you lactating?" in Spanish.[9] Table 8.5 lists other translation slip-ups in international marketing. Another problem is choosing the appropriate language within a country that has more than one. For example, in Haiti, a company might use Creole to reach the general population but French to reach wealthier consumer segments.[10]

Legality

Advertising that qualifies as legal in one country may be illegal elsewhere. Indeed, a curious aspect of international business is that any given business practice is likely illegal someplace in the world. In any event, differences in

Translation Slip-Ups in International Marketing		Table 8.5
Original Brand Name or Promotion Message	**Mistranslation or Misperception**	

Original Brand Name or Promotion Message	Mistranslation or Misperception
Johnson Wax company named its flagship product Pledge "Pliz" in the Netherlands.	The Dutch pronunciation of Pliz sounds like "piss."
Ford branded one of its low-cost pickup trucks the "Fiera."	Spanish consumers interpreted Fiera as "ugly old woman."
Adolph Coors Co. used the message "Turn It Loose" to promote Coors Light Beer.	*Turn it loose,* when translated into Spanish, means "Drink Coors and get diarrhea."
PepsiCo, at one point, used the message "Come Alive with Pepsi."	In Germany, this message translated into "come out of the grave with Pepsi."
Kentucky Fried Chicken uses the promotion pitch of "finger licking good" wherever it goes.	Translated into Chinese, this pitch turned into "eat your fingers off."
Ford branded one of its small cars the "Pinto."	In Portuguese, *pinto* is slang for "small male appendage."
Budweiser used the promotion pitch "Delicious, less filling" around the world.	Translated into Spanish, this pitch turned into "filling, less delicious."
3M branded its synthetic sponge, a personal care product, the Buf-Puf.	In France, "Buf" is slang for a house of prostitution, whereas in Germany, it is a colloquial term for homosexuality.
Parker Pen sells a ballpoint pen, the Jotter, in many countries.	In Latin American markets, *jotter* sometimes refers to a jockstrap.
Frank Perdue Chicken Company used the message "It Takes a Tough Man to Make a Tender Chicken."	In some markets, this message turned into "it takes a sexually excited man to make a chick affectionate."
Dairy company Pet brands its products with its company name.	In France, *pet* can refer to breaking wind.

legally acceptable promotions chiefly result from varying national views on consumer and competitive protection. In terms of consumer protection, laws differ on the amount of deception permitted, what can be advertised to children, whether companies must list warnings on products of possible harmful effects, and the extent to which they must list ingredients. Competitive protections, while less widespread, still pop up. The United Kingdom and the United

States, for instance, allow direct comparisons with competing brands (such as Pepsi versus Coca-Cola in the notorious Pepsi Challenge Taste Test), whereas the Philippines prohibits them.

Some countries regulate advertising because of social and cultural standards. That is, practically all governments have distinct views on advertising and the promotion of civil rights, standards of morality, and expression of nationalism. Presently, few countries regulate sexism in advertising, but some governments restrict the advertising of certain products (such as contraceptives and feminine hygiene products) because they feel such ads are in questionable taste. Elsewhere, governments restrict ads that might prompt children to misbehave or people to disobey laws (such as advertising automobile speeds that exceed the speed limit) and those that show scantily clad women. New Zealand banned a Nike advertisement in which a rugby team tackles the coach because it thought the message threatened violence.

Finally, e-business over the Internet creates new challenges for companies trying to design effective e-promotions in the face of government regulation. At the least, a company's Internet ads and prices must comply with the laws of each country in which the company actually sells a product. This poses problems because a company's Web page easily reaches Internet users everywhere and anywhere. For example, Land's End, a U.S. merchandiser, has long used its unconditional lifetime guarantee to help promote its merchandise. German law, however, forbids such a guarantee on the grounds that it is a gimmick hidden in the sales price. Land's End, therefore, must either change this pivotal part of its marketing philosophy or exclude Germany from its Internet sales.[11] Clearly, the Internet creates new opportunities for companies to promote their products internationally, but it also moves them into uncharted legal seas.

Message Needs

An advertising theme may not be appropriate everywhere because of national differences in how well consumers know the product, how they perceive it, who will make the purchasing decision, and what qualifies as an effective appeal. For instance, companies report that different nations find the same product attribute appealing in dissimilar ways. Green Giant, thus, advertises canned corn according to the main way it is eaten in different countries—as a hot side dish in the United States, a pizza topping in the United Kingdom, a cold addition to salads in France, an after-school treat in Japan, and a topping for ice cream in South Korea.[12]

Branding

A **brand** is an identifying mark for a product. When a company registers a brand legally, it becomes a **trademark.** A well-designed brand gives a good or service instant consumer recognition, thereby reducing the need for specialized product promotions over the long term. For example, the Disney brand is immensely powerful; stamping this brand on virtually any product in most markets in the world gives consumers automatic assurance of quality, appropriateness, and value. Generally, all companies have to deal with four major branding decisions: (1) brand versus no brand, (2) manufacturer's brand versus private brand, (3) one brand versus multiple brands, and (4) worldwide brand versus local brands. Only companies that operate in foreign markets must resolve the latter decision.

Some companies, such as Coca-Cola, Disney, and Microsoft, opt to use the same brand and logo globally. Other companies house many of their products within the same family of brands, such as the Nestea and Nescafé brands for Nestlé, or Panasonic, Quasar, and Technics for Matsushita. While sometimes a set of brand names is a legacy of earlier acquisitions, at other times it reflects a company's plan to share the collective goodwill of the brand family with individual brands. Whatever reasons motivate using brands the same or similar way abroad, companies run into problems with language, brand acquisition, late-mover penalties, and country-of-origin effects.

Language Factors

Perhaps the most vexing challenge to a global brand is language. Despite the best intentions of marketing managers, some brand names simply have a different meaning in another language. For instance, Coca-Cola tries to use global branding wherever possible, but it discovered that the word *diet* in Diet Coke suggests illness in Germany and Italy. Rather than accept the expensive challenge of trying to change cultural outlooks, Coca-Cola rebranded this product as Coca-Cola Light outside the United States. Other companies find points of brand standardization that are immune to possible language distortions. Unilever, for example, translated the brand name of its fabric softener Snuggle into many variations, such as Kuschelweich in Germany, Cajoline in France, Coccolino in Italy, Mimosin in Spain, and even "Huggy" in English-speaking Australia. Unilever, however, insisted that every packaging label prominently display the brand symbol of Snuggle, a trademarked image of a cuddly bear cub.

Pronunciation presents other problems to building a global brand. Different languages may lack some of the sounds of a particular brand name. More commonly, the pronunciation of a brand name may unintentionally sound different. For example, McDonald's uses Donald McDonald in Japan because many Japanese struggle to pronounce the letter *R*. Marcel Bich dropped the *H* from his name when branding Bic pens because of the fear of mispronunciation in English. Finally, the alphabets of different languages pose strange barriers to building a brand. Often, consumers judge English brand names by whether they sound appealing or exotic. Brand names in Mandarin and Cantonese must have visual appeal, however, because the Mandarin and Cantonese alphabets are pictograms. Some companies in China have sought names that people perceive as lucky, such as a brand with eight strokes in it and depicted in red rather than blue.[13]

Brand Acquisitions

Companies often expand internationally by buying foreign companies that have products with strong local brand identities. For example, when Avon acquired the Justine Company in South Africa, it kept the Justine brand, given its high local status. Similarly, Sunbeam acquired several brand names in Italy (including Rowenta, Oster, Cadillac, Aircap, and Stewart) that it uses to market products there and in other markets. Brand acquisition, as we mentioned above, can complicate international marketing management. Generally, managers have to be careful about brand name proliferation. Managing the promotion of 50 small local brands versus five major international brands tends to be much more difficult and costly. For example, Sunbeam found that stretching its marketing skills and the promotional budget over so many brands raised the odds that its promotions were not as effective as they might have been with fewer, larger brands that enjoyed more significant positive recognition.[14]

Legal Problems

Occasionally, companies develop a brand only to find upon entering foreign markets that someone else has already legally claimed the local right of use. For example, Acer Inc., the computer manufacturer from Taiwan, began with the brand name of Multitech. As it expanded into other nations, it did so as Multitech. However, upon its entry into the United States, Acer discovered that an American company had already registered the Multitech name. In recourse, the company adopted the Acer brand.[15] This problem has taken on a new level of seriousness with respect to the Internet. Specifically, many companies have entered foreign markets only to discover that their preferred Web address belongs to someone else. So far, the legal implications of the ownership rights of registered domain names on the World Wide Web are still unfolding. In some cases, companies have resolved matters out of court by buying the right to use their name on the Internet from the original registrant.

Country-of-Origin Images

MNEs have to decide whether to create a local or a foreign image for their products. The products of some countries, particularly industrial countries, tend to have a higher-quality image than do those from other countries.[16] There are also image differences concerning specific products from specific countries. For example, the French company BSN-Gervais Danone brews Kroenenbourg, the largest-selling bottled beer in Europe. Despite its French ownership, the company's director general frankly admits that the Kroenenbourg brand was chosen because it "sounds German"; customers perceive Germany as the source of great beer and France as the home of fine wines.[17] Similarly, Avon uses English or French brand names, given consumers' positive associations with them and cosmetics. Besides these direct effects, country-of-origin stereotypes also limit a company's freedom in setting prices. Exporters in emerging economies often must promote their products primarily through low prices because of negative perceptions about the products' quality. But there are dangers in lowering prices in response to adverse stereotypes: A lower price may reduce the product image even further.

Country-of-origin images can and do change. The label "Made in Japan" suggested poor quality in the 1950s and 1960s. By the 1980s, the same label signified supreme quality. Korean companies have gone through a similar evolution. In the 1970s and 1980s, many Korean companies sold their products abroad under private labels or under contract with well-known companies, given consumers' reluctance to trust Korean-made goods. Some of these Korean companies, such as Samsung and Daewoo, now emphasize their own trade names, and the quality of Korean products has opened up markets around the world. Presently, we see elements of these perceptions with products bearing the "Made in China" stamp. In all likelihood, this stamp will eventually signify high quality that commands a premium price.

Distribution Policy

A company may accurately assess market potential, design goods or services for that market, price them appropriately, and promote them to likely consumers. However, it has little chance to meet its sales targets if it does not make the good or service conveniently available to customers. Put simply, companies need to place their products where people want to buy them. For example, does a man prefer to buy shampoo in a grocery store, barbershop, drugstore, or some other type of outlet? Does a company in a worldwide manufacturing supply chain look to buy components from local wholesalers, business-to-business Web services, or a new supplier halfway around the world? **Distribution** is the course—actual physical path or legal title—that goods and services take between production and consumption. In international marketing, a company must decide on its method of moving products among countries, as well as of moving products within the country where the final sale occurs.

Companies may limit early distribution in some foreign countries by trying to sell regionally before moving into national markets. Many products and markets lend themselves to this sort of gradual development. In some cases, unique topographies split a single country into local markets. Mountain ranges divide Colombia, for example, whereas a desert splits Australia. In other countries, such as Albania or Zimbabwe, scant wealth or few potential sales may lie outside the large metropolitan areas. In still others, advertising and distribution may be handled effectively on a regional basis. For example, most multinational consumer goods companies have moved into China one region at a time.[18]

Chapter 3 discussed operating forms for foreign market penetration, and Chapter 7 looked at the idea of global supply chain management. This section complements these ideas by reviewing the features of product distribution within foreign countries from the point of view of an international marketer delivering goods to the end customer. Table 8.6 identifies important issues to consider when devising a distribution policy for international markets.

Difficulty of Standardization

Within the marketing mix of product, price, promotion, and distribution, MNEs find distribution one of the most difficult functions to standardize internationally. Granted, the fundamental purpose of distribution is crystal clear—to efficiently move goods to the ultimate consumer. As in other aspects of international business, however, cultural, economic, and legal conditions create idiosyncratic distribution situations in various nations. MNEs, consequently, must try to devise cost-efficient distribution plans in the face of physical and psychological challenges.

Common factors that influence how goods are distributed in a given country include citizens' attitudes toward owning their own stores, the cost of paying retail workers, labor legislation that affects chain stores and individually owned stores differently, legislation restricting the operating hours and size of stores, the trust that owners have in their employees, the efficacy of the postal system, and the financial ability to carry large inventories. For example, Finland has few stores per capita because general-line retailers predominate there, whereas Italian distribution has to deal with a fragmented retail and wholesale structure that is built on a politically powerful coalition of mom-and-pop storeowners. In the Netherlands, buyer cooperatives deal directly with manufacturers. Japan has cash-and-carry wholesalers for retailers that do not need financing or delivery services. In Germany, mail-order sales are important, but not so in Italy because of the country's unreliable postal system.[19] China has banned door-to-door sales, complicating the expansion plans of push-oriented companies such as Avon and Amway.[20]

Table 8.6

International Distribution Policy: Issues to Consider

When Going Alone

- Are there any barriers—physical or psychological—that divide the national market into regional or local markets?
- How much can we standardize our distribution setup from market to market?
- Should we build a distribution system from scratch or hire local agents to do the job?
- Does outsourcing distribution to local agents fit with our long-term strategy?
- To what degree can we transfer our distinctive distribution skills from our home market to foreign markets?
- What, if any, are the hidden costs of distribution within a nation?

When Hiring a Local Distributor

- How many field salespeople does the representative or distributor have?
- Would it need to expand to accommodate our account properly? If so, would it be willing to do so?
- What is the average sales volume per outside salesperson?
- What sales territory does it now cover?
- Does it have any plans to open additional offices?
- How many product lines does it represent?
- Are these product lines compatible with ours?
- Would there be any conflict of interest?
- Is it willing to alter its present product mix to accommodate ours?
- Does it have adequate warehouse facilities?
- What communications facilities does it have (fax, modem, telex, Web site, etc.)?
- Does it plan to develop Web commerce capabilities?
- What software does it run to manage accounts? Is it compatible with ours?
- How does it compensate its sales staff?
- Does it have special incentive or motivation programs?
- How does it monitor sales performance?
- What kinds of customers does it currently contact?
- Who are the key accounts?
- How many principals does it currently represent?
- Would we be its primary supplier?
- What media does it use, if any, to promote sales?
- How much of the budget does it allocate to advertising?
- Will we be expected to contribute funds for promotional purposes?
- If necessary, can it translate our advertising copy?

Choosing Distributors and Channels

An early operational decision for MNEs is whether to try to set up their own distribution network or to contract with independent companies to do it for them.

Setting Up a Distribution System

The general rule of thumb is that high sales volume in a particular market makes it more economical for a company to build its own distribution system.

In the short term, this plan can prove expensive because start-up from scratch in foreign markets requires lots of management time and company funds. In the long term, however, if sales continue to grow, the company will be able to leverage its early investment into a powerful competitive advantage. Besides the raw measure of total sales, several other conditions prod MNEs to set up their own distribution systems. For example, products that are high priced, are high tech, or need lots of after-sale service lead customers to demand a direct relationship with the seller. Microsoft, for instance, would have a tough time selling consumers on the idea that if they have a question about a software problem, they should contact their local retailer for assistance. Indeed, the more complex and expensive the product, the more important is after-sales service. In this situation, companies may need to invest in service centers for groups of distributors that serve as intermediaries between producers and consumers.

Similarly, many companies define their competitive advantage in terms of the superior distribution skills they built in their home market. These companies typically try to transfer this skill abroad even in the face of potential barriers. Amway, Avon, and Tupperware are examples of companies that have successfully transferred their house-to-house distribution methods from the United States to many of their foreign operations. Too, Matsushita relies on its 20,000 storefronts—which stock only its branded products—to reach customers in Japan. Its success there has led it to transfer this distribution approach to China; Matsushita is on the way to a network of 3,000 company-owned retail outlets there. Similarly, Dell Computer has successfully transferred its direct mail-order distribution network from the United States to Europe and plans ultimately to serve the world with a comparable distribution system. Finally, some Internet companies, notably Yahoo!, Amazon.com, and eBay, see the potential of the Internet as perhaps the ultimate distribution network. Specialized distribution expertise increasingly determines the success of many business-to-consumer e-companies.

Buying a Distribution System

Low sales volume in a particular market makes it more economical for a company to outsource its distribution function to specialized services. Again, in the short term, this plan pays off by removing an expensive part of international expansion. In the long term, however, the company's success can put it in a position in which it has to come up with a great deal of cash to buy out its subcontractors. Managers should periodically reassess whether sales have grown to the point at which they justify insourcing distribution.

The company that opts to outsource its international distribution function can typically choose from numerous qualified distributors. Marketing managers looking for the best distributor should carefully review each candidate's financial strength; supply connections; extent of other business commitments; current status of personnel, facilities, and equipment; and—increasingly—e-business capability. The distributor's financial strength is important because of the potential long-term relationship between company and distributor and because of the assurance that money will be available for such things as maintaining sufficient inventory. Good connections are particularly important if sales must be directed to certain types of buyers, such as governmental procurement agencies. The extent of other business commitments can indicate whether the distributor has time for the company's product and whether it currently handles competitive or complementary products.[21] The status of the distributor's personnel, facilities, and equipment indicates not only its ability to deal with the product, but also how quickly start-up can occur. Too, the burst in e-commerce and potential of networked supply chain management has made e-business skills a necessary competency of any distributor. For example, a company's Web advertisements and prices reach customers everywhere. E-customers' expectation of delivery in "Internet time" means a company must find distributors that can quickly deliver what it sells in any number of countries.

The belief that a company should do what it does best and outsource the rest moves many companies to jump at the chance to hire world-class distribution skills. And just as companies evaluate the merits of potential distributors, distributors too must choose which companies and products they will represent. Both wholesalers and retailers have limited storage facilities, display space, working capital to finance inventories, and transportation and personnel to move merchandise. Therefore, they try to carry only those products that have the greatest profit potential. A company expanding into a new market must sell possible distributors on its products as well as on itself as a reliable company. This process can be hard in international markets. A company that is new to a country and wants to introduce products, that some competitors already sell may find it impossible to find distributors to carry its brands. Even established companies sometimes struggle to gain distribution for their new products. Often, though, they benefit from their established brand image and the ability to offer existing profitable lines only if distributors accept new, unproven products. A company planning to use existing distribution channels must analyze competitive conditions to offer effective incentives to help sign up distributors. Companies can offer such incentives as higher profit margins, after-sales servicing, and promotional support—any of which may be offered on an introductory or permanent basis. In the final analysis, however, incentives are only as attractive as the company's products.

The Hidden Costs in Foreign Distribution

Because of structural differences among nations' distribution systems, the cost of getting products to consumers inevitably varies from country to country. Our preceding discussion looked at prominent sources of distribution expenses in international business. International markets, however, are teeming with hidden costs that, if not planned for, can ruin the efficiency of even the best-designed distribution system. In particular, managers need to anticipate the indirect costs of the following factors.

Infrastructure Conditions
In many countries, poor roads and few warehouse facilities make it tough to get goods to consumers quickly, at a low cost, and with minimum damage or loss while in transit. For example, in Nigeria, Nestlé had to build small warehouses across the country instead of depending on the central warehouse that would normally be justified by the country's size. Roads are in such poor condition that travel is slow and trucks are prone to breakdowns. Further, because of crime, Nestlé posts armed guards on its delivery trucks, which are then allowed to travel only during daylight hours.[22]

Number of Levels in the Distribution System

Many countries have multitiered wholesalers that sell to each other before the product reaches the retail consumer. For example, national wholesalers sell to regional ones, which sell to local ones, and so on. This sometimes occurs because wholesalers are too small to cover more than a small geographic area. Japan typifies such a market. On average, there are 2.21 wholesale steps between producer and retailer in Japan, compared to 1.0 in the United States and 0.73 in France. Because each intermediary has to add a markup to cover its costs and generate a profit, product prices gradually rise higher and higher.

Retail Inefficiencies

In some countries, particularly emerging economies, low labor costs and a basic distrust by storeowners of all but family members result in inefficient retail practices that raise consumer prices. This distrust is evident in customers' preference for personalized counter service instead of self-service. In the former, customers wait to be shown merchandise. A customer who decides to purchase something gets an invoice to take to a cashier's line to pay. Once the invoice is stamped as paid, the customer must go to another line to pick up the merchandise after presenting the stamped invoice. Some companies have counter service for purchases as small as a pencil. The additional personnel add to retailing costs, and the added time that people must spend in the store means fewer people can be served in the given space. In contrast, most retailers in some (mainly industrialized) countries have equipment that improves the efficiency of handling customers and reports, such as electronic scanners, cash registers linked to inventory control records, and machines connecting purchases to credit-card companies.

Size and Operating-Hour Restrictions

Many countries, such as France, Italy, Germany, and Japan, protect small retailers with a panoply of unique laws. Some regulations effectively limit the number of large retail establishments and, thus, the efficiencies they would bring to supply chains. Many countries also limit operating hours as a way to protect employees from working late at night or on weekends. At the same time, such limits keep retailers from spreading the fixed cost of their space over more hours. Ultimately, they try to pass these costs onto consumers. In Sweden, 7-Eleven stores cannot use longer opening hours as a competitive advantage because Swedish law prohibits sales of a full range of goods between midnight and 6 A.M.[23]

Inventory Stock-Outs

Where retailers are small, as is true of grocers in Spain and Italy, there is little space to store inventory. Wholesalers must incur the cost of making small deliveries to many more establishments and sometimes may have to visit each retailer more frequently because of stock outages.

Summary

Perfecting the best possible marketing mix in any situation is an intellectual challenge and operational struggle. Marketing managers have to find ways to combine the rigorous sciences of product policy, pricing strategy, promotion approach, and distribution design with the art of figuring out how to encourage people to buy their particular product. Going international, expectedly, complicates this task. Certainly, many elements stay the same. However, this chapter showed that many elements vary dramatically from country to country. While international marketing managers continue to tangle with these tasks, the hard-earned wisdom of many companies helps others navigate the ever-changing tides of foreign consumers' needs and wants.

endnotes

[1] "Wal-Mart to Expand into Argentina, Brazil," United Press International, June 3, 1994; Leslie Kaufman, "Its Prices, and Its Reach, Push Wal-Mart to Top," *New York Times,* October 22, 2000; www.clarin.com/diario/98-05-18/o-02401d.htm; "Germany to Retailers: Raise Prices," Associated Press, September 8, 2000; and www.walmart.com.

[2] Tara Parker-Pope, "Nonalcoholic Beer Hits the Spot in Mideast," *Wall Street Journal,* December 6, 1995, p. B1+.

[3] Nina Munk, "The Levi Straddle," *Forbes,* January 17, 1994, pp. 44–45.

[4] Matthew B. Myers, "The Pricing of Export Products: Why Aren't Managers Satisfied with the Results?" *Journal of World Business,* Vol. 32, No. 3, 1997, pp. 277–289.

[5] Alicia Swasy, "Venezuela Sets Price Controls," *Wall Street Journal,* Jan 11, 1994, p. A10.

[6] "New Delhi Suspends Sale of Pepsi, Coke," *BC Cycle,* January 20, 1996.

[7] Miriam Jordan, "In Rural India, Video Vans Sell Toothpaste and Shampoo," *Wall Street Journal,* January 10, 1996, p. B1+.

[8] Kevin Goldman, "Prof. Levitt Stands by Global-Ad Theory," *Wall Street Journal,* October 13, 1992, p. B7.

[9] Rick Wartzman, "Read Their Lips," *Wall Street Journal,* June 3, 1999, p. A1.

[10] Michael Christie, "Marketing Overseas: When Translating Isn't Enough," *Export Today,* March 1995, pp. 16–17.

[11] Brandon Mitchener, "Border Crossings," *Wall Street Journal,* November 22, 1999, p. R41.

[12] Tara Parker-Pope, "Custom-Made," *Wall Street Journal,* September 26, 1996, p. R22.

[13] Bernd H. Schmitt, "Language and Visual Imagery: Issues of Corporate Identity in East Asia," *Columbia Journal of World Business,* winter 1995, pp. 28–36.

[14] Myron M. Miller, "Sunbeam in Italy: One Success and One Failure," *International Marketing Review,* Vol. 7, No. 1, 1990, pp. 68–73.

[15] Christopher A. Bartlett and Anthony St. George, "Acer, Inc: Taiwan's Rampaging Dragon," Harvard Business School Case No. 9-399-010, revised April 26, 1999.

[16] John S. Hulland, "The Effects of Country-of-Brand and Brand Name on Product Evaluation and Consideration: A Cross Country Comparison," in T. S. Chan (ed.), *Consumer Behavior in Asia: Issues and Marketing Practice* (New York: The Haworth Press, 1999), pp. 23–39.

[17] William H. Flanagan, "Big Battle Is Brewing as French Beer Aims to Topple Heineken," *Wall Street Journal,* February 22, 1980, p. 16.

[18] Sally D. Goll, "Few Retailers in China Carry Modern Goods," *Asian Wall Street Journal,* April 11, 1995, p. A1+.

[19] Cecilie Rohwedder, "U.S. Firms Go After Europeans," *Wall Street Journal,* January 6, 1998, p. A15.

[20] Craig S. Smith and Ian Johnson, "China, Worried About Direct Marketers' Growth, Bans Practice," *Wall Street Journal,* April 22, 1998, p. A16.

[21] See for example, "The International Supplier Selection: The Relevance of Import Dependence," *Journal of Global Marketing,* Vol. 9, No. 3, 1996, pp. 23–45.

[22] Greg Steinmetz and Tara Parker-Pope, "All Over the Map," *Wall Street Journal,* September 26, 1996, p. R4+.

[23] Hugh Carnegy, "Swedish 7-Eleven Stores Lose Some of Their Convenience," *Financial Times,* March 29, 1996, p. 1.

1. To appreciate how international business activity gives rise to a variety of payment and collection issues

2. To learn about the different forms of payment in international business

3. To understand the trade-off between risk and return for various forms of payment in international business

4. To learn about collection challenges in international business

5. To understand the role of foreign currency in making and collecting payments

6. To appreciate the public and private agents who help companies manage their payments and collections cycles

Trying to Trade in Sub-Saharan Africa

C ompanies prefer to manage their payments and collections cycles in cash or guaranteed credit—both are efficient means of exchange that do away with the risk of fraud or default. In many places, though, neither cash nor credit is an option. Many markets in Africa, Asia, Eastern Europe, and South America, for instance, have tremendous demand for products but little or no access to the cash or credit needed to buy them.

Consider the case of sub-Saharan Africa, a set of 48 nations that stretches eastward from Senegal to Somalia and southward from Nigeria to South Africa. Sub-Saharan Africa's population constitutes about 10 percent of the world's total yet produces just a bit more than 1 percent of the world's gross domestic product. Nations in this region endure shortages of easily converted currencies, restrictive foreign currency regulations, cumbersome bureaucracies, balance-of-payment problems, and politically risky environments.

These hardships put up high trade barriers, mostly in local buyers' ability to get the cash to buy goods from foreign suppliers. The typical solution to this problem—to borrow money from banks—is often unavailable. Commercial lenders are reluctant to finance business with sub-Saharan Africa, given their judgment of high risk, a view that is hardened by a history of loan defaults in this region. Overall, the area's debt markets need major changes before banks will routinely finance local buyers and sellers.

Not surprisingly, exporters, particularly those from nations with easily converted currencies such as the U.S. dollar, Japanese yen, or German mark, rate the unavailability of financing as a key challenge to expanding into sub-Saharan Africa. In certain markets, exporters have used intermediaries, such as banks and government agencies, to help them do business. For instance, Citicorp addressed the shortage of financing in sub-Saharan Africa by developing the Africa Trade Finance Facility. This trade program created a pool of African trade finance that increased the market flexibility of U.S. exporters.

Potential demand in these markets has led some exporters to use alternative methods. Many companies have used **countertrade,** whereby an exporter takes

Payments and Collections

chapter 9

A Korean mask of papier mache.

payment in goods instead of cash from a local buyer. Philosophically, counter-trade fits with African norms—as Krish Govender, professor at Technikon Witwatersrand of South Africa, explained, "barter and trade" are part of an African tradition that is reluctant to conform to "Euro-centric" methods of cash payment. The Foreign Ministry of Thailand, following the example of Singapore, Malaysia, and India, has opened a portal (www.mfa.go.th/Africa) to promote countertrade with Africa. The Thai Foreign Ministry noted that some African countries have energy resources that could be traded for Thai products.

Besides countertrade, exporters and multinational enterprises (MNEs) use other methods of payment, such as finance leasing, factoring, project finance, forfait financing, and escrow accounts, to get paid in sub-Saharan Africa. While mysterious sounding, these alternative techniques are creative yet practical means of collections and payments in international business. More important, these financial tools give companies the means to do business in countries that, if forced to rely on cash or credit, would otherwise not happen.[1]

Introduction

An international company, whether a small exporter or large MNE, relies on global pro-duction and supply chains to do business in different nations. The immediate outcome of cross-national transactions is a multitude of financial obligations that can quickly span the globe. For instance, consider the travels of a Nokia cell phone. A consumer in Italy can buy a Nokia phone from any number of outlets, ranging from shopping mall kiosks to office supply stores and, of course, thousands of different e-tailers. In each case, the seller purchases the phone from a distributor, which in turn had purchased the phone from Nokia O.Y., based in Finland. Nokia, in making the phone, used materials and com-ponents that it had bought from suppliers around the world, ranging from circuit boards from Germany to keypads from Taiwan. In turn, these suppliers had sourced materials and components from chip companies in the United States and capacitors from China. Each of these transactions, beginning with the wire makers in China and culminating with the customer in Italy, created a financial obligation between a buyer and a seller. By doing so, each company entered into a payment and collection relationship that spanned nations. Inherent in each of the many links in this supply chain is the buyer's concern about collecting payment and the seller's concern about making payment.

Involvement in international business opens up a variety of payment and collection issues (see Figure 9.1). A company, whether a small exporter or large MNE, must figure out how and with whom it should finance its transactions in the least-risky but most effi-cient way. At the least, international traders must determine which financing technique, given the specific circumstances of the transactions, ensures that moneys and goods go where and to whom they are expected. The complexity of these dealings leads many inter-national traders to seek help in setting up systems for payments and collections. Popular points of assistance include commercial banks, export intermediaries, and governmental agencies. Then again, a daring exporter could opt to go it alone and use alternative forms of financing, such as countertrade or factoring, to complete the deal.

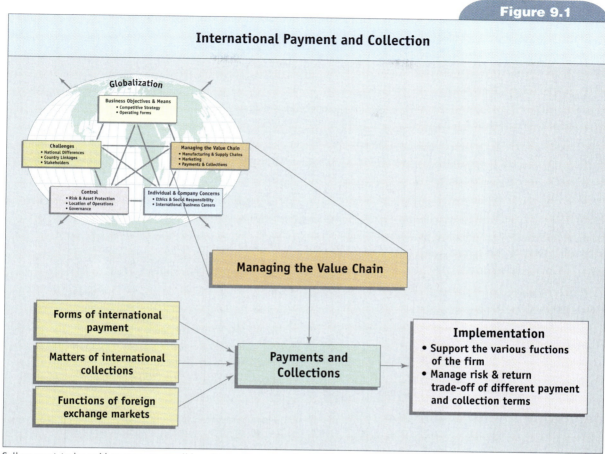

Figure 9.1

International Payment and Collection

Sellers want to be paid as soon as possible, whereas buyers prefer to delay payment until they have at least received and, where possible, resold the goods. Companies design their payment and collection cycles to try to achieve this goal with a range of viewpoints and tools.

Larger companies also need to arrange payments and collections to gain advantages, as well as prevent problems. Regarding the former, the geographic spread of an MNE's business units across nations gives it access to many capital markets. At any given time, some foreign capital markets may offer better financing terms than those available in the MNE's home nation. Easier access to more liquid capital markets, whatever nation they happen to be in, lets an MNE borrow money at a lower price. The MNE can then capitalize on this advantage by authorizing more flexible collection terms or accepting greater payment risks for its international trades.

Regarding potential problems, the fact that an MNE buys and sells things in different nations, as we saw with Nokia, means its collections and payments will involve many different national currencies. For example, buying integrated circuits from German suppliers requires Nokia to make payment in German marks, whereas selling cell phones in Italy requires Nokia to collect Italian lire. Given that Nokia buys and sells goods in more than 100 nations, each with its own currency, it ends up with a rich mix of different moneys.

Figure 9.2

Doing business means companies transact the purchase and sale of raw materials, components, and finished products between different parties. Transactions can take place from business to business (B2B) or business to consumers (B2C). Whatever the form of transaction, it automatically creates a payment and collection relationship. Managing these transactions, especially when they span different nations, requires that consumers and companies consider a variety of issues.

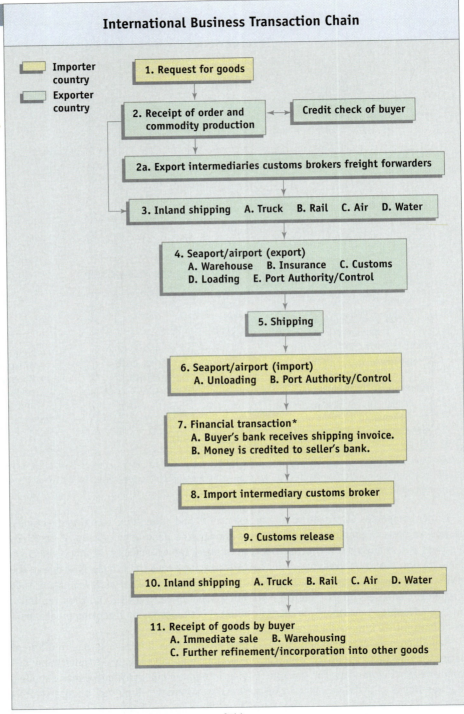

International Business Transaction Chain

Importer country
Exporter country

1. Request for goods

2. Receipt of order and commodity production ← Credit check of buyer

2a. Export intermediaries customs brokers freight forwarders

3. Inland shipping   A. Truck   B. Rail   C. Air   D. Water

4. Seaport/airport (export)
   A. Warehouse   B. Insurance   C. Customs
   D. Loading   E. Port Authority/Control

5. Shipping

6. Seaport/airport (import)
   A. Unloading   B. Port Authority/Control

7. Financial transaction*
   A. Buyer's bank receives shipping invoice.
   B. Money is credited to seller's bank.

8. Import intermediary customs broker

9. Customs release

10. Inland shipping   A. Truck   B. Rail   C. Air   D. Water

11. Receipt of goods by buyer
    A. Immediate sale   B. Warehousing
    C. Further refinement/incorporation into other goods

* Financial transactions occur at every stage of this process.

source: *Export America*, Vol. 1, November 1999, p. 17.

Figure 9.3

"O.K. The forward rate for marks rose in March and April, combined with a sharp increase in German reserves and heavy borrowing in the Eurodollar market, while United States liquid reserves had dropped to fourteen billion dollars, causing speculation that the mark might rise and encouraging conversion on a large scale. Now do you understand?"

source: ©The New Yorker Collection 1971, James Stevenson from cartoonbank.com. All Rights Reserved.

Therefore, Nokia must prudently manage its pool of national currencies or else watch its payments and collections quickly run into costly problems.

This chapter looks at the ways, both common and unusual, that international traders, whether a one-person exporter or a large MNE, deal with the matters of payments and collections. We start from the viewpoint that how a company decides to pay its bills or collect payment for its sales can be a remarkably profitable or costly decision. This chapter, therefore, gives a sense of the pros and cons of the many ways international traders can manage, finance, and control their payments and collections across different markets. We then look at a recurring bit of intricacy that frequently tangles the best-laid plans of international traders—namely, how they manage payments and collections in a world of different currencies whose exchange values are always changing. We wrap up this review by profiling prominent sources of international finance assistance.

A Point of Perspective

An axiom of business is that sellers want to be paid as soon as possible, whereas buyers prefer to delay payment until they have at least received and, where possible, resold the goods. Historically, the clear-cut simplicity of these goals made the payments and collections humdrum functions of business. By and large, companies assigned these responsibilities to a staff unit with the unstated mission not to muddle things up by accepting too much collection risk or agreeing to tough payment terms. Recent trends in payments and collections, however, create tremendous incentives for companies to rethink this mission. Communications and software innovations give enterprising managers many tools to transform payments and collections from a tedious obligation of doing business into a powerful source of revenues and international competitiveness.

This change in view largely follows from our improving understanding of the financial implications of better managing global manufacturing and supply chains. Specifically, more and more companies try to boost the number of times they turn over their inventory, an accomplishment that then reduces the need to tie up costly working capital in idle inventory. Perfectly tuned, managers can create a system that needs zero working capital precisely because before a good is built, the company has already collected payment from its buyer. Dell Computer, for example, has made such payment and collection innovations a key part of its strategy. More precisely, Dell's business design, whether in the United States or Europe, taps credit cards and requires electronic payments to convert the typical sale of computer equipment from the customer's actual order to cash payment in less than 24 hours. This distinctive competency lets Dell get the best possible financing outcome—guaranteed payment; short-term, interest-free use of the customer's funds; and hence the need to borrow less working capital.

In contrast, Compaq Computer, which sells principally through independent distributors and local retailers, needs more than 30 days to go from building and shipping a personal computer to collecting payment on the sale. Over that time, Compaq has to keep its books open, thereby exposing it to change in customer demand, threat of unanticipated changes in exchange rates, and random distribution snafus.

In sum, innovative views of the payments and collections can lead to terrific outcomes, such as minimizing financing costs, reducing the size of warehouses and inventories, and reducing the overhead associated with managing inefficient practices in credit and payables. And by the same token, seeing payments and collections as tedious obligations of doing business perpetuates costly inefficiencies that hamper the performance of global supply chain management.

Unquestionably, international traders will always worry that moneys and goods go where and to whom they are expected. The following sections will show that exporters and importers can choose from a range of options to guide their payments and collections. However, evolving competitive conditions in globalizing markets increase the potential payoff of innovative management of these activities. Globalization therefore obligates companies to impose a strategic perspective on their ideas of managing, financing, and controlling payments and collections around the world.

In practice, managers can initiate a strategic perspective by speaking to the following points as they design their payment and collection systems:

- **The Period of Financing.** A seller's policy on the length of time it will finance a product sale is crucial to many buyers. Customers in sub-Saharan Africa, for instance, struggle with the stipulation of Western companies for cash in advance or guaranteed credit transfers. In the case of integrated supply chain links, such as those in Nokia's phone manufacturing network, buyers generally look for a seller offering credit terms that let them effectively buy and sell a good before they are obligated to make payment. Intricate supply relationships, like those in Dell or Toyota's network, influence buyers' tolerance of complicated or expensive methods of financing.

- **The Need for Financing to Make the Sale.** If the competition offers better terms and has a similar product, a sale can be lost for reasons that have nothing to do with the quality of the product. Instead, buyers may choose a comparable or even inferior product, given the leeway of its more flexible financing terms. Therefore, companies often opt to make a product more competitive by modifying credit terms to meet a buyer's particular preferences or constraints. In other cases, buyers may prefer to do business with a particular company but might choose a different supplier, given the option of better credit terms. Too, a seller may offer customers incentives to pay promptly.

- **The Cost of Different Methods of Financing.** Interest rates, administrative fees, and general overhead can differ dramatically for different forms of payments and collections. Government agencies, a useful source of export financing, charge less than commercial banks but require much more documentation and lead time for applications. Variation in other nations' capital markets and government export–import programs amplify these differences. Some methods of financing, such as a letter of credit from a commercial bank, loans from export management companies, or export financing from a government, can impose higher costs in some countries than in others.

- **The Capacity for E-Finance.** Payments and collections over the Internet are increasingly powerful aspects of international trade. E-finance gives buyers and sellers the capacity to reduce the costs of transacting with each other, speedily process documents online, and quickly access pertinent information. Both parties can use online tools to improve efficiency. As a simple example, companies can use e-mail versus the postal system to transact contracts. In more complex examples, companies can use e-finance tools to decrease the costs of functions such as invoice generation, account management, contract compliance, and time-and-billing procedures. Also, emerging forms of e-finance, such as so-called e-cash, will reshape international traders' view of payments and collections.

- **The Risks of Financing the Transaction.** A principle of finance holds that the riskier the transaction, the harder and more costly it will be to fund. Buyers in economically and politically unstable nations often make sellers wonder about the strength of the security of contract terms or guarantee of completing the transaction. Too, unstable countries, such as those in sub-Saharan Africa, tend to have unstable currencies. Therefore, international traders facing these situations may opt to install safeguards such as requiring potential buyers to make a secure payment in a hard currency, present a binding letter of credit, or arrange export credit insurance. Ultimately, though, sellers that are reluctant to extend credit to foreign buyers may lose the sale to a more risk-tolerant rival.

In sum, buyers and sellers press each other for payment and collection terms that favor their position and, as such, disfavor the position of the other. Other things being equal, rivalry in the global market results in liberal financing and flexible payment terms significantly enhancing the international competitiveness of a good or service. For instance, in the ongoing aircraft contest between Airbus and Boeing, the deciding point for many buyers often boils down to the financial package offered by each company. Therefore, international traders must devise prudent financing policies that both satisfy their payment and collection standards and, with an eye toward the future, position them to translate their policies into an advantageous strategic relationship.

Forms of Payment for the International Trader

Financing plays a key role in virtually every international trade. Sellers trading across national borders naturally dislike placing goods on a ship or airplane and then waiting for the buyer to inspect the goods and decide how much, if at all, to pay and when. Therefore, obtaining cash immediately is a high priority for exporters, given the inevitable risk in extending credit to foreign buyers. Importers, meanwhile, do not want to pay in advance for fear of the purchased goods not being shipped as specified. Complicating matters for both exporters and importers are the effects of logistical snarls, variability in currency exchange rates, and customs regulations on the flow of money across national borders.

Over the years, exporters have developed several financial methods to improve the odds that they get paid. These forms of payment include cash in advance, documentary collection or draft, letters of credit, an open account, and alternative forms of payment. We will look at the fine points of each payment option in just a moment. Before doing so, it is important to keep in mind the key moderator that usually shapes a seller's preference for a particular form of payment—namely, his or her judgment of the trustworthiness of the buyer. Trust is the crucial element in whatever form of payment an exporter agrees to extend to the foreign buyer. Put simply, the more the seller and buyer trust each other, the more willing each is to accept payment terms that substitute good faith for cold cash. Figure 9.4 illustrates this relationship, showing that international traders need to negotiate the risk and return of the various forms of payment when developing their financing plans.

Cash in Advance

The seller that wants to receive payment before shipping the good or performing the service strongly prefers payment by cash in advance. Besides enjoying no collection worries, in the style of Dell Computer, the exporter can put the money to work much sooner. Operationally, cash in advance is easy to do: A buyer can make payment with a wire transfer, check, credit cards, or, increasingly, e-cash over the Internet. Whatever the form used, though, the seller must always verify the transaction.

Cash in advance, expectedly, disfavors the buyer. It can open the door to fraud, as well as provoke cash flow problems for the buyer. Also, outside the United States, cash in advance of delivery is uncommon for several reasons, including legal (there is little recourse if the foreign seller does not honor the

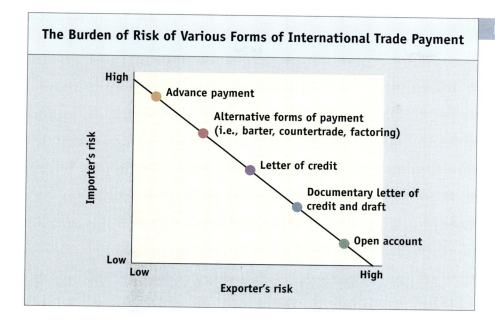

The Burden of Risk of Various Forms of International Trade Payment

Figure 9.4

deal), cultural (a legacy of nonshipments of goods), and technological (limited credit-card and e-cash availability).

Letter of Credit

Essentially, a **letter of credit** is a loan from a bank. However, instead of lending you money, a bank "lends" you its stability, reputation, and creditworthiness. For its trouble, the bank receives a fixed fee for the specific transaction instead of a stream of interest payments on the debt component of the transaction. Operationally, a letter of credit obligates the buyer's bank in the importing country to accept a draft (a so-called **commercial bill of exchange**) when it is presented, provided the draft comes along with the prescribed documents and proof that the exporter has complied with all the terms and conditions that are explicitly stipulated in the letter of credit. Naturally, guaranteed payment through a letter of credit has terrific benefits for international traders; explained an importer of Oriental rugs, "Letters of credit enable a small company like ours to compete very successfully abroad against much larger companies that have an internal source of funds. It puts us on an equal basis with these companies from the supplier's point of view."[2] Not surprisingly, letters of credit have become the "quintessential international instrument" that has enjoyed an "unprecedented expansion" around the world over the past 30 years.[3]

When an exporter requires a letter of credit, the importer is responsible for arranging it at the importer's preferred bank. An exporter that receives this guarantee from an importer's bank can rely on the established credit history of that bank rather than placing its faith in the creditworthiness of the importer. This arrangement enables the seller to draw a bill of exchange on the importer's bank rather than on the specific importer. As a result, the seller has little difficulty in selling or discounting the draft. Figure 9.5 shows the

Figure 9.5

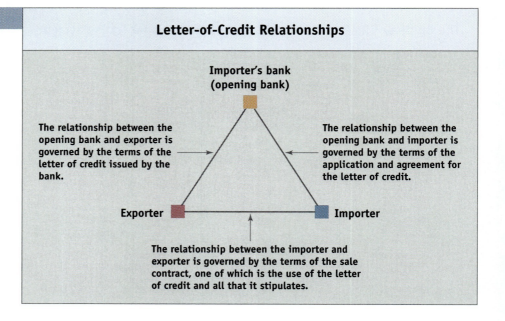

Letter-of-Credit Relationships

Importer's bank
(opening bank)

The relationship between the opening bank and exporter is governed by the terms of the letter of credit issued by the bank.

The relationship between the opening bank and importer is governed by the terms of the application and agreement for the letter of credit.

Exporter

Importer

The relationship between the importer and exporter is governed by the terms of the sale contract, one of which is the use of the letter of credit and all that it stipulates.

general workings of a letter of credit among an importer, exporter, and bank. Table 9.1 outlines the step-by-step sequence of the typical letter-of-credit transaction.

In practice, common types of letters of credit include:

- A **confirmed letter of credit** is guaranteed by both the exporter's bank in its home nation and the importer's bank in the country of import. Essentially, "confirmed" means a bank that is acceptable to the exporter promises to pay the bill if the importer's bank is unable or unwilling to do so.

- A **revocable letter of credit** can be modified by the issuing bank without approval from either the exporter or the importer.

- An **irrevocable letter of credit** cannot be canceled or changed in any way by any single party without the consent of all parties to the transaction. This type of letter obligates the importer's bank to pay, as well as accept, any drafts (bills of exchange) at sight. Thus, as soon as the correct documents are presented to the bank, it must honor the terms of the letter.

Whatever form of letter of credit is used, each and every condition that is formally stipulated—such as the method of transportation, description of the merchandise, and scope of insurance coverage—must be met by the exporter. If not, the letter is invalid, the banks will halt the financing process, and the deal will go into limbo or simply terminate.

Typically, an exporter asks the buyer to pay the fees for the letter of credit. Some buyers may not agree to this added cost. In such cases, the exporter can try to negotiate a compromise or else absorb the costs of the letter of credit if not doing so risks losing the sale. Generally, letters of credit for smaller amounts can be expensive because fees can be high relative to the sale.

Table 9.1

The Step-by-Step Sequence of a Letter of Credit

1. The exporter and buyer agree on the terms of a sale.
2. The buyer instructs a bank (the issuing bank) in its own country to open a documentary credit for a foreign seller that specifies the documents needed for payment. The buyer determines which documents will be required to satisfy its concerns about the sale.
3. The buyer's bank issues, or opens, its letter of credit that stipulates all instructions to the seller relating to the shipment of the goods.
4. The issuing bank then instructs a bank in the seller's country (the correspondent bank) to accept, negotiate, or pay an amount specified on the buyer's draft to the seller, provided that the seller presents certain shipping and sales documents to the correspondent bank. The exporter can request that a particular local bank be the confirming bank, or the foreign bank may select a correspondent bank in the seller's country.
5. The buyer's bank sends its letter of credit to the seller's chosen bank and requests confirmation.
6. The seller's bank prepares a letter of confirmation to forward to the seller that specifies which documents the seller must deliver (or "present") before the correspondent bank will accept and pay (or "honor") the buyer's draft.
7. The seller reviews all conditions in the letter of credit. The seller asks its shipping department or independent freight forwarder whether the shipping date can be met. If the exporter cannot comply with one or more of the conditions, it immediately notifies the customer.
8. The exporter arranges with the shipping department or freight forwarder to deliver the goods to the appropriate seaport or airport. When the goods are loaded, the shipping department or freight forwarder completes the necessary documentation.
9. The bank reviews the documents. If they are in order, the documents are sent to the buyer's bank for review and then transmitted to the buyer.
10. The buyer (or the buyer's agent) uses the documents to claim the goods.
11. After performance by the seller under the contract with the buyer, and after the seller then presents conforming documents to the correspondent bank, the correspondent bank pays the seller.
12. In some situations, the actual goods may not be in the hands of the buyer at the time the seller presents conforming documents to the correspondent bank. In this situation, the correspondent bank's obligation to pay the seller is not conditional on the buyer's prior receipt of the goods or on the actual quality or quantity of the goods in transit.

Documentary and Drafts

Buyers and sellers use this form of payment to further protect their respective interests. Documentary drafts stipulate that a bank will make payment on the material basis of formal documents, such as an ocean **bill of lading, consular invoice,** or **bill of exchange.** Effectively, the presentation of documents to the bank confirms the title and the stipulated steps (such as shipment, insurance, and delivery) that have taken place since the exporter shipped the goods and the importer accepted the shipment.

Documentary drafts can be paid immediately or at a later date. Drafts that are paid upon presentation are called **sight drafts,** whereas those paid at a later date, often after the buyer receives the goods, are called **time drafts** or date drafts. There is higher risk when a sight draft is used to transfer the title of a shipment from the buyer to seller. In some cases, the buyer's ability or willingness to pay might change from the time the goods are shipped until the time the drafts are presented for payment. Problems then arise because there is no bank agreement to honor the buyer's obligation. Additionally, local political or economic disruptions in the importing country, such as a security crisis, can also interfere with the transfer of control to the buyer. If the buyer cannot or will not pay for and claim the goods, returning or disposing of the products then becomes the seller's responsibility.

Open Account

An exporter occasionally may sell on an **open account,** in which it extends unsecured credit to the buyer. With an open account, the exporter simply bills the customer, which is expected to make payment under the agreed terms at a future date. Operationally, an open-account arrangement means the necessary shipping documents are mailed to the importer before any payment from or definite obligation on the part of the buyer. Releasing goods in this manner is somewhat unusual for the small international trader because it risks default by the buyer. Open accounts are an especially convenient method of payment if the buyer is trustworthy and has an established credit history with the seller. In particular, this form of payment is customary among larger, established exporters. Many MNEs set up their payments and collections to make purchases only on open account, especially when the importer and exporter are subsidiaries within the same company or established links in the global supply chain.

Naturally, open-account sales carry lots of risk. The lack of binding documents and banking agents to govern the transaction makes it hard to legally document disputed claims. Furthermore, in the event of a dispute, an exporter often has to pursue collection efforts abroad, which can be difficult, costly, and time consuming. Another problem is that receivables may be harder to finance, because the seller does not have drafts or other evidence of the debt. This risk can be especially troublesome in the face of potential political, economic, and exchange risks. Chapter 10 looks at ways in which international traders can reduce these risks.

Alternative Forms of Payment

Table 9.2 lists alternative forms of financing that a company can use to trade internationally. Overall, these forms of payment generally involve arrangements whereby the buyer and seller do not exchange cash or credit but rather goods, services, or other instruments of trade in partial or whole payment for the transaction. The gap between the straightforward efficiency of cash or credit and the outwardly peculiar techniques listed in Table 9.2 prompts an explanation of why most companies—which prefer not to use alternative forms of payment—must often do so if they aim to complete the transaction in the face of extenuating circumstances.

Naturally, there are many reasons why companies avoid alternative forms of payment. At the least, these forms of payment are always less efficient than cash-for-goods exchanges. Furthermore, rather than simply looking at the foreign exchange table in the local newspaper or relevant Web site, buyers and

Table 9.2

Forms of Alternative Financing in International Business

Barter	The direct trade of goods and services without the use of any form of money.
Countertrade	An agreement in which goods and services are paid for with other goods and services.
Finance leasing	A full-payout, noncancelable agreement in which the lessee is responsible for maintenance, taxes, and insurance.
Factoring	The factor assumes responsibility for the credit, collections, and record-keeping functions for the supplier client.
Forfaiting	A financing institution absorbs the risk of collecting payment from the buyer, independent of the seller, by discounting the negotiated bills of exchange or promissory notes.
Buyback	The export of industrial equipment in exchange for products eventually made by that equipment.
Offset	A company agrees to offset a hard-currency sale to a nation by making a hard-currency purchase of a to-be-determined product from that nation in the future.
Consignment sales	The goods are shipped to a foreign distributor that sells them on behalf of the exporter. The exporter retains title to the goods until they are sold, at which point payment is sent to the exporter. The exporter has the greatest risk and least control over the goods with this method.
Escrow account	A mechanism to insulate collateral and disburse to lenders, according to contractual terms, the hard-currency revenues generated by the project that is being financed by a loan.
Project financing	A technique to fund projects that require large sums of cash and protracted debt servicing. Lenders look to the project's expected cash flow to repay the debt and the project's hard assets for collateral.

sellers must enter complex and time-consuming negotiations to reach a fair value for the exchange. In some situations, such as those involving barter or countertrade, the goods that are sent as payment may be poor quality, packaged unattractively, or difficult to sell and service. Also, there is a lot of room for price and financial distortion in alternative forms of payment, given that non-market forces set the prices of these goods or contract terms. Ultimately, alternative forms of financing threaten free-market forces with protectionism and price fixing that can complicate trade relations with other nations. In sum, alternative forms of financing have many drawbacks that, as economic theory is quick to point out, are inefficient trade mechanisms that "pollute" an open and free-trade system.

Still, as we saw with respect to sub-Saharan Africa, the harsh reality of international trade means that alternative forms of payment are often unavoidable for companies that want to do business with companies that have limited access to cash or credit. Complicating matters is the fact that as much as companies may dislike them, many developing nations prefer alternative forms of financing as low-risk ways to preserve their monetary assets, generate foreign exchange, and improve their balance of trade. In addition, these methods help developing nations reduce their need to borrow working capital, as well as allowing them to access the technology and marketing expertise of MNEs. More significantly, benefits beyond financing the immediate transaction do accrue to companies. Accepting alternative forms of financing shows managers' good faith and flexibility in the face of onerous conditions. These sensitivities can position the firm to gain preferential access to emerging markets.

Collection Problems in International Trade

In a perfect world, sellers would promptly ship the right product and buyers would promptly pay. In international trade, though, perfection seldom comes to pass. Just as in a company's domestic business, exporters encounter problems with buyers that default on their payment for actual performance problems or, as we see in the following discussion of videotapes, negative perceptions of product attributes. No matter what the source of buyer discontent, however, dealing with collection problems in international trade is difficult, costly, and time consuming.

Illustrative Case: Collection Trouble in the Video World[4]

The popularity of American entertainment, particularly television and cinema, creates a great deal of international demand. Essentially, broadcasters in other nations, looking to fill their viewing schedules, buy videotapes of U.S. shows to televise in their local market. In the early 1990s, amid growing demands for U.S. entertainment, collections emerged as a vexing problem in the international trade of videotapes. As one distributor explained, "Business is great . . . I can sell everything—the problem is getting paid." Similarly, the leading trade magazine, *Movie/Video Age,* reported that the "industry is experiencing a major collection problem, which, in the case of some of the smaller distributors and sales agents, is creating a severe cash flow hang-up." Problems had grown so large so quickly that a major U.S. distributor reported at the Monte Carlo Festival and Market that it had formed a new unit just to try to collect on its growing international receivables.

   In a few situations, buyers failed to pay U.S. exporters due to unplanned cash shortages or credit mix-ups. Many buyers, though, chose not to pay their bill because, explained a European agent, they believed that American distributors had shipped poor-quality products. "How do you expect to get paid when the material is sent late or it is sent with technical defects?" he asked. Going on, he observed that "certain countries in Europe are very demanding. To them, quality is uncompromising." Displeased with the quality of the product, buyers either tried to convince U.S. exporters to correct the problem or, in some cases, canceled the deal and returned the opened material. Others, however, disagreed with the quality allegations. Francesca Santini of Croce del Sud, one of Italy's largest voice dubbing companies, maintained that "Americans pay attention to quality." Ms. Santini conceded, "Yes, the Germans are very demanding, but they also can be too fastidious, overzealous, and uncompromising. Once we returned a tape to Germany, which was sent back to us with a long list of 'defects.' The second time around, the tape was accepted and we had not even unpacked it. There was nothing wrong with it." Whatever the source of buyers' regret, their decision created tough collection problems for U.S. exporters, especially those following the popular notion that the "customer is always right."

Sellers' Concerns

Some risk-averse exporters buy insurance from private companies or governmental agencies to cover the risk that buyers will fail to make payment. Insurance, though, is not a great initial solution. Besides hiking the seller's transaction costs, it takes time to file a claim and await reimbursement in the event a buyer fails to pay the bill. Thus, as in most areas of international business, an exporter is best served by doing the best possible due diligence, prudently gauging the risk of the payment terms, and taking the necessary precautions. Considering the worst-case scenario, while sometimes unpleasant, is especially helpful in pinpointing potential collection problems.

If initial collection efforts go awry for ill-defined reasons, such as we saw with German distributors' judgment of the quality of U.S. video products, then the exporter has two practical options. One, it can give the buyer the benefit of the doubt and replace the product with no questions asked. This solution, the idealized customer service philosophy, pays off if the seller believes compromise may save a valuable customer in the long run. If compromise is out of the question, then a company should obtain the assistance and advice of qualified experts, whether in the form of international collections specialists at its bank, an international trade attorney, or government agencies.

Seasoned exporters generally prefer to avoid using the judicial system to settle disputes. Commercial disputes often provoke prolonged legal dealings to reach a settlement. In international collections disputes, questions of jurisdiction (should the dispute be resolved by the judicial system of the home nation of the exporter, importer, or somewhere else?) and applicable law (should civil or common law apply to this dispute?) can further confuse an already confused matter. Therefore, experienced exporters, anticipating the worst-case scenario, try to include an arbitration provision in the sales contract. Arbitration is often faster and less costly than legal action. Moreover, the International Chamber of Commerce, a transnational organization that is not affiliated with any single country and handles the majority of international arbitration, is usually agreeable to companies around the world. As a last resort, an exporter can sell its receivables to a international collections agency or collections agency in the debtor's country. This option, though, typically returns only a small share of the total outstanding debt to the exporter.

Buyers' Concerns

Sellers are not the only ones that need to worry about collection problems. Buyers too must worry about "collecting" the good or service that they bought. For instance, letters of credit have become indispensable tools for conducting international trade. Along with their increased use, though, has come a growing volume of fraud. The basis of the problem is somewhat subtle, but a genuine risk to buyers. Specifically, letters of credit, especially sight drafts, ostensibly guarantee payment to the seller and delivery to the buyer. But in so doing, letters of credit shift certain commercial risks from the seller to the buyer.

For instance, international shipment creates many points for product casualty. The seller's goods might be negligently damaged in transit, say, or spoiled through unexpected delays in clearing customs. Then again, the seller may mistakenly send the wrong items to the buyer. Finally, just as some buyers may order goods with no intention of paying for them, some sellers might knowingly ship damaged or worthless goods to customers that live in faraway lands. In each of these scenarios, once the seller presents documents from the shipper that seem to establish the performance of the seller's contractual obligations to the buyer as specified in the letter of credit, the bank is obligated to pay the exporter. At this point, the foreign buyer must hope the seller made an honest mistake. Still, there are many cases where buyers in one country, alleging fraud on the part of sellers in another, have tried to stop the issuing banks from honoring the seller's payment demand. Sometimes the buyers are successful, but often they are not.

The Importance of Guidelines

Whether they are buying or selling, international traders should follow universal guidelines of effective collections. Specifically, rather than presume that buyers in foreign nations adhere to the same business standards, traders should study potential markets with particular attention to customary payment times for business debts, laws governing debt collections, legal jurisdiction for business debts, and the accepted standards of arbitration. This information will then help exporters and importers devise the best form of payment and, where necessary, craft a sales agreement that prevents intractable collection disputes. International traders should also check with banks, public agencies, and other international commerce groups to identify external events that may prevent a debtor from paying. For example, the transition to democracy in Nigeria has slowed payments to foreign oil companies. Eventually, the Nigerian National Petroleum Corporation will likely honor its debts, but, until then, a prudent exporter would insist on cash in advance or an irrevocable letter of credit before doing business with it. If, after these steps, collection problems still occur, the buyer or seller should quickly seek restitution. Waiting too long may cause you to lose an opportunity to collect. Finally, where possible, pursue arbitration—it saves aggravation, time, and money.

Foreign Currency

There is a fundamental difference between payments and collections in the domestic versus international market. In a domestic transaction, companies use only one currency; in a foreign transaction, however, companies can use two or more currencies. That is, when a company sells goods or services to a foreign customer and receives foreign currency, it needs to convert the foreign currency into its domestic currency. When importing, the company needs to convert the domestic currency to the foreign currency to pay the foreign supplier. For example, a U.S. company that exports $100,000 worth of computer chips to a Finnish phone maker will ask the Finnish buyer to remit payment in dollars, unless the U.S. company has a specific use for Finnish marks, such as paying a different Finnish supplier. Therefore, a buyer and a seller that are in different countries rarely use the same currency to complete a transaction. Payment is usually made in either the buyer's or the seller's currency or in a third, mutually agreed-upon, currency.

Elements of Foreign Exchange

Simply put, **foreign exchange** refers to money denominated in the currency of another nation or group of nations. The market in which international traders buy and sell different national currencies is known as the foreign exchange market. Foreign exchange can be cash, funds available on credit cards and debit cards, traveler's checks, bank deposits, or other short-term claims.[5] An **exchange rate** is the price of a currency. It is the number of units of one currency that is needed to buy one unit of another currency. For example, on June 26, 2001, a Finnish exporter could exchange 1 Finnish mark for 15 U.S. cents. The exchange rate, then, is the link among different national currencies that makes international price and cost comparisons possible, and ultimately makes international trade a reality.

In quick terms, the traditional foreign exchange market consists of the spot, forward, and swap markets. Spot transactions involve the exchange of currency the second day after the date on which the two traders agree to the transaction. Outright forward transactions involve the exchange of currency three or more days after the date on which the traders agree to the transaction. Other key foreign exchange instruments are currency swaps, options, and futures. Chapter 10 looks at how international traders use these tools to manage the risk of exchange rate instability.

The Mechanics of Currency Exchange

Operationally, the foreign exchange process follows standard steps. That is, assume you are a U.S. importer that has agreed to purchase a certain quantity of German-made circuit boards and to pay the German exporter 10,000 marks for them. Assuming you had the money, how would you go about paying? First, you would go to the international department of your local bank to buy 10,000 marks at the going market rate. On June 26, 2001, the mark/dollar exchange rate was 2.268 marks per dollar. On that date, your bank then would charge your account for $4,413.45 (10,000 ÷ 2.268) plus the transaction costs and give you a special check payable in marks made out to the exporter. The exporter would deposit it in a local German bank, which then would credit the exporter's account with 10,000 marks. The transaction would be complete.

One of the risks associated with foreign trade is the uncertainty of future exchange rates. The relative value between the two currencies could, and typically does, change between the time the deal is concluded and the time payment is received. If the exporter is not suitably protected, devaluation or depreciation of the foreign currency could cause the exporter to lose money. For example, if the buyer has agreed to pay 500,000 French francs for a shipment and the franc is valued at 20 cents, the seller would expect to receive U.S. $100,000. If the franc later decreased in value to 19 U.S. cents, payment under the new rate would be only U.S. $95,000, a loss of U.S. $5,000 for the seller. On the other hand, if the foreign currency increases in value to 21 U.S. cents, the exporter would get a windfall of $5,000 in extra profits. Nonetheless, few people profitably speculate on foreign exchange fluctuations on a regular basis.

One of the simplest ways for a U.S. exporter to avoid this type of risk is to quote prices and require payment in U.S. dollars. Doing so shifts the burden of foreign exchange risk onto the buyer. Exporters should also be aware of potential challenges to converting one currency into another. Not all currencies are freely or quickly converted into U.S. dollars. The U.S. dollar is widely accepted as an international trading currency, a characteristic that makes it a so-called **hard currency.** As such, American firms can often secure payment in dollars.

If the buyer asks to make payment in a foreign currency, the exporter should consult an international banker before negotiating the sales contract. Banks can offer cost-effective advice on the foreign exchange risks that exist with a particular currency. Some international banks can also help hedge against such a risk by agreeing to purchase the foreign currency at a fixed price in dollars, regardless of the currency's value at the time the customer pays. Banks will normally charge a fee or discount the transaction for this service. If this mechanism is used, the bank's fee should be included in the price quotation.

How Companies Use Foreign Exchange

Most foreign exchange transactions take place within the realm of the international department of commercial banks. This office helps exporters and importers manage many financial transactions. In the matter of financing international trade, an international department performs three essential functions: It buys and sells foreign exchange, collects and pays money in transactions with foreign buyers and sellers, and lends money in foreign currency. In performing collections, the international department serves as a vehicle for payments between its domestic and foreign customers. Lending usually takes place in the currency of the bank's headquarters, but the bank might be able to provide loans in a foreign currency if it has a branch in that country.

Commercial banks buy and sell foreign currency for many purposes. At the most basic, travelers going abroad or returning from a foreign country need to purchase or sell foreign currency. Also, residents of one country wanting to invest directly in other nations need to purchase foreign currency from a commercial bank. Further, suppose a Finnish exporter, such as Nokia, receives payment from a U.S. importer of cell phones in U.S. dollars and wants to use the dollars to buy raw materials from wire makers in China. Nokia's bank would simultaneously serve as a collector and act as a dealer in a foreign exchange transaction.

There are a number of reasons why companies use the foreign exchange market. The most obvious is for import and export transactions. For example, a U.S. company importing products from an overseas supplier—again, like Nokia—might have to convert U.S. dollars into a foreign currency to pay Nokia. In addition, international traders traveling abroad in search of new markets or new products must use foreign exchange to pay for their local expenses.

Besides conducting export and import deals, companies also use the foreign exchange market for a multitude of different financial transactions. For instance, a U.S. company opts to establish a manufacturing plant in Mexico to produce toasters for export back to the United States. At the outset, this company has to convert dollars into pesos to make the foreign direct investment into Mexico. After the Mexican subsidiary generates a profit, the company might then wish to convert pesos to dollars in order to send some of its profits back to its U.S. parent.

Traveling abroad, let alone working abroad, often creates moments of uncertainty. Here we see a shopper trying to decipher the currency exchange rates posted outside of a change shop in the Czech Republic. The exchange rate board shows a subtle but potentially costly difference between the United States and Europe. Whereas the former uses a period to denote a decimal point, Europeans use a comma. If not careful, companies and people can easily make a costly mistake.

Sources of Foreign Exchange

The foreign exchange market is made up of many different players, including but not limited to investors, exporters, importers, companies, governments, and transnational institutions. Some players buy and sell foreign exchange because they are involved in the export and import of goods and services. Others buy and sell foreign exchange because of foreign direct investments—both investing capital into and remitting dividends out of a country. Others are portfolio investors—they invest money in foreign stocks, bonds, and mutual funds in order to earn a return. These players have different objectives for buying and selling foreign currencies, but they all are part of the supply and demand for those currencies.

When a company needs foreign exchange, it typically goes to its commercial bank for help. If that bank is a large market maker, such as Citibank or Bank of America, the company can get its foreign exchange fairly easily. However, if the company is located in a small market using a local bank, where does this bank get its foreign exchange? A bank, either dealing on its own account or for a client, can trade foreign exchange with another bank directly or through a broker. In the broker market, it can use a voice broker or an electronic brokerage system.

Gradually, foreign exchange transactions are moving onto the Internet. Although the implications of such Internet use are still a matter for speculation, its adaptability raises the possibility that international traders will eventually be able to bypass the bank intermediaries to meet their need for foreign exchange. For instance, as of fall 2000, about $1.5 trillion of foreign currencies were traded every day on the world market, more than the total volume of stocks that change hands in an entire month on the New York Stock Exchange and NASDAQ combined. During 2000, a handful of marketplaces for foreign exchange opened. For example, Currenex of California began operations in April 2000; by October 2000, it was handling $375 million worth of transactions per day by mediating the exchange of currency among many foreign exchange buyers and the 25 banks that act as sellers. Currenex's system is direct. For example, say Intel wants to buy $5 million of Japanese yen. Under any circumstances, Intel stipulates that its finance staff must consider a minimum of three quotes for every foreign exchange deal.[6] Therefore, the finance staff of Intel logs on to Currenex.com and places an order; the member banks are instantly alerted. Within 25 seconds (for major currencies), the banks post their offers. Currenex then pops up a window to Intel that shows the offers in best-price-to-worst-price order. Intel then has five seconds to choose its seller and lock in the quote. So far, the results have been worthwhile. Others banks are moving into this market. In June 2000, a consortium of 13 banks announced plans for their own exchange, called FXall. In August 2000, wire services reported that Citigroup, Chase, Deutsche Bank, and Reuters would follow suit with a system of their own called Atriax.

As the cost competitiveness of Internet-based foreign exchange trading improves, more international traders will shift more of their trade from bricks-and-mortar currency dealers to the click-and-computer agents of the Internet. In all likelihood, given the performance of the Internet so far, international traders will get better foreign exchange quotes from e-finance outlets on the Internet than they could get from traditional currency dealers. In any event, we can foresee a wired world of currency exchange that gives international traders faster and cheaper access to foreign currencies. Indeed, in October 2000, only about 12 percent of foreign exchange trading was done electronically, yet some project the volume to grow to 75 percent by 2002.[7] As banks solve security issues associated with Internet trading, activity should pick up.[8]

Sources of Help for International Traders

Making sense of the various forms of international payment is tough under the best of circumstances. Adding the uncertainty created by changing foreign exchange rates poses even more difficulties. Companies typically have many options from both private and public sectors to help them figure out the best financing option. Specifically, international traders can consult national, state, and local trade offices; freight forwarders; international banks; export intermediaries; or general trade consultants. We will look at the three most popular resources—governmental agencies, export intermediaries, and commercial banks—that traders turn to for guidance.

Governmental Agencies

National, state, and local governments, seeing the benefits of international trade, actively aid the efforts of potential and active exporters and, to a lesser degree, protect the interests of struggling importers. Japan, for instance, relies on several offices, such as the Small and Medium Enterprise Agency, Agency of Industrial Science and Technology, and **Ministry of International Trade and Industry.** The latter, often referred to as MITI, plays a vital role in developing a strategic policy and providing operational assistance in order to help Japanese companies profitably trade internationally.

Programs in the United States give a sense of the financial help that is available to the international trader. The **Export–Import Bank (Exim Bank)** and Small Business Administration, for instance, directly help international traders get private sector loans to finance their export transaction. More precisely, these federal agencies help arrange the financing of the manufacturing costs of goods for export, purchase of goods or services, foreign accounts receivable, and standby letters of credit. Similarly, most states and several cities fund and operate export financing programs, including preshipment and postshipment working-capital loans and guarantees, accounts receivable financing, and export insurance.

The limited reserves of some states and cities push them to make their assistance contingent upon the exporter's proof that they do not risk losing much if the deal falls apart. An exporter need only provide proof of a letter of credit or sufficient credit insurance to satisfy this requirement. Too, in some situations, states and cities require the exporter do some part of the export deal within the jurisdiction of the funding authority. Often, meeting this call for local content can be done by using transportation facilities, such as an air- or seaport, in the city or state.

More strategically, the **Overseas Private Investment Corporation (OPIC)** finances the investment portion of an overseas transaction for U.S. businesses interested in a long-term investment in developing markets. OPIC uses a range of financial tools, including equity, debt (institutional, intercompany, and private), management agreements, and technical assistance to help a company finance its international operations. Recently, OPIC-supported funds have made direct equity and equity-related investments in emerging, expanding, and privatizing companies in sub-Saharan Africa, India, the New Independent States, Latin America, and Asia. Typical projects included ones in manufacturing and distribution, power generation, telecommunications, agribusiness, hotels, and banking.

Export Intermediaries

Export intermediaries, notably the so-called **export management company** and **export trading company** are practical recources. Export intermediaries can vary in size, ranging from specialized, small one-person operations to international trading companies with staff located around the world. Whatever their size, export intermediaries provide international traders with several ways to deal with payments and collections, particularly with respect to the more complex forms of financing such as countertrade.

In the extreme case, the export intermediary takes full responsibility for the export end of a company's business, leaving the manufacturer to worry simply about making enough products to fill international orders. Although attractive, this option can result in the company losing control over its foreign sales. If this is a concern, companies can opt to employ export intermediaries in any number of less comprehensive ways, including using them to provide short-term financing for the goods in transit or managing the exchange of national currencies. These choices efficiently deal with the matters of financing sales and extending credit. The price for this service, however—depending on whether the export intermediary is working on salary, commission, or retainer plus commission—can be high.

Commercial Banks

The same commercial banking tools that companies use to finance domestic activities, including revolving lines of credit for working capital, are often sought to finance export sales until the trader receives payment. A logical first step for a trader seeking to finance short-term international sales is to approach its local bank, given this bank's familiarity with the trader's financial standing, credit needs, repayment record, and ability to perform. Most banks can set up the paperwork to cover export and import transactions; however, smaller banks may charge particularly high fees for such services.

Therefore, a trader may consider consulting a commercial bank that has an active international department. This sort of bank usually has specialists who are familiar with exporting and importing and provide several services that help organize international trade financing (see Table 9.3). Such banks tend to have their own overseas branches or correspondent relationships with foreign banks. Also, this sort of bank can help many areas of payments and collections, particularly with respect to dealing with letters of credit. Finally, there is a straightforward solution to the trader's dilemma of whether to retain a relationship with the local bank without an international department or open one with the commercial bank that does. The trader can retain the local bank relationship while arranging a referral to the other bank; this referral then opens a correspondent relationship between the two banks.

Table 9.3

Payment and Collection Support Services Provided by Commercial Banks

- Exchange of currencies
- Assistance in financing exports
- Collection of foreign invoices, drafts, letters of credit, and other foreign receivables
- Transfer of funds to other countries
- Letters of introduction and letters of credit for travelers
- Credit information on potential representatives or buyers overseas
- Credit assistance to the exporter's foreign buyers

Often, an exporter shipping capital goods, such as Nokia exporting cell phones to its North American distributors, may ask its commercial bank to make medium-term loans directly to the foreign buyer to finance the sale. Generally, these loans are available for well-established foreign buyers in stable markets. Where there is an element of risk, banks typically require a standby letter of credit, recourse on the exporter in case of default, or similar sorts of repayment reinforcement.

Summary

The catalyst for trade between people of different nations is a powerful, self-sustaining force: People around the world need and want goods and services that are often only available from other nations or available there for a lower price than domestic producers charge. The financial mechanics of meeting this demand, however, are not quite self-sustaining or, if challenged, even self-maintaining. Managers must work hard to make sure payments and collections go as planned, especially when they must take into account factors such as the possibility of fraud and default, fluctuating foreign exchange rates, and the odd political or social disruption. The importance of prudent planning is perhaps most compelling in the matter of getting paid for what you do and making sure that what you bought is what you receive. Effective payments and collections help international traders deal with these issues. Fortunately, as this chapter showed, exporters and importers can use many financial tools and trade resources.

endnotes

[1] Paula Mitchell, "Alternative Financing Techniques in Trade with Sub-Saharan Africa," *Business America,* Vol. 118, No. 1–2, January–February 1997, p. 29; "Barter, Trade 'Are African Tradition,'" Africa News Service, February 2, 2000, p. 1; "Thailand Opens Homepage to Promote Thai-African Trade," Xinhua News Agency, August 11, 2000; and David Greybe, "South Africa Arms Deal Expected To Create 65,000 New Jobs," *Business Day,* September 17, 1999; Africa News Service, Inc.

[2] Len Karpen, "Your Company's Ticket Abroad: A Letter of Credit Can Help Small Companies Do Business with Foreign Suppliers," *Nation's Business,* Vol. 83, No. 8, August 1995, p. 47.

[3] James E. Byrne, "The Task Force on the Study of the UCC Article 5 (Letters of Credit)," *Business Law,* 1990, pp. 1521, 1538.

[4] "Some Blame Collection Problems on Material U.S. Is Sending Buyers," *Video Age International,* Vol. 11, No. 4, April–May 1991, p. 49.

[5] Ibid.

[6] Stated by Tim Power, cash manager at Intel Corporation, in Alix Nyberg, "Foreign Exchange: Getting Current Online," *CFO,* Vol. 16, October 2000, p. 25.

[7] Ibid.

[8] "Life After Execution," *Euromoney,* May 1999, p. 89.

Objectives

1. To appreciate the difference between risk and uncertainty

2. To grasp the idea of managing risk as an opportunity versus risk as a hazard

3. To learn about foreign exchange risk and the tools that traders and companies use to manage it

4. To understand the idea of political risk, its principal types, and active versus passive management approaches

5. To profile competing views of the scope of intellectual property rights

6. To realize how companies establish and protect intellectual property rights

Matsushita Deals with Foreign Exchange Risk

Beginning in 1974, Japan's Matsushita Electric Industrial Company, the world's biggest consumer electronics maker, steadily expanded its high-tech operation in the United Kingdom into a profitable export base to Europe. In September 2000, however, Matsushita announced plans to move most of its color TV production out of Britain. The growing risk of excessive economic exposure facing the U.K. subsidiary threatened to erode the value of continued operations in that country. Explained Yukio Shohtoku, Matsushita's managing director for overseas operations, "We are now facing the choice of moving color TV production out of the U.K.... It's only a question of time, not whether we will move.... We cannot continue to stay there and make money."

Matsushita blamed its decision on the increasing strength of the British pound against the euro, the recently created single European currency. Indeed, in August 2000, the president of Matsushita, Kunio Nakamura, had voiced concern about the growing currency risks of staying in Britain and speculated that, sooner or later, global companies would have no choice but to move their operations out of that country. More precisely, Matsushita, which sells products under the Panasonic, Technics, Quasar, and National brands, exports many products from the United Kingdom to Europe. Therefore, a rise in the pound's value against the euro makes its products more expensive and, thus, less competitive in other nations. By early September 2000, the British pound was rising in strength against that of the falling euro, a slide that had taken it to lifetime lows just 18 months after its momentous debut.

Mindful of the importance of host-government support and local consumers' positive image of its brands, Matsushita tried to minimize the fallout of its unpopular decision. Shohtoku emphasized that his company wanted to make up for the lost U.K. jobs but that the strength of the pound versus the euro created a growing hazard of currency risk. Ultimately, Matsushita could not remain in the United Kingdom and expect to make money.

Risk Management and Asset Protection

chapter 10

A mask of a human skull with protruding eyes used in the Day of the Dead festival in Mexico.

Shohtoku said any new foreign direct investment (FDI) would likely be in Eastern Europe—already, Matsushita planned to make many of its color TVs for the European market in the Czech Republic. The growth opportunities in this region promised to improve the company's competitive position. Offsetting these opportunities, however, were the hazards of disruptions in business regulations that could depress profits, along with the greater threat of intellectual property violations. Unlike the United Kingdom, social and economic changes in Eastern Europe had made political stability an ambitious quest. In addition, unlike the United Kingdom, these nations had not yet developed the systems to register, protect, and enforce the protection of intellectual property rights. Matsushita believed, though, that it still made better sense to trade the safety of the United Kingdom for the opportunities of Eastern Europe. In any event, Matsushita planned to set up safeguards to prevent possible theft of its technology.[1]

Introduction

FDI, particularly in the economies of emerging markets, offers many opportunities. Taking advantage of this growth has put many companies in new, exciting places. Many, though, have discovered that these environments can quickly become unkind, if not downright hostile. Therefore, a conspicuous by-product of international expansion is the exposure to greater and different forms of risk. Certainly, under many business circumstances, wherever managers go, they run into risk, whether in the form of competitive risk, market risk, financial risk, operating risk, technological risk, environmental risk, regulatory risk, or litigation risk. As we saw with Matsushita, the dynamic nature of international business only throws fuel onto this fire, adding the major risks of changing foreign exchange values, political disruption and turmoil, and violation of intellectual property rights (see Figure 10.1). Two facets of international business especially complicate these matters, namely (1) the difficulty of applying conventional risk management techniques to the stunning variety of international markets and (2) the fact that more things change than stay the same in many nations.

This chapter looks at those sources of risk that especially menace international operations: Fluctuations in foreign exchange values, political disruption and turmoil, and intellectual property violations. More important, we review the tools that managers use to define and contain these risks. Before turning to these topics, though, we take a closer look at the idea of risk management. This discussion gives a sense of the outlooks that companies use to raise the odds of success and reduce the chance of failure in their international activities.

The Idea of Risk Management

The best-laid plans of managers and companies run into challenges when things do not go as planned. Challenges can arise from internal conditions, such as an abrupt shortage of money to finance expansion. More commonly, managers face challenges that arise from unforeseen changes in the market-

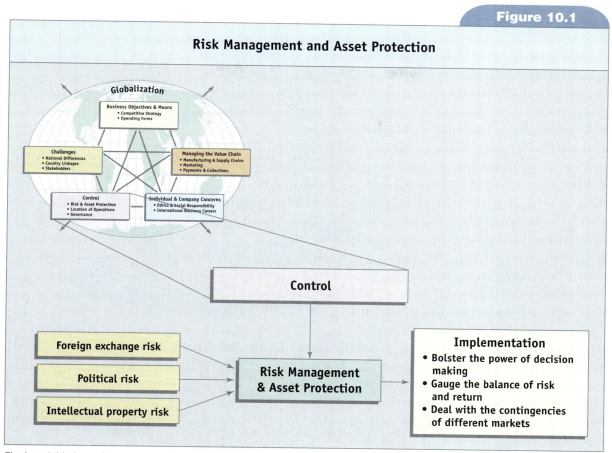

Figure 10.1

Risk Management and Asset Protection

The best-laid plans of managers and companies can run into unexpected operational and environmental challenges. Managers use a range of tools to protect their assets from excessive exposure to these risks.

place. Generally, we think of these changes in terms of uncertainty or risk. Although related, fundamental differences distinguish these ideas.

Uncertainty comes from changes in economic, social, and political trends (such as a spike in oil prices or interest rates), the arrival of new technologies (like the Internet), or shifts in consumer demand (preference for personal computers in Day-Glo colors versus traditional beige). These macro-events fundamentally alter the business environment for all companies in a market. In contrast, *risk* is the chance that a specific company will gain or lose money on a particular investment activity. For example, emerging markets such as Russia and China offer high growth potential but also high degrees of risk that will affect companies doing different things in different ways.

Unquestionably, it is useful to study the significance of uncertainty in a given country. However, forecasting the future ultimately tends toward speculation. For instance, although the Internet had been around for more than 20 years, its emergence into the business world in the mid-1990s surprised virtually all companies and quickly increased uncertainty in the marketplace. So

"Come <u>on</u>, Louis. No risk, no reward."

although prudent managers try to prepare for uncertainty, its random behavior and sweeping impact make it virtually impossible to manage it.

In contrast, the idea of risk is measurable and, therefore, manageable. Specifically, it is well within the realm of managers to define, measure, and predict the degree of risk of a specific activity—such as the probability of profitably entering a new market, building a plant in a foreign nation, or selling a different type of product. Without question, uncertainty surrounds all of these activities when first proposed. However, guided by their idea of risk, managers can rigorously estimate the likelihood that the company will run into particular types of challenges. Managers can then use this information to forecast whether the potential returns of an activity exceed its potential risks.

The most important step in the idea of risk management is the first one—namely, stipulating a clear-cut definition of risk that can effectively guide how managers then gather data, process information, and frame decision making. Generally, managers start this process by defining the idea of risk management in terms of risk as an opportunity or risk as a hazard.

Risk as Opportunity

This view of risk follows from the notion that a basic relationship exists between risk and return: The higher the risk of an activity, then the higher its potential return ought to be. For example, virtually any measure of risk would rate most proposals to invest in emerging markets, such as Nigeria, Russia, or

Vietnam, as speculative bets. Indeed, emerging countries' propensity toward regulatory and bureaucratic obstacles, infrastructure gaps, and vulnerability to natural disasters make many companies simply avoid them. However, the United Nations Conference on Trade and Development (UNCTAD) reported that, over the past decade, foreign investment in the world's 44 poorest countries has risen steadily, from an annual average of less than $1 billion in 1987–1992 to nearly $3 billion in 1998. Asked why, companies replied that these investments return far more profits than most of their other foreign investments. More precisely, UNCTAD reported that from 1990, the rate of return on FDI in Africa averaged 29 percent, a performance that was higher than in any other region in the world.[2]

To some degree, these superb returns reflect companies' investment in only the most potentially lucrative business opportunities in high-risk markets. Still, the rising tide of globalization inexorably raises the income levels of all people, whether they happen to live in stable developed markets or in risky emerging markets. For instance, Microsoft's business in Africa is growing by about 30 percent a year because emerging markets have many laptop-toting citizens who look for the latest and greatest software innovations. Thus, to paraphrase an age-old aphorism, the view of risk as an opportunity sees high-risk markets as simply half-filled glasses. Therefore, the idea of managing risk for opportunities is an offensive, proactive outlook that moves managers to take actions that achieve positive gains rather than avoid possible losses.

Prudently managed, risky markets promise terrific growth opportunities and great profit potential for the confident multinational enterprise (MNE). Still, the critical premise of this statement is "prudently managed." As we will see later in this chapter, companies apply various tools to manage risks that they believe increase the likelihood of positive returns within the constraints of a particular market. Finally, while approaches to managing risks as opportunity vary from company to company and situation to situation, they all center on collecting useful information to create knowledge that supports prudent risk taking.

Risk as Hazard

This idea of risk is typically what people think of when they hear the term *risk*. That is, the idea of risk as a hazard conjures images of negative events such as the devastating financial loss that can follow extreme change in exchange rates (as befell Barings Bank), a costly product recall due to unforeseen problems (like the tire recall that affected Bridgestone, Firestone, and Ford), or an environmental di-saster (as happened to Union Carbide in Bhopal, India). These sorts of disruptions inevitably command lots of headlines, provoke public debate, and terrify managers.

In practice, however, MNEs worry a lot about the nagging day-to-day risks that touch upon issues ranging from their abstract corporate image to the precise details of their business operations. Regarding the former, for example, Nike and McDonald's increasingly run the risk of a public backlash for the working conditions in East Asian companies that they use to make, respectively, athletic shoes and Happy Meals toys. Furthermore, MNEs monitor the potential risks of all sorts of operational hazards. For instance, the fear of being unable to run their business in an efficient, legal manner significantly shapes managers' foreign investment strategies. A survey of 121 European and American firms found that more than 40 percent had walked away from an oth-

These images spotlight a basic dilemma of intellectual property rights (IPRs). One photo shows street vendors open for business across the street from the U.S. Embassy in Beijing. Flagrantly defying the law, these vendors sell fake Beanie Babies at much lower prices than the genuine articles. In the second photo, we see Chinese officials in Guangzhou trying to enforce the IPRs of Japanese companies. They are supervising the destruction of more than 11,000 fake Casio, Citizen, and Seiko wristwatches that had been confiscated in a series of raids on counterfeiters.

erwise attractive foreign investment option due to the country's reputation for fraud, embezzlement, or corruption.[3]

Just like managing risk as an opportunity, managing risk as a hazard pushes managers to come up with methods to reduce the odds of a negative event—subject to the goals of not incurring excessive insurance expenses, prevention costs, or growth restraints. That is, managing risk to avoid possible penalties is a defensive approach that tends to use formal policies, procedures, and systems to prevent excessive exposure to business hazards. As we will see later in this chapter, managers use a range of internal and external techniques, such as currency hedging strategies or political risk insurance coverage, to minimize their exposure to potential investment losses.

Interestingly, globalization steadily pushes firms to see risk more as the price of better opportunities—as exemplified in Matsushita's move from the safety of the United Kingdom to the emerging economies of Eastern Europe. Increasingly, the market premium awarded to fast revenue growth can punish a company that plays it safe and frets too much about the hazards of an overseas opportunity. Furthermore, worrying too much about what can go wrong—the glass must be half empty for a reason—can constrain the natural entrepreneurship of managers. Therefore, perhaps the greatest irony of risk management is that going to great lengths to manage the risk of failure can ultimately lead to the failure of a company for the simple reason that business success depends on taking risks in the pursuit of opportunity.

Foreign Exchange Risk

To many, the most striking operating difference between domestic and international business is the financial basis of exchange. Chapter 9 showed that payments and collections in a domestic market differ greatly from their international counterparts. In a domestic transaction, companies use only one currency and need not worry about intermediaries, exposures, and inefficiencies. In a foreign transaction, companies use two or more currencies and care about each of these contingencies. The seemingly direct exchange of one currency for another, therefore, creates extensive risk for international traders.

Companies try to forecast exchange rate changes in the effort to reduce their possible costs. Fearful of the hazardous risk of making a bad call, most managers consult with outside experts to help them determine whether they have tapped important factors or need to rethink their forecast model. No matter how carefully the company prepares its forecast or how many experts it consults, however, estimates of currency trends and exchange rate changes are ultimately educated guesses.

For example, consider the turn of events that ravaged Hitachi, the Japanese conglomerate. In November 1998, Hitachi's management estimated its fiscal year fourth-quarter 1998 earnings (which ended on March 31, 1999, the typical close of the fiscal year for Japanese companies) based on a prediction of an exchange rate of 125 yen to the U.S. dollar. Although this forecast accurately called the direction of change in this set of exchange rates, it missed the magnitude of the strengthening of the yen relative to the dollar. As events unfolded, the yen actually averaged 117.9 to the dollar from October to early February. This change limited Hitachi's ability to export from Japan, depressed the yen value of its overseas earnings, and ruined its profit forecasts. By the time Hitachi closed its books for 1999, exchange rate changes turned its projected profits for 1998 into losses of more than $3 billion.

Sources of Foreign Exchange Risk

Companies such as Hitachi try to limit the downside of currency fluctuation by modeling currency trends and forecasting exchange rate movements. Justifying their efforts are the findings of many studies that link the value of a currency to any combination of circumstances, including but not limited to changes in foreign exchange reserves, inflation, balance of payments, money supply growth, interest rates, and economic growth rates on the supply, demand, and price of national currencies. In the realm of theoretical models, these variables can reasonably forecast currency trends and exchange rates for national currencies—presuming that the law of supply and demand behaves in practice as its does in theory.

In reality, though, several factors violate the law of supply and demand. The most notable lawbreaker is national governments. Governments intervene in the foreign exchange market to influence the direction and magnitude of change in the value of their currency for many reasons. For instance, a government may want to conserve its scarce reserves of a particular foreign currency—such as the U.S. dollar—in order to finance its purchase of petroleum from OPEC. Therefore, the government may impose exchange restrictions on companies or individuals that want to exchange the national currency for U.S. dollars. For instance, the aim of better controlling the rate of growth of its economy prompted the Central Bank of Russia to demand that exporters deposit 75 percent of their hard-currency proceeds with the Central Bank; it later added that it might increase this to 100 percent. This policy enabled the Central Bank to tighten its grip over foreign exchange operations and, by controlling exporters' access to working capital, the performance of the economy.[4]

Typically, governments intervene in the foreign exchange markets by using their reserves of other currencies to buy their own currency. This transaction effectively creates more demand, lower supply, and, therefore, higher exchange prices for the national currency. Governments have several means of intervention, including import licensing, multiple exchange rates, import deposit requirements, and quantity controls (see Table 10.1).

Business Implications of Exchange Rate Risk

The irony of government intervention in the foreign exchange market is that it is theoretically impossible for any form of intervention to permanently alter the value of a national currency. Without question, intervention can temporarily halt a slide in the value of the national currency. However, intervention can-

Table 10.1

Common Forms of Government Intervention in the Foreign Exchange Market	
Method of Intervention	**Outcome**
Artificially fix the exchange rate	Requires all recipients, exporters, and others who receive foreign currency to sell it to its central bank at the official buying rate. Then the central bank rations the foreign currency it acquires by selling it at fixed rates to those needing to make payment abroad for essential goods.
Multiple exchange rate system	The government determines which kinds of transactions are to be conducted at which exchange rates. Countries with multiple exchange rates often have a very high exchange rate for luxury goods and financial flows and a lower exchange rate for other trade transactions, such as imports of essential commodities and semimanufactured goods.
Government-imposed inconvertibility of currency	This setback effectively prohibits a company from converting its profits or capital from the local currency into a different currency.
Advance import deposit	The government tightens the authorization of import licenses and requires importers to make a deposit with the central bank, often for as long as one year and interest free, covering the full price of manufactured goods they would purchase from abroad.
Quantity controls	Limits the amount of currency that a local resident can purchase from the bank, usually for foreign travel. The government sets a policy on how much money a tourist is allowed to take overseas.

not force the market to move the long-term exchange rate to a value that has no economic basis. Consequently, government intervention tends to happen in hazardous styles that create extensive foreign exchange risk for international companies. In particular, exchange rate changes can affect companies' marketing, production, and financial decisions.

Marketing Decisions

Marketing managers watch exchange rates because their dramatic effect on consumer demand for a company's products can influence price, promotion, distribution, and product policies. For instance, if Hitachi sold its new TV set for 325,000 yen, it would cost $2,500 in the United States when the nominal exchange rate was 130 yen to the dollar. At a forecast rate of 120 yen, the TV would cost $2,708. If the yen continued to strengthen and the relative inflation rate held steady, Hitachi would worry even more. In reality, in the late 1990s, the dollar actually approached 100 yen and the U.S. price of the TV rose to $3,250. At this point, Hitachi's marketing people wondered whether American consumers would pay $3,250 for a TV or simply wait for the price to fall. In the meantime, Hitachi had to figure out if it should pass the price increase onto consumers or reduce the U.S. price and absorb the loss. Depending on the answer to these questions, Hitachi had to adjust its promotion and distribution policies. Ultimately, if the yen eventually strengthened beyond 100 to the dollar, Hitachi would need to rethink the ongoing feasibility of its product policy.

Production Decisions

Exchange rate changes affect several aspects of international manufacturing. For example, a company in a country in which wages and operating expenses are high might consider moving production to a country with a currency that is rapidly losing value, as we saw earlier in Matsushita's move from the United Kingdom to Eastern Europe. The company's home currency would buy lots of the weak currency, thereby letting the company effectively pay lower prices to setup and supply its plant. Furthermore, the lower costs of production would yield goods that would be relatively cheaper in other national markets. The experiences of German automaker BMW highlight other facets of the effect of exchange rates on production decisions. In the mid-1990s, BMW decided to build a new factory to make cars in South Carolina due to the then unfavorable exchange value of the German mark in terms of the U.S. dollar. Moving auto production to the United States solved this dilemma by letting BMW build and sell cars to American consumers without direct concern for exchange rates. However, as events unfolded, renewed strength in many European currencies allowed BMW to use its U.S. factory to serve the American market and also supply cars, via export, to Europe.[5]

Financial Decisions

Exchange rates especially affect financial decisions, primarily in the areas of sourcing of financial resources, remittance of funds across national borders, and reporting of financial results. In the first area, a company might be tempted to borrow money where interest rates are lowest. However, global money markets are remarkably efficient in quickly eliminating interest rate differentials among countries through exchange rate changes. In the matter of managing cross-border financial flows, a company prefers converting its holdings of a local currency into its home-country currency when favorable exchange rates give it the opportunity to exchange fewer local currency units for more of its home currency. However, countries that rely on strict currency controls make it difficult to do so.

Exchange rate movement can impact a company's cash flow. For example, if a U.S. company's Mexican subsidiary earns 1 million pesos when the exchange rate is 3.12 pesos to the dollar, the dollar equivalent of its income is $320,513. If the peso depreciates to 8 pesos per dollar, the dollar equivalent of that income falls to $125,000. The opposite takes place if the local currency appreciates against that of the company's home country. As we saw above, this type of exchange rate risk punished Hitachi. The yen equivalent of Hitachi's dollar earnings in the United States continued to fall as the value of the dollar fell against the yen. Finally, as we will elaborate in the following discussion, exchange rate changes can materially influence the character of the financial results that a company reports.

Forms of Foreign Exchange Risk Exposure

If all exchange rates were permanently fixed in relation to one another, there would be no foreign exchange risk. However, currency values change frequently. A change in the exchange rate can result in three different exposures for a company: translation exposure, transaction exposure, and economic exposure.

Translation Exposure

We refer to the risk created by the present measurement of past activity as **translation exposure.** That is, periodically, a company must translate its foreign currency financial statements into a single reporting currency in order to build its consolidated financial statements. Exposed accounts—those translated at the balance sheet rate or current exchange rate—either gain or lose value when the conversion from the foreign to the reporting currency takes place. The combined effect of the exchange rate change on all assets and liabilities is either a net gain or loss.

It is important to note that the gain or loss does not represent an actual cash flow effect—the cash is simply translated into dollars, not actually converted into dollars. The problem is that reported earnings can either rise or fall against the dollar because of the translation effect. This volatility can affect earnings per share and stock prices.

Transaction Exposure

The risk that exchange rate fluctuations materially change the expected income from a transaction that is denominated in a foreign currency is **transaction exposure.** Until a company settles the accounts receivable or payable that it holds in a foreign currency, it carries exposure to the risk that exchange rate movements will either penalize it (in the event that its home currency grows weaker relative to the other currency) or reward it (in the event that its home currency grows stronger relative to the other currency). Unlike the "paper" gains or losses of translation exposure, transaction exposures materially change the actual cash flows for the buyer and seller.

Economic Exposure

This source of risk refers to the degree that changes in exchange rates, as we saw in our opening discussion of Matsushita, materially influence a firm's future earning power. Whereas transaction exposure deals with mostly short-term risks, **economic exposure** refers to the long-run effects of exchange rate changes on the future pricing of products, the sourcing and cost of inputs, and the location of investments. Often, dealing with economic exposure leads a company to rethink the way it runs its international operations, seeking to locate plants and offices in nations with a more supportive exchange rate environment. For instance, the remarkable strength of the Japanese yen during the 1980s and 1990s discouraged foreign firms from manufacturing products there. Instead, most opted to build plants in Korea, China, or Taiwan, all nations then with relatively more competitive currency rates, to access regional resources and supply Japanese consumers.

Managing Foreign Exchange Exposure

Managers and their firms, whether they treat risk as a hazard or as an opportunity, apply several methods to protect their investments from translation, transaction, and economic exposure.

Translation and transaction exposure can be covered by protecting short-term cash flows from adverse changes in exchange rates. Typically, managers use a mix of the major tools of the foreign exchange market, namely, the spot exchange rates, forward exchange rates, and currency swaps.

Spot Exchange Rate

When a buyer and a seller agree to execute their deal right then and there, or "on the spot," they then must arrange the immediate exchange of money (in reality, spot transactions involve the exchange of currency up through the second day after the date on which the two foreign exchange traders agree to the transaction). They do so by determining the **spot exchange rate,** the rate at which a foreign exchange market would, at that moment, willingly convert one currency into another currency. Given that exchange rates change continually, the timing of the spot exchange can greatly influence the relative value of the parts of the transactions.

Forward Exchange Rate

To minimize the hazard of picking a bad "spot" to complete a deal, a buyer may arrange a forward exchange whereby it persuades the seller to transfer the good and exchange currencies by a specific future date. We call the exchange rates that govern this sort of future deal the **forward exchange rate.** The natural reluctance of sellers to wait too long limits how far into the future they will agree to a specified exchange rate. Although there are exceptions, most sellers will allow buyers to use the 30-day, 90-day, or 180-day forward exchange rate. Naturally, the longer the time span, the greater the odds that an unexpected event, either good or bad, might happen. Therefore, depending on whether the buyer sees opportunities or hazards in the forward exchange rate market, it will negotiate its preferred time span. Reality, though, does restrict the flexibility of this option. There is a forward exchange market for a limited number of national currencies, principally those of Britain, Canada, France, Germany, Japan, Switzerland, and the United States.

Currency Swap

This instrument refers to the simultaneous purchase and sale of a given amount of foreign exchange for different value dates—sort of like a complex forward con-

> **Table 10.2**

Exchange Rates, Thursday, April 5, 2001

Currency	Foreign Currency in Dollars Thu.	Wed.	Dollars in Foreign Currency Thu.	Wed.	Currency	Foreign Currency in Dollars Thu.	Wed.	Dollars in Foreign Currency Thu.	Wed.
f-Argent (Peso)	1.0005	1.0003	.9995	.9997	Jordan (Dinar)	1.4065	1.4085	.71098	.70998
Australia (Dollar)	.4909	.4894	2.0371	2.0433	Lebanon (Pound)	.000660	.000660	155.00	1515.00
Austria (Schilling)	.0652	.0655	15.340	15.258	Malaysia (Ringgit)	.2632	.2632	3.7995	3.7996
c-Belgium (Franc)	.0222	.0224	44.97	44.73	z-Mexico (Peso)	.106123	.106213	9.4230	9.4150
Brazil (Real)	.4616	.4596	2.1665	2.1760	Netherlands (Guilder)	.4072	.4092	2.4555	2.4435
Britain (Pound)	1.4932	1.4343	.6697	.6972	N. Zealand (Dollar)	.4045	.4068	2.4722	2.4582
30-day fwd	1.4920	1.4395	.6702	.6947	Norway (Krone)	.1103	.1106	9.0660	9.0416
60-day fwd	1.4906	1.4381	.6709	.6954	Pakistan (Rupee)	.0163	.0163	61.40	61.43
90-day fwd	1.4895	1.4370	.6714	.6959	y-Peru (New Sol)	.2836	.2837	3.526	3.525
Canada (Dollar)	.6348	.6363	1.5754	1.5717	z-Philippines (Peso)	.0199	.0200	50.17	50.01
30-day fwd	.6347	.6372	1.5756	1.5694	Poland (Zloty)	.2475	.2469	4.04	4.05
60-day fwd	.6346	.6371	1.5758	1.5695	Portugal (Escudo)	.004474	.004498	223.50	222.30
90-day fwd	.6346	.6371	1.5758	1.5695	a-Russia (Ruble)	.0347	.0347	28.8600	28.8600
y-Chile (Peso)	.001674	.001673	597.45	597.65	SDR (SDR)	1.27140	1.26740	.7865	.7890
China (Yuan)	.1208	.1208	8.2771	8.2772	Saudi Arabia (Riyal)	.2666	.2666	3.7503	3.7504
Colombia (Peso)	.000432	.000432	2316.50	2314.25	Singapore (Dollar)	.5520	.5511	1.8115	1.8145
c-Czech Rep (Koruna)	.0260	.0259	38.44	38.60	Slovak Rep (Koruna)	.0207	.0206	48.33	48.51
Denmark (Krone)	.1207	.1210	8.2830	8.2617	South Africa (Rand)	.1237	.1241	8.0822	8.0553
Dominican Rep (Peso)	.0629	.0629	15.90	15.90	South Korea (Won)	.000732	.000732	1365.20	1365.20
d-Egypt (Pound)	.2594	.2594	3.8550	3.8550	Spain (Peseta)	.005394	.005420	185.39	184.49
Europe (Euro)	.89730	.90200	1.1145	1.1086	Sweden (Krona)	.0984	.0979	10.1653	10.2124
30-day fwd	.89790	.90270	1.1137	1.1078	Switzerland (Franc)	.5877	.5904	1.7015	1.6938
90-day fwd	.08993	.90420	11.1198	1.1059	30-day fwd	.5893	.5914	1.6969	1.6908
Finland (Mark)	.1509	.1517	6.6248	6.5928	60-day fwd	.5896	.5928	1.6961	1.6870
France (Franc)	.1368	.1375	7.3087	7.2722	90-day fwd	.5921	.5943	1.6888	1.6827
Germany (Mark)	.4586	.4612	2.1804	2.1683	Taiwan (Dollar)	.0303	.0303	32.98	32.96
Greece (Drachma)	.002632	.002647	379.88	377.83	Thailand (Baht)	.02204	.02215	45.38	45.15
Hong Kong (Dollar)	.1282	.1282	7.7983	7.7997	Turkey (Lira)	.000001	.000001	1245000	1215000
Hungary (Forint)	.0034	.0034	295.87	297.57	U.A.E. (Dirham)	.2723	.2723	3.6728	3.6727
y-India (Rupee)	.0215	.0215	46.590	46.590	f-Uruguay (New Peso)	.0781	.0781	12.8000	12.8000
Indonesia (Repiah)	.000093	.000094	10705.00	10610.00	Venezuela (Bolivar)	.0014	.0014	707.7000	707.5000
Ireland (Punt)	1.1390	1.1451	.8780	.8733					
Israel (Shekel)	.2376	.2362	4.2080	4.2330	a-Russian Central Bank rate.				
Italy (Lira)	.000463	.000466	2158.61	2146.64	c-commercial rate, d-free market rate, f-financial rate, y-official				
Japan (Yen)	.008062	.007970	124.04	125.47	rate, z-floating rate.				
30-day fwd	.008097	.008019	123.50	124.71	Prices as of 3:00 P.M. Eastern Time from Dow Jones Telerate				
60-day fwd	.008125	.008046	123.07	124.28	and other sources.				
90-day fwd	.008160	.008080	122.55	123.76					

tract. Whereas the spot and forward exchanges are open to almost anyone, currency swaps are intricate arrangements that usually involve transactions within a company. For example, consider the U.S. electronics company that buys parts from its Japanese subsidiary. The U.S. parent must pay its Japanese subsidiary when the latter transfers the parts. However, presume that the U.S. parent plans to receive Japanese yen in 90 days when its subsidiary sells the finished good in the Japanese market and remits the sale receipts to the parent. In this scenario, a currency swap gives the U.S. parent the option to exchange dollars on the spot market for the yen that it will need to pay its outstanding debt to the subsidiary but also buy a forward contract to sell Japanese yen in 90 days at the quoted 90-day forward rate for the yen. Therefore, this currency swap lets the U.S. parent lock in the future yen/dollar exchange rate, thereby reducing its exposure to the risk of unforeseen exchange rate movement. As a general rule, companies use currency swaps when they believe it makes sense to move out of one currency into another for a period without incurring any additional foreign exchange risk.

Managing Economic Exposure

The spot, forward, and swap tools of the foreign exchange market enable companies to manage translation and transaction exposure. These tools, however, do not help a company deal with economic exposure. Managing this source of foreign exchange risk requires that a company carefully review its idea of risk and assemble the optimum mix of countries within which to build and operate its plants. Preparing for economic exposure compels a company to think and, as we saw earlier with Matsushita's move from the United Kingdom to Eastern Europe, to review its international strategy carefully. Again, the general rule for managing economic exposure is configuring assets in the mix of countries that best protects the firm's long-term financial soundness from adverse change in foreign exchange rates.

Japanese firms' recent transfer of manufacturing from Japan, their preferred production base, to other countries spotlights their effort to avoid having the exchange value of the yen determine their product pricing policies. Making products in different countries lets Japanese firms shift production out of Japan, when the long-term value of the yen rises too high. This strategy, incidentally, would have helped Hitachi avoid its $3-billion foreign exchange penalty. Therefore, the best protection against economic exposure is to avoid putting all of your eggs into the country whose rising currency value threatens to eliminate your price competitiveness and strategic flexibility in other foreign markets.

Political Risk

Investing overseas exposes a company to new sources of risk. Perhaps the most potentially damaging of these risks arises from the quirks of national politics or, as commonly called, political risk. Generally, **political risk** is the chance that political decisions, events, or conditions in a particular nation will affect the business environment in ways that lead investors to lose some or all of the value of their investment or be forced to accept a lower-than-projected rate of return. A variety of actions, events, and situations create political risk (see Table 10.3). Although the sources of political risk differ from country to country, the net effect is the same around the world: The actions of political actors, forces, or trends create a climate of risk that reduces the company's rate of return or possibly destroys the value of the company's local assets.

General Types of Political Risk

There are several types of political risk, ranging from those that create the routine hardships of international business to those problems that can escalate

Table 10.3

Profile of Leading Sources of Political Risk

Type	Outcome
Expropriation or nationalization	A government or political faction unilaterally takes ownership of the company's local assets. Compensation to the company, if at all forthcoming, is generally a trivial percent of the assets' value. This event was common in the 1960s and 1970s (e.g., Cuba, Chile, Venezuela, Uganda, Zambia, Ethiopia, Iran) but is rare today. However, in any event, the losses are immense.
International war or civil strife	Damages or destroys the company's local assets.
Unilateral breach of contract	Decision of a government to repudiate the original contract that it had negotiated with the foreign company. The revision penalizes the firm and rewards the nation by reallocating the profits of the local operations. In addition, this extends to government approval of a local company's choice to breach its contracts with its foreign partner.
Destructive government actions	Actions such as the unilateral imposition of nontariff barriers in the form of greater local content requirement, which interferes with the transfer of goods between supply links or the distribution of goods to local consumers.
Harmful actions against people	Directed toward the local staff of the company; often involves kidnapping, extortion, and terrorism.
Restrictions on repatriation of profit	Limits on the gross amount of profits a company can remit from its local operation to a nonlocal unit of the company.
Differing points of view	Differing interpretation of human and labor rights and environmental obligations that create backlash problems in the foreign company's home market.
Discriminatory taxation policies	A foreign company bears a higher tax burden than the local firm, or in some cases, the more favored foreign company, because of its nationality.

toward doomsday scenarios. This section looks at the most common types: systemic, procedural, distributive, and catastrophic political risks.

Systemic Political Risks

Generally, the political process within a particular nation does not routinely subject foreign operations to discriminatory treatment. If it did, few companies would accept the excessive hazard of investing in such countries—no matter how attractive the market opportunity. More commonly, domestic and international companies alike face political risks created by significant shifts in public policy. For instance, new political leadership in a nation may impose a radically different approach to the regulation of private investment than had its predecessor. These regulations can alter the business system for all companies. Then again, a government may target its public policy initiatives toward a specific economic sector that it believes foreign companies unduly dominate—as has happened with bananas in Guatemala, copper in Chile, and oil in Iran. In both situations, change in the political system created systemic risks that changed a company's view of the opportunities and hazards in a national economy.

Systemic changes do not always result in higher political risks that reduce potential profits. Elections and subsequent policy shifts can create opportunities, although risky, for foreign investors. In Argentina, for example, a newly elected government initiated radical programs in the 1990s that transformed the 40-year-old protectionist, highly regulated, state-centered economy into a system marked by deregulation, private enterprise, and international competition. Companies that accepted the risk of these new opportunities were able to prosper as Argentina moved from socialism to capitalism.

Finally, a major source of political risk comes from international systemic events that are beyond the control of a national government. As we noted in Chapter 4, the waves of economic and financial crisis that engulfed emerging markets in the late 1990s led governments in East Asia, Russia, and South America to depreciate their national currencies and adopt austerity programs. These decisions spurred massive capital flights of liquid assets from these countries, which in turn triggered further currency devaluations and soaring interest rates. As consumers stopped buying goods and companies stopped building plants, growth ground to a halt. These types of dramatic shifts in monetary policy can quickly trigger economic disruption, social discontent, and political turmoil, all of which can boost the level of political risk for companies caught in these markets.

Procedural Political Risk
Each day, people, products, and funds move from point to point in the global market. Each move creates a procedural transaction between units, whether within a company, a country, or region. In a risk-free environment, these transactions work efficiently and effectively. Political actions, however, sometimes create frictions that interfere with these transactions.

On one level, government corruption, labor disputes, election fraud, and a partisan judicial system can significantly raise the costs of getting things done for an MNE. For instance, corruption among customs officials can influence the export or import operations of a foreign firm by making it difficult to clear goods through customs unless the company consents to pay for "special assistance." Similarly, the low bidder for a public works project may lose to the firm that is disposed to make a "campaign contribution" to an influential government minister. In these sorts of situations, political risk changes the procedures of the business game. The net effect is to raise the cost of business such that the company looking for growth has to adjust the projected returns of the opportunity against the higher operating costs, whereas the firm managing risk as a hazard finds justification to stay away.

Distributive Political Risk
People in many nations see the foreign company, at its most glorious, as an agent of profits and prosperity. As an MNE achieves greater success over time,

however, some nations question the distributive justice of the rewards, wondering whether they are getting their "fair" share. Often, nations decide they are not and begin a game of creeping intervention that aims to redirect a greater share of rewards to local interests—but in ways that do not provoke the company to close shop and flee. Generally, nations do so by revising their tax codes, regulatory structure, and monetary policy to capture greater benefits from foreign companies. The immediate outcome of these changes is to enrich the host nation. Eventually, though, nations that hike distributive risk to extreme levels pay the price by developing reputations or installing barriers that discourage other foreign investors.

This form of political risk can be quite subtle. For instance, few think of the United States as a nation with high levels of distributive political risk. However, like every other nation in the world, the U.S. government uses its policy tools to achieve political goals via economic activity. For example, the United States has perhaps the highest degree of political risk in the world for companies that manufacture and market cigarettes. The U.S. government has fought domestic and international cigarette companies on matters of taxation, regulation, business practice, and liability. Its numerous successes thus far have imposed direct costs of tens of billions of dollars and indirect costs that some in the industry claim are incalculable. In recourse, cigarette companies are seeking growth in foreign markets that show a better trade-off between political risk and financial returns.

Catastrophic Political Risk
This type of political risk includes those random political developments that adversely affect the operations of all companies in a country but especially punish MNEs' local operations. Catastrophic political risk arises from the usual flash points of national crisis, such as racial and ethnic discord, civil strife, terrorism, civil war, international quarrels, and national collapse. Generally, the catalyst for such risk is a politically motivated disagreement that fuels conflict at the local, national, or international level. Although uncommon, catastrophic political risk's impact immediately disrupts the business environment. If it spirals out of control, such risk can devastate companies and countries.

For instance, in 1998, civil strife swept through Indonesia and eventually culminated in the downfall of the long-running Suharto government. The revolution that surrounded Suharto's fall, besides costing MNEs billions of dollars in lost revenues, extensively damaged their local facilities. Moreover, those foreign companies that had prospered under Suharto especially suffered when their patron fell from power. We see similar situations at play in the ethnic discord, civil war, and international conflict that plague parts of the former Soviet Union and Yugoslavia, as well as hot spots throughout Africa, South America, and East Asia. In each nation, the resulting political risk has crippled local operations and deterred other MNEs from even looking at potential opportunities.

Finally, most often, the press reports the political catastrophes that hit companies. However, the visibility of foreign companies and their local managers may inspire terrorist activities, such as kidnapping and assassinations of executives, that can lead to personal catastrophes. Indeed, the matter of personal safety is a growing source of political risk for more and more companies (see Figure 10.3). For instance, as of fall 2000, the U.S. government listed 74 coun-

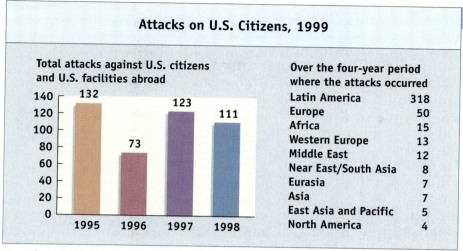

Attacks on U.S. Citizens, 1999

Total attacks against U.S. citizens and U.S. facilities abroad

Year	Attacks
1995	132
1996	73
1997	123
1998	111

Over the four-year period where the attacks occurred

Latin America	318
Europe	50
Africa	15
Western Europe	13
Middle East	12
Near East/South Asia	8
Eurasia	7
Asia	7
East Asia and Pacific	5
North America	4

source: September 21, 1999. © 1999, USA Today. From *USA Today,* Reprinted with permission.

Figure 10.3

The attacks include those on tourists and government employees but indicate the widespread nature of violence that expatriates can encounter.

tries that it believed posed a local threat to the physical security of U.S. citizens. Increasingly, expatriates' residences in crime-torn cities such as Lagos, Bogotá, or Johannesburg come equipped with a phalanx of security devices. Some foreign firms in South Africa even offer "pre-rape counseling" to female expatriates and their daughters.[6] Besides the human cost of lost lives and lost opportunities, protecting managers from this sort of political risk is costly. Some firms, for instance, spend between 5 and 10 percent of their budgets on security in nations such as Algeria, South Africa, and Colombia that exhibit high political risk.

An Illustrative Example: Political Risk Management at Hewlett-Packard[7]

Hewlett-Packard has extensive exposure to political risk, given that it makes computers and business machines at 60 locations in 16 countries and sells goods and services to another 120 countries. In addition, Hewlett-Packard's leveraged, interdependent global supply chain links many subcontractors spread across numerous locations. Therefore, Hewlett-Packard particularly worries about the hazard of the "domino effect" of a business interruption at any one site moving along its global supply chain. Cedric Hughes, corporate risk manager for Hewlett-Packard, explained that the company's goal is to "manage the political risk, not transfer it."

Practically, Hughes explained that Hewlett-Packard's philosophy of actively managing its political risk rather than transferring it to third-party agencies or insurance companies reflects an "aggressive risk identification and mitigation" approach that proactively looks for problems before they flare into crises. In other words, Hewlett-Packard tries to manage its political risk exposure by asking managers to identify and recognize their real exposures, directing its strategic planning process to make risks obvious, and devising business continuity and business recovery plans.

Hewlett-Packard concedes that perfectly forecasting political risk is impossible and that no matter how well it prepares, political risks can quickly emerge and escalate into crises. Consequently, Hewlett-Packard maintains three global crisis management teams: A corporate team in the United States and regional teams based in Europe and East Asia. The regional teams operate as an early-warning system whereby any incident at a particular subsidiary or site is reported to the regional office and then to the corporate crisis management team.

Political Risk Management

The actions of host governments and local political institutions and actors directly shape the success or failure of overseas operations. MNEs try to deal with these challenges by working with local partners, choosing locations in the safest part of an unsafe nation, configuring plants and offices in ways that create barriers to government interference or takeovers, or building alliances with powerful local supporters. Each of these methods is a politically keen response to political risk management. However, given the choice, MNEs would prefer to do business in ways that make economic rather than political sense. Nonetheless, political distortions in many countries simply do not give an MNE a choice. Therefore, political risk management is an essential component of any profitable foreign investment strategy.

In principle, as we saw with Hewlett-Packard, each company has to deal with several issues in managing political risk. Important questions include the choice of actively or passively managing political risks, fully or partially hedging them through insurance, or simply ignoring them. We will look at the two most common political risk management methods: active management and passive management.

Active Political Risk Management

Managers who see risk as an opportunity, like those at Hewlett-Packard, tend to take an active approach to manage the company's exposure to political risk. This outlook typically leads them to choose between two political risk management methods: Trying to quantify the precise degree of political risk versus relying on the judgment of experts to estimate the general degree of political risk in a country.

Managers who believe in the power of rigorous quantitative analysis assume that positive and negative political events in any nation are neither independent nor random events. Rather, they believe political events unfold in observable patterns that can be detected by statistical methods, which can thus measure and predict future instances of political risk. In summary, this method of political risk management reasons that if you measure the right set of discrete events, you should be able to calculate the degree of political risk in a particular country and estimate the odds that politically risky disruptions—civil strife, contract repudiation, redistribution of benefits, financial controls, disruptions in regimes, and so forth—will happen.

An active approach depends on identifying the indicators that best measure political risk. Often, these indicators include such things as the number of generals in political power, pace of urbanization, timing of government crises, ethnolingual fractionalization, and degree of literacy. For instance, the Political System Stability Index uses time-series analysis to create three equally weighted indices: Socioeconomic Characteristics Index, Governmental Process Index, and Societal Conflict Index, each of which is made up of several indicators. Upon collecting the needed data, managers can objectively look at and compare the level of political risk within and across nations.

Other companies tinker with this approach and try to assess political risk with qualitative measures. That is, they shy away from simply counting and analyzing political events in favor of the presumably more insightful judgment of country experts. Granted, country experts often rely on quantitative measures of political risk. However, they add their sense of the situation to include subjective elements of political risk. Dow Chemical was an early user of this method. Its managers ran standardized interviews to determine key events in a country over a specified period. They would then develop likely scenarios and assign probabilities for a five-year period. Hewlett-Packard, as we saw previously, also applies a qualitative approach to political risk management.

Presently, there are several political risk management services, such as Institutional Investor, Euromoney, Economist, and the PRS Group, that report risk measures for individual countries. For instance, the PRS Group offers 18-month and five-year risk forecasts for more than 100 nations using models that try to capture political risk in terms of regime stability, financial transfer, direct investment, and export markets. PRS relies on three to seven country experts per nation to estimate the trend for a menu of *political variables* (such as corruption in government, military in politics, organized religion in politics, racial and nationality tensions, and political terrorism), *financial variables* (such as delayed payment of suppliers' credits, repudiation of contracts by governments, losses from exchange controls, and expropriation of private investments), and *economic variables* (such as inflation, debt service as a percentage of exports of goods and services, and international liquidity ratios). Table 10.4 shows PRS's 2000 report of the riskiest and least-risky countries for business in 2000.

Passive Political Risk Management

Many companies refrain from directly managing the political risk of their operations. Instead, they treat political risk as an unpredictable hazard of international business and seek ways to hedge their exposure. Typically, these companies shield themselves from political risk by buying insurance that protects

Table 10.4

THE PRS GROUP Top-Ranked Countries for Political Risk	
Ten Least-Risky Countries	**Ten Riskiest Countries**
1. Singapore 2. Luxembourg 3. Finland 4. Norway 5. Switzerland 6. Netherlands 7. Brunei 8. Denmark 9. Ireland 10. Canada	1. Sierra Leone 2. Somalia 3. Yugoslavia 4. Guinea-Bissau 5. Congo, Dem. Republic 6. Angola 7. Iraq 8. Korea, DPR 9. Congo, Republic 10. Liberia

source: www.polrisk.com/commonhtml/toprank.html

their operations from any number of sources of political risk, including but not limited to government expropriation, involuntary abandonment, or damage to assets due to political violence. Presently, government agencies like the Overseas Private Investment Corporation (OPIC) in the United States, international organizations such as multilateral development banks, and private sector insurance companies provide political risk insurance. We look at each in turn.

OPIC. This U.S. governmental agency assists U.S. FDI in emerging markets. OPIC encourages U.S. investment projects overseas by offering political risk insurance, all-risk guarantees, and direct loans. OPIC's political risk insurance protects U.S. investment ventures abroad against civil strife and other violence, expropriation, and inconvertibility of currency. Insurance, which is limited to U.S. businesses, is available for up to $200 million per investment, and both debt and equity are eligible for coverage. In 1990, for example, OPIC paid a claim to Chase Manhattan Bank for losses that it incurred due to the Dominican Republic government's refusal to let it convert its pesos into dollars. Similarly, in 1999, OPIC, along with various syndicates of Lloyd's of London, paid MidAmerican Energy $290 million in accordance with its political risk insurance policies. This payment covered MidAmerican Energy's losses on its Indonesian energy projects when Persero Perusahaan Listruik Negara, the Indonesian state electric corporation, reneged on its contracts.[8]

Multilateral Development Banks (MDBs). These banks are international financial institutions funded and owned by the member governments. Examples of MDBs include the African Development Bank, Asian Development Bank, European Bank for Reconstruction and Development, Inter-American Development Bank, and World Bank Group. MDBs aim to promote economic and social progress in their developing member countries by providing financial incentives that make opportunities more attractive or hazards less intimidating. Historically, MDBs fulfilled this mission by providing loans, technical cooperation, grants, capital investment, and other types of assistance to governments, governmental agencies, and other entities in their developing member countries. MNEs' record as powerful engines of economic growth has led MDBs to also provide funds to private companies for FDIs in their national markets. From an MNE's point of view, this pool of capital lets it tap an MDB's funds to expand into politically risky environments—if political risk dilutes or destroys the project, then at least the company has prudently reduced its potential loss.

Private insurance. Several private insurers underwrite political risk—for a price. Many private insurers cover "routine" political risk that involves property and income loss such as contract repudiation or currency inconvertibility. However, private suppliers of political risk coverage are especially risk averse when it comes to possible catastrophic events. They offer limited coverage prior to the investment, but not after bullets start flying or governments begin falling. To fill these gaps, some companies offer esoteric services. For instance, Air Partner, a British aircraft-charter firm, offers a "global evacuation service" that whisks expatriates and their families from trouble spots to safety.

Intellectual Property Rights

Intellectual property (IP) is the creative idea, innovative expertise, and intangible insight that gives an individual, company, or country a competitive advantage. Officially, there are two classes of IP: Industrial property and copyright. The former includes inventions (patents), trademarks, proprietary databases, industrial designs, software, fashion designs, and chip masks, whereas the latter includes literary and artistic works such as novels, poems, and plays; films; musical works; artistic works such as drawings, paintings, photographs, and sculptures; and architectural designs. Table 10.5 profiles the major forms and forums of IP. The term **intellectual property rights (IPRs)** refers to rights of the registered owner of the particular invention, literary or artistic work, symbol,

Table 10.5

Forms and Forums of Intellectual Property Rights		
Form of Intellectual Property Rights	**Subject Matter**	**Primary Areas of Use**
Patents	New, nonobvious, applicable inventions	Chemicals, drugs
Copyrights	Original work of authorship that is publishable in a medium that can be circulated	Software, entertainment (audio, video, motion picture), printing, broadcasting, Web tools
Trademarks, service marks, and trade dress	Words, logos, or design that identifies the source and origin of a good or service	All industries
Integrated circuits	Original layout and design of a computer chip	Electronics semiconductor manufacturers
Trade secrets	Secret and proprietary business information, such as chemical formulations, compounds, compilation of information (i.e., client list), industrial processes, formally undisclosed company information	All industries
Industrial design	Ornamental or nonfunctional design feature	Clothing, automobiles, accessories, household goods, electronics, etc.
Plant breeders' rights	New, stable, homogeneous, and distinguishable varieties	Agricultural, food, and seed industries

name, image, or design. Importantly, IPRs grant the owners of any form of IP the right to exclude others from access to or use of their property.

Long a tame topic, the growing power of ideas in the global economy has made IPRs a source of extreme risk. In Adam Smith's time, economies drew power from agriculture prowess. Later, smokestack industries defined a nation's prosperity and power. Now nations are competing on the strength of their brainpower to create might, prestige, and wealth. In the United States, for instance, the Patent and Trademark Office registered 70 percent more patents—about 170,000—in 1999 than it did a decade ago.[9]

The rising importance of ideas creates all kinds of international risks for companies. Books, music, designs, brand names, and software are tough to come up with but ever so easy to copy. Indeed, the range of copied products is mind boggling, including but by no means limited to books, music CDs, videotapes, aircraft parts, cigarettes, wristwatches, razor blades, batteries, motorcycles, shampoo, pens, toys, wine, shoes, clothing, luggage, medicines, foods, beer, perfume, cleaning supplies, and on and on and on. The costs of IPR violations—whether lost sales, ruined brand reputation, dangerous products, policing, or legal proceedings—are immense.

For example, consider the situation in the global software industry. The Business Software Alliance and Software Publishers Association estimates that approximately 45 percent of new business software was pirated worldwide from 1994 through 1997 and that this piracy cost the software industry almost $50 billion in lost revenue.[10] In the United States alone, software piracy cost 109,000 jobs in 1998 and is projected to cost an additional 175,700 jobs by 2008. In 1999, U.S. Patent and Trademark reported that the U.S. software industry lost more than $22 billion to piracy. At the national level, the Interactive Digital Software Alliance has suggested that more than 90 percent of entertainment software is pirated in China and Russia. China, in particular, is seen as a virtual counterfeiting machine—at the end of 2000, there were more than 25 CD and laser disc factories in central and southern China manufacturing 50 million pirated CDs annually for export to Taiwan and Southeast Asia.

However, as we see in Table 10.6, with respect to software, few nations can plead not guilty to violating IPRs. Regrettably, few expect these piracy rates for software in specific or IP in general to drop soon. The Internet makes it immensely easy for people to swap and copy music, movies, electronic books and records, and software—if it can be digitized, it can be easily stolen. Therefore, many anticipate that the use of IP has emerged as major battle for coming decades because of its role as economic fuel. Greatly complicating any negotiations is the basis and scope of disagreement between nations on the very idea of IPRs.

The Basis of Disagreement

The first international treaties covering IPRs, the Paris Convention for the Protection of Industrial Property and the Berne Convention for the Protection of Literary and Artistic Works, were created in the 1880s and have been updated many times since. The **World Intellectual Property Organization (WIPO),** a United Nations agency established in 1967, administers these agreements. Despite these and other treaties, tremendous intellectual risks for international companies result from the fact that an IPR granted by, say, a U.S. patent, trademark registration, copyright, or design registration extends only through the United States and its territories and possessions. An IPR confers no

Table 10.6

Piracy Rates and Losses in the Global Software Industry for Select Nations and Regions, 1997

	Piracy Rate	Estimated Revenue Losses (Retail $1,000)		Piracy Rate	Estimated Revenue Losses (Retail $1,000)
Western Europe			**Asia/Pacific**		
Austria	40%	$41,620	Australia	32%	$129,414
Finland	38%	$37,754	China	96%	$1,449,454
France	44%	$407,900	India	69%	$184,664
Germany	33%	$508,884	Indonesia	93%	$193,275
Ireland	65%	$46,847	Japan	32%	$752,598
Italy	43%	$271,714	Korea	67%	$582,320
Spain	59%	$167,288	Philippines	83%	$49,151
Sweden	43%	$127,051	Singapore	56%	$56,599
Switzerland	39%	$92,898	Other Asia/Pacific	83%	$31,974
U.K.	31%	$334,527	TOTAL Asia/Pacific	52%	$3,916,236
TOTAL Western Europe	39%	$2,518,726			
			Middle East		
Eastern Europe			Israel	54%	$57,060
CIS less Russia	92%	$44,276	Saudi Arabia	74%	$22,541
Czech Rep	52%	$51,972	Turkey	84%	$64,306
Hungary	58%	$25,488	UAE	60%	$5,325
Russia	89%	$251,837	Other Middle East	73%	$27,774
Other Eastern Europe	62%	$25,474	TOTAL Middle East	72%	$206,003
TOTAL Eastern Europe	77%	$561,355			
			Africa		
North America			Egypt	85%	$12,890
U.S.	27%	$2,779,673	Kenya	72%	$302
Canada	39%	$294,593	Nigeria	72%	$2,509
TOTAL North America	28%	$3,074,266	South Africa	48%	$69,833
			Other Africa	71%	$95,414
Latin America			TOTAL Africa	60%	$185,507
Argentina	65%	$105,194			
Brazil	62%	$394,994	**TOTAL WORLD**	**40%**	**$11,381,746**
Chile	56%	$33,147			
Colombia	62%	$65,085			
Guatemala	86%	$7,867			
Mexico	62%	$133,102			
Uruguay	74%	$13,613			
Venezuela	64%	$54,905			
Other Latin America	47%	$34,848			
TOTAL Latin America	62%	$919,653			

source: SPA's Report on Global Software Piracy, *1998 Software Publishers Association.*

protection in a foreign country. Furthermore, there is no shortcut to worldwide protection—you cannot register with an organization like the WIPO for a "global" patent, trademark, or copyright. Certainly, international agreements give companies time to register in other countries once they have registered in their own. But again, an individual or company can claim rights in any particular country only by registering for an IPR in that country.

Scope of Disagreement

Few question the challenge of coming up with an ingenious idea. However, IPRs are and will continue to be a recurring focus of fierce international negotiation over who has what rights to use an idea. By and large, a country's level of economic development, national cultural attitudes, and social and economic institutions influence its view of IPRs.

Level of Economic Development

Mostly, the wealthier nations of the world provide greater protection of IP than do their poorer counterparts. High-income countries have lower piracy rates than those in emerging parts of the world (see Table 10.6). Consistently, the data show that the vigor of IPR protection is dependent on a country's stage of economic development. Developed nations argue that forceful IPRs promote innovation and economic growth. Effective protection of ideas, they say, is the only way to energize the incentive to innovate. For instance, one analyst explained that "if stuff you create can be misappropriated, your incentive for continuing to create valuable intellectual property diminishes significantly."[11] Emerging nations counter that strict protection of IPRs restricts the diffusion of new technologies, inflates the prices they pay for products available only from wealthier nations, and inhibits economic development by restricting the use of existing knowledge.

Emerging nations are quick to point out the irony of wealthy nations' current calls for stricter regulation of IPRs. Notably, the United States and Japan spearhead the current campaign to force emerging nations to adopt their own IPR standards. However, in the early stages of their economic development, both nations rejected then prevailing ideas of IPRs. The United States refused to join the Berne Convention, the first international treaty on copyright use, upon its passage in the 1880s. The United States, in defense, claimed that as a newly industrialized country, it needed easy access to foreign works; it did not become a signatory to the Berne Convention until 1989. Similarly, in the 1950s, Japan disregarded IPR legislation and adapted Western technologies. Only upon its national success did it begin to call for IPR protection.

National Cultural Attitudes

Some commentators suggest that cultural attitudes help explain differences in the inclination of people to respect or violate IPRs. Western countries anchored in Judeo-Christian norms have individualist cultures that respect individual ownership of IP. In such cultures, it makes complete sense that a copyright means that if you create it, then you have the right to say who gets to copy it or who gets to use it for what purpose. In contrast, many cultures with a group orientation, such as those in East Asia, have collectivist norms and values that extol the virtue of sharing over individual ownership. As a result, these cultures are reluctant to adopt Western conceptions of the individual ownership of an idea. For instance, asked about software piracy in his country, the South Korean ambassador to the United States explained that "historically, Koreans have not viewed intellectual discoveries or scientific inventions as the private property of the discoverers or inventors. New ideas or technologies were 'public goods' for everybody to share freely. Cultural esteem rather than material gain was the incentive for creativity."[12]

Social and Economic Institutions

Others note that national differences in the treatment of IPRs reflect broader differences in social and economic institutions. Nations with strong institutions that enforce contracts and safeguard traditional physical property usually have strong institutions to protect IP. Therefore, nations ruled by governments that unilaterally repudiate contracts, foster corruption in the bureaucracy, or expropriate assets cultivate a disrespect of personal property, contracts, and law and order.

Protection of IPRs

Presently, many organizations are trying to set minimum standards for the protection and enforcement of IPRs. WIPO and the World Trade Organization are trying to establish and enforce international antipiracy standards. As we noted earlier, WIPO administers the two major IPR treaties, the Paris Union and the Berne Convention. Other organizations are helping here and there. For instance, the European Commission financed efforts to promote IPRs by giving 700,000 euros to Bangladesh as part of its five-year economic cooperation program with nations of South Asia to protect IP.[13] Nations are also joining in the effort. For instance, Hong Kong passed legislation to control the manufacture of optical discs and prevent smuggling. This law led to the seizure of 16.5 million pirated optical discs, shutdown of 14 production lines, and arrest of 2,700 people for copyright infringement in 1999 in Hong Kong.[14] We expect to see more nations doing the same in order to ensure the confidence of foreigner investors. As the director general of IPRs at the Indonesia Ministry of Law and Legislation explained, "If Indonesia is known worldwide for promoting property rights, then investors will feel assured in expanding their business here."[15]

Company Response and Action

So far, greater specification and enforcement of local regulations and international norms by political authorities and trade groups has a spotty performance record. Many companies see these efforts as largely ineffective—a sentiment borne out by the massive monetary losses of IPR violations. For instance, Microsoft advised the U.S. House of Representatives' International Economic Policy and Trade Subcommittee to refrain from trumpeting any more major new policy initiatives. Instead, it petitioned the subcommittee to dedicate more resources to existing enforcement mechanisms that could and would actually protect IP.[16]

The basis and scope of disagreement among nations on IPRs creates fundamental gaps that will not be easily resolved. Companies, therefore, are trying to devise ways to manage this risk, notably through employee relations, dealings with outside parties, and a tough reputation.

Employee Relations

The most common sources of IP losses are employees, whether they are lab assistants or outside advisers such as lawyers or consultants. The unauthorized release of ideas can occur through carelessness, such as someone leaving valuable documents lying on an unattended desk or researchers inadvertently divulging secrets in a public question-and-answer session. Increasingly, companies use their employee handbook and employment contracts to stipulate what items must be protected and how to protect them, who owns what, preexisting conditions, obligations of departing employees, stock ownership in suppliers or competitors, illegal practices, and prohibitions on postemployment recruiting of company employees. Less common is the premeditated theft of IP secrets, such as when an employee leaves to start a business or sells secrets to the competition. Generally, companies are imposing tougher procedures and constant education to reduce these risks. No matter how vigilant, though, it is hard to predict and preempt corporate espionage.

Dealing with Outside Parties

Day-to-day business matters often require that outside parties have access to a company's IP. This is particularly true for companies that have built networked supply chains, such as Toyota, Dell, and Hewlett-Packard. In these situations, a company can reduce the risk of IPR violations by limiting the degree of involvement between itself and another supply chain link. Reconciling this aim with the vital need for open information exchange with other supply chain links is a growing problem. Increasingly, MNEs try to manage this risk by working with a smaller set of trustworthy suppliers that have willingly signed nondisclosure agreements or agreed to the stipulation that, in the event of a disagreement, U.S. law applies.

A Tough Reputation

Some companies develop a reputation as someone you do not want to mess with—prime examples include Disney, Intel, and Microsoft. Having a reputation as a company that vigorously protects its IPRs may not eliminate violations, but it will help deter them. Intel, for instance, has fought le-gal battles with NEC, AMD, DEC, Cyrix, NextGen, IBM, and Chips & Technologies, to name just a few, over domestic and international applications of its IPRs.

Summary

The management of risk—whether it involves foreign exchange, political disruption, or IP—is emerging as a central strategic practice that focuses as much on opportunity as on hazard. Whatever outlook an MNE adopts, the ideal method of risk management is organizational planning, sound knowledge, due diligence of business environment and policy risks, and careful review of possible options. Finally, as the old saying goes, "The best-laid plans of mice and men often go astray." The defining element of risk management in international business, therefore, is to expect the unexpected.

endnotes

[1] Retrieved on September 7, 2000, on the World Wide Web: www.matsushita.com; retrieved on September 7, 2000, on the World Wide Web: www.meluk.co.uk/panasonic.htm; and "Matsushita Chief Bemoans Pound's Strength vs. Euro," dailynews.yahoo.com/h/nm/20000907/tc/matsushita_dc_1.html, September 7, 2000.

[2] Retrieved on April 1, 2001, from UNCTAD, Foreign Direct Investment in Africa: Performance and Potential, on the World Wide Web: www.unctad.org/en/pub/pubframe.htm.

[3] "Risky Returns," *Economist* (U.S.), Vol. 355, No. 8171, May 20, 2000, p. 85.

[4] Jeanne Whalen, "Russia's Putin Tips Hand by Voicing Support of Lower Rates, More Foreign-Exchange Control," *Wall Street Journal,* January 7, 2000, p. A12.

[5] Oscar Suris, "BMW Expects U.S.-Made Cars to Have 80% Level of North American Content," *Wall Street Journal,* August 5, 1993, p. A2.

[6] "Risky Returns."

[7] Retrieved on September 22, 2000, on the World Wide Wed: www.hp.com; Edwin Unsworth, "Political Risk Creates Need to Choose Strategy," *Business Insurance,* Vol. 32, No. 19, May 11, 1998, p. 43; and William E. Dugan, "Global Dangers: Political Risk Management," *Business Insurance,* Vol. 46, No. 9, September 1999, p. 13.

[8] Mealey Publications, Inc., "Indonesia Doesn't Pay Awards; MidAmerican Energy Gets $290 Million on Political Risk Claim," *Mealey's International Arbitration Report,* Vol. 14, No. 12, December 1999.

[9] "The Creative Economy," *Business Week,* August 28, 2000, p. 76.

[10] Business Software Alliance and Software Publishers Association, *1997 Global Software Piracy Report* (Washington, DC: Business Software Alliance and Software Publishers Association, 1998).

[11] Stephanie Sanborn, "Protecting Intellectual Property on the Web—The Internet Age Is Making Digital Rights Management Even More Important," *InfoWorld,* Vol. 22, No. 25, June 19, 2000, p. 40.

[12] "A High Cost to Developing Countries," *New York Times,* October 5, 1986, p. 2.

[13] EC to Help Promote Intellectual Property Rights in Bangladesh," Xinhua News Agency, July 19, 2000.

[14] "HK's Intellectual Property Protect Efforts Fruitful," Xinhua News Agency, July 26, 2000.

[15] "Intellectual Property Rights Key to Investor Confidence," *Jakarta Post,* July 20, 2000.

[16] "Microsoft, Others Want Better Piracy Enforcement," *Newsbytes,* July 21, 2000.

Mattel: Where to Sell and Produce?

Mattel, one of the world's largest toy companies, is best known for its lines of Barbie dolls and miniature toy vehicles, such as Matchbox and Hot Wheels. In 1998, its chief executive officer (CEO) announced that the company expected to increase sales by $6 billion over the next five years (125 percent growth) and that two-thirds of this increase would come from Japan and Europe. This plan called for Mattel's international sales to grow from 35 percent to more than 50 percent of total sales. Mattel's CEO decided to emphasize growth more in Japan and Europe than in the United States for two reasons. First, she felt more opportunities existed abroad than at home because only 3 percent of the world's children are in the United States. Second, she felt it would be easier to increase sales per child in Europe and Japan than in the United States because Mattel sells four dolls per year per child in the United States, two in Europe, and only one in Japan.[1]

Mattel's managers have to allocate marketing budgets and efforts among regions, such as deciding how much marketing budget to spend in Europe versus Asia. Then they must decide how much of the European budget to spend in each European country. They must also decide where (in what countries) to secure the new supplies of toys necessary to achieve the 125 percent growth in five years. The source of supplies is different from the market location. Mattel depends heavily on Asia—primarily China, Indonesia, Malaysia, and Thailand—for supplies produced through its own and other companies' facilities.

Choosing Where to Operate

chapter 11

A Cherokee tribe mask
from North America.

Introduction

Like Mattel, all companies must determine where to market and where to produce. They must also determine where to locate specific company operations such as research and development (R&D) and financial management, as well as overall and product group headquarters. A company should choose locations based on the questions, "Where can we best leverage our already developed competencies?" and "Where can we go to best sustain, improve, or expand our competencies?" Because companies seldom have enough resources to take advantage of all opportunities, their commitments of human, technical, and financial resources to one locale may mean forgoing projects in other areas. Consequently, location decisions are an integral part of a company's allocation of resources. Figure 11.1 shows how companies' strategies, national differences, linkages among countries, and stakeholders' concerns influence their decisions of where to locate.

Managers must set geographic strategies so that their operating locations can shift as conditions change and as results deviate from expectations. Location strategies must be flexible enough to let a company both respond to new opportunities and withdraw from less profitable activities. Managers must decide not only where to operate, but also the

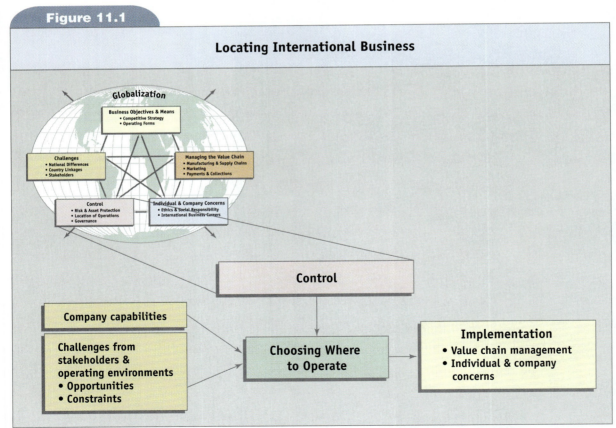

Figure 11.1

Locating International Business

Managers need to choose where to sell and where to produce based on their strategies, their capabilities, and the constraints facing them. Companies encounter different opportunities and risks in different countries. The choice of country also influences the company's operating mode and how managers must adjust operations.

order of entry among countries and how much of their operations to place within each. Determining the order of entry is important if the company cannot or does not want to go everywhere at once. Thus, managers should first allocate company resources to more desirable locations. But once the company has entered many countries—perhaps all that are feasible—managers must allocate expenditures and efforts among those countries.

The Location Decision Process

To make optimum location decisions, managers normally take three steps: (1) Scan globally to choose a reasonable number of countries that seem to offer the best possibilities, (2) examine the prioritized countries in much greater detail, and (3) form entry plans, such as entering by joint venture with a specific partner, assembling imported components, and selling output within a regional trading group of countries. We'll emphasize the first two steps in this chapter inasmuch as we discussed entry method alternatives in Chapters 2 and 3.

Scanning and Detailed Examination Compared

Scanning involves comparing countries on the basis of broad variables. Scanning is useful because managers might otherwise consider too few or too many alternatives. In terms of considering too few alternatives, there are approximately 200 countries today, so many that managers might easily overlook some good opportunities simply because they never think to scrutinize conditions in certain countries. Further, managers sometimes lump certain countries together—such as Central American or African countries—and reject all of them as a possibility for business before they examine individual ones sufficiently. For instance, they might not consider Turkey because "the Middle East is too risky," even though Turkey may lack the risk that is prevalent in some of its neighbors. In terms of considering too many alternatives, managers' detailed analyses of 200 countries would be overly expensive and time consuming. Scanning allows managers to examine most or all countries broadly so that they can then take a more detailed look at a reasonable number of the most promising opportunities in much greater detail. In scanning, managers compare country data that are readily available, inexpensive, and fairly comparable. Managers can usually complete the scanning process without having to incur the expense of visiting foreign countries. Instead, they rely on analyzing published information and communicating with people familiar with the foreign countries. Generally, in scanning, they compare countries on a few conditions that could significantly affect the success or failure of their business.

Once managers determine the most promising countries, they need to compare the feasibility and desirability of each. At this point, they almost always need to analyze and collect more specific information on location. Take a situation in which managers need to decide where to place their sales efforts. Through scanning (such as comparing various countries' average incomes, economic growth, and cultural compatibility with the company's product), they might determine that countries A and B will most likely offer them the best markets. They will then visit the countries to conduct market research and contact distributors in each before choosing between A and B and before committing significant resources in either. Or take a situation in which managers need to decide where to locate their production. Through scanning (such as comparing many countries' labor rates, unemployment, and infrastructure development), they might determine that countries C and D will likely offer them the least-cost production locations. They will then visit C and D to collect such specific information as what land and suppliers are available before choosing between them and committing significant resources to either.

Risk–Opportunity Considerations

Managers should decide where to allocate resources by estimating the combinations of opportunities and risks that exist in different countries. Figure 11.2 illustrates how countries can compare on these dimensions. Countries E and F are high-opportunity and low-risk countries in comparison to countries A, B, C, and D. Thus, countries E and F are better candidates for detailed analysis than the others. In reality, however, managers may have to choose between two countries, one with high risk and high opportunity, another with low risk and low opportunity. They are apt to make their decision based on their tolerance for risk and on the portfolio of countries in which the company is already operating. Further, although A, B, C, and D are less appealing than E and F, the company may nevertheless find opportunities in A, B, C, and D without necessarily making a large commitment. For example, they may be ideal candidates for licensing or shared ownership arrangements.

But how can managers plot values on such a matrix? They must determine which factors are good indicators of their company's risk and opportunity and weight them to reflect their importance. For instance, on the risk axis, they might give 40 percent (0.4) of the weight to expropriation risk, 25 percent (0.25) to foreign exchange controls, 20 percent (0.2) to civil disturbances and terrorism, and 15 percent (0.15) to exchange rate change, for a total allocation of 100 percent. They would then rate each country on a scale of 1 to 10 for each

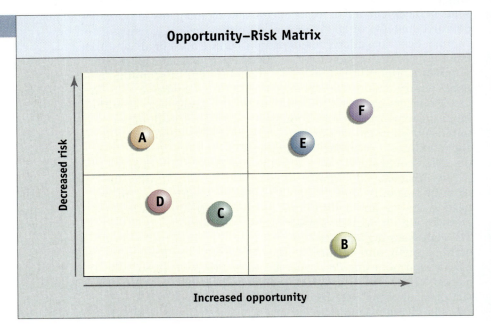

Figure 11.2	**Opportunity–Risk Matrix**

Countries E and F are most preferable because they have the most opportunity and the least risk. Nevertheless, A and B may have opportunities if the company does not need to commit many resources to the country. If managers had to choose between A and B, their tolerance for risk would be a factor.

variable (with 10 indicating the best score and 1 the worst) and multiply each variable by the weight they allocate to it. For instance, if they give country A a rating of 8 on the expropriation risk variable, the 8 would be multiplied by 0.4 (the weight they assign to expropriation) for a score of 3.2. They would then sum all of country A's risk variable scores to place it on the risk axis. They would plot the location of country A on the opportunity axis similarly. Once they determine the scores for each country, they can ascertain the average scores for all countries' risks and opportunities and divide the matrix into quadrants.

A key element of this kind of matrix, and one that managers do not always include in practice, is the projection of where countries will be in the future. Such a projection is obviously useful. Thus, managers may rely on forecasters who are knowledgeable not only about the countries, but also about forecasting methods.

Some types of information are more important to one company or for one product than another. For example, managers in a company selling a low-priced consumer product might heavily weigh population size as an indicator of market opportunity, whereas those in a company selling tire retreading services might heavily weigh the number of vehicles registered. In terms of production location, managers in one company may be most concerned about the wage rates of low-skilled workers and managers in another with the local production of supplies.

We discussed international business risk in Chapter 10. In summary, *political risk* refers to political actions that may affect company operations adversely, such as governmental takeover of property, operational restrictions that impede the company's ability to take certain actions, and agitation that disrupts sales or causes damage to property or personnel. Such actions may come about because of changes in opinions of political leaders (most likely when the government's leadership changes), civil disorder (most likely when there are poor economic conditions, human rights violations, and group animosity within society), and adverse relations with other countries, such as conflict between the home and host governments or war that causes property damage or inability to deliver supplies or products. Managers usually assess political risk by examining past patterns, published opinions of political leaders and potential leaders, and underlying conditions (such as poverty or class and ethnic differences) that may cause instability. Managers may also rely on a number of commercial risk assessment services.[2]

In summary, *economic risk* refers to economic conditions that may adversely affect a company's ability to operate profitably and use its funds to meet its strategies. In essence, economic risk occurs because currencies' purchasing powers change (either locally through inflation or internationally through exchange rate changes) and because governments control the conversion and movement of their currencies. Changes in currencies' purchasing powers affect business because companies' market potentials grow or contract, because companies' potential least-cost production location may change from one country to another, and because companies' asset values may increase or decrease. Governmental currency controls affect companies because they cannot easily move funds where they can use them most effectively. To assess economic risk, companies need to look not only at current conditions and trends, but also at underlying conditions that may affect a currency's strength. These underlying conditions include countries' trade balances, official reserves, price levels, and external debts.

Managers may rely on different indicators of opportunity and risk, depending on whether they are deciding where to sell or where to produce. In terms of opportunity, if managers are looking for a country to sell baseballs, they would rely on indicators of the sport's popularity and of people's income to buy baseballs. On both counts, they would find Haiti a low-opportunity country. However, if managers are looking for a place to produce baseballs, they would rely on indicators of available inexpensive and productive labor for stitching the balls and of reliable and low-cost means of transporting the balls to the countries that buy them. On these counts, they would find Haiti a high-opportunity country. In fact, Haiti produces baseballs entirely for export markets. In terms of risk, if managers are looking for a place to sell, a country with a weakening currency would be unattractive because purchasing power is falling. However, if managers are looking for a production location, a country with a weakening currency may be attractive because its production costs may fall compared to production costs in countries with stable or strengthening currencies.

Despite these differences, many conditions affect both sales and production locations. For example, higher personal income levels are indications of higher market potential. They are also usually associated with better infrastructure (transportation and communications) and a better-educated workforce. Thus, a company should encounter better operating efficiencies where incomes are higher. In fact, these efficiencies may more than counteract any savings realized by tapping low-wage labor in a low-income country. Political risks, such as civil disruptions in a country, have a negative effect on both sales and production.

Further, managers' market and production location decisions are often intertwined, particularly if a company must produce in the country in which it sells because of trade barriers or transportation costs. For example, Indian tariffs on the import of automobiles make automobile exporting to India impractical. Thus, automobile manufacturers must consider Indian conditions that might affect both sales and production.

Ease and Compatibility of Operations

In addition to risk and opportunity, managers usually put some weight on how easy it will be to operate in different countries. The ease of operating is usually based on: (1) the degree of closeness of countries to companies' home country, (2) the ability of companies to use their preferred operating methods, (3) the ability of companies to get local resources to complement their own, and (4) the number of government hurdles to cross in order to operate.

Closeness of Countries

Managers in the home and foreign facilities need face-to-face communication with each other to exchange information and so that headquarters managers can control global operations. Physical proximity facilitates this communication. Further, a company can normally move products and components less expensively and more quickly among nearby than distant foreign units. From a marketing perspective, a company may more easily sell to people in a nearby foreign country because those people will more likely be familiar with its products and services. For example, many U.S. companies' advertisements reach people near the U.S. borders in Canada and Mexico.

However, closeness among countries encompasses more than physical distance. It also involves closeness of language, culture, and economic level. When a company operates in a foreign country that speaks its home-country language, its personnel can communicate more easily with employees, suppliers, and customers there than where the language is different. When a company locates in a country whose culture is similar to its home-country culture, it will more likely find that customers view its products favorably and employees accept its operating methods. (Figure 11.3 depicts a manager's performance problem in a very different culture.) Similarly, if it operates in a country with a similar economic level to that in its home country, it will increase the likelihood of finding consumers who want to buy the same type of products the company has developed for its domestic market.

Using Preferred Operating Methods

Managers need to ensure that country-specific conditions allow the company to use its competencies and preferred operating practices to achieve objectives. For example, assume a company's primary marketing competence is based on house-to-house selling. Managers might narrow their list of the most attractive

Figure 11.3

Performance may suffer when the company operates in an environment very different from its managers' experience. They may have to spend so much time learning the nuances of the environment that they cannot fully utilize their own or their company's competencies.

source: Roger Beale. Reprinted by permission. © Roger Beale.

countries by examining indicators of potential household access by sales personnel. Although they may find precise data unavailable, they can easily pose a few simple questions to people who have lived in the country. For example, they might ask, "Do people with purchasing power tend to live in homes behind locked gates? Do many live in apartment buildings with guards posted at elevators?" A yes answer would indicate more difficulty in gaining access to potential buyers. Managers might also prefer locales where the company needs to alter its products minimally and where it can use production technologies with which its present personnel are experienced. If managers have a strong preference for 100 percent ownership in foreign operations or if they feel strongly that they should be able to remit a certain targeted portion of profits, they may ascertain information on ownership and remission restrictions during the scanning process so that they eliminate unacceptable countries before engaging in expensive on-site feasibility studies.

Similarly, companies depend on certain operating forms and develop core competencies in managing them. Naturally, managers would like to use these same forms abroad so that they enjoy the same advantages in managing their foreign operations as at home. For example, if a company has expanded domestically through franchise operations, its managers will likely want to expand abroad primarily through franchising as well because they know how to sell to and control the operations of franchisors. They will likely favor those countries in which the concept of franchising is already well developed because they can more easily transfer franchising there.

Getting Complementary Resources

Managers should also consider the local availability of resources in relation to the company's needs because companies must often combine local inputs with resources they bring in. For example, the company may need to hire local personnel who are sufficiently knowledgeable about the type of technology it will bring in. Or it may need to add local capital to its own investment. If few local people are available with needed skills or if local capital is scarce, management may consider locating elsewhere. Likewise, managers may prefer for the company to expand abroad by buying companies that have production facilities and labor forces in place. Scanning should help managers determine where existing production and companies are already located.

Hurdles to Cross

Managers frequently compare the hurdles (red tape) they must cross to operate in given countries because these hurdles increase operating costs. Such hurdles include difficulties in getting permission to operate or bring in expatriate personnel, in obtaining licenses to produce and sell certain goods, and in satisfying governmental agencies on such matters as taxes, labor conditions, and environmental compliance. For example, Ukraine (like many other countries) has thousands of government employees who have the power to block exports, ban sales, levy licensing fees, seize money from private bank accounts, and generally cause trouble for foreign businesses. They act not only in what they think is the national interest, but also to protect friends and state companies from competition. They often want to receive bribes for favors.[3] Where corruption is widespread, companies are less prone to make foreign direct investments (FDIs). When they do, they are more prone to make them with local joint venture partners that better know how to operate within the system.[4] The degree of red tape is not directly measurable, so managers commonly rate countries subjectively on this factor.

Diffusion Versus Concentration of Expansion

Thus far, we have emphasized managers' need to prioritize countries for their companies' international expansion. However, over a period of time, companies (particularly for market-seeking operations) may gain a sizable presence and commitment in most countries. But, managers may move their companies along different paths to reach that position. At one extreme, they may move the company rapidly into most foreign markets and gradually increase commitments within each of them—a so-called *diffusion path.* At the other extreme, they may move the company to only one or a few foreign countries until they develop a strong commitment and competitive position there before moving to other countries—a so-called *concentration path.* Of course, managers may move in combinations of these two extremes, such as by moving the company rapidly into most markets but increasing the commitment in only a few.

Generally, managers prefer a diffusion path when the company has little lead time over competitors and when it will gain advantages by being in markets early to line up the best suppliers, distributors, and local partners. However, a diffusion path strains a company's available resources. Thus, when managers decide to follow a diffusion strategy, they are more prone to seek partnerships with other companies that can supply some of the resources. Generally, managers prefer their company to follow a concentration path when it must incur high fixed costs in each foreign country in which it operates. High fixed costs could occur because of technological requirements to build a large capacity or because local preferences require it to alter its products substantially. Further, managers are more likely to decide on a concentration path strategy when they want full control over foreign operations, such as because they fear partners will become competitors or because they want to achieve global objectives that might undermine performance in a given country.

Specific Market-Seeking Considerations

Although managers consider some of the same conditions when deciding where to sell and where to produce, there are some specific considerations for sales locations. These include sales potential, experience in other countries, competitive risk, and how to respond to unsolicited requests for their products.

Sales Potential

Sales potential is probably the most important reason that managers choose one country versus another when determining where to expand their company's sales abroad. Managers assume, of course, that prices will exceed costs. Thus, where the company can sell, it will find profits.

In some cases, managers may be able to obtain past and current sales figures on a country-to-country basis for the type of product they plan to sell. If they cannot get these figures, they may be able to get information on a related product that serves as an indicator. For example, managers of Blockbuster Video obtained information by country on the number of homes with VCRs. This information gave them an indication of video rental potential, and they used this information to help decide Blockbuster's order of expansion by country.[5] In many cases, however, managers may not be able to get useful figures even for a related product, especially if the product is new. Nevertheless, they must make projections about what will happen to future sales. They may use broad indicators of market size and opportunity such as data on population (broken down by age groups for some products), gross domestic product, per capita income, growth rates, income distribution (for example, consumers pass through thresholds of disposable income that enable them to buy certain products), and level of industrialization.[6]

However, income is not enough to generate demand. Culture, for example, often hampers market accessibility because consumers will not accept certain products, such as pork products in Islamic countries. Further, if a country contains more than one culture, a company may need to target each cultural group separately. Two variables are useful for scanning if there is a multicultural situation: the size of the largest language group and the size of the largest religious group relative to the total population. The larger these are, the more likely a company can target a large enough segment to justify entering the market.[7]

Managers also consider whether the company can tap market potential effectively and safely. For example, many emerging economies lack efficient and extensive distribution systems and effective means to protect intellectual property rights. For this reason, many managers choose for their companies to be followers rather than leaders into these markets. By being followers, they can "wait and see" the experience of other companies.[8] Or managers may decide to enter one region at a time in certain countries because there is little national distribution and because a regional entry reduces the resources they put at risk. For example, many companies are now entering China one region at a time.

Analogies with Other Countries

Sales of a product in one country may follow earlier patterns from other countries because of sequential conditions affecting demand. One such condition is per capita income: As incomes change, the demand for a product may change. For example, Korean demand for apparel, cosmetics, and automobiles has grown with increased per capita income—a trend that closely parallels the experience of some other countries that reached high economic levels in earlier years.[9] Managers, thus, may infer that demand for a product will grow as a country's per capita income grows and in a pattern resembling what has happened in other countries. They may collect demand information on different countries, such as per capita consumption at different income levels, and estimate future demand based on projections of income and population growth.

Examining what has happened in different countries may be particularly useful when sales of one product or service precede another as incomes grow. For example, the demand for televisions, VCRs, and videotapes has grown in most countries as per capita incomes have grown and passed certain thresholds. But videotape sales and rental growth followed growth of VCR sales, which followed the growth of television sales.

Nevertheless, countries' product demands do not necessarily follow other countries' patterns. We have already discussed factors, such as culture, that cause demand to differ among countries. Further, as technology and prices change, a country may adopt products much earlier or later than other countries did during the growth process. For example, in industrial countries, consumers typically bought wired phones before they bought wireless phones. However, in many emerging economies, most people are buying wireless phones first because cellular technology developed before they had traditional phones and because they must often wait a long time (sometimes years) to get a traditional phone installed. Further, even if a change in income level triggers a change in consumption, a late-adopting country may increase its demand faster or slower than an early-adopting country did.[10]

Competitive Risk

A company's innovative advantage may be short lived. Even when the company has a substantial lead time, this time may vary among markets. In such a situation, managers may try to preempt competition by moving to those countries most likely to develop local production themselves before moving to other countries. What factors help managers predict possible local production? Three are local availability of technology, high international freight costs, and high import restrictions. If technology is available in a country, local producers may start manufacturing quite fast. If freight costs or import restrictions are high for exports to the country, a local producer may, despite inefficiencies, be able to gain a cost advantage over imported goods.

Managers also may adopt strategies whereby they concentrate efforts on those countries in which they are least likely to face significant competition. For example, Kao, Japan's top maker of toiletries and home cleaning products, has concentrated its international expansion in Southeast Asia because that market has been growing and because U.S. and European competitors are less entrenched there.[11] Over time, however, managers are less likely to avoid significant competition because fewer frontiers remain and competitors follow them into markets. This type of strategy also implies possibly avoiding markets that may be too big and too competitive. For example, few foreign retailers have managed to succeed in the U.S. market because few can make a high enough commitment to gain a sufficient presence and because they must face so many formidable and entrenched U.S. competitors.[12]

Passive Involvement

In actuality, managers make many market location decisions passively because they receive unsolicited export requests from other companies or individuals who have seen or heard of their products. Fortunately, much of companies' passive expansion turns out to be successful, and managers go on to actively commit resources to expand in those same countries. In these situations, managers avoid the sometimes high cost of comparing countries through feasibility studies. Relatedly, some companies are now experiencing foreign market success by advertising and selling on the Internet, which gives them worldwide exposure. They sell wherever they receive orders, and they expand their commitments where demand for their products grows the most.

However, there are problems in using a passive approach inasmuch as companies concentrate most of their later efforts in areas in which sales happened to develop with very little earlier effort—which may not be their optimum markets. Passive sales are most likely to develop where their advertising programs spill over from the home to a foreign country, such as U.S.-directed television advertising that reaches foreign viewers. Or if there are more Internet users in one country than another, the company may put emphasis on markets that do not have the highest potential for its products. For example, about 42 percent of the Finnish population is connected to the Internet, but only about 13 percent of Spaniards are connected.[13] Even if Spain were a bigger potential market, a company would nevertheless put more emphasis on Finland. Of course, if the company's advantage domestically is in distributing through Internet sales, such as Amazon.com's for book sales, a passive approach to location decisions has more merit. But even in a company like Amazon.com, managers must decide how to allocate marketing budgets among countries, such as deciding the budget for newspaper ads in France versus Britain to entice consumers to seek out its Web page.

Specific Production Location Considerations

Although managers consider many of the same conditions when deciding where to sell and where to produce, there are some specific considerations for production locations. These include the cost and availability of resources, the location of competitors, and the existence of governmental incentives.

Cost and Availability of Resources

As trade restrictions have diminished, companies have more alternatives for locating their production because they can more easily export into markets. The reduction in trade restrictions is also enabling companies to take greater advantage of economies of scale by building large facilities that can serve markets in more than one country. This creates a countervailing pull in terms of optimum location.[14] On the one hand, managers would like to locate company production near markets to save on transportation costs. On the other hand, they would like to locate where production costs are lowest. Generally, the location choice involves a trade-off. For example, Mattel depends heavily on Asian production because of low manufacturing costs. However, when U.S. demand suddenly surged for the 2000 Christmas season, Mattel had to shift from inexpensive sea transportation to expensive air transportation to get toys to market in time.[15]

A company whose foreign objective is to acquire resources, such as a petroleum company seeking crude oil supplies, must get them where they exist. Nevertheless, managers in companies such as Shell do not depend only on geological reports to determine where to drill. Once they determine which countries have likely reserves, they compare political risk situations among them. In other words, companies can usually secure resources from multiple locations, and they should compare locations to determine which best fit their needs. In addition to risk, managers must consider total production and transportation costs. Generally, a company's least-cost production location depends in some part on its process technology. For example, if its process requires high inputs of labor, then locating where labor costs are low is apt to be most important, whereas if capital (machinery) costs are the primary input, then the company might consider locating where labor is flexible enough that the company can use its machinery fully by operating 24-hour shifts, seven days a week.

Labor compensation is an important manufacturing cost for most companies. However, capital intensity is growing in most industries. Capital intensity reduces labor as a percentage of total costs, decreases the cost advantage of locating in a low-wage country, and increases the importance of being near the market.[16] Nevertheless, labor costs in some industries remain the critical factor for determining total cost. Managers may use current labor costs, trends in those costs, and unemployment rates to help estimate cost differences among countries. Labor, however, is not a homogeneous commodity. If a country's labor force lacks the specific skill levels a company requires, the company may have to implement an expensive means to use the labor, such as training, redesigning production, or adding supervision. For this reason, managers may choose to operate in a country with a higher-paid but highly skilled labor force. For example, Germany has some of the world's most expensive workers and longest vacations, but such companies as Micro Devices, Guardian Industries, and Motorola located foreign investments there because of the high skill level and productivity of German workers.[17] In the case of new technical processes, companies need specific skills at the production site. For example, Lego, the Danish toy maker, has kept its toy making in high-wage countries because it can use its factories to develop unique capabilities in molding design and plastics that necessitate having skilled engineers at the production site.[18]

The importance of examining total costs is illustrated by a comparative analysis of producing sewn bags within Yucatán in Mexico and North Carolina in the United States. The production process is highly standardized and needs semiskilled workers, who comprise more than two-thirds of employees. Despite much lower labor rates in Mexico, Mexican production is more expensive. Companies must spend more on training in Mexico because they must hire workers with lower entry skills and because there is a high labor turnover. They face higher utility costs in Mexico, and they must hire a higher ratio of supervisors to laborers.[19] In the absence of precise information on comparative costs, managers may make estimates by looking at other production in the area. If the area is already turning out competitive products embodying inputs similar to those required for the production being considered, total costs of the planned operation will probably be sufficiently low.

Linkages of Companies

Increasingly, suppliers and industrial customers need to locate near each other and in an area in which the infrastructure will allow them to move their supplies and finished products efficiently. Industrial customers are simply leery of depending on supplies that come from too far away because delivery problems increase with distance. To counteract the possible delivery problems, industrial customers might maintain higher inventories of supplies, but this is expensive. Given the need for proximity, suppliers often follow their customers into foreign markets, which results in agglomerations of vertically linked manufacturers in the same foreign locale.[20]

Managers also find advantages in locating where they have several competitors. A cluster of competitors can usually attract multiple suppliers and employees with specialized skills to the area as well. This gives companies more flexibility for switching suppliers and less dependence on any single supplier. It also gives them greater assurance that their supply costs do not

Managers' decisions on where to produce and sell should be based on their objective assessment of companies' opportunities and risks. Managers can often devise tactics to increase opportunities or decrease risks, but these tactics usually increase operating costs. For example, the photo shows Coca-Cola protecting against the risk of robbery and hijacking by hiring an extra employee to "ride shotgun" on the side of its delivery truck in Guatemala.

exceed those of their competitors. Further, clustering gives all the competitors better access to information about new developments because managers hear things about other companies informally. Companies also get sales advantages because customers like to go where they can visit multiple potential suppliers on the same trip. Finally, peer pressure amplifies competitive pressure, which leads to production improvement.[21]

Companies benefit by locating their corporate or international product headquarters near specialized private and public institutions such as banks, factoring firms, insurance groups, public accountants, freight forwarders, customs brokers, and consular offices, all of which handle certain international functions. For example, such large South African companies as Anglo American and South African Breweries moved their headquarters to London in order to have better access to capital and other resources they need for their international expansion.[22]

Governmental Incentives

Chapter 6 discussed governments' attempts to attract foreign investors by offering them incentives for their operations. These include tax holidays, employee training, R&D grants, accelerated depreciation, low-interest loans, loan guarantees, subsidized energy and transportation, exemption from import duties, and the construction of rail spurs and roads. Incentives lower a company's operating and investment costs. However, acceptance of incentives may bring a company problems. If the government rescinds its incentives, which is always a possibility, a company may then be in a high-cost location. Further, the company may have difficulty exporting because other countries may view the output as being subsidized.

Corporate income tax rates also affect location decisions, especially when rates differ among countries in the same trading group. In fact, tax rates lead to big differences in FDI movements.[23] Companies may even move their headquarters because of taxes. A survey of Sweden's 500 largest companies revealed that many might move their headquarters abroad because of high Swedish taxes on companies and their employees. High taxes on employees create barriers for Swedish companies to bring in needed employees from abroad.[24]

Data Collection and Analysis

Thus far, we have discussed types of information that managers find useful when deciding where to locate their companies' operations. Before committing resources to a foreign location, managers will probably collect information from external sources and from studies they make abroad themselves. We shall now examine information sources and comment on their cost, accuracy, and comparability.

External Sources of Information

There are simply too many external sources of information to examine them all. For example, a routine search on the Internet often yields thousands of sources, and LEXIS-NEXIS gives full-text citations from about 5,000 newspapers and magazines. Thus, we will highlight the major types of external information sources in terms of their completeness, reliability, and cost.

Individualized Reports

Market research and business consulting companies will conduct studies for a fee in most countries. Naturally, the quality and the cost of these studies vary widely. They are generally the most costly information source because the individualized nature restricts prorating costs among a number of companies. However, the fact that managers can specify what information they want often makes the expense worthwhile.

Specialized Studies

Some research organizations prepare fairly specific studies that they sell to any interested company at costs much lower than for individualized studies. They sometimes print these specialized studies as directories of companies operating in a given locale, perhaps with financial or other information about the companies. They may also publish studies about business in certain locales, forms of business, or specific products. They may combine any of these elements as well. For example, they might issue a study on the market for imported auto parts in Germany.

Service Companies

Most companies that provide services to international clients—for example, banks, transportation agencies, and accounting firms—publish reports. These reports are usually geared toward either the conduct of business in a given area or some specific subject of general interest, such as tax or trademark legislation. Because the service firms intend to reach a wide market of companies, their reports usually lack the specificity managers may want for making their companies' final location decisions. However, the data may give them useful background information. Some service firms also offer informal opinions about such things as the reputations of possible business associates and the names of people to contact in a company.

Governmental Agencies

Governments and their agencies are another source of information. Different countries' statistical reports vary in subject matter, quantity, and quality. When a government or governmental agency wants to stimulate foreign business activity, the amount and type of information it makes available may be substantial. For example, the U.S. Department of Commerce publishes the National Trade Data Bank, which includes such basic data as news about and regulations in individual foreign countries and product/location-specific information. Personnel in the U.S. Department of Commerce also will help set up appointments with businesspeople abroad.

International Organizations and Agencies

Numerous organizations and agencies are supported by more than one country. These include the United Nations, the World Trade Organization, the International Monetary Fund, the Organization for Economic Cooperation and Development, and the European Union. All of these organizations have large research staffs that compile basic statistics, as well as prepare reports and recommendations concerning common trends and problems. Many of the international development banks even help finance investment-feasibility studies.

Trade Associations

Trade associations connected to various product lines collect, evaluate, and disseminate a wide variety of data dealing with technical and competitive factors in their industries. Many of these data are available in the trade journals published by such associations; others may or may not be available to non-members.

Information Service Companies

A number of companies have information retrieval services that maintain databases from hundreds of different sources, including many of those already described. For a fee, or sometimes for free at public libraries, managers can obtain access to such computerized data and arrange for an immediate printout of studies of interest.

Internal Generation of Data

Managers may have to conduct many studies abroad themselves. Sometimes the research process may consist of no more than observing keenly and asking many questions. Investigators can see what kind of merchandise is available, can see who is buying and where, and can uncover the hidden distribution points and competition. In some countries, for example, the competition for ready-made clothes may be from seamstresses working in private homes rather than from retailers. The competition for vacuum cleaners may be from servants who clean with mops rather than from other electrical appliance manufacturers. Surreptitiously sold contraband may compete with locally produced goods. Traditional analysis methods would not reveal such facts. In many countries, even bankers have to rely more on clients' reputations than on their financial statements. Shrewd questioning may yield very interesting results. But such questioning is not always feasible. For example, Bass's managers think that women in Saudi Arabia consume most of their well-selling Barbicon Malt with Lemon. But they cannot be sure because they cannot hold focus groups to discuss products, rely on phone books for random surveys, stop strangers on the street, or knock on the door of someone's house in Saudi Arabia.[25]

Often, managers must be extremely imaginative, extremely observant, or both. For example, managers of one soft drink manufacturer wanted to determine their Mexican market share. They could not estimate reliably from the final points of distribution because sales were so widespread. So they hit on two alternatives, both of which turned out to be feasible: The bottle cap manufacturer revealed how many caps it sold to each of its clients, and customs supplied data on each competitor's soft drink concentrate imports.

Problems of Accuracy and Comparability

Although managers may examine thousands of information sources, the information they get from these sources may be inaccurate. Further, the information may not be comparable with what they collect from other countries.

Most problems of inaccuracy are caused by difficulty in collecting information. For example, a government may lack the funds or skills to carry out an accurate census. Or people may hide information because they mistrust how the information will be used, particularly if they wish to hide illegal activities or taxable income. But some inaccuracies are intentional. For example, a government or service company might purposely mislead because it wants to attract investment or tourism. Finally, managers must rely on forecasts because they need to make decisions based on an uncertain future. Because different organizations forecast differently, projections can vary substantially. There is some evidence that economic forecasts by private groups are more accurate than those by governments and international organizations. Governments and international organizations may simply manipulate data for political purposes.[26] Even if figures are accurate, managers may have trouble comparing those from different countries. One problem is that definitions may differ, such as for *family, unemployment,* and *literacy.* Differences in accounting rules, such as permissible depreciation, also lead to comparison problems. Further, governments and organizations collect information at different times. For example, two countries may conduct a census every 10 years. But if one conducts it in 2000 and another in 2005, managers need to extrapolate what has happened in the interval. Finally, countries count only legal activities and those that are formally sold in the economy, so country differences in crime and in nonmarket activities—producing for personal household consumption such products and services as vegetables, haircuts, and clothing—make comparisons among countries imperfect.

Noncomparative Strategies

Although managers compare locations before expanding abroad, they also decide to expand abroad on a noncomparative basis. Noncomparative location decisions occur primarily in two types of situations: go–no-go decisions and reinvestment decisions.

Go–No-Go Decisions

Managers often must make a commitment or not on stand-alone proposals, a situation known as a **go–no-go decision.** This situation sometimes occurs because they receive proposals from another company to set up a joint venture or distribution arrangement or to sell or buy one of the company's business units. This situation also occurs because governments request bids for companies to buy state-owned enterprises, to supply equipment to them, or to construct facilities for them. Thus, managers must make a quick decision even though they may have no other proposals with which to compare. To delay or forgo a decision is the same as saying no.

Managers can conduct only so many foreign feasibility studies simultaneously. Of those they do conduct simultaneously, some are apt to be in various stages of completion at a given time. For example, managers may have just completed a study for a possible project in Australia, but they are still researching possible projects in New Zealand, Japan, and Indonesia. They probably cannot afford to wait for completion of all the studies before making a decision about the Australian project. They will go ahead or not with the Australian project based on whether expected results meet some minimum threshold criteria for acceptance.

Reinvestment Decisions

Once committed to a given locale, a company may have to **reinvest** a substantial portion of its earnings there—to do otherwise would endanger the continued success in that locale. For example, it may need to expand there or risk losing market share and incurring higher unit costs than its competitors. Aside from competitive factors, a company may need several years of almost total reinvestment and allocation of new funds to one area in order to meet its objective, particularly if its objective is to move from regional to national distribution. Over time, a company may use its local earnings to broaden its product line there, to integrate its production, and to expand into export markets. Therefore, managers usually give precedence to reinvestment in existing markets over entries into countries for the first time. Another reason headquarters managers treat reinvestment decisions differently from new investments is that they believe their experienced personnel abroad may be the best judges of what their country operations need.

Dynamics of Locational Emphasis

Managers need to reassess their companies' locations almost continuously. They may eliminate or downscale operations in a given country. They may also place more growth emphasis on some countries than on others.

Divestment Decisions

Companies commonly **divest** some products or country operations (reduce their commitments) because their managers see better performance prospects elsewhere. Divestment shifts companies' emphasis among countries. For example, if managers decide to restructure their product line by shedding some products, they eliminate foreign sales or production of those products. Corning did this when it sold its consumer products division. PepsiCo did this when it spun off its fast-food division. These divestments included Corning's facilities to make Corning Ware and Pyrex in Europe and PepsiCo's to sell fast food in Japan.

Companies also divest because managers see better performance opportunities in other countries. For example, Woolworth sold all its German stores because its managers forecasted lower German earnings than what they forecasted they could earn by investing the proceeds in Latin America and elsewhere in Western Europe.[27] But if managers expect performance to be poor, they may not easily sell the facilities. For example, Ben & Jerry's Homemade entered the Russian market with a 70 percent joint venture stake to produce ice cream. However, Ben & Jerry's encountered operating problems there that caused it to lose money for its first five years. Ben & Jerry's simply abandoned the market by turning over its ownership to one of its Russian partners.

Further, if managers foresee poor future performance because of economic and political conditions in a host country, chances are that managers in other companies see the same thing. It is difficult to sell a facility at a good price under these circumstances.

Still another reason to divest is political pressure.[28] For example, Texaco sold its stake in Myanmar after the United States imposed investment sanctions against the military-ruled nation.[29] Managers may also divest because of pressure from stakeholders, especially if the pressure can hurt the company's reputation and sales elsewhere. This is particularly true if the companies' operations are in a country with a poor human rights record. However, managers are never quite sure how shareholders will react to their relinquishing assets in and future cash flows from such countries. For example, shareholder reaction was quite mixed for U.S. companies that withdrew from South Africa because of its racial policies.[30]

Not all companies divest when political and economic conditions seem bad within a given country. Much depends on the time horizon managers have set for the investments. For example, at the same time that Ben & Jerry's was moving out of Russia, many other foreign investors in Russia were also experiencing poor performance and outlooks. But managers in such companies as Unilever, Siemens, and Campofrío indicated a willingness to endure short-term losses in order to capture expected long-term gains from building market share.

There are indications that companies might fare better by planning divestment better and by developing divestment specialists. Managers have tended to wait too long before divesting, trying expensive means of improving performance instead. Local managers, who fear losing their positions if the company abandons an operation, propose additional expenditures, which they claim will improve performance. These may include money for training, equipment, new-product development, and sales promotion. Thus, companies' decisions to invest are different from their decisions to divest. Ideas for investment projects typically originate with middle managers or with managers in foreign subsidiaries who are enthusiastic about collecting information to accompany a proposal as it moves upward in the organization. After all, the evaluation and employment of these people depend on growth. They have no such incentive to propose divestment.

Change in Country Emphasis

In an international divestment, managers reduce a company's presence in a foreign country. However, much of the dynamics of location simply involves growing more rapidly in some countries than in others. For example, Mattel's five-year plan to become more dependent on international sales, especially those in Europe and Japan, does not imply any downsizing of U.S. facilities. Mattel plans to continue growing in the United States, but not as fast as in foreign markets.

Whereas Mattel's five-year plan emphasizes changes in market location, companies also change production locations. Cost is usually the driving force. For example, in 1980, Nike depended, respectively, on Korea and Taiwan for about 70 percent and 20 percent of its sneaker supplies. But by 1996, China and Indonesia each accounted for about a 30 percent share of its sneaker supplies. Nike entered Vietnam in 1996, and within a year, Vietnam accounted for 10 percent of supplies.[31]

Summary

Clearly, location decisions and strategies—for both market and production—are important for optimizing performance. Managers risk overlooking viable alternatives on the one hand and spending too much time and capital by examining too many alternatives on the other hand. Scanning to reach a reasonable number of alternatives for detailed feasibility studies helps them sequence their companies' order of entry and to allocate resources among countries. However, for either scanning or final feasibility, managers might consider an enormous number of useful variables. They should choose and weigh these variables according to their companies' own special situations, including objectives, products, and operating experience.

endnotes

[1] Lisa Bannon, "Mattel Plans to Double Sales Abroad," *Wall Street Journal,* February 11, 1998, p. A3+.

[2] Different services and their methods are described in Llewellyn D. Howell and Brad Chaddick, "Model of Political Risk for Foreign Investment and Trade," *Columbia Journal of World Business,* fall 1994, pp. 71–91; and William D. Coplin and Michael K. O'Leary (eds.), *The Handbook of Country and Political Risk Analysis* (East Syracuse, NY: Political Risk Services, 1994).

[3] Matthew Brzezinski, "Ukraine's Bureaucrats Stymie U.S. Firms," *Wall Street Journal,* November 4, 1996, p. A14.

[4] Alan Beattie, "Investors See Corruption as a Barrier," *Financial Times,* October 17, 2000, p. 8, citing a World Bank study of foreign direct investment in 22 Eastern European and former Soviet countries.

[5] John D. Daniels and Lee H. Radebaugh, "Bockbuster Video," in *International Business: Environments and Opportunities* (Upper Saddle River, NJ: Prentice Hall, 2001), pp. 441–443.

[6] Robert T. Green and Ajay K. Kohli, "Export Market Identification: The Role of Economic Size and Socioeconomic Development," *Management International Review,* Vol. 31, No. 1, 1991, pp. 37–50.

[7] Philip M. Parker, "Choosing Where to Go Global: How to Prioritize Markets," *Financial Times,* Mastering Marketing section, November 16, 1998, pp. 7–8.

[8] David J. Arnold and John A. Quelch, "New Strategies in Emerging Markets," *Sloan Management Review,* fall 1998, pp. 7–20.

[9] Michael Schuman, "U.S. Companies Crack South Korean Market," *Wall Street Journal,* September 11, 1996, p. A14.

[10] Parker.

[11] Mayayoshi Kanabayashi, "Japan's Top Soap Firm, Kao, Hopes to Clean Up Abroad," *Wall Street Journal,* December 17, 1992, p. B5.

[12] Anil Gupta and Vijay Govindarajan, "How to Build a Global Presence," *Financial Times,* As Business Goes Global section, January 30, 1998, p. 10.

[13] Ernest Beck, "E-Business," *Wall Street Journal,* October 16, 2000, p. B1+.

[14] Mary Amiti, "Trade Liberalisation and the Location of Manufacturing Firms," *The World Economy,* Vol. 21, No. 7, September 1998, pp. 953–962.

[15] Bill Mongelluzzo, "The Peak Season Game," *Journal of Commerce,* December 11, 2000, p. 9.

[16] Alan David MacCormack, Lawrence James Newman III, and Donald B. Rosenfield, "The New Dynamics of Global Manufacturing Site Locations," *Sloan Management Review,* summer 1994, pp. 69–79.

[17] "Germany Appeals to U.S. Companies," *New York Times on the Web* (www.nytimes.com), A.P. Online news report, November 12, 1997.

[18] Kasra Ferdows, "Making the Most of Foreign Factories," *Harvard Business Review,* March–April 1997, pp. 73–88.

[19] Douglas M. Sanford Jr. and David Fink, "Can US Locations Compete with Low-Cost Mexican Labor? A Location Cost Analysis of North Carolina and the Yucatán in the Sewn Bag and Case Industry," *International Executive,* Vol. 39, No. 6, November–December 1997, pp. 805–829.

[20] A. J. Venables, "Equilibrium Locations of Vertically Linked Industries," *International Economic Review,* Vol. 37, No. 2, 1996, pp. 341–359.

[21] Michael E. Porter, "Clusters and the New Economics of Competition," *Harvard Business Review,* November–December 1998, pp. 77–90.

[22] "Anglo Goes Global," *Financial Times,* October 16, 1998, p. 21; and Robert Block, "South Africa's Corporate Exodus Picks Up," *Wall Street Journal,* December 7, 1998, p. A26.

[23] James Hines, *Tax Policy and the Activities of Multinational Corporations* (Cambridge, MA: National Bureau of Economic Research Working Paper No. 5589, 1996).

[24] Greg McIvor, "Ericsson HQ May Quit Sweden This Year," *Financial Times,* March 27, 1998, p. 2.

[25] Tara Parker-Pope, "Nonalcoholic Beer Hits the Spot in Mideast," *Wall Street Journal,* December 6, 1995, p. B1.

[26] Stephen Fidler, "Study Finds Private-Sector Predictions More Accurate," *Financial Times,* September 23–24, 2000, p. 3, referring to a study by Roy Batchelor.

[27] Richard Tomkins and Graham Bowley, "German Woolworth Stores to Be Sold," *Financial Times,* September 23, 1998, p. 19.

[28] Betsy McKay, "Ben & Jerry's Post-Cold War Venture Ends in Russia with Ice Cream Melting," *Wall Street Journal,* February 7, 1997, p. A12.

[29] Ted Bardacke, "Texaco Considers Sale of Stake in Burmese Gas Field," *Financial Times,* June 11, 1997, p. 16.

[30] Martin B. Meznar, Douglas Nigh, and Chuck C. Y. Kwok, "Announcements of Withdrawal from South Africa Revisited: Making Sense of Contradictory Event Study Findings," *Academy of Management Journal,* Vol. 41, No. 6, 1998, pp. 715–730.

[31] Tony Tassell, "Nike's Trainers Grace Fittest Tigers in Asia," *Financial Times,* April 2, 1997, p. 16.

Lincoln Electric Restructures International Operations

Lincoln Electric, a U.S.-based manufacturer of factory welding equipment, began operating more than a century ago. Its 1999 sales of $1.1 billion came from manufacturing sites in 17 countries. In the early 1990s, Lincoln's non-U.S. activities lost money because the company had built too much capacity at a number of foreign locations in the late 1980s. It also had to customize U.S. products at a high cost to sell them abroad. Further, the company lacked mechanisms to capitalize on capabilities from outside the United States. Lincoln's governance has evolved to rectify these problems.

Until 1995, Lincoln Electric was an entirely family-owned company, after which it sold 65 percent of its shares to the public. Subsequently, Lincoln brought in a new chief executive officer (CEO) from a different industry, a head of international operations from Westinghouse, and an Australian to direct its U.S.-based global product development activities. Lincoln closed some foreign plants so that the remaining ones could operate at closer to full capacity. At the same time, Lincoln added other plants, mainly in Asia, where it expects better growth rates than elsewhere. Lincoln has also realigned the relationship between its U.S. and foreign operations by placing foreign country managers at the same level as U.S. managers; they were formerly responsible to U.S. domestic managers. It has also integrated plants in different countries and developed products specifically for important non-U.S. markets—particularly for Europe.[1]

Governance of Operations

chapter 12

Bare chested Dogon man of Mali wearing a carved wooden mask that is used to evoke ancestors.

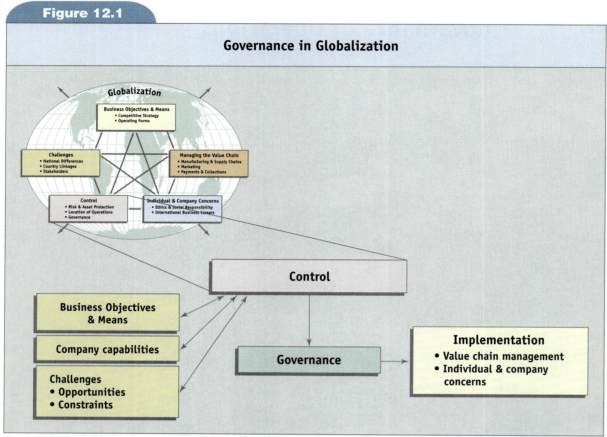

Once companies decide their strategies, they must control operations in order to implement the strategies. In turn, the very things that influenced the strategies—company capabilities and challenges—influence how companies can control their global operations. Governance is a major means of control.

Introduction

Lincoln Electric, like other companies operating internationally, uses a number of governance mechanisms to help meet company performance objectives. This chapter examines four major means of governance: (1) location of decision making, (2) organizational structure, (3) selection and development of key personnel, and (4) control instruments. We conclude the chapter by discussing situations and conditions that create problems for international business governance. Figure 12.1 shows the place of governance in the internationalization of business.

Location of Decision Making

The higher within an organization that managers make decisions, the more the decisions are **centralized**; the lower, the more they are **decentralized**. We can examine centralization or decentralization within a company's foreign subsidiaries, such as how top managers of a U.S. company's Swedish and Mexican subsidiaries delegate decision making to their subordinates. They may well delegate differently because the Swedish and Mexican managers may have different personal management styles and because their subordinates may have different capabilities and experience. We can also examine centralization and decentralization between headquarters and foreign subsidiaries, which is our focus. For purposes of this discussion, we consider decisions made by the foreign subsidiary managers to be decentralized, whereas those made by managers above the foreign subsidiary are centralized. Complete centralization and decentralization are extremes on a continuum. In actuality, companies neither centralize nor decentralize all decisions. Instead, they vary decision making by issue, by circumstance, and over time.

Basically, companies should base their choice of decision location on a combination of three trade-offs: (1) balancing pressures for global integration versus pressures for local responsiveness, (2) balancing the capabilities of headquarters versus capabilities of subsidiary personnel, and (3) balancing the expediency versus the quality of decisions.

Pressures for Global Integration Versus Local Responsiveness

The higher the pressure for global integration, the greater the need to centralize decision making. The higher the pressure for responsiveness to local conditions, the greater the need to decentralize decision making. We shall now discuss the reasons for pressures one way or the other.

Resource Transference

A company may move its products or resources—capital, personnel, or technology—from its facilities in one country to its facilities in another. For example, it may produce only part of its product line in a given country while exporting its other products to that country. Or it may produce different components in different countries, which it ships elsewhere for assembly. Managers may split production among countries to take advantage of country differences in costs, capabilities, and market size. They may move resources internationally to improve the return on them, such as by moving earnings from country A to country B because B has better opportunities. Or they may move resources—technology and key personnel—from country A to country B so that B gains capabilities that A developed.

Companies usually centralize decisions involving resource transfers because good decisions require someone to assimilate information from all potential operating units before deciding which alternatives will best achieve overall company objectives. Such information is usually available only at a centralized location. Otherwise, managers in virtually all the company's operating units would need to exchange reports so that each could determine whether its units could use resources from another country. Such determination would still not guarantee that managers from another country would transfer the resources. Similarly, if a company needs to export among subsidiaries to maintain a continual production flow (for example, with vertical integration or rationalized production), it may need centralized control to assure this flow. Also, it will usually centrally control jurisdiction over export markets. For example, if a company has manufacturing facilities in the United States and Germany, headquarters managers will likely decide which facility will export to South Africa.

The company makes such a decision centrally to avoid price competition among the subsidiaries and to consider comparative production costs, transportation costs, tax rates, foreign exchange controls, and capacity utilization.

Standardization

Worldwide uniformity of a multinational enterprise's (MNE's) products, purchases, methods, and policies may reduce its global costs substantially, even if some costs increase for a particular subsidiary. Such standardization is highly unlikely if managers in each subsidiary make their own decisions. For example, if an MNE standardizes machinery used in the production process, it may gain savings from quantity discounts on purchases, consolidation of mechanics' training, maintenance of manuals, and carrying of spare parts inventories. The company may realize economies, not only in scale production, but also in activities such as advertising, research and development (R&D), and the purchase of group insurance. Product uniformity gives a company greater flexibility in filling orders when supply problems arise because of strikes, disasters, or sudden increases in demand. The company can simply expand in one country to meet shortages elsewhere.

However, the downside of standardization is that revenue losses may exceed gains from cost savings because some subsidiaries end up with products and processes that do not quite fit their particular needs. Therefore, a company can justify standardization only if its global gains exceed the sum of its local losses. Of course, some products or processes are more suitable to global standardization than are others. For example, General Electric's jet engines require no local adaptation, whereas some of Nestlé's food products do because of differences in national tastes and regulations. Nevertheless, managers can usually assess cost savings from standardization more accurately than they can project changes in revenues.

Systematic Dealings with Stakeholders

Increasingly, stakeholders (government officials, employees, suppliers, consumers, and the general public) are aware of what the company does everywhere. For example, they know the company's concessions in other countries on labor rates and conditions, environmental responses, and product safety. The result is that a company may easily grant concessions in one country that stakeholders then demand in other countries in which the company cannot afford them. Centralized control is, therefore, useful so that a company's decisions in one country will not have a bad effect in another.

Even product and pricing decisions in one country can affect demand in other countries. With the growing mobility of consumers, especially industrial consumers, a good or bad experience with a product in one country may eventually affect sales elsewhere. This is especially true if industrial consumers themselves want uniformity in their end products. If prices differ substantially among countries, consumers may even find that they can import more cheaply than they can buy locally. Centralized decision making is necessary to ensure that operations in different countries go toward achieving global objectives.

Global competition also may cause managers to make decisions in one country to improve performance elsewhere. For example, managers may give price concessions to an industrial customer in Brazil so that they may more easily gain business with that customer in other countries. (The industrial customer may prefer to deal with the same supplier worldwide.) Usually, such dealings with potential global customers or competitors need centralized decision making because headquarters personnel are the only ones with information on all the countries in which the company operates, such as information on what a global competitor is doing in one country that may have an impact elsewhere. However, in some cases, the subsidiary may be the best place to make decisions about the customer or competitor. For example, IBM's top management feared that its eroding Japanese market share would spill into other markets because Japanese competitors would have resources and confidence to fight IBM elsewhere. IBM, thus, gave its Japanese subsidiary decision-making power. The subsidiary increased its manufacturing capacity substantially, and it developed new products specific to the Japanese market.[2]

Relationship to Corporate Strategy

In Chapter 2, we discussed three international strategies: multidomestic, global, and transnational. These strategies relate closely to the needs of subsidiaries. For example, subsidiaries have different needs to integrate with operations in other countries through resource transfer, global standardization, and systematic dealings with stakeholders. Their needs also differ when it comes to local responsiveness, such as having to differentiate their products and operating methods to fit unique country needs.[3] Figure 12.2 illustrates that the need for either integration or local responsiveness varies substantially among subsidiaries.

Subsidiaries in the bottom left-hand quadrant of Figure 12.2 have both a low need for integration and a low need for local responsiveness. These subsidiaries—called *replication subsidiaries*—usually replicate operations in the home country, though often on a smaller scale. Companies usually establish them because trade barriers and high transportation costs prevent them from

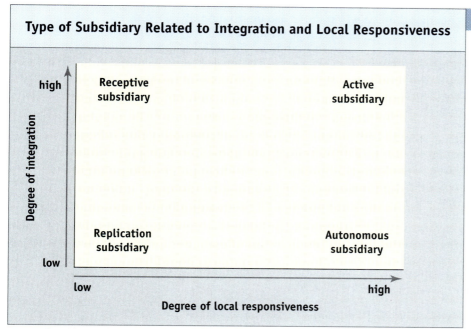

Type of Subsidiary Related to Integration and Local Responsiveness

Figure 12.2

Because subsidiaries have different needs to integrate with activities in other countries and to adapt products and operating methods to unique country needs, their relationships to corporate strategies differ.

source: Adapted from J. H. Taggart, "Strategy Shifts in MNC Subsidiaries," *Strategic Management Journal,* Vol. 19 (1998), p. 666.

exporting to the markets. Management in the replication subsidiary usually makes decisions quite autonomously, and the subsidiary usually follows a multidomestic strategy. A replication subsidiary may, over time, develop and export some products of its own; however, it generally lacks the resources to become globally competitive with those products that replicate home-country production. Instead, it sells these products almost entirely in its domestic market, such as to industrial customers that the company services globally. If the replication subsidiary becomes too disconnected from what is happening in other countries, it may innovate insufficiently to continue to be competitive even within its local market. Further, the replication subsidiary may not survive if reductions in trade restrictions allow imports to enter more easily. For example, when the German government reduced trade restrictions, Lincoln Electric then closed its German production facility because it could export from the United States to Germany.[4]

Autonomous subsidiaries are in the lower right-hand quadrant of Figure 12.2. These also typically follow multidomestic strategies because they have high local responsiveness needs and low integration needs. Autonomous subsidiaries usually have well-developed R&D that focuses on adapting and developing new products for their local markets. Because of this focus on their own markets, these subsidiaries typically export very little. The overall percentage of subsidiaries that are autonomous is falling because subsidiaries cannot afford to incur high R&D cost to develop products for only one country.

Receptive subsidiaries have a low local responsiveness need and a high international integration need. We show them in the upper left-hand corner of Figure 12.2. These subsidiaries are part of a company's vertically integrated or rationalized production network. Their operations usually fit within global strategies because companies need to manage the flow of materials and components that they largely standardize internationally.

Finally, *active subsidiaries,* which we show in the upper right-hand quadrant of Figure 12.2, have a high need for both local responsiveness and international integration. These subsidiaries generally conduct extensive R&D, but they consider the needs in other countries when they develop new products or processes. Thus, they may develop international competencies apart from those the company develops in the headquarters country. To take advantage of these competencies, the company usually follows a transnational strategy. In some cases, companies have even placed some divisional headquarters in foreign countries. For instance, AT&T moved its corded telephone division from the United States to France; Siemens moved its air traffic management division from Germany to the United Kingdom; and Hyundai shifted its personal computer division from Korea to the United States. Although these divisional headquarters still report to corporate headquarters, other global operations, including those in the home country, must report to them.[5] An active subsidiary may become globally competent by developing an important new product, by buying a local firm with a leading-edge product, or by developing collaborative agreements with key customers.[6]

Capabilities of Headquarters Versus Subsidiary Personnel

Headquarters managers' perception of their own competence versus foreign subsidiary managers' competence influences the decisions that each will make. Although there are rational factors affecting this perception, unrealistic attitudes may lead to excessive control at either headquarters or abroad. Unrealistic attitudes include, for example, a belief that only the on-the-spot person knows the situation well enough to make a decision or that the corporate managers are the only individuals capable of making decisions. But there are real differences in capabilities as well. Decentralization may be warranted when the local management team is large rather than lean, when local managers have worked a long time with the company, and when local managers have developed successful track records. However, headquarters managers may underestimate and not fully understand the resources and capabilities of subsidiary units, in which case they will underutilize decision making by managers in the subsidiary. Thus, subsidiary managers may need to exert initiative to enhance the flow of information about subsidiary capabilities.[7]

Motivation and Development

Although headquarters managers can clearly make some decisions efficiently, this efficiency must be weighed against morale problems they create by taking responsibility from local managers. When they prevent local managers from acting in the best interest of their own operation, the local managers may think, "I could have done better, but corporate management would not let me." If local managers cannot participate in developing global strategies, they may lack the positive attitude to "go the extra mile" to implement global strategic decisions.[8] If they lose commitment to their jobs, they may not gain the experience needed to advance within the company.

By giving groups of overseas employees a great deal of autonomy in certain areas, an MNE may more easily attract high-caliber personnel. In essence, high-caliber personnel may come from anywhere in the world, and many are willing to work only in their own countries and in jobs that give them considerable autonomy. For example, Pfizer established a small U.K. laboratory to attract British scientists who wanted to work in Britain. They have been responsible for many of Pfizer's discoveries.[9] A company may give subsidiaries autonomy over such activities as development of a specific product or technology or performance of certain test marketing.

Changes in Competencies

Small companies, especially those that are fairly new to international operations, may have little if any specialized support staff in foreign countries. Further, small companies typically have narrow product lines and lean structures. Thus, they may be able to get key headquarters players in different functions—marketing, production, and legal—to work closely with each other and with foreign customers or suppliers. For example, such headquarters involvement helped Cisco, when it was a small U.S. manufacturer of networking gear, to gain contracts with Japan's Nippon Telegraph & Telephone. And headquarters involvement helped Pall, a small U.S.-based maker of filters, develop extensive offshore manufacturing. However, as a company grows abroad, its foreign management group becomes more capable of operating more independently of headquarters in the overseas markets. Simultaneously, corporate managers may no longer be able to deal as effectively with international business operations because their efforts are spread more thinly as the company enters more foreign markets. Thus, these changes in competencies encourage more decentralization.

Still, there are opposing pressures. As foreign operations become more significant to total global performance, headquarters managers become more preoccupied with the foreign operations.[10] Over time, people with foreign expertise move into headquarters positions, and headquarters managers can afford staff specialists to deal with the company's multiple international operations. Thus, centralization again becomes more suitable. Nevertheless, a very large foreign country operation, such as Nestlé's U.S. operation, can afford its own staff specialists and will likely have considerable autonomy.

Decision Expediency and Quality

Cost and Expediency

Although corporate personnel may be more experienced in advising on or making certain decisions, the time and expense involved in centralization may not justify the so-called better advice. A company cannot put off certain decisions. If headquarters personnel are to make effective decisions about subsidiary questions, they may need face-to-face communication with subsidiary managers or on-the-spot observation. Bringing in corporate personnel may not always be warranted.

Importance of the Decision

Any discussion of location of authority must consider the importance of the particular decisions. This question is sometimes asked: "How much can be lost through a bad decision?" The greater the potential loss, the higher in the organization the location of control usually is. In the case of marketing decisions, for example, local autonomy is not nearly as prevalent for product design as for advertising, pricing, and distribution. Product design generally necessitates a considerably larger capital outlay than do the other functions; consequently, a company may lose more from a wrong decision. Further, a company can more easily reverse advertising, pricing, and distribution decisions if managers have made an error in judgment. Rather than delineating the decisions that can be made at the subsidiary level, the company can set limits on expenditure amount, thus allowing local autonomy for small outlays while requiring corporate approval on larger ones.

Organization Structure

The organization structure defines how companies group individuals and operating units to carry out their activities. Such groupings are companies' formal structure and lines of communication. They indicate where companies count and consolidate profit and loss. Organization structures reflect the *major* but not the *only* lines of communication within an organization. In addition, informal communication networks are very important in disseminating information within an organization.

Separate Versus Integrated International Structures

A company may group its international activities separately from its domestic ones (for example, in an international division) or integrate them into the product, geographic, or functional structure the company relies on domestically. Figure 12.3 shows simplified structures for international business. Most companies basically use one of these approaches. However, no form is without drawbacks.

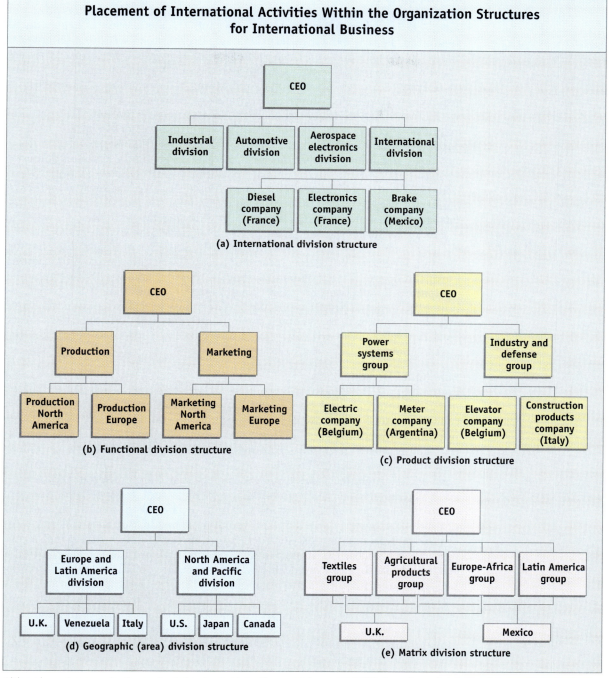

Figure 12.3

Placement of International Activities Within the Organization Structures for International Business

(a) International division structure

- CEO
  - Industrial division
  - Automotive division
  - Aerospace electronics division
  - International division
    - Diesel company (France)
    - Electronics company (France)
    - Brake company (Mexico)

(b) Functional division structure

- CEO
  - Production
    - Production North America
    - Production Europe
  - Marketing
    - Marketing North America
    - Marketing Europe

(c) Product division structure

- CEO
  - Power systems group
    - Electric company (Belgium)
    - Meter company (Argentina)
  - Industry and defense group
    - Elevator company (Belgium)
    - Construction products company (Italy)

(d) Geographic (area) division structure

- CEO
  - Europe and Latin America division
    - U.K.
    - Venezuela
    - Italy
  - North America and Pacific division
    - U.S.
    - Japan
    - Canada

(e) Matrix division structure

- CEO
  - Textiles group
  - Agricultural products group
  - Europe-Africa group
  - Latin America group
    - U.K.
    - Mexico

Although most companies have mixed structures, these five examples are simplified versions of the most common organization structures for international businesses.

source: From *International Business Environments and Operations, 9e* by Radebaugh and Daniels © 2001. Reprinted by permission of Pearson Education, Inc., Upper Saddle River, NJ 07458.

International Division

By grouping international activities into their own division, companies put specialized personnel together to handle such diverse matters as export documentation, foreign exchange transactions, and relations with foreign governments. They also create a large enough critical mass of personnel who can wield power to promote international business within the organization. In contrast, integration of international operations within product or functional groups may so disperse the people promoting international business that they are ineffective at prodding the company to aggressively promote international business development. However, an **international division** might have to depend on the domestic divisions for products to sell, personnel, technology, and other resources. Further, because companies generally evaluate domestic division managers on their domestic performance, these managers may withhold their best resources from the international division to improve their own performances. Given the separation between domestic and foreign operations, this structure is probably best suited for multidomestic strategies.

Figure 12.3(a) shows an example of an international division. Companies such as Lincoln Electric, which we described at the beginning of this chapter, use this structure. Although international divisions are not popular among European international companies, they are popular among U.S. international companies. One apparent reason for this difference is that U.S. companies typically depend much more on their domestic markets than do their European counterparts. Having a separate international division allows a U.S. company to gain the critical mass of internationally oriented personnel discussed above.

Functional Division

Figure 12.3(a), (b), and (c) shows organization structures in which companies integrate international operations rather than handling them separately. Companies with a narrow range of products are the ones most likely to use **functional divisions,** such as those we show in Figure 12.3(b). Most companies begin with functional structures; however, as they add new unrelated products, this structure becomes cumbersome. For example, in a company such as Westinghouse (which produces more than 8,000 different products in such diverse areas as real estate finance, nuclear fuel, television production, electronic systems, and soft drink bottling), it is hard to imagine that a head of production could understand all the diverse needs. But many oil and mineral extraction companies, such as Exxon, basically use a functional structure. This structure is ideal when products and production methods are essentially undifferentiated among countries. For example, oil companies may need to differentiate methods of extraction by terrain, but not by country. Thus, global responsibility over production assures that each country has access to the same state-of-the-art production methods. Ford, in an attempt to narrow regional differences in automobile design (thus moving toward a global rather than a multidomestic strategy), first returned to the global functional structure and then to a global product structure. In recent years, many companies have been spinning off unrelated businesses by either selling them or turning them into separate companies. As companies narrow their product lines, we might expect many to move back to the functional structures they abandoned earlier.

Product Division

Companies with diverse product lines, such as Motorola, are the ones most apt to use **product divisions,** as illustrated in Figure 12.3(c). Product divisions are especially popular among companies that have become diverse primarily through acquisitions. Because these product groups may have little in common, even domestically, they may be highly independent of each other. As is true for the functional structure, the product division structure is well suited to companies pursuing a global strategy because both the foreign and domestic operations report to the same head.

The product structure is not without shortcomings. First, one product division will likely duplicate international functions performed by another division. For example, each product division may have its own personnel to complete export documentation. Second, divisions cannot easily learn from each other's international experience because of a lack of formal communication among them. Finally, different subsidiaries within the same foreign country will report to different product divisions at headquarters. Thus, a company can lose synergy within countries if different subsidiaries don't communicate with each other or with a common manager. For example, at one time in Westinghouse, one subsidiary was borrowing funds locally at an exorbitant rate, while another in the same country had excess cash.

Geographic (Area) Division

Companies using **geographic divisions,** as shown in Figure 12.3(d), generally have very large foreign operations that are not dominated by a single country or area. This structure is more common among European international companies, such as Nestlé, than among U.S. international companies because no one country dominates their production or sales. The U.S. market dominates the sales and production of most U.S. companies. This structure is probably more suited to multidomestic strategies than to global strategies. Moreover, it is useful when companies can obtain maximum economies in production on a regional rather than a global basis. However, companies might engage in costly duplication among areas. For example, when Rockwell spun off Goss Graphic Systems, Goss had two plants each in the Americas, Asia, and Europe. Each of these three areas developed its own products. Goss later abandoned its regional structure so that personnel from all six plants worked together for a unified technical and marketing program.[11]

Matrix

Because of the problems inherent in either integrating or separating foreign operations, many companies, such as Tenneco Automotive, are moving toward **matrix** organizations, illustrated in Figure 12.3(e). In this organization structure, a subsidiary reports to more than one group (functional, product, or geographic). This structure is based on the premise that the groups will become more interdependent, exchange information, and exchange resources with each other because they share responsibility. For example, product group managers must compete among themselves to ensure that R&D personnel responsible to a functional group, such as production, also develop technologies for their product groups. These product group managers also must compete to ensure that geographic group managers emphasize their lines sufficiently. Not only do product groups compete, but functional and geographic groups must also compete among themselves to obtain resources held by others in the matrix. For example, as Figure 12.3(e) shows, the resources available for development of textile products in Mexico depend partly on the competition for resources between the Europe–Africa group and the Latin America group and partly on the competition between the textiles group and the agricultural products groups.

Companies using a matrix organization nevertheless encounter drawbacks. One drawback concerns how groups compete for scarce resources. When lower-level managers fail to agree, upper management must decide which operating method to follow and how to allocate the resources, which takes time. Further, for whatever reasons, upper management may favor a specific executive or group. As others in the organization see this occurring, they may perceive that power lies with that individual or group. Consequently, other group managers may think it futile to push their own group's unique needs, thus eliminating the multiple viewpoints that a matrix is supposed to bring. Or a superior may neglect control of subordinates because of assuming wrongly that someone else is overseeing them. This was a factor in the collapse of Barings, a British investment bank, after a futures trader in Singapore lost about $1.3 billion through speculative and fraudulent trading.[12] For these reasons, some companies that adopted dual-reporting systems have gone back to conventional structures with clear lines of responsibility. These include Dow Chemical, Digital Equipment, and Citibank.[13]

Dynamic Nature of Structures

A company's structure can evolve as its business evolves. When a company is only exporting, it may attach an export department to a product or functional division. (In most companies, departments are subordinate to divisions.) But if international operations continue to grow—say, the company starts foreign production in addition to exporting—an export department may no longer be sufficient. Perhaps an international division replaces the department, or perhaps each product division takes on worldwide responsibility for its own products. Or if the international division becomes very large, the company may divide it into geographic divisions.

Mixed Nature of Structures

Because of growth and unique country, product, or functional circumstances, companies' organizational relationships seldom, if ever, correspond to the simplified organization structures described here; most have a mixed structure. For example, a company may require a recent acquisition to report to headquarters until it can consolidate that division efficiently within existing divisions. Or a company may handle a particular country, product, or function apart from the overall structure because of special circumstances. For example, a company with an area structure may have a facility in one country report directly to headquarters (instead of to the area division) because it supplies a product or service to countries in more than one of its area divisions. A company may own some foreign operations wholly, thus enabling it to develop a denser network of communication than in others in which it has only partial or no ownership of an operation. Further, the overall structure gives an incomplete picture of companies' divisions. For example, PepsiCo is organized by product lines—soft drinks and snacks—which would seem to imply that each product line is integrated globally. However, each line has its own international division, which separates it from domestic operations.[14]

Selection and Development of Key Personnel

Companies need good personnel to formulate and implement effective strategies to achieve superior performance. Of course, not all employees will have the same qualifications, but a successful international company's total employment force must include sufficient people with (1) functional expertise (such as marketing and production), (2) abilities to integrate functions (such as marketing with production), and (3) vision to plan for an uncertain future. The company must additionally have personnel who will take a global rather than national orientation to operations, will understand the importance of both national responsiveness and cross-national integration, and will have the interpersonal skills to bring diverse cultural viewpoints together.

Headquarters–Subsidiary Relationship

International staffing is two tiered. First, subsidiaries need people who can manage well locally. Second, headquarters needs people who can effectively coordinate and control worldwide and regional operations. These two staffing dimensions are closely related because headquarters managers usually choose and evaluate subsidiary managers. Figure 12.4 illistrates humorously that headquarters managers maintain upper hierarchical positions regardless of companies' structure. Both headquarters and subsidiary managers must be sufficiently aware of and willing to accept trade-offs between global integration and national responsiveness.

Figure 12.4

Although foreign subsidiaries may have a great deal of autonomy, headquarters is ultimately responsible for what they do.

source: Roger Beale. Reprinted by permission. © Roger Beale.

The Global–National Trade-Off

Although we talk about global objectives for the international company, the world is partitioned into countries. We are all products of our nationalities and are taught from an early age to give our allegiance to national rather than global interests. Thus, most of us have national rather than global mind-sets, which companies sometimes strengthen inadvertently through philosophies that are excessively ethnocentric or polycentric. Also, shared ownership in foreign operations—such as in joint ventures—is increasingly widespread. If a company transfers managers to these operations, the managers may not be able to act in their employer's global interests because they are also accountable to the operations' other owners. Finally, most people perceive that their well-being is primarily determined by circumstances within their home countries rather than in the world as a whole. After all, most employees' compensation and retirement plans are based on their home-country conditions. Further, companies may evaluate employees' performance mainly on their operating unit's results rather than on global performance.

However, companies need to get personnel to think globally much less when their strategy is multidomestic than when their strategy is global or transnational.[15] Regardless of the strategy, the company may have technologies, policies, and managerial styles that work better in some countries than in others. International managers, at headquarters and in subsidiaries, are responsible for introducing (or not introducing) practices in each country.

Matching Style to Operations

Where there is a need for cross-border integration, whether between headquarters and subsidiaries or among subsidiaries, *feeling-type managers* (those concerned with how their decisions will affect others, particularly others' feelings) are apt to be more effective than *thinking-type managers* (those concerned with processing information analytically and impersonally). The reason is that the collaborative nature of integration requires a high level of cooperation. Cooperation is enhanced by understanding and considering the feelings of people who can expedite or impede the integration.[16]

There is also a need to manage in a style that subordinates will accept. There are different national norms in terms of employee preferences, such as between authoritarian and participatory leadership and individualism versus collectivism in the workforce. Although any country has successful managers whose styles vary, there is substantial anecdotal evidence of a better chance of success when managerial actions conform to subordinates' preferences and expectations.[17] Thus, managers may improve their performance by adapting to the preferred management styles of the people with whom they are working.

Developing a Global Mind-Set

Unless headquarters management has a global mind-set, the company may be excessively **ethnocentric** or **polycentric.** In the former case, it would assume that whatever works at home will work abroad. In the latter, it would assume that every country must have unique operations. Keep in mind that a global presence is different from a global mind-set. A global mind-set implies that management is willing for the company to go anywhere to avail itself of the best resources and to increase sales. It is willing to transfer successful products and practices from one country to another—including transfer from foreign to domestic operations. It considers global costs and benefits when deciding whether and how much to adapt to country-specific environmental differences.

Sometimes a company shifts from being too ethnocentric or polycentric because of poor performance abroad. For example, IKEA, a global Swedish furniture retailer, entered the U.S. market by replicating its Swedish operations, which included no home delivery and the use of metric sizes. At the time, IKEA's entire senior management team was Swedish, and all senior managers had to be fluent in Swedish. Because of the problems in the United States, the company took steps to integrate different nationalities into its management and decision making, such as by relaxing its Swedish-fluency requirement.[18]

Companies use three approaches to build a global mind-set. First, they mix nationalities within the organization so as to create a greater likelihood that managers will consider diverse national viewpoints when making decisions. They may mix them on the board of directors, within subsidiaries, at headquarters, and on committees or task forces. To achieve more of a mix, a company must give foreign subsidiary managers opportunities to move into regional- or corporate-level positions rather than reaching a ceiling within their own countries. Second, companies may assign managers temporarily to foreign countries so that they learn to work in a variety of social systems and can better mesh domestic and foreign operations when they take on corporate responsibilities. For example, Nestlé moves management trainees around Europe so that they learn to react like Europeans rather than like any specific nationality. Matsushita brings foreign employees to Japan, partly to train them in the company culture but primarily to get Japanese employees to develop more of a global mind-set.[19] Third, companies include global in addition to national results in their evaluations of managers for compensation and advancement purposes. However, there is some evidence that the shift from a domestic to a global mind-set comes more quickly at the headquarters level than at the subsidiary level.[20]

Developing a Corporate Culture

Any company has certain common values that its employees share. These values constitute the **corporate culture** and form a means of governance that is implicit and helps enforce the company's explicit bureaucratic governance mechanisms. International companies have more difficulty relying on a corporate culture for control because managers from different countries may have different norms pertaining to the management of operations and little or no exposure to the values and attitudes prevalent at corporate headquarters. Nevertheless, many companies encourage a worldwide corporate culture by promoting closer contact among managers from different countries. They aim to convey a shared understanding of global goals and norms for reaching those goals. Frequent transfers of managers among operations in different countries help develop increased knowledge of and commitment to a common set of values and objectives. Thus, the company needs fewer procedures, less hierarchical communication, and less surveillance.

Control Instruments

In addition to developing managers, companies use a variety of instruments to govern their international operations. These include coordinating mechanisms and reports. We shall now describe these.

Coordinating Mechanisms

Because each type of organization structure has advantages and disadvantages, companies in recent years have developed mechanisms to pull together some of the diverse functional, geographic (including international), and product perspectives without abandoning their existing structures. These mechanisms include the following:

- Developing teams with members from different countries for planning by building scenarios on how the future may evolve[21]
- Strengthening corporate staffs (adding or creating groups of advisory personnel) so that headquarters and subsidiary managers with line responsibilities (decision-making authority) must listen to different viewpoints—whether or not they take the advice
- Keeping the international and domestic personnel in closer proximity to each other, such as by placing the international division in the same building or city as the product division
- Establishing liaisons among subsidiaries within the same country so that different product groups can get combined action on a given issue
- Giving all divisions and subsidiaries credit for business resulting from cooperative efforts so that they are encouraged to view activities broadly
- Basing reward systems partially on global results so that managers are committed to global as well as local performance

Companies also use staff departments (for example, legal or personnel) to centralize activities common to more than one subsidiary. For instance, some companies use a single expatriate transfer-and-compensation policy to minimize duplicated effort.

Reports

Headquarters needs timely reports to allocate resources, correct plans, and reward personnel. Decisions on how to use capital, personnel, and technology are almost continuous, so reports must be frequent, accurate, and up to date to assure meeting the MNE's objectives. Headquarters uses reports to evaluate the performance of subsidiary personnel so as to reward and motivate them. These personnel prepare reports and try to perform well on what they are asked to report so that they receive more rewards. They also seek feedback so that they know how well they are performing and can alter their performance accordingly.[22]

Not all information exchange occurs through formalized written reports. Within many MNEs, corporate staff spend much time visiting subsidiaries. Although this attention may alleviate misunderstandings, there are some "rules" to conducting visits properly. On the one hand, if corporate personnel visit the tropical subsidiaries only when there are blizzards at home, the personnel abroad may perceive the trips as mere boondoggles. On the other hand,

Geographic distance used to create a big barrier to companies' governance of international operations than it poses today. This factor matters less and less, given that companies can communicate more easily and more cheaply with their foreign operating units, customers, and suppliers. The photo of traditional Papua New Guinea villagers watching television in a retail store demonstrates how up-to-date communications now reach people worldwide.

if a subsidiary's managers offer too many social activities and not enough analyses of operations, corporate personnel may consider the trip a waste of time. Further, if visitors arrive only when the corporate level is upset about foreign operations, local managers may always be overly defensive.

MNEs should evaluate subsidiary managers separately from their subsidiary's performance so as not to penalize or reward them for conditions beyond their control. For example, a company may decide not to expand further in a country because of its slow growth and risky economic and political environment, yet still reward that country's managers for doing a good job under adverse conditions. However, what is within a subsidiary manager's control varies from company to company because of decision-making authority differences, and from subsidiary to subsidiary because of local conditions. Take currency gains or losses. Who is responsible depends on whether working capital management decisions occur at headquarters or at the subsidiary level, and whether there are instruments such as forward markets in a particular country that allow for hedging against currency value changes.

Headquarters should evaluate subsidiaries and their managers on a number of indicators rather than relying too heavily on one. Financial criteria tend to dominate the evaluation of foreign operations and their managers. Although many different criteria are important, the most important for evaluating both the operation and its management are budget compared to profit and budget compared to sales value, because these immediately affect consolidated corporate figures. Many nonfinancial criteria are also important, such as market share increase, quality control, and managers' relationships with host governments.

Special Governance Problems

Acquisitions, shared ownership, networks with other companies, and changes in strategies create control problems. We shall now discuss each of them.

Acquisitions

A policy of expansion through acquisition can create some specific control problems. At Nestlé, for example, some of its U.S. acquisitions resulted in overlapping geographic responsibilities and markets, as well as new lines of business with which corporate management had no experience. Another control problem is that the acquiring company's criteria for evaluating performance may be different from those of the acquired company. For example, U.S. executives tend to focus more on profitability than market potential, whereas the opposite is true in Korean companies.[23] When a U.S. company acquires a Korean company, it must communicate and implement new performance standards. Still another problem is that existing management in an acquired firm is probably accustomed to considerable autonomy.

Attempts to centralize certain decision making or to change operating methods may result in distrust, apprehension, and resistance to change on the part of the acquired company. Moreover, resistance may come not only from the personnel, but also from governmental authorities wanting to protect their domestic economies. These authorities may use a variety of means to ensure that decision making remains vested within the country.

Shared Ownership

Ownership sharing limits the flexibility of corporate decision making. For example, Nestlé shares ownership with Coca-Cola in a joint venture for the production and sale of canned coffee and tea drinks, and Nestlé has less autonomy for this operation than for those it owns wholly because Coca-Cola has an equal voice in decision making. Nevertheless, there are administrative mechanisms to gain control even with a minority equity interest. These mechanisms include spreading the remaining ownership among many shareholders, contract stipulations that board decisions require more than a majority (giving veto power to minority stockholders), dividing equity into voting and nonvoting stock, and side agreements on who will control decision making. A company can also maintain control over some asset the subsidiary needs, such as a patent, a brand name, or a raw material. In fact, maintaining control is a motive for having separate licensing or franchising agreements or management contracts with a foreign subsidiary.

When a joint venture is with a competitor, control issues transcend the joint venture itself. Employees in the partner's organization may have been conditioned over the years to conspire against the other. It becomes difficult to get them to cooperate for the success of the joint venture.[24]

Network Organizations

No company is fully independent. Each is a customer of and a supplier to other companies. Such interdependence is known as a **network alliance.** Each company must decide which products, functions, and geographic areas it will own and handle itself and which it will outsource to others. A company can control what it handles itself with clear superior–subordinate relationships, known as hierarchies. However, when it depends on another company—say, as an essential supplier—which is the superior and which is the subordinate is not clear. Therefore, the location of control in a network alliance is ambiguous and is known as a **heterarchy.**[25] Corning is a good example of a heterarchy because so much of its earnings come from alliances. Corning management cannot dictate what its alliance partners must do. Instead, it serves as a broker, conflict negotiator, and facilitator for them.[26]

Changes in Strategies

Most recent changes in strategies have involved movements from multidomestic to transnational or global operations. But regardless of the type of change, there will be a need for new reporting relationships, changes in the type of information collected, and a need for new performance appraisal systems.[27] For example, when Citibank moved from a multidomestic to a regional strategy within Europe, it needed to introduce interdependence among operations and to collect results not only on a country-by-country basis, but also by product and customer.[28] In addition to the practical problems of changing systems, there are human resource problems as well.

It is difficult to remove control from operations when managers are accustomed to much autonomy. Within Europe, for example, many U.S. companies owned very independent operations for decades in the United Kingdom, France, and Germany. These companies often faced difficult obstacles when integrating these operations because the country managers perceived that integration would bring personal and operating disadvantages. Managers who fear losses through a changed strategy continue to guard their autonomy and functional specialties and maintain existing allegiances.

International Governance Difficulties

We have discussed factors affecting international governance, but we want to emphasize that governance is usually more difficult in international than in domestic operations. The reasons are as follows:

- *Distance.* Despite the growth in e-mail and fax transmissions, much communication is still best handled by face-to-face or voice-to-voice contact. The geographic distance (especially when operations span multiple time zones) and cultural disparity separating countries increase the time, expense, and possibility of error in cross-national communication.

- *Diversity.* This book has emphasized the need for an MNE to adjust to each country in which it operates. When market size, type of competition, nature of the product, labor cost, currency, and a host of other factors differentiate operations among countries, the task of evaluating performance or setting standards to correct or improve business functions is extremely complicated.

- *Uncontrollables.* Evaluating employees' and subsidiaries' performance is of little use in maintaining control unless there is some means of taking corrective action. Effective corrective action may be minimal because many foreign operations must contend with the dictates of outside stakeholders, whose objectives may differ somewhat from those of the parent, and with government regulations over which the company has no short-term influence.

- *Degree of certainty.* Control implies setting goals and developing plans to meet those goals. Economic and industry data are much less complete and accurate for some countries than for others. Further, political and economic conditions are subject to rapid change in some locales. These factors impede planning, especially long-range planning.

Summary

Companies must include a structure by which foreign operations report. Whether they separate or integrate international operations, they usually develop additional mechanisms to prevent duplication of efforts, ensure that resources will be shared, and include insights from anywhere in the organization that can benefit performance. They must also decide who in the structure will make which decisions. Important considerations are trade-offs between needs for global integration and local responsiveness, capabilities of headquarters and subsidiary managers, and expediency versus quality of decisions.

The selection and development of key personnel are important for governing international operations, especially choosing people who can match management styles to operating needs and development of managers' global mindsets. Control instruments, such as a corporate culture and reports, are important in implementing company actions effectively.

Governance of international operations is especially problematic in acquisitions, shared ownership arrangements, and network organizations. Some factors leading to governance difficulties of foreign operations are distance, diversity, uncontrollables, and uncertainty.

endnotes

[1] Peter Marsh, "Change to Global Approach," *Financial Times,* February 13, 1998, p. 12; Jamie O'Connell, "Lincoln Electric: Venturing Abroad," Harvard Business School Case No. 9-398-095, April 22, 1998; and Donald F. Hastings, "Lincoln Electric's Harsh Lessons from International Expansion," *Harvard Business Review,* May–June 1999, pp. 163–178.

[2] Edward E. Lucente, "Managing a Global Enterprise" (Pittsburgh: Carnegie Bosch Institute for Applied Studies in International Management, 1993), Working Paper 94-2.

[3] James H. Taggart, "Strategy Shifts and MNC Subsidiaries," *Strategic Management Journal,* Vol. 19, 1998, pp. 663–681.

[4] Hastings.

[5] Joann S. Lublin, "Firms Shift Unit Headquarters Abroad," *Wall Street Journal,* December 9, 1992, p. B1.

[6] Karl Moore, "How Subsidiaries Can Be More than Bit Players," *Financial Times,* Mastering Global Business issue, February 10, 1998, pp. 14–15.

[7] Julian Birkinshaw, Neil Hood, and Stefan Jonsson, "Building Firm-Specific Advantages in Multinational Corporations: The Role of Subsidiary Initiative," *Strategic Management Journal,* Vol. 19, March 1998, pp. 221–241.

[8] W. Chan Kim and Renee A. Mauborgne, "Making Global Strategies Work," *Sloan Management Review,* spring 1993, pp. 11–28.

[9] Stephen D. Moore, "Pfizer's English Site Is Research Boon, Developing Some of Firm's Major Drugs," *Wall Street Journal,* September 6, 1966, p. D8.

[10] Nitin Nohria and Sumantra Ghoshal, "Differentiated Fit and Shared Values: Alternatives for Managing Headquarters–Subsidiary Relations," *Strategic Management Journal,* Vol. 15, July 1994, pp. 491–502.

[11] Marsh.

[12] John Gapper and Nicholas Denton, "The Barings Report," *Financial Times,* October 18, 1995, p. 8.

[13] "The Discreet Charm of the Multicultural Multinational," *Economist,* July 30, 1994, pp. 57–58.

[14] Robert Frank, "Excitement Brews in Beverage Industry as Enrico's Rise at PepsiCo Stirs Market," *Wall Street Journal,* February 26, 1996, p. B8.

[15] Jan M. Hannon, Eing-Chung Huang, and Bih-Shiaw Jaw, "International Human Resource Strategy and Its Determinance: The Case of Subsidiaries in Taiwan," *Journal of International Business Studies,* Vol. 26, No. 3, third quarter 1995, pp. 531–554.

[16] Kendall Roth, "Managing International Interdependence: CEO Characteristics in a Resource-Based Framework," *Academy of Management Journal,* Vol. 38, No. 1, 1995, pp. 200–231.

[17] Martin J. Gannon, "Overcoming Culture Shock," *Export Today,* Vol. 10, No. 4, 1994, pp. 12–16.

[18] Anil K. Gupta and Vijay Govindarajan, "Success Is All in the Mind-Set," *Financial Times,* Mastering Global Business issue, February 27, 1998, pp. 2–3.

[19] "The Glamour of Gaijins," *Economist,* September 21, 1991, p. 80.

[20] Thomas P. Murtha, Stefanie Ann Lenway, and Richard T. Bagozzi, "Global Mind-Sets and Cognitive Shift in a Complex Multinational Corporation," *Strategic Management Journal,* Vol. 19, 1998, pp. 97–114.

[21] Daniel Erasmus, "A Common Language for Strategy," *Financial Times,* April 5, 1999, Mastering Information Management section, pp. 7–8.

[22] Anil K. Gupta, Vijay Govindarajan, and Ayesha Malhotra, "Feedback Seeking Behavior Within Multinational Corporations," *Strategic Management Journal,* Vol. 20, 1999, pp. 205–222.

[23] Michael A. Hitt, Beverly B. Tyler, Camilla Hardee, and Daewoo Park, "Understanding Strategic Intent in the Global Marketplace," *Academy of Management Executive,* Vol. 9, No. 2, 1995, pp. 12–19.

[24] For a discussion of the difficulties of bringing competitors together, see John Hunt, *Structural and Organizational Changes in Global Firms* (Pittsburgh: Carnegie Bosch Institute for Applied Studies in International Management, 1993), Working Paper 94-4.

[25] Gunnar Hedland, "The Hyper-Modern MNC—A Heterarchy?" *Human Resource Management,* spring 1986, pp. 9–35.

[26] James R. Houghton, "Chairman Reflects: The Age of the Hierarchy Is Over," *New York Times,* September 24, 1992, pp. 31–44.

[27] Mahmoud Ezzamel, Simon Lilley, and Hugh Willmont, "The 'New Organization' and the 'New Managerial Work,'" *European Management Journal,* Vol. 12, No. 4, 1994, pp. 454–461.

[28] Thomas W. Malnight, "The Transistion from Decentralized to Network-Based MNC Structures: An Evolutionary Perspective," *Journal of International Business Studies,* Vol. 27, No. 1, first quarter 1996, pp. 43–65.

Objectives

1. To appreciate why ethical and socially responsible behavior is important for individuals and companies operating internationally

2. To realize that there are different norms internationally in what people perceive to be ethical and socially responsible behavior

3. To see that national environments may dictate that companies take different ethical and socially responsible actions

4. To understand some of the major areas of disagreement on what ethical and socially responsible behavior should be internationally

5. To conceive approaches companies can take to avoid criticism about their ethical and socially responsible behavior

H. D. Fuller Company: Damned If You Do, Damned If You Don't

The H. D. Fuller Company, a manufacturer of specialty chemicals, says in its corporate mission statement, "The company will conduct business legally and ethically, support the activities of its employees in their communities and be a responsible corporate citizen." The company gives 5 percent of its profits to charity in each country in which it operates. Through its commitment to a safe environmental operation, it uses practices that are often more stringent than those required by local governments. Overall, a number of nongovernmental organizations (NGOs) give the company high marks for corporate conduct. One such NGO is the Interfaith Center for Corporate Responsibility, an organization that coordinates investments worth about $50 billion from approximately 275 religious groups. Nevertheless, critics have bombarded H. D. Fuller about some of its practices. For example, they object to its sale of adhesives to the tobacco industry because the tobacco industry makes health-hazardous products. They criticize its sale of paint with high lead levels in Central America because the paint is a risk for children.

In both the above cases, H. D. Fuller's sales are legal, as are its Central American sales of the glue Resistol. Critics object to Resistol because thousands of Central American children sniff glues to get intoxicated. When children sniff glue repeatedly, they damage their brains. Television networks, magazines, and newspapers have presented exposés of glue sniffing. Protestors have demonstrated outside Fuller's annual meetings, and NGOs have bought Fuller shares in order to complain at annual meetings about the sale of glue in Central America. Fuller has responded by discontinuing its glue sales to retailers and small-scale users in Central America, thus making purchases by children more difficult. It has also changed the product's formula by substituting a less sweet-smelling and less toxic chemical for the one it used before. Nevertheless, critics argue that Fuller either should not sell glue at all in these markets or should make the glue smell really noxious. The company has argued against abandoning the market because important industries, such as shoe manufacturing, need the glue. Fuller has also resisted making a noxious-smelling glue because a reconstituted formula will reduce the glue's effectiveness and make it irritating to legitimate users.[1]

Ethical and Socially Responsible Behavior

chapter 13

A mudman of the Mendi tribe in the south highlands of Papua New Guinea.

Introduction

The experience of H. D. Fuller illustrates that even if a company has an overall exemplary record of civic behavior, it may nevertheless face costly criticism. Further, a company may be criticized because of its association with another company—in this case, its sales to the tobacco industry—in addition to what it does directly. And a company may be criticized regardless of the alternative it pursues. For example, if Fuller were to make noxious-smelling glue to suppress glue sniffing, it would undoubtedly be criticized for selling a less effective product that makes workers sick.

The concepts of ethical and socially responsible behavior are closely related. *Ethical behavior* conforms to accepted moral standards of conduct. *Socially responsible behavior* is more proactive, rather than reactive to current social pressures. It implies that a company or individual has a behavioral obligation that is honorable, generous, and responsible in terms of long-term benefits to society. Nevertheless, the concepts of ethical and socially responsible behavior are so similar that we'll discuss them together in this chapter.

Why Study Ethical and Socially Responsible Behavior?

Both individuals and companies need to consider what is ethical and socially responsible behavior. Figure 13.1 illustrates that their opinions impact what they consider their employers should do; thus, they influence what companies can and will do.

From an individual standpoint, your concept of what is ethical or socially responsible may differ from some other individuals' concepts. In fact, your beliefs may differ from the dominant viewpoint within the company in which you work or within the society in which you live. In such a situation, you have four alternatives. First, you may go along with what the majority believes—a course you are most likely to take when you do not feel very strongly about the issue in question. Second, you may try to persuade others in your company or society to accept your beliefs—a course you are most likely to take when you believe there is a chance that you can influence others about the issue. Third, you may decide to leave your employer or not live in the society with dominant beliefs different from your own—a course you are most likely to take when you feel very strongly about the issue *and* you see little chance of changing the opinions of those with whom you disagree. Fourth, you may reach a compromise, but this is not always possible.

A company's dominant belief system may also differ from that of some other companies or the society in which it wishes to operate. Like individuals, it may go along with what society seems to want, try to persuade others of its viewpoint, avoid places where it cannot operate according to its own concept of what is ethical and socially responsible, or reach a compromise.

The Individual

We base our individual beliefs about what is right and wrong on our family and religious teachings, the laws and social pressures of the societies in which we live, our observations and experiences, and our own economic circumstances. Our individual ethical beliefs tend to be deep seated and developed when we are young. Developmental psychologists believe that by age 10, most children

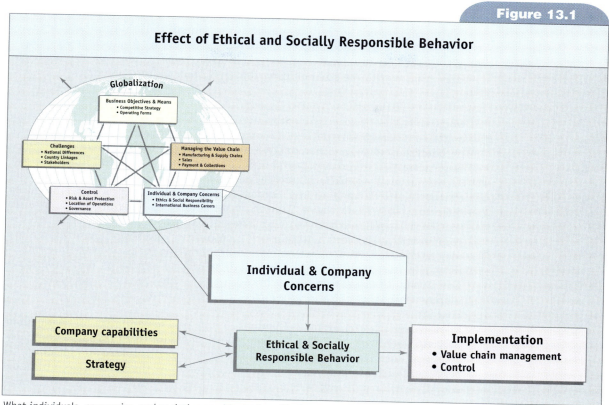

Figure 13.1

Effect of Ethical and Socially Responsible Behavior

Globalization

Business Objectives & Means
• Competitive Strategy
• Operating Forms

Challenges
• National Differences
• Country Linkages
• Stakeholders

Managing the Value Chain
• Manufacturing & Supply Chains
• Sales
• Payment & Collections

Control
• Risk & Asset Protection
• Location of Operations
• Governance

Individual & Company Concerns
• Ethics & Social Responsibility
• International Business Careers

Individual & Company Concerns

Company capabilities

Strategy

Ethical & Socially Responsible Behavior

Implementation
• Value chain management
• Control

What individuals, companies, and societies consider to be ethical and socially responsible behavior influences companies' capabilities, strategies, and implementation of practices to carry out strategies.

have their basic value systems firmly in place, after which they resist changing them. These basic values include such concepts as evil versus good, dirty versus clean, ugly versus beautiful, unnatural versus natural, abnormal versus normal, paradoxical versus logical, and irrational versus rational.[2] Given the firmness of value systems, we have no intention of trying to persuade you of what your ethical or socially responsible behavior should be. Rather, we shall describe ways that individuals and companies can and do determine their behavior when opinions differ on what ethical and socially responsible behavior should be. There are, of course, myriad ethical issues in any domestic context; however, we shall concentrate on those issues you may encounter in international operations.

As an individual, you should examine your values to see which are deep seated and which are superficial. This will help you determine your relative flexibility on different issues. As an individual, you are bound to disagree sometimes with others on what is right and wrong—especially in foreign operations in which cultures and values are different. But even domestically, people's views differ. For example, people in the United States have recently disagreed about abortion, women's roles, gay rights, flag burning, capital punishment, gun control, euthanasia, organ transplants, marijuana usage, and welfare payments. People often voice such disagreements emotionally. As individuals, we may avoid working for, becoming shareholders in, or buying products from companies that follow practices countering our deep-seated values—*or* we may try to work from within the companies so that they change those practices.

The Company

Companies have two possible objectives from ethical and socially responsible behavior: to create competitive advantages and to avoid negative consequences by being perceived as irresponsible. In terms of the former, there is evidence that being perceived as equitable leads to strategic and financial success because it leads to trust, which leads to commitment.[3] For example, the chief executive officer (CEO) of Levi Strauss has argued that its practices (including the refusal to operate where there are substantial human rights violations or to buy from suppliers whose work or safety measures are poor) have enabled the company to attract and maintain better employees and suppliers, to gain more consumer loyalty, and to maintain credibility during times of crisis. In terms of the latter, the same CEO said, "In today's world, an exposé on *60 Minutes* can undo years of effort to develop brand loyalty. Why squander an investment when, with foresight and commitment, reputational problems can be prevented?"[4]

However, companies face dilemmas in how best to capitalize on responsible behavior and avoid criticism. To begin with, behavior that prevents a company from making adequate short-term profits jeopardizes its future and its ability to serve any of its long-term stakeholder interests. At the same time, although socially responsible behavior may help the company over the long term, some practices that many people would consider unethical may help the company's performance in the short term. Additionally, companies largely evaluate managers on short-term results and prod them to improve their short-term performance. Thus, managers may be encouraged to behave in socially irresponsible ways because they figure rightfully that they will not be blamed—they will move on to other jobs before their actions have negative consequences on their companies' performance. For example, if they engage in such practices as untruthful advertising or the irresponsible discharge of toxic chemical waste, they may increase short-term profits through increased revenue or decreased prices. It may take years before the public discovers these practices—long after the managers responsible have retired or taken better positions. Or managers may make less drastic decisions, such as forgoing assistance to local community efforts. These decisions may increase short-term performance by reducing costs. But they may have adverse longer-term effects by reducing sales, which are difficult to connect to earlier decisions.

Further, a company often faces a "damned if you do, damned if you don't" situation. As we discussed in Chapter 6, a company's decisions must satisfy conflicting stakeholders. Operating internationally, trade-offs create situations whereby different groups can simultaneously praise and criticize the company. For example, if the company transfers some production from a high-wage to a low-wage country, groups in the former country may criticize it, whereas groups in the latter praise it because of the impact on employment. If the company pays above the going rate in a low-wage country, some groups may praise it for not exploiting labor, whereas other groups criticize it for upsetting the economic and social structure of the society. If the company invests in productive equipment, groups may praise it for increasing productivity and for reducing the drudgery of work (for example, allowing workers to carry heavy loads by forklift rather than by hand), but other groups may criticize it for employing fewer people where unemployment is a problem.

International Differences

Thus far, we have discussed ethics and social responsibility from an individual and company perspective. But these perspectives can vary substantially from country to country. Figure 13.2 illustrates the relationships among individual, company, and societal values that determine what is ethical and socially responsible behavior.

Cultural Norms

Although individuals within any society have different values from others, there are norms that link people within a given society and differentiate their norms from those in other societies. How companies and businesspeople should react to cultural practices that run counter to their own values is itself a value judgment. On the one hand, *relativism* affirms that ethical truths are relative to the groups holding them; thus, intervention would be unethical. A company holding to relativism would probably follow Saint Ambrose's fourth-century advice: "When in Rome, do as the Romans do." In addition, any company faces pressures to operate in accordance with the prevailing value system in a foreign country. These pressures may include laws in that country that permit or even require the company to follow certain practices, lost sales to competitors that adapt to local norms when the company does

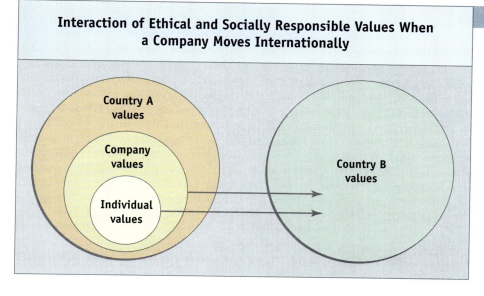

Interaction of Ethical and Socially Responsible Values When a Company Moves Internationally

Country A values

Company values

Individual values

Country B values

Figure 13.2

When an individual and company move into another country, they bring their own perceptions with them of what is ethical and socially responsible behavior. If these clash with the dominant values in the host country, the individual and company must decide whether or not to adapt.

not, or general ill will if a company tries to impose practices based on its home-country values rather than those of the foreign country. For example, the United States and Saudi Arabia have widely divergent values concerning women's behaviors. Both U.S. and Saudi Arabian companies have followed relativism concerning those behaviors when operating in each other's countries. Pizza Hut (from the United States) built two dining rooms in its Saudi Arabian restaurants—one for single men and one for families (women are not allowed to go out without their families)—because the Saudi value system holds that female interaction with males outside the family is immoral. Aramco, the Saudi Arabian–based oil giant, has made no attempt to separate females and males in its U.S. workplace. If Pizza Hut had attempted to have one dining room in Saudi Arabia as it does in the United States, or if Aramco had attempted to place partitions between men and women in its U.S. workplace as it does in Saudi Arabia, the companies would undoubtedly have failed in their foreign operations.

Normativism holds that there are universal standards of behavior that individuals and companies should uphold; thus, nonintervention that allows noncompliance with these standards would be unethical. There are also pressures to follow normativism. First, some business standards are, indeed, universal. For example, killing a competitor to gain a performance advantage goes against the dominant value system of all countries. Second, company stakeholders, particularly NGOs, have pressured companies to follow certain universal standards. Further, companies' home governments have sometimes imposed standards, and consumers have threatened to boycott products and spread adverse publicity about companies that do not follow certain standards. Third, pressures come from companies' own ethical values, which are a composite of the dominant values of the individuals they employ.

In actuality, most companies and their managers follow combinations of relativism and normativism. In other words, they adjust to host-country values when doing so will likely increase their global profits *and* when the adjustment does not infringe on their own deeply held values. They must calculate the likely effect on global profits by estimating what they might gain or lose in the host country, as well as in other countries, by following or not following the ethical norms of the host country. At the same time, a host society may not expect foreign companies and their managers to adhere to all the practices that they consider ethical. For example, many practices that home-country cultures consider "wrong" are either customary or only recently abolished and libel to be reinstated in many host societies. These include slavery, polygamy, concubinage, child marriage, and the burning of widows.[5] Although host societies do not expect foreign companies and their managers to participate in these "wrong" practices, some companies have avoided operating in locales in which such practices occur because their managers find the mere exposure to them too traumatic. Others have operated by ignoring the practices. Still others have pressured a host country to change the "wrong" practices.

Home-country personnel at headquarters sometimes impose normativism. If a company's foreign operations grow as a percentage of its total operations, a company might attempt to develop a normativist ethical policy based on a composite of ethics from the different countries in which it operates.

Legal Differences

Some people argue that the legal justification for ethical behavior is the only important one. By this standard, a person or company can do anything that is legal. However, the legal argument is insufficient. First, not everything unethical is illegal, particularly many dimensions of interpersonal behavior. Second, laws are often based on moral concepts that are not precisely defined; therefore, we need to interpret what they mean. Nevertheless, the law is usually the minimum adequate guide for proper conduct: Companies and individuals are generally afraid to break the law because of their potential liability if they did.[6]

A company may encounter laws abroad that give it either narrower or greater latitude in making decisions than it may experience in its home country. Differences in some cases may be due to uneducated or corrupt governmental leadership that either does not understand or does not care about the consequences. For example, the governments of some emerging economies allow—in fact, they promote—the import of hazardous toxic waste for a fee. Little, if any, of the fees benefit their general populations. At the same time, their general populations face additional health risks because of the waste's presence. Therefore, international companies may face criticism elsewhere if they follow only the minimum standards of the laws they encounter.

Of course, not all individuals or companies adhere to every aspect of the law. Laws are usually slow to be enacted; they are also slow to be repealed. The slowness in repealing means that every country has some laws that few people consider to be based on current standards of ethical or socially responsible behavior. Further, these are often the laws that have little likelihood of enforcement. For example, many U.S. cities still have laws against putting cut Christmas trees inside buildings—laws that were enacted when cut trees created a much greater fire hazard than they do today. These laws are simply no longer enforced. Similarly, countries have laws relating directly to business, such as certain tax laws and government procurement laws, that de facto are inoperative. When operating in a foreign country, companies, thus, face a dilemma in whether to break laws that nearly everyone else seems to be breaking. On the one hand, they can be criticized and convicted for noncompliance. In fact, a government may convict a company for breaking such a law because it cannot punish the company for its legal, but socially irresponsible, behavior. On the other hand, companies can face competitive disadvantages if they comply and their competitors do not.

Individuals sometimes consider some other factors when deciding whether or not to adhere to a law. First, they consider the degree to which they break a law. For example, many individuals feel it is acceptable to exceed a speed limit by a small amount, but not by a large amount. (They also feel less likely to be fined for a minor excess of speed.) Similarly, many people in business feel that small gifts to governmental officials to help secure an order are morally acceptable, but large gifts are not. Second, they consider whether the end justifies the means. For example, some people who would never disregard a red light in normal circumstances have no qualms in running through one to get someone to the hospital. Similarly, many people in business feel that a legal violation that brings more benefits than costs is more justifiable than one that does not. For example, the head of a French company, KIS, spent $134,000 to bribe a French government official who saved the company approximately $1.8 million.[7]

Different Realities

Companies from industrialized countries own most foreign investments. Most NGOs that criticize multinational enterprises' (MNEs') practices in emerging economies use conditions within industrial countries as benchmarks for socially responsible behavior. However, societies and companies within emerging economies often must choose between the lesser of two evils. For example, higher-income countries ban the use of the pesticide DDT in order to protect the environment. These higher-income countries have few problems of adequate food supply or sufficient incomes for people to purchase food. By these standards, NGOs have criticized companies for selling DDT in emerging economies. Yet leaders of emerging economies claim that without DDT they would have insufficient or too expensive food supplies because of using less efficient pesticide alternatives.[8] Further, without DDT, many emerging economies cannot effectively kill malaria-carrying mosquitoes, which are responsible for killing sizable portions of their populations.[9]

Another difference in reality concerns the environment. Environmentalists worry that cutting tropical rain forests will cause irreparable damage to the world's ecology. They have pressured tropical countries, such as Brazil, to disallow it. They have also pressured international companies not to exploit the forests. For example, protestors marched at the 1999 World Trade Organization's meeting in Seattle to condemn Boise Cascade's cutting of trees in the rain forests. They seized microphones at Home Depot stores to announce that Home Depot was destroying the global environment by selling products from rain forests. The Forest Stewardship Council, an NGO, advertised with such celebrities as Pierce Brosman and Olivia Newton-John to coerce Home Depot, Lowes, and Wickes not to sell wood products that were grown or harvested in ways that injure the forest or its inhabitants.[10] Nevertheless, many critics have questioned this pressure because (1) most industrial countries have grown economically by harvesting their own virgin forests and (2) the trade-off for tropical countries may be to withhold a higher standard of living from their people.[11]

Some ethicists argue that managers should make decisions based on the greatest good for the greatest number of people. But managers cannot easily make such an assessment. Further, even if they could assess how many people are helped and hurt, they may have difficulty in persuading society to accept their assessment. Consider the following example. Just prior to Christmas, an NGO, the Animal Liberation Front, announced that it had put rat poisoning into a few of the Christmas cakes that Nestlé manufactured in Italy. The group did this to protest Nestlé's genetic tests on animals.[12] Although it poisoned less than 1 percent of the cakes, Nestlé's managers had no way to determine which cakes were contaminated. So they quickly decided to recall all of the cakes at a cost of about $30 million. In addition to the ethics involved, bad publicity and legal suits from not recalling would undoubtedly have cost Nestlé more than the $30 million it lost from the recall. Further, Italians were not about to risk consuming rat poison by buying and eating a Nestlé Christmas cake. After

You might be wondering—What are alligators doing in a book on globalization and business? Simply put, globalization creates economic development and business opportunities in previously inaccessible areas, such as the one in the photo of the Pantanal, the world's largest wetland that stretches over portions of Argentina, Bolivia, Brazil, and Paraguay. For example, dredging channels will give economic and international business impetus to the region. But, ecologists argue the potential cost may be irreparable damage to natural areas that may adversely affect the well-being of the entire world.

all, they had enough alternative food supplies—even cakes they could buy for Christmas. Hypothetically, Nestlé's managers could have considered shipping the recalled cakes to Rwanda, where hunger was rampant. A simple statistical analysis would show that many more people would be saved from starvation in Rwanda than would be killed from the rat poisoning if they ate the cakes. (Thus, Nestlé would serve the greatest good for the greatest number of people by shipping the cakes to Rwanda.) Nevertheless, neither Nestlé nor any other large company would likely consider such an option because the possibility of negative publicity from sending poisoned cakes to the starving poor in a war-ravaged country would far outweigh any positive publicity that the company would likely receive.

Some Ethical and Social Issues

Managers must deal with hundreds of ethical issues internationally. In most cases, people disagree about what is ethical. Therefore, they face dilemmas over what they should do. The following discussion highlights the major issues.

Labor Issues

Companies have been heavily criticized for their labor practices in emerging economies. For example, two NGOs, Banana Link and the World Development Movement, took up the cause of banana workers in Costa Rica by sending post-cards to Del Monte, gathering a petition of 8,000 signatures from European con-sumers, and delivering a ton of banana skins to Del Monte's U.K. headquar-ters.[13] In another case, critics have singled out Nike because of its shoe manufacturing contracts in Asia, which employ about 350,000 workers.[14] Critics have argued that Nike's contractors pay labor rates too low, relative to the price of Nike's products and relative to what Nike pays celebrities to adver-tise them. For example, Nike's contractors pay Indonesian workers a little over $2 a day, while Nike sells Indonesian-made shoes for more than $100. At the same time, it pays sports figures, such as Tiger Woods, millions of dollars to advertise them. Critics argue that companies produce merchandise in so-called sweatshops. However, there is disagreement among companies, unions, and human rights groups on what constitutes a sweatshop. In trying to develop a voluntary code of conduct for the apparel industry, some people contend that it is sufficient for companies to pay the local prevailing wage, but others argue for paying wages high enough to meet basic needs. Some contend that compa-nies should require employees to work no more than 48 hours per week, and others argue for a 60-hour-per-week standard.[15]

Critics also argue that MNEs exploit women in many emerging economies in which they have less formal education than men, have been trained since childhood to perform tasks requiring manual dexterity, and are willing to accept lower wages than are men. Their qualifications are, thus, ideal for cer-tain labor-intensive activities. Without the constraints of sex discrimination legislation, companies sometimes advertise openly that they want female workers. Some governments even encourage the practice. In addition, the mass media that shows people enjoying more material wealth has helped to entice more women into the workplace in emerging economies. They sometimes leave rural areas to live in company-provided dormitories in urban areas.

Critics argue that emerging economies' social costs have increased because of resultant family-unit instability and because of increased unemployment among the traditional male heads of households. Companies argue that they create jobs and better income opportunities, as well as contribute to women's independence from their traditional subservient roles.

Many people contend that MNEs' hiring of children in emerging economies is unethical because children then lack access to the education they need for their future development. The International Labor Organization (ILO), a multilateral organization promoting the adoption of humane labor conditions, estimates that a quarter of all children between ages 5 and 14 in emerging economies are engaged in economic activity; in Africa, the figure is one out of three.

But what if the choice isn't between working and education? For many poor children in these countries, there is no opportunity for education, whether they work or not. Without the chance to work, many join the legions of abandoned street children, such as those we have discussed in Central America who sniff glue to kill hunger pains and who must steal to subsist. For these children, work would enable them to live better. Relatedly, the government of Bangladesh criticized the United States for restricting importation of child-made products, arguing that such a law could force thousands of children into begging or prostitution. The ILO agrees that trade sanctions on child-made products might endanger rather than protect children. Nevertheless, some private groups, such as FIFA, the world soccer governing body, have adopted policies of not using or selling merchandise made by child labor. UNICEF acknowledges that children need to work in poverty situations, but it has called for the elimination of child labor that is hazardous or exploitative.

Pollution of the Environment

Pollution of the air, land, and sea clearly poses a threat to the future of the planet. Governments, companies, and individuals are concerned about the present and future effects of pollution on the environment. Although many pollution problems are national in nature, they have cross-national ramifications that may require cross-national cooperation. In turn, environmentalists scrutinize companies' global practices to determine and publicize any that have negative effects on the environment. For example, a group of shareholders presented a resolution at Shell's annual meeting in London because of its pollution in Nigeria—oils spills that despoil farmlands and fishing areas, and oil flares that affect people's health. Companies' responses are complicated because critics and experts disagree on how best to handle pollution problems. Further, national regulations vary and are evolving. Thus, companies must engage in costly piecemeal compliance rather than taking standard approaches that would be less costly and the same in all countries.[16]

Consumer Protection

Critics argue that MNEs develop products for industrial country consumers that are superfluous to the needs of emerging economies. By marketing these products in emerging economies, they claim that MNEs shift spending from necessities and contribute to the enhancement of elitist distinctions. For example, they question making soft drinks available to consumers who lack funds for pharmaceuticals. Soft drink companies have responded that consumers should make their own choices, that introducing sanitary bottling operations has aided other industries (including pharmaceuticals), and that attempts to add vitamins or nutrition to tasty food have failed in the marketplace.[17] Nevertheless, critics question whether this is sufficient justification. Even if products reach only affluent customers, companies may be criticized. For example, Benetton has been taken to task for opening hard-currency-only shops for tourists in Cuba and North Korea because the shops are an affront to the local population, who are economically and legally prohibited from buying the merchandise.[18]

Critics have also complained that MNEs promote products to people (particularly in emerging economies) who do not understand the products' negative consequences. In some cases, a company's home government may even prohibit domestic sales, such as of an unapproved pharmaceutical. Relatedly, pharmaceutical companies perform human trials in emerging economies in which critics claim poorly educated patients do not understand the dangers of medicines they take. Nevertheless, the pharmaceutical trials speed new drugs to marketplaces in industrial countries.[19] In other cases, such as with tobacco products, the company can sell domestically, but only under heavy marketing restrictions. The most famous product case has involved infant formula sales in emerging economies, in which infant mortality increased when bottle-feeding supplanted breast-feeding. Because of low incomes and poor education, mothers frequently overdiluted formula and gave it to their babies in unhygienic conditions. Critics argued that promoting infant formula increased bottle-feeding. Infant formula manufacturers claimed that other factors increased bottle-feeding—specifically, more working mothers and fewer products and services being made in the home. The promotion, they argued, persuaded people to give up their "home brews" in favor of the most nutritious breast milk substitute available. Regardless, the World Health Organization passed a voluntary code to restrict formula promotion in emerging economies. Critics hit Nestlé hardest because it had the largest share of infant formula sales in emerging economies and because its name-identified products facilitated the organization of a boycott. The company ceased advertising that could discourage breast-feeding, limited free formula supplies at hospitals, and banned personal gifts to health officials.[20] Despite the criticism of bottle feeding, few governments have prohibited infant formula sales or promotion. The infant formula controversy has heightened by revelations that HIV can be transmitted through breast milk, a particular problem in Africa where many women are HIV/AIDS infected.[21] In the absence of regulations (for infant formula and other products), how far companies should go to protect consumers is unclear. For instance, should companies now promote infant formula as an AIDS prevention?

Critics also complain that MNEs sometimes keep prices artificially high in their home markets in order to sell them more cheaply in foreign markets. For example, pharmaceutical companies have been criticized for selling prescription drugs more cheaply abroad than in the United States. At the same time, they have lobbied to keep the drugs they produce abroad from being imported to the United States. Some pharmaceutical companies also decided to make AIDS-combatant drugs available to African governments at a very low cost because of the rampant epidemic there and the lack of funds to buy medicines. They have subsequently been criticized for charging high prices in industrial countries, which effectively subsidize the sales to Africa.

Bribery

Using gifts and flattery to gain business advantages may seem unethical to some people. But in many countries, particularly in Asia, your business counterparts may interpret your failure to bring a small gift as both a breach of etiquette and a signal of your lack of interest in doing business with them. The difference arises because most Westerners express gratitude verbally, and most Asians, particularly Chinese, express appreciation tangibly, such as with gifts. Giving gifts to government officials may be particularly perplexing to Westerners. In many places, such gifts or payments are customary in obtaining governmental services or contracts. Although this practice may be condemned officially, it is so embedded in local custom that it has nearly the prescribed enforcement of common law. In Mexico, for example, companies commonly give tips once a month to the mail carrier; otherwise, the carrier simply loses the mail. Companies can rather easily ascertain the going rate of payment, which is usually graduated on the ability to pay. The practice of making payments to government officials is, in effect, a fairly efficient means of taxation in countries that pay civil servants poorly and do not have the means for collecting income taxes.

Transparency International, a German-based NGO, surveys businesspeople annually to determine how prevalent they perceive bribery to be in different countries. Table 13.1 shows the results for the year 2000. Note that the extent of bribery is much higher in emerging economies than in industrial countries.

Despite custom, many managers in MNEs consider payments to government officials to be wrong. Further, home-country constituents frequently view payments as so unethical that they successfully lobby for laws that their governments enforce against their MNEs in foreign environments. The situation is complicated by cross-national differences in the rules governing political payments. For example, some countries prohibit corporate payments to political parties, but other countries do not. Also, even if two countries have similar laws regarding payments, one may enforce them and the other may not.

One motive for bribery is to secure government contracts that otherwise might not be forthcoming at all or to obtain them at the expense of competitors. Another is to facilitate governmental services that the companies are entitled to receive but that officials otherwise might delay, such as product registrations, construction permits, and import clearances. Companies have also made government payments to reduce tax liabilities, to keep a competitor from getting permission to operate, and to prevent harm to their employees and facilities.

The **Foreign Corrupt Practices Act (FCPA)** makes certain payments by U.S. companies to foreign officials illegal. Critics claim the act is inconsistent because payments to officials to expedite their compliance with the law are legal, but payments to other officials who are not directly responsible for carrying out the law are not. For example, a large payment to a customs official to clear legally permissible merchandise is legal, but even a small payment to a government minister to influence the customs official is illegal. The FCPA allows the former payment because governmental officials in many countries delay compliance of laws indefinitely until they do receive payments, even though such payments may be illegal in those countries.

Many U.S. critics of the FCPA have contended that U.S. firms lose business because competitive countries lack similar laws against foreign bribery by their companies. But countries belonging to the Organization for Economic Cooperation and Development (OECD) now disallow their companies from taking

Table 13.1

International Corruption: A Survey of Business Perceptions

Country Rank	Country	2000 CPI Score	Country Rank	Country	2000 CPI Score	Country Rank	Country	2000 CPI Score
1	Finland	10.0	32	Hungary	5.2	63	China	3.1
2	Denmark	9.8		Tunisia	5.2		Egypt	3.1
3	New Zealand	9.4	34	South Africa	5.0		Burkina Faso	3.0
	Sweden	9.4	35	Greece	4.9	65	Kazakhstan	3.0
5	Canada	9.2	36	Malaysia	4.8		Zimbabwe	3.0
	Iceland	9.1	37	Mauritius	4.7	68	Romania	2.9
6	Norway	9.1		Morocco	4.7	69	India	2.8
	Singapore	9.1	39	Italy	4.6		Philippines	2.8
9	Netherlands	8.9		Jordan	4.6		Bolivia	2.7
10	United Kingdom	8.7	41	Peru	4.4	71	Ivory Coast	2.7
11	Luxembourg	8.6	42	Czech Republic	4.3		Venezuala	2.7
	Switzerland	8.6		Belarus	4.1	74	Ecuador	2.6
13	Australia	8.3		El Salvador	4.1		Moldova	2.6
14	USA	7.8	43	Lithuania	4.1		Armenia	2.5
15	Austria	7.7		Malawi	4.1	76	Tanzania	2.5
	Hong Kong	7.7		Poland	4.1		Vietnam	2.5
17	Germany	7.6	48	South Korea	4.0	79	Uzbekistan	2.4
18	Chile	7.4	49	Brazil	3.9	80	Uganda	2.3
19	Ireland	7.2	50	Turkey	3.8	81	Mozambique	2.2
20	Spain	7.0	51	Croatia	3.7	82	Kenya	2.1
21	France	6.7		Argentina	3.5		Russia	2.1
22	Israel	6.6		Bulgaria	3.5	84	Cameroon	2.0
23	Japan	6.4	52	Ghana	3.5	85	Angola	1.7
	Portugal	6.4		Senegal	3.5		Indonesia	1.7
25	Belgium	6.1		Slovak Republic	3.5	87	Azerbaijan	1.5
26	Botswana	6.0	57	Latvia	3.4		Ukraine	1.5
27	Estonia	5.7		Zambia	3.4	89	Yugoslavia	1.3
28	Slovenia	5.5	59	Mexico	3.3	90	Nigeria	1.2
	Taiwan	5.5		Colombia	3.2			
30	Costa Rica	5.4	60	Ethiopia	3.2			
	Namibia	5.4		Thailand	3.2			

The CPI score relates to perceptions of the degree of corruption as seen by businesspeople, risk analysts, and the general public, and ranges between 10 (highly clean) and 0 (highly corrupt).

source: Transparency International, 2000.

tax deductions for overseas bribes. Additionally, the U.S. government monitors bribery payments by non-U.S. companies and puts diplomatic pressure on foreign governments to stop the practices. However, the view that the FCPA has caused U.S. companies to engage less in bribery than their foreign competitors is questionable. Transparency International also surveyed local executives, bankers, accountants, lawyers, and chambers of commerce in 14 emerging economies to determine how prevalently companies from 19 leading exporting countries pay bribes. Figure 13.3 shows that U.S. companies fall in the middle of this ranking.[22] The Organization of American States has also adapted a Convention Against Corruption, which calls for criminalizing bribery and extraditing offenders.[23]

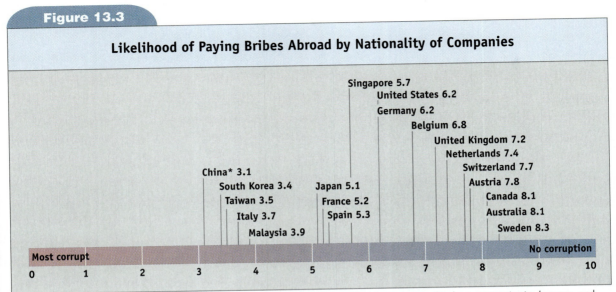

Figure 13.3

Likelihood of Paying Bribes Abroad by Nationality of Companies

Singapore 5.7
United States 6.2
Germany 6.2
Belgium 6.8
United Kingdom 7.2
Netherlands 7.4
China* 3.1
Switzerland 7.7
South Korea 3.4   Japan 5.1   Austria 7.8
Taiwan 3.5   France 5.2   Canada 8.1
Italy 3.7   Spain 5.3   Australia 8.1
Malaysia 3.9   Sweden 8.3

Most corrupt
No corruption
0   1   2   3   4   5   6   7   8   9   10

Transparency International used Gallup International to collect opinions of local executives, bankers, accountants, lawyers, and chambers of commerce in 14 emerging economies. The scales are 1 to 10. Higher scores indicate a lower incidence of paying bribes. (For the latest rankings, see www.transparency.delwelcome.html.)

source: The BPI is based on surveys undertaken by Gallup International for Transparency International among leading domestic and foreign business executives in 14 leading emerging market countries. (www.transparency.org)

Transactions with Related Entities

A **transfer price** is a price on goods and services sold by one member of a corporate family to another, such as from a parent to its subsidiary in a foreign country. A company may establish arbitrary transfer prices because of differences in tax rates between countries. For example, if the corporate tax rate is higher in the parent country than in the subsidiary country, the company could set a low transfer price on exports to the subsidiary to shift profits to the subsidiary where tax rates are lower. A company may also set arbitrary transfer prices to avoid currency controls. For example, if the government in which the subsidiary is located has currency controls on the remission of dividends, the company may manipulate transfer prices so that it locates profits where there are no currency controls. Further, a company may understate the invoice value of exports so that it will pay a lower ad valorem tariff rate when entering a foreign country.

Countries vary in how they regulate transfer prices. For example, Canada, France, Germany, the United Kingdom, and the United States are strict. They require companies to charge **arm's-length prices**—the prices that unrelated companies would charge each other. Their tax authorities can fine companies and allocate profits between two taxing jurisdictions when companies manipulate prices to avoid taxes. However, at the other extreme, some countries such as Ireland and Puerto Rico have no transfer pricing policies. So the MNE needs to determine whether it is ethical to set arbitrary transfer prices. For example, by shifting profits to a low-tax country, it is not harming tax collections in that country. In fact, that country will collect more taxes. But it is harming tax collections in the country from which the taxes are shifted.

Relatedly, in some countries most companies believe that all transactions should be arm's length. They deter purchasing managers from making contracts with companies owned by their relatives for fear contracts will violate the independence needed to buy the best quality at the lowest prices. However, in some other countries employees consider such deterrence unethical because they value family relationships so highly and because they trust relatives more to comply with contractual requirements. Clearly, companies face dilemmas in whether and how to deal with related entities in different countries.

Using Intermediaries

To avert adverse publicity about questionable ethical practices abroad, some companies have used intermediaries to avoid their direct involvement in the practices. They may or may not be aware of what the intermediaries do. For example, a company might buy from foreign suppliers rather than owning foreign facilities in which sweatshop labor is prevalent. A company might use a contractor to dispose of its hazardous waste where disposal often causes environmental damage. Or a company might hire a middleman to secure orders in a country in which such orders normally require the bribing of government officials. For example, critics have uncovered examples in which companies paid higher-than-normal fees to middlemen abroad and have claimed that the middlemen used part of the fees to bribe government officials.

However, the transfer of these activities does not prevent unethical practices; rather, it helps a company conceal its connection to them. Critics increasingly detect these distancing gimmicks and criticize international companies for not adequately overseeing their intermediaries. Companies using foreign contractors must now incur added costs to monitor intermediaries.[24] For example, IKEA, a Swedish furniture retailer with worldwide sourcing and sales, contracted an Indian exporter to supply it with rugs. IKEA required the Indian exporter to sign a contract stipulating that no child labor would be used in making the rugs. However, a German television documentary traced the supply chain and exposed that an IKEA rug supplier in India hired 10-year-olds, made them work 16 hours a day, and beat them if they arrived late to work or performed poorly. IKEA immediately withdrew the rugs from sale, but the documentary and publicity about it caused consumers to boycott IKEA in Europe and Hong Kong. Belatedly, the documentary turned out to have been a fraud. Nevertheless, IKEA now monitors its entire supply chain to assure that intermediaries fulfill their contracts requiring socially responsible behavior. Still, it is not easy for companies to monitor suppliers in a foreign country because the foreign suppliers may find many ways to conceal their practices. Figure 13.4 shows the monitoring problem humorously.

Some Positive Alternatives

Our preceding discussion emphasized problems for companies in avoiding consequences from being perceived as ethically or socially irresponsible. We shall now discuss how companies may gain advantages from their behaviors.

Picking Complementary Projects

Most companies help finance community projects, ranging from support of the arts to support of social services. Companies receive more requests for contri-

Figure 13.4

Problems of Monitoring
Intermediaries
Monitoring suppliers for
their ethical and socially
responsible behavior is a
problem. The cartoon
shows how interpreters can
mislead monitors.
Additionally, suppliers may
subcontract questionable
practices to other
suppliers. They may also
reform conditions only in
anticipation of a visit.

source: Doonesbury © G.B. Trudeau. Reprinted with permission of Universal Press Syndicate. All rights reserved.

butions to worthwhile causes than they can fulfill; therefore, they often choose those causes that might give them the most positive publicity and help their business the most. For example, Avon, which depends almost entirely on female clients, targets its support worldwide toward breast cancer prevention, a worthy cause its customers find important. Johnson & Johnson, a pharmaceutical company, sends Kenyans abroad to study nursing, thus possibly creating opinion leaders who view its products favorably. Merck, another pharmaceutical company, gives away millions of doses of a drug to fight river blindness in Africa, thus countering negative publicity that claims pharmaceutical companies do too little to combat health and disease problems in the poorer countries of the world because people lack incomes to spend much on pharmaceuticals.

Another possibility is to use excess capacity to help worthwhile programs. For example, Coca-Cola has established an African foundation. One of its initiatives is to lend logisitcs managers to charities in Africa when they are not busy so that they can help them develop routes to deliver literature, condoms, and testing kits for AIDS prevention. The company is also lending them space in its warehouses, trucks for transport, and is enlisting support from the 100,000 people who work for marketing and bottling companies that are affiliated with Coca-Cola.[25]

Move to Rural Areas

The migration of families from rural to urban areas in many emerging economies has resulted in unfulfilled expectations for many of the migrants. In desperation, many families have had to send their children to work to supplement family earnings enough to buy food. An integrative governmental program in Thailand encourages foreign companies to locate in rural areas, in which they tap adult labor supplies so that families need not migrate or send their children out to work. Such companies as Bata, American Express, and 3M have availed themselves of the program by locating in rural Thailand.[26] They have built local allies as a result.

Local Involvement

Companies, especially in extractive industries, sometimes locate in remote parts of emerging economies, in which few people live. These few local inhabitants often see little self-benefit from the business projects. In fact, they fear that the projects will adversely affect their way of life. Companies traditionally handled these situations through paternalism. In other words, companies gave people what they thought would be good for them, rather than what the people actually wanted. This sometimes proved disastrous because companies spent heavily without quelling opposition to their entry. Further, NGOs have sometimes sided with the local people to impede companies' operations, such as in Papua New Guinea.

However, more recently, oil companies in the Orinoco delta of Venezuela and mining companies in the Andes of Peru have hired anthropologists to determine what is really important to local people. Companies have also contracted international nonprofit agencies, such as Care, and local NGOs to carry out programs to appease local critics. For example, people in the community of Yanacocha, Peru, worried that a U.S.–Peruvian gold mining joint venture would invade sacred mountains and contaminate their water sources. With help from an anthropologist, the company implemented cheap and simple answers to their worries and turned critics into supporters. In brief, the joint venture donated two sheep to the local community for each test hole it drilled. The community sacrificed one sheep to appease the mountain gods and added one sheep to its communal flock. Later, the company developed projects in Yanacocha and nearby communities. These projects included drinking water systems, latrines, schools, medical posts, and training programs in agricultural and stock-raising techniques.[27]

High Versus Low Profile

Companies have two trains of thought concerning publicity about their socially responsible behavior. One train of thought is to widely publicize the positive things the company is doing. For example, General Motors publishes a public interest report to highlight its involvement in a wide array of activities globally, such as environmental cleanup programs in Mexico and Eastern Europe, cancer research, AIDS education, and global celebration of Earth Day. Some firms also feel that all companies will eventually have to adhere to high social responsibility standards. Thus, if they can be in the forefront, such as by developing more environmentally friendly production methods, they can gain competitive advantages by publicizing what they do. Further, they believe they can gain cost advantages if they become efficient before slower-moving competitors adapt high social responsibility standards. However, publicity also puts a company in the spotlight so that the general public (particularly NGOs) watches it more closely. For example, H. D. Fuller is not the only company selling glue in Central America. However, publicity about H. D. Fuller's good citizenship made it a visible target when the public learned about glue sniffing among Central American children. A lower profile may have lessened the attention directed at H. D. Fuller.

Avoiding Locations or Not

MNEs face a dilemma on whether to locate where they cannot operate in a socially responsible way. Some people argue that MNEs should not operate in these areas because they are so powerful and important that countries will alter their policies to attract them. Others argue that MNEs are better able to bring about change by locating in these countries and working within the systems. For example, because of apartheid (racial separation) policies, consumers outside South Africa boycotted international companies so that they would leave South Africa. Many did leave, but many stayed as well. Between 1986 and 1991, 235 of 360 U.S. foreign investors left South Africa. South Africa ended its apartheid policies. For example, it rescinded laws that disallowed equal pay for equal work. But observers continue to debate whether companies' departures from South Africa had affected the termination of apartheid. In another example, Carlsberg, a Danish brewery, reluctantly gave in to Danish trade union and consumer pressures to discontinue a joint venture in Myanmar because of the country's military dictatorship. A company manager pointed out that Carlsberg was not in business to pursue Danish foreign policy and that the decision might weaken its future competitive position in Myanmar because Anheuser-Busch remained there.

Guidelines

Many multilateral agreements exist that can help companies make ethical and socially responsible decisions. These agreements deal primarily with employment practices, consumer protection, environmental protection, political activity, and human rights in the workplace. The U.S. government issued a voluntary code for U.S. companies' operations abroad, which interestingly calls for U.S. companies to publicize their positive accomplishments in the workplace abroad. Also, the U.K. government established an office to promote socially responsible behavior by its companies abroad. Nevertheless, despite a growing body of agreements and codes, no set of workable corporate guidelines is universally accepted and observed.

The OECD, a multilateral organization of industrial countries, approved a code of conduct for companies' international operations. The code is necessarily vague so that governments and groups they represent could reach a consensus. Various groups have also issued codes of conduct dealing with specific activities, such as infant formula sales and environmental practices. Some codes deal only with specific areas of the world, such as employment practices in northern Mexico and in Northern Ireland. In some cases, industry groups, such as the International Council of Toy Makers, have agreed on codes to provide good working conditions and avoid the use of child labor. Because codes are voluntary, adoption does not guarantee enforcement. However, codes help clarify a collective attitude toward specific company practices that could ease governments' abilities to pass restrictive legislation without fear that the legislation would be greatly out of step with world public opinion.

Summary

Clearly, when companies do business internationally, they face disagreements on what constitutes ethical and socially responsible behavior. Individuals may face situations in international business that challenge their ethical beliefs. They may react by forgoing their desired behavior, by convincing others to accept their positions, by leaving their employers or operating locations in order to avoid conflicts, or by compromising with others whose opinions are different. Because companies represent a conglomeration of individuals, they face the same alternatives. In the final analysis, ethical and socially responsible behavior requires judgment, which makes it relative and subjective.

endnotes

[1] Diana B. Henriques, "Black Mark for a 'Good Citizen,'" *New York Times,* November 26, 1995, p. 1F+.

[2] Geert Hofstede, *Cultures and Organizations* (London: McGraw-Hill, 1991), p. 8.

[3] Larue Tone Hosner, "Response to 'Do Good Ethics Always Make for Good Business?'" *Strategic Management Journal,* Vol. 17, 1996, p. 501.

[4] Robert D. Haas, "Ethics in the Trenches," *Across the Board,* Vol. 31, No. 5, May 1994, pp. 12–13.

[5] Bernard Lewis, "Western Culture Must Go," *Wall Street Journal,* May 2, 1988, p. 18.

[6] John R. Boatright, *Ethics in the Conduct of Business* (Inglewood Cliffs, NJ: Prentice Hall, 1993), pp. 13–18.

[7] "A Charter to Cheat," *Economist,* February 15, 1997, p. 61.

[8] Michael Harvey, "Marketing of Banned Pesticides and Unapproved Pharmaceuticals to Developing Countries," *Journal of Global Marketing,* Vol. 93, No. 3, 1996, pp. 67–93.

[9] Lorraine Moody, "A DDT Ban Would Be Deadly," *Wall Street Journal,* September 2, 1999, p. A14.

[10] Joseph A. Massey, "Guide to the Art of Lobbying," *Financial Times,* March 27, 1998, Mastering Global Business section, p. 5+.

[11] "Technology Dilemma Over Old Cultures," *South China Morning Post,* February 20, 1995, p. 13, quoting opinions of Newt Gingrich.

[12] Paul Betts, "Poisoning Halts Production of Nestlé's Italian Christmas Cake," *Financial Times,* December 14, 1998, p. 14.

[13] James Wilson, "Del Monte Sidesteps Banana Skin Pile," *Financial Times,* February 20, 1998, p. 3.

[14] G. Pascal Zachary and Samantha Marshall, "Nike Tries to Quell Exploitation Charges," *Wall Street Journal,* June 25, 1997, p. A16.

[15] Steven Greenhouse, "Voluntary Rules on Apparel Proving Allusive," *New York Times,* February 1, 1997, p. 1+.

[16] Elizabeth Howard, "Keeping Ahead of the Green Regulators," *Financial Times,* March 27, 1998, Mastering Global Business section, p. 8.

[17] Mark Turner, "Feasting on Famine Food," *Financial Times,* November 24, 1998, p. 6.

[18] "Benetton Opens a Havana Boutique Aimed at Tourists: Exile Groups Protest," *Wall Street Journal,* January 26, 1993, p. A10.

[19] Joe Stephens, "Testing Drugs: Overseas Trials Lack Oversight," *Miami Herald,* January 7, 2001, p. L1+.

[20] "Cause for Concern; With Nestlé in the Spotlight Again Over Its Advertising Tactics," *Marketing Week,* February 11, 1999, pp. 28–31.

[21] Michael Waldholz, "Sparks Fly at AIDS Meeting Over Breast-Feeding," *Wall Street Journal,* July 12, 2000, p. B2.

[22] *Toronto Sun,* October 27, 1999, p. 2, reporting data from Transparency International.

[23] Nancy Dunne, "Kanter Calls for Bribery Action," *Financial Times,* July 26, 1996, p. 3.

[24] Philip Rosenzweig, "How Should Multinationals Set Global Workplace Standards?" *Financial Times,* March 27, 1998, Mastering Global Business section, pp. 11–12.

[25] Donald G. McNeil, Jr., "Coca-Cola Joins AIDS Fight in South Africa," *New York Times,* June 21, 2001, p. A6.

[26] Deborah Leipziger and Pia Sabharwal, "Companies That Play Hide and Seek with Child Labor," *Business in Society Review,* Vol. 95, 1996, pp. 11–13.

[27] Raymond Colitt, "Oilmen Struggle to Become Good Jungle Citizens," *Financial Times,* May 24–25, 1997, p. 4; and Sally Bowen, "People Power Keeps Peru's Investors in Check," *Financial Times,* February 6, 1998, p. 6.

Objectives

1. To appreciate the challenges and rewards of a career in international business

2. To grasp the balance between technical competency and personal mind-set in shaping an individual career plan in international business

3. To discern the ethnocentric, polycentric, and geocentric mind-sets and their implications for international business careers

4. To understand the major issues of working aboard as an expatriate—being selected for the position, negotiating a motivating compensation plan, and planning the return home

5. To learn about approaches that a pending or current expatriate can take to manage the foreign assignment

The Challenges and Opportunities of International Business Careers

In August 2000, eBay, the leading online auction site, announced plans to revolutionize the way people around the world bought and sold goods. Essentially, eBay planned to convert developing nations into virtual marketplaces with its online audience for native handicrafts, thereby infusing remote villages with cash that could improve their standard of living. "It's fascinating," chief operating officer Meg Whitman explained. "There is a real frontier here that would truly make global trading a reality. You think about the third world, villagers in Guatemala and Africa who have handicrafts to sell, who could list in their currency and their language and sell to the industrialized world. As that seller community makes more money for their town or village, they then have more purchasing power to buy more products and services from the more developed world. . . . Certainly it has the power to transform countries and cities and villages and empower people to make a living in ways they could not before. . . . eBay is creating new trade on a global basis that the world has never seen—that's what gets us up in the morning." Despite the many skeptics, Whitman summed up eBay's outlook by saying, "The fun thing about eBay is that we're pioneering a whole new marketplace. . . . It's going to be tremendous."[1]

Moving from a global outlook to heading overseas is a major career move. Like eBay's vision, a long time can pass from ambition to starting the foreign assignment. For example, Honeywell tried to identify and develop potential candidates years before their transfer abroad. Early on, Honeywell briefed potential expatriates on their cross-cultural skills and prescribed training paths. Explained Manfred Fiedler, vice president of human resources, "We give them a horizon, a perspective and, gradually, we tell them they are potentially on an international path. . . . We want them to develop a cross-cultural intellect, what we call 'strategic accountability.'"[2] Toward this end, Honeywell might advise an employee to study another language or informally explore areas in which he or she might be at odds with foreign cultures.

Careers in
International Business
chapter 14

Mask used by witch doctors in
the Gia tribe of Liberia.

Laying the foundation for a possible career in international business is hard work. Many people who have worked overseas, though, note that the early challenges were just the beginning. Working internationally compels people to develop richer management repertoires than they used while working in their home nation. Consider Mrs. Joan Pattle, a Microsoft marketing manager who worked at corporate headquarters for three years before accepting a post as product manager for direct marketing in Britain. While in the United States, Pattle had been in charge of direct marketing. Her U.K. job came with much wider responsibilities. She explained, "At home, my job was very strictly defined. I basically had to know everything about managing a database. But when I got to London, I was also in charge of direct marketing and press relations. I was exposed to a much broader set of experiences."[3]

Finally, once overseas, virtually all managers eventually return home. You would think this would be a snap—pack the bags, say good-bye to colleagues, board the plane, and return to a hero's welcome. In many cases, everything but the hero's welcome happens. Observed Tom Schiro of Deloitte & Touche, "Some companies just send somebody overseas and forget about them for two years."[4] Expectedly, wise career planning can make a world of difference. For example, following a four-year assignment in Tokyo, Bryan Krueger returned to a promotion to president of Baxter Fenwal North America. When he had left to start his job in Tokyo, his company had not guaranteed him a promotion upon his return. Thus, while he was away, he kept up to date with the goings-on at headquarters. Later, Mr. Krueger credited his particularly smooth return to his intensive networking. During his stint in Tokyo, he returned to the United States four to five times a year in order to see colleagues and friends. As he explained, "I was definitely proactive. Anyone who's not is doing himself a disservice. I made a conscious effort to stay in touch, and it paid off."[5]

Careers in international business span many environmental, company, and individual conditions. From defining brave new markets to returning home, international business careers take any number of directions. At the center of all, though, is the individual facing unprecedented challenges that often lead to amazing opportunities. The contest between challenges and opportunities, as we will now see, is the spirit of a career in international business.

Introduction

This chapter looks at a simple question: How do you develop a career in international business? As with most simple questions, the answer tends to be complicated. For example, consider this puzzle. Generally, people think of an international business career as filled with terrific learning opportunities, munificent compensation, glamorous mystique, and a ticket to leadership positions. Nonetheless, convincing people to accept a foreign assignment is a tough sell. Many companies struggle to fill long-term international slots. Indeed, more companies now try to outsource part or all of their international management functions.[6] Convincing people to go abroad is just half the problem. When they return, most seem less than thrilled about their new assignments. Many returning expatriates feel that their companies really don't value or know what to do with their hard-won international experience.[7] To complete this doom and gloom, more multinational enterprises (MNEs) talk about filling local slots with host-country citizens in place of high-priced expatriates.

In contrast, other data show that careers in international business are flourishing. Several groups report the long-running growth in expatriate posts in Western Europe, the United States, Central and Eastern Europe, China, and South America will not only continue but in fact accelerate.[8] Even MNEs that use local personnel to staff international operations still rely on expatriates to help out. For instance, at any given time, Ford Motor Company has 1,500 to 2,000 U.S. employees working abroad, whereas Royal Dutch Shell stations 5,500 employees outside their home country.[9]

As Figure 14.1 suggests, this chapter explains this puzzle. It does so by taking the view that international business experience adds value to a person's skills and outlook. Specifically, we consider why people who work internationally believe that, upon return-

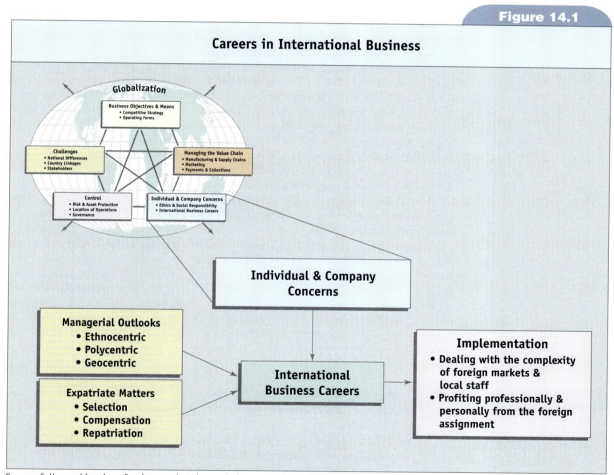

Figure 14.1

Careers in International Business

Successfully working in a foreign market demands both a unique attitude and specialized aptitudes. No fixed rules stipulate the correct outlook or best set of skills. Managing expatriate matters spurs companies to develop meaningful guidelines that prepare the executive to meet personal and professional goals.

ing home, they have something special on their résumé. And if they sometimes don't believe so, others do. For instance, one observer noted, "A foreign posting sometime in your career is now almost required for senior-level jobs."[10] Another concluded, "If you've got global skills, you're definitely seen as a hot ticket."[11]

Whether your ambition is to be an entrepreneurial exporter or expatriate executive for a large MNE, this chapter gives you a sense of the ways that careers in international business evolve. The chapter begins by addressing a notable shift in our idea of careers in general and a career in international business in particular. We then discuss the notion of a mind-set and how your particular idea of the world powerfully influences your potential for a career in international business. The chapter then evaluates vital issues in the realm of expatriates: The matters of their selection, compensation, and repatriation. Throughout all, we look at environmental, business, and managerial trends that shape how a person starts and sustains a career in international business.

A Point of Perspective

Traditionally, discussing careers in international business started and ended with the tasks of international human resource planning (see Table 14.1). These issues still fundamentally shape how we understand careers in international business, and throughout this chapter, we look at each. However, others parts of this text have reported that many events and trends hasten the globalization of business. Consequentially, people who work in international business are rethinking what they do in search of ways that better fit a progressively interlinked world.

More precisely, if we went back 20 years or so, we would find many large, centralized MNEs that focused on a few national markets. Career paths at this time were clear-cut. Although most included the occasional international trip, few asked people to take a career detour with a long-term foreign assignment. Today, a look around the business world finds different career patterns in the face of growing globalization. Managers now seek international jobs to develop the experiences needed for a world with freer-moving people, ideas, products, and capital.

Earlier chapters showed that institutional changes and technological innovations push companies to rethink their global manufacturing strategy and supply chain management. Consumers are reacting in kind, buying things from companies—whether a one-person firm on eBay or the thousands running General Electric Supply—in ways that we did not even imagine a decade ago. These and other changes show that careers in a globalizing market rely on many traditional notions of business but increasingly must deal with new ideas about products, consumers, companies, markets, cultures, and institutions.

Table 14.1

Principal Issues of International Human Resource Management

- Selection and recruitment of qualified individuals
- Training and development of personnel
- Assessment and compensation of performance
- Repatriation and retention of competent personnel
- Management of the interface between labor and management

We are duty bound to note that pinpointing specific international business career plans in the face of such change is tough. Even in stable times, career patterns are notoriously difficult to discern for people who are actually implementing them. Moreover, research shows that individuals' perceptions of how they are doing in their careers can vary markedly from an observer's appraisal.[12] Besides the jumble created by globalizing markets, any notion of a specific career plan must also allow that fewer and fewer people spend their working lives within a single company. Therefore, we refrain from specifying discrete career plans that arguably lead to or away from international activity. Instead, this chapter takes its cue from the current work environment and presumes that people blaze their own trails, making choices and pursuing opportunities in ways that are consistent with their career ambitions.

We do qualify this presumption with a word of caution to those who may reply, "Yeah, whatever, a career in international business is not in my plans." Consider that since the 1980s, many companies have had to transform themselves or die. Although many trends fueled these efforts, the globalization of business ignited the fire. Eventually, even those companies that thought they had built impervious firewalls felt the heat of international business. In case after case, successful MNEs like Caterpillar, Intel, ABB, Sony, and Citibank reviewed their business outlook, questioning how they had and how they should interpret globalization. We see the same chain of events happening to individuals' career paths. Technology, institutions, and consumer behavior continually throw more fuel onto the globalization fire. As more firewalls fall, more people must deal with the new faces and forces of international markets.

More practically, consider people who will likely never leave their home nation for a foreign assignment but, for various reasons, see learning a foreign language as a career plus, and sometimes a career must. The freer movement of people among nations means that individuals with particular jobs or certain ambitions find foreign-language skills give them a competitive edge in their own hometown. These careers run the gamut. Besides traditional executive

Welcome

Figure 14.2

slots, foreign languages are being spoken by more and more customers or colleagues at banks, health care facilities, telephone companies, police departments, and construction sites.

In sum, change in the old and new ways of working in a globalizing market has tremendous implications for all sorts of careers. Change, moreover, applies to all, whether you are an expatriate in an MNE, an entrepreneur who reaches overseas markets through your Web site, or someone who comes into contact with immigrants. Still, despite all the unfolding changes in the idea of an international business career, one basic principle endures: Career paths start from the same point of perspective, namely, the mind-set that you use to make sense of the many varied situations of international business.

The Idea of a Mind-Set

Every day we see and read reports of developments in the world of business. For instance, Matsushita moves VCR production to Eastern Europe, Citicorp launches a commercial lending program for sub-Saharan Africa, or the World Trade Organization mediates a trade dispute between the United States and China. These sorts of events fit our particular understanding of the structure and behavior of consumers, companies, markets, and institutions. Others, though, defy routine interpretation. For instance, Zara redefines competitive standards in the global retail industry, or eBay plans to change the idea of international trade. Whatever the case, each of us tries to make sense of change with our particular *mind-set*—essentially the interpretative framework that guides how we classify and discriminate change in ways that let us understand what we perceive to have happened and, therefore, anticipate what now may happen.

More so than ever before, an individual's mind-set creates the possibility for and shapes the potential of an international business career. Plainly put, success in international business careers increasingly depends on your attitude as much as, if perhaps not more than, your technical aptitude. For instance, Peter Drucker, a leading management authority, stated that a truly multinational company "demands of its management people that they think and act as international [businesspeople] in a world in which national passions are as strong as ever." More directly, McKinsey & Company, a prominent management consultant company, reported that technical competence is now a given but that "global market pioneers must have a particular mindset."[13]

This situation results from quirks in beginning a career in international business. Notably, "international business" is not a traditional entry-level point or career track within a company. Moreover, while some schools offer specialized international business training, few students formally study to be an exporter or expatriate, and far fewer go directly from graduation to a foreign assignment. Once you begin your career, either on your own or with a company, you will come across very few doors boldly labeled "Push Here for an International Business Career." Indeed, as we saw with Honeywell in our opening discussion, the time from expressing an interest in working abroad to actually departing for a foreign assignment can span years. Therefore, a career in international business is, within both start-ups and established corporations, a function of a lot of hard work and a dash of inspiration.

Figure 14.3

The fact that you have gotten to this point in the text testifies to your diligence. The matter of inspiration that turns your knowledge into a career in international business, however, is impossible to define. Rather, the catalytic role of inspiration depends on your evolving interpretation of events in a globalizing world. For instance, if one day an e-mail in your in-box lists a message from Switzerland regarding your posted auction on eBay, your mind-set about international business could lead you to say, "This might be interesting"—and you then reply to the inquiry. More easily, however, you may ask yourself, "Why bother dealing with this strangeness?" hit the delete key, and move on to things that better fit your mind-set about how the business world works for you. Similarly, as your career unfolds within an MNE, opportunities will arise that let you show your interest in the company's foreign markets. A recently repatriated executive may recount her experience to you and, eventually, relay your interest to the expatriate selection committee. Alternatively, you can easily opt to avoid hearing a bunch of tired war stories about bizarre places that may be strategic to the firm but are not part of your current responsibilities or idealized career path.

These scenarios, while overly simplified, try to depict how your mind-set about events rather than some generic checklist ultimately shapes the likelihood of a career in international business. Findings by McKinsey & Company amplify this theme: "When you look behind the success stories of leading globalizers, you find companies that have learned how to think differently from the herd. They seek out different information, process it in a different way, come to different conclusions, and make different decisions. Where others see threats and complexity, they see opportunity. Where others see a barren landscape, they see a cornucopia of choices."[14]

Types of Mind-Sets

The mind-set of people in international business is an enduring curiosity. Research spotlights three types: The ethnocentric mind-set, the polycentric mind-set, and the geocentric mind-set. We now turn to the fine points of each. First, though, a quick note. As you review each type, keep in mind that there is no fundamentally superior outlook. Rather, each mind-set has strengths and weaknesses that make it, depending on the individual, company, or market situation, a useful way to start and guide a career in international business.

The Ethnocentric Mind-Set

Ethnocentrism is the belief that the values, practices, and behaviors of the home country are intrinsically superior to those in other nations. Executives with an ethnocentric mind-set believe that successful business practices at home need not change when transferred to foreign markets. Instead, they assume that if their business design has already proven successful at home, then it will work anywhere in the world.

Advantages of ethnocentrism. An ethnocentric view helps a company transfer its unique competitive skill overseas. Chapter 2 showed that an individual or firm often earns success in the home market from a superior competency. Sustaining this edge when they move overseas tends to make managers interpret the company's unique skills as the best way to get things done right. An ethnocentric outlook sees tinkering with a prized formula just to go overseas as unreasonably risky.

Often, an ethnocentric framework is a useful way to make sense of foreign markets when a company has built a unique business design that is hard to articulate plainly or specify precisely. Like a technological innovation, a hard-to-copy business design helps a firm challenge better-positioned rivals in foreign markets. Transferring ethnocentric managers from the home office to the foreign subsidiary, therefore, ensures that the preferred message makes it overseas. From the point of view of the home office, the local company can now leverage the company's competitive advantages with the kind of home-country hands-on knowledge that made the company successful in the first place.

Finally, earlier chapters noted the formidable task of working in odd, exotic places. An individual, guided by an ethnocentric mind-set, often endures less stress in making sense of foreign situations. For instance, many Japanese firms transfer their management mind-set and business design to their foreign opera-

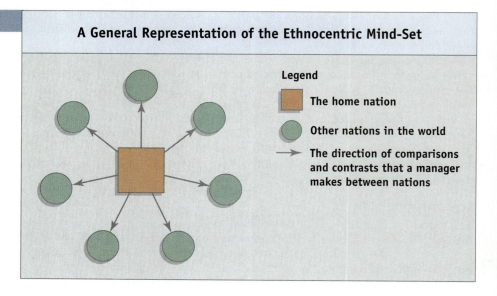

Figure 14.4

A General Representation of the Ethnocentric Mind-Set

Legend

☐ The home nation

⬤ Other nations in the world

→ The direction of comparisons and contrasts that a manager makes between nations

tions no matter what part of the world that they happen to be in. Asked why, Japanese companies typically reply that the unique mind-set of their company is the foundation of their global success. So whether Komatsu, Inc., makes tractors in Tokyo, Japan or Peoria, Illinois, its managers typically interpret business events with an ethnocentric outlook.

Disadvantages of ethnocentrism. As the adage goes, "Vices are simply virtues taken to extreme," so too with an ethnocentric mind-set. International business, if anything at all, is about differences among people, places, and processes. Trying to make all foreign situations fit one outlook runs the risk of managers slamming circular and triangular pegs into square slots. Granted, eventually, a company can make its foreign operation mirror the outward appearance of the home office. Success, however, often carries the price of ruinous change, high costs, and lost opportunities. Inevitably, companies have good reasons when asked why they tried to transfer their mind-set abroad. They explain that there was usually no shortage of brainpower in a particular nation, just a shortage of people with the right mix of technical skills and a willingness to accept their particular style of doing business. Continuing on, they add that if you rely heavily on locals, you're going to have a local culture, not the corporate culture that made your company great.

A benefit of international business is exposure to different, possibly better, ways of doing things. Reluctance to consider this possibility can dull the competitive edge of an individual or firm. An ethnocentric mind-set is especially prone to this risk. At some point, in making sense of different people, places, and processes, an ethnocentric manager will reject the claim that consumers, markets, or institutions in foreign markets have innovations that are worthy of accommodation or emulation. In doing so, an ethnocentric mind-set can impose blinders upon an individual or firm.

The Polycentric Mind-Set

A **polycentric** outlook accepts the importance of adapting to differences, real or imaginary, between the home and host country. A polycentric manager champions the ways of foreign markets as just as enlightened as the practices of the parent company and home nation, if not more so. To a lesser degree, we can see this philosophy in the notion, "When in Rome, do as the Romans do."

Advantages of polycentrism. The simple economics of staffing international operations fit best with a polycentric mind-set. The choice to hire local managers eliminates the expense of expatriates. Consider, for example, FedEx, the U.S.-based express delivery company. With 210 expatriates out of 140,000 worldwide employees, FedEx fills as many overseas slots with local executives as possible because expatriates almost always cost more. Similarly, local managers should perform better sooner, given that they have the mind-set to make sense of their local colleagues, customers, markets, and institutions. As another example, when operating outside the United States, Microsoft tries to hire foreign nationals rather than use expatriates. "You want people who know the local situation, its value system, the way work gets done, the way people use technology in that particular country, and who the key competitors are. . . . If you send someone in fresh from a different region or country, they don't know those things," explained the chief operating officer of Microsoft.[15] In addition, Bill Gates of Microsoft suggests that a polycentric mind-set is some-

Figure 14.5

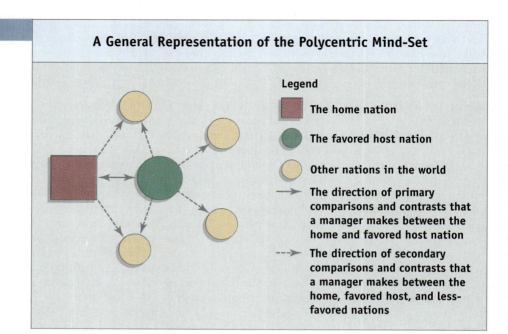

A General Representation of the Polycentric Mind-Set

Legend

■ The home nation

● The favored host nation

○ Other nations in the world

→ The direction of primary comparisons and contrasts that a manager makes between the home and favored host nation

--→ The direction of secondary comparisons and contrasts that a manager makes between the home, favored host, and less-favored nations

what of a moral obligation of international business, declaring that, when staffing an international office, "It sends the wrong message to have a foreigner come over to run things."

Disadvantages of polycentrism. The temptation to champion the ways of a foreign nation can, if unchecked, lead to the "Going Native" phenomenon—people abandon their home-country mind-set in favor of the favored host country's. Difficulties emerge when a person or company intent on local assimilation makes poor sense of events both at home and within the adopted foreign country. Another risk of a polycentric mind-set is the flip side: A polycentric individual or firm tends to place great faith in the local staff in the charitable belief that if you cannot rely on the locals, then who can you rely on? This belief can lead to delegating a lot of authority to local managers. In theory, local managers ought to be able to balance the competing demands of making sense of events from a local and home-office view. In practice, however, they may believe national concerns ought to be more important than the needs of a faraway home office. Finally, entrepreneurs with a polycentric mind-set direct their energy toward discovering and serving opportunities in their preferred market. So, for example, an Anglophile U.S.-based seller of Web design services likely would direct marketing efforts toward the United Kingdom, Canada, and Australia to the neglect of potentially more lucrative national markets that seem less interesting.

The Geocentric Mind-Set

Unlike the ethnocentric and polycentric mind-sets, the **geocentric** mind-set is not tied to a particular home or host nation. As a result, the geocentric framework can be a hard idea to visualize. A helpful way to grasp this idea is to imagine the many national markets of the world as separate but interdependent pieces of a mosaic. In totality, there is a picture of a huge market that shares common features such as goods, attitudes, competition, and institutions. However, making up this mosaic are more than 200 different individual pieces, each representing a particular nation with unique characteristics. Therefore, geocentrism holds that all nations have inalienable traits that are neither superior nor inferior but simply there.

Advantages of geocentrism. A geocentric mind-set offers terrific advantages in an international business career. A geocentric outlook does not automatically presume that a particular nation provides a universal solution to every problem or perfect explanation for every action. Instead, geocentrism maintains that interpretation is in the national eye of the beholder. The geocentric manager then tries to figure out how people have made sense of what they have seen in order to understand and manage what they do.

Therefore, geocentrism spurs people to appreciate the beliefs, values, behaviors, and business practices of individuals and organizations from any nation. More colorfully, some people talk about a new type of international manager—so-called cosmopolitan managers. These folks are viewed as a special type of men and women who are rising to leadership positions in their companies by "finding commonalties . . . [and] spread[ing] universal ideas and juggl[ing] the requirements of diverse places."[16] Whether called geocentric or cosmopolitan, the outcome is the same: People and companies with this mind-set seek and see commonalties across nations.

A geocentric mind-set can tap learning opportunities around the world by pushing a manager to seek new business ideas—irrespective of their national origin or cultural heritage. Whether the innovation arises in Tokyo, Timbuktu, or Toronto is irrelevant. What matters is the individual's or firm's choice to try to understand the event, identifying which points are opportunities and which are threats. Once this is done, the person or company can then make better sense of consumers, competitors, markets, and institutions around the world. For instance, Fujio Mitarai, president of Canon, Inc., observed, "Until recently,

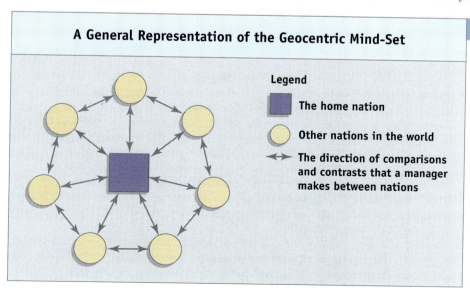

A General Representation of the Geocentric Mind-Set   Figure 14.6

Legend

■ The home nation

○ Other nations in the world

↔ The direction of comparisons and contrasts that a manager makes between nations everything we did overseas was an extension of what we were doing in Japan. From now on, we want to give birth to new value abroad. We want to make the best of the different kinds of expertise available in different countries."[17]

In sum, the challenge of a geocentric mind-set is (1) accepting the premise that bright people of all nationalities are doing bright things around the world and (2) developing an understanding of the interaction between the many things that are alike and the many things that are different among nations. Once done, a manager has a mind-set that, while not perfect in any nation, functions well in every nation.

Disadvantages of geocentrism. The geocentric mind-set is hard to develop and costly to maintain. Difficulty follows from the need to keep a sense of who you are and still be able to understand the views of a diverse range of people. For instance, at Gillette, only 15 percent of the company's expatriates are natives of the United States; 85 percent come from 27 other countries. Similarly, J. P. Morgan, the investment bank, employs more than 50 nationalities in its London office.[18] Making sense of all the mind-sets that potentially bear on a decision can overwhelm the best intentions. If done poorly, geocentrism can erode the sense of common purpose. Like the Tower of Babel, the clarity of the task can get lost in a hodgepodge of different outlooks. Similarly, the logistics of geocentrism are costly. Exposing people to different ideas and places gets expensive very quickly.

Which Mind-Set When?

Declaring which mind-set is best suited for a career is international business is unwise. At the least, going from this text to the real world is a big jump. Once in the marketplace, neatly categorizing the particular mind-set of an individual or firm is unrealistic—indeed, just like the idea of beauty, few of us can define it, but we all think we know it when we see it. To blur matters, the ethnocentric, polycentric, and geocentric mind-sets have particular strengths and weaknesses (see Table 14.2). Therefore, as with many aspects of international business, the "best" mind-set often depends on what else is going on within the market, company, or an existing career.

The issue of which mind-set when ultimately raises the question: "Can mind-sets change?" That is, if you currently identify with the polycentric outlook, can you aspire to adopt the ethnocentric or geocentric mind-set if either one offers more career advantages? Historically, many thought that changing outlooks was infeasible. That is, the conventional wisdom in international business regarded individual mind-sets largely as it did national culture, essentially as the expression of latent, or innate, psychological values (such as, individuality versus collectivism), norms (femininity versus masculinity), and attitudes (risk averse or risk affinitive). This viewpoint effectively holds that an individual's outlook is anchored in attitudes and convictions that emerged early in life as the result of socialization within a family, community, and country. Therefore, changing your outlook, given these circumstances, is akin to changing your identity. Consequently, this viewpoint allows little possibility of adopting a different outlook.

Recent research on the idea of cultural cognitivism suggests otherwise. There is growing evidence that your mind-set is a cognitive (rather than psychological) framework that shapes how you perceive, relate, and interpret

Table 14.2

Properties of the Mind-Sets of International Business

Mind-Set	Assumption	Advantages	Drawbacks
Ethnocentric	Presumes that the values, practices, and behaviors of the home country are superior to those in other nations.	Leverages an individual's or company's unique competence to foreign markets. Gives people a strong point of perspective. At some point, all people experience this mind-set; requires little effort to maintain.	Can inspire belief that the home market is intrinsically better at everything. Can result in cultural arrogance. May blind people to innovations in other countries.
Polycentric	Accepts unquestionably the importance of adapting to any differences, real or imaginary, between the home and host countries.	Helps people see the special virtues of a particular nation. Removes most barriers to adapting to the chosen local market.	Can lead to the "Going Native" effect. May lead people to give too much credit to attitudes and practices in a favored nation.
Geocentric	All nations are created equal and possess inalienable characteristics that are neither superior nor inferior but simply there.	Is a socially adept way to deal with different people in different nations. Helps people see points of commonality across different nations. Opens up tremendous learning opportunities.	Can lead to a loss of national identity. Tough to develop and hard to maintain.

information. Thus, rather than being locked into a particular way of seeing the world, you can use your interpretative framework to guide how you engage new ideas and make sense of new experiences. Indeed, as the doctrine "Cogito, ergo sum" (I think, therefore I am) suggests, you have the innate capacity to think about why you adopt a particular outlook and, where deemed desirable, to change it to better deal with a changing world. Thus far, studies of the views and attitudes of managers in many nations, such as Britain, France, Germany, the United States, India, Japan, Hong Kong, and Singapore, support this view.[19]

The idea that how you make sense of information shapes your outlook creates the mechanisms by which you can purposefully change your mind-set.

Plainly put, a mind-set is not a given; you can change your outlook through any number of methods, ranging from the elementary (such as by reading news of foreign events reported in local and international papers), intermediate (inviting an international student from the local university for dinner), or complex (traveling to foreign nations to see how other people live). Needless to say, the same goes for an MNE—it can opt to monitor developments in foreign markets, support the local world trade club, sponsor cross-cultural training programs for its workers, design management teams composed of people of different nationalities, or mix nationalities among its headquarters staff. Whichever way is chosen, new experiences and new ideas stimulate individuals and companies to rethink their mind-sets.

Staffing International Operations: Expatriates or Locals?

Talk of virtual companies operating in cyberspace free of the bounds of national borders may eventually become reality. Presently, though, international business takes place within a world marked by geographic borders and populated by bricks-and-mortar companies. Indeed, as we noted in Chapter 5, in 1999, there were more than 63,000 MNEs with more than 690,000 foreign affiliates spread across the 200-plus nations of the world.

Staffing these thousands of home offices and foreign affiliates is a major aspect of international business careers. No matter what the strength of their product or process innovations, MNEs must ultimately find and move managers among the various units of their global enterprise if they are to gain the benefits of globalization. The range of MNEs and their strategic goals prevents stating a universal rule of which career paths ought to culminate in an international job. The vast majority of MNEs resolve this issue by deciding whether to staff their international operations with local workers in the host nation or expatriates sent from home or a third nation.

Reasons to Staff with Locals

Various points in this chapter touch on the challenge and expense of staffing international operations with expatriates. More than a few trends suggest that MNEs will progressively rely on local managers in place of expatriates. Specifically:

- Staffing foreign operations with locals has indisputable competitive advantages (see Table 14.3).
- Information and communication technologies make it progressively cheaper and easier to have real-time connections with plants and offices around the world.
- Some nations simply do not like the idea of expatriates. Governments discourage or legally restrict the number of allowable expatriates within a nation for political, cultural, and economic reasons.
- If executives need to visit foreign operations, faster and more accessible air and rail travel lets them reach more and more places within a day.
- Greater access to foreign business education increasingly creates larger pools of skillful local managers.

Table 14.3

Leading Reasons to Staff Foreign Operations with Locals	
Cost containment	The most compelling reason is cost. Due to tax equalization, housing allowance, cost-of-living adjustment, and other benefits, the typical expatriate compensation package is three to five times base salary at home and several times that of a local hire.
Nationalism	Host countries that dislike foreign-controlled operations regard local managers as "better citizens" because they likely put local interests ahead of the company's global objectives. Too, host governments can restrict expatriate headcounts in order to develop indigenous talent pools.
Management development	MNEs that consistently award top jobs to expatriates often struggle to attract, motivate, and retain good local employees.
Employee morale	Many subsidiary employees prefer to work for someone who is from their own country.
Expatriate failure rates	Failure rates for overseas postings, falling typically between 10 and 25 percent, can reduce performance, sidetrack careers, and corrode morale.*
Product issues	The greater the need for local adaptations, the more advantageous it is for companies to use local managers, because they arguably interpret local conditions better than an expatriate.

* Bross and J. S. Matte, *Selecting International Employees—A Corporate Investment* (Toronto: Family Guidance International, 1997).

- Moving from an international company (a host-country company with many independent foreign offices) to a global company (one company with interlinked offices around the world) lessens the need to have home-country managers personally supervise local activities.

- Not everyone aspires to be an expatriate—people increasingly decline foreign assignments for reasons that would have rarely been acknowledged a generation ago (see Table 14.4).

Reasons to Staff with Expatriates

Companies have been moving expatriates around the world for centuries. The evidence suggests that this trend will continue largely due to the significant benefits that expatriates produce (see Table 14.5). Although few dispute the intrinsic advantages of local staffs, some argue for better understanding the operational cost versus strategic benefit of expatriates. Specifically, this view holds that although expatriates make poor financial sense, they have tremendous strategic value. Global competition increasingly requires that a company's leaders understand the reality of working with different business, cultural, and political practices. Speculation about how things work "over there" is a poor substitute for the insights earned through personal experience. Hence, expatriate assignments are indispensable to companies' strategic success in global markets. Therefore, the MNE that sees foreign assignments as the training ground for its future leadership also sees the operational cost of an expatriate as simply a necessary expense of management development. As such, letting cost concerns determine the use of expatriates can create a risky "penny wise but pound foolish" dilemma.

Table 14.4	
Leading Reasons Why People Don't Work Abroad	
Family	Most often, managers reject a foreign assignment given their belief that it will impair their family's lifestyle due to inferior living conditions, inadequate educational opportunities for their children, and the inability to be near aging parents.
Career concerns	A foreign assignment may take the manager outside the corporate mainstream for advancement, thereby actually slowing his or her career trajectory.
Legal barriers	Governments often prohibit or restrict the use of expatriates. Less dramatically, national licensing requirements often prevent companies from using expatriate accountants and lawyers.
Spouse issues	Spouses rarely get a permit to work in a comparable job abroad. If the couple is unmarried, the "significant other" may be unable to get permission to live in the foreign location.
Travel fatigue	The fatigue of extensive travel may cause emotional anxiety, physical illness, and subpar professional performance.
Location disapproval	The political, cultural, religious, and security characteristics of some nations may inspire little or no interest.

A Pragmatic Resolution

There is no fixed rule to the expatriate versus local staffing dilemma. Each choice has advantages and disadvantages. Some MNEs, such as FedEx, use expatriates sparingly, whereas others, like Royal Dutch Shell and Ford, use them extensively. The crucial thing to note is that all MNEs use expatriates—just to varying degrees.

The Realm of the Expatriate

In principle, few MNEs question the need for qualified expatriates to supervise, assist, and monitor local operations. For instance, at a roundtable discussion of chief executives on how the world is changing and what, if anything, management can do to regulate change, the chairman of Unilever observed, "The single most important issue for us has been, and will continue to be, organization and people."[20] Translating this belief into effective expatriates compels an MNE to find those people who are prepared for an international business career, devise ways to motivate them to perform well, and capitalize on their new skills and improved outlook when they are ready for their next assignment. Therefore, we review the matters of expatriate selection, compensation, and repatriation.

Expatriate Selection

Screening executives to find those with the highest performance potential for a foreign assignment is the process of *expatriate selection*. This process can be quite difficult. Few MNEs have the luxury of a large corps of mobile and

Table 14.5

Leading Reasons to Staff Foreign Operations with Expatriates

Command and control	Home-country expatriates are used to doing things the "headquarters' way" and, thus, will transfer the "correct" systems to foreign operations.
Local talent gaps	Shortage of qualified local candidates, particularly given the need to transfer specialized technologies overseas, compels sending abroad highly skilled managers.
Social integration	Transferring people to different national slots helps all parties understand the global corporate entity.
Ownership structure	Joint ventures with local partners spur foreign companies to insist on using their personnel to fill key positions in order to protect their property.
Local implementation	Transferring best practices between the home country and foreign subsidiaries usually breaks down in the details of local implementation. Expatriates can quickly resolve breakdowns or bottlenecks.
High turnover among locals	MNEs face high turnover among local employees in foreign markets, particularly with highly trained professionals with technical skills. Each person who leaves is a risk of an intellectual property leak.
Management development	International experience and exposure to many nationalities encourage a manager's development of a global outlook.

experienced expatriates. Moreover, there is no specific set of technical indicators of a good versus a poor expatriate. This problem is especially complicated by the difficulty of judging a potential expatriate's adaptability to foreign places, people, and processes. Some companies try to deal with these constraints by selecting a team of expatriates. Nortel, for instance, sends three expatriates to start operations in emerging markets: An expert in international finance, an entrepreneurial sales manager, and a line manager with the softer skills needed to handle personal relationships.[21] This approach, while a solution, still depends on identifying those people in the company with the necessary skills and outlook. Therefore, the struggle to select the right expatriates continually pushes MNEs to assess their talent pool through all sorts of subtle indicators. Generally, companies look for people with skills and outlooks in the following areas: Functional expertise, cross-cultural sensitivity, leadership ability, language proficiency, and enthusiasm.

Functional Expertise

MNEs have the most difficulty filling local positions in sales and marketing. An innate understanding of local markets and consumer preferences is hard to pick up on the flight to the foreign assignment. Marketing experience with multicultural sensitivity is part of the mind-set most prized by companies and lucrative for entrepreneurs. In a reversal of fortune, there are fewer and fewer expatriate slots in finance and accounting. Historically, MNEs filled these jobs

The inevitable by-product of an international business career is traveling the world. Here we see the two sides of the coin: Traveling with the masses as each person tries to navigate his or her particular journey versus the rarefied realm of executive travel on private jets. No matter the style or type of travel taken, traveling to foreign markets puts business-persons face to face with an ever-changing mix of challenges and opportunities.

with a trustworthy manager from the home office: Headquarters essentially needed some-one to watch the money who was steadfastly loyal to the home office. Today, thanks to information technology and enterprise software, the home office can closely monitor the financial performance of overseas units. As a result, companies tend to fill these slots with host-country nationals who have knowledge of local accounting principles and financial practices.

Cross-Cultural Skills and Sensitivity

Exposure to other nations and cultures, the reasoning goes, is the best preparation for deal-ing with the challenges of culture shock (namely, the initial disapproval of the host cul-ture that can deteriorate into homesickness, depression, irritability, arrogance, and dis-dain). Therefore, culturally sensitive expatri-ates generally stand a far better chance of local success. An open mind to different ideas, atti-tudes, and beliefs positions an expatriate to take advantage of more opportunities and get through the inevitable challenges of the foreign assignment.

This view is a recent change in perspective. Historically, MNEs invested a lot of effort in improving their employees' technical skills but generally left it up to the individuals to develop their cross-cultural competence. Often, people interested in interna-tional business visited other countries, studied world events, and sought peo-ple of different ethnicities, cultures, and nations. Over time, these people developed mind-sets that boosted their performance during subsequent for-eign assignments. As we saw in our opening look at Honeywell, more compa-nies address managerial mind-sets by preparing expatriates for the overseas assignment with cross-cultural training. Asked why, most companies reply that these programs make sense as well as save cents. Cross-cultural training reduces the odds of a costly expatriate failure (defined as the manager's early trip home due to poor job performance). The direct cost of each failure can easily reach $1 million when you add the time and money spent in selection, visits to the location before the executive moves, and lost productivity as things fall apart.

Finally, family spirit greatly influences an expatriate's local success. Research shows a foreign assignment is usually more stressful for the family than for the transferred employee. Indeed, the leading cause of expatriate failure is the inability of a spouse to adapt to the host nation.[22] Abrupt sepa-ration from friends, family, and career can isolate the spouse and children. In recourse, they look to the working spouse or parent for more companion-ship and support. Almost always, the working spouse has less time because of the new job. This may cause family stress, which then affects work performance. Therefore, potential expatriates should appraise the cultural versatility of the family members who will accompany them. If a foreign assignment is not imminent, think about improving family members' cross-cultural sensitivity.

Leadership Ability

Most executives believe that personal leadership is the key to success in a career in international business.[23] Asked why, most note that expatriates often find themselves as senior managers in their foreign assignment; communication skills, motivation, self-reliance, courage, risk taking, and diplomacy quickly become essential qualities. More precisely, McKinsey & Company found that successful expatriates had an interesting set of mind-set attributes. In descending order of importance, managers registered optimism (believes future challenges can be overcome), drive (has passion to succeed), adaptability (handles ambiguity well), foresight (imagines the future), experience (has seen and done a great deal), resilience (recovers quickly from failure), sensitivity (adjusts management style to cultural differences), and organization (plans ahead, follows through).[24]

We saw with Joan Pattle of Microsoft in our opening discussion that working abroad requires you to wear many hats. Besides superb technical competency, you need a mind-set that understands cultural differences in problem solving, motivation, leadership, use of power, consensus building, as well as being able to make sense of trade rules and regulations, business practices, joint venture methodology, and similar market realities. Overall, this knowledge and flexibility can breed tremendous self-confidence and pave the road to greater success in the business world.

Language Skills

Debate continues over the importance of language competency to an individual's success in international business. On the one hand, proponents of language skills point out that nations have different cultural and business expectations. Consequently, those who rely solely on their native language, or even the pretense of English as the worldwide business language, will be cut off from local business information and excluded from influential business networks, will struggle to conduct negotiations, and will be unable to chat with their local colleagues. Moreover, there is a subtle but consequential cultural dimension to language competency. Explained the American Council on the Teaching of Foreign Languages, "Just making an effort to say a few words in the native tongue can make a good impression . . . it sends a subliminal message that we are equal."[25] Moreover, life abroad is a struggle; language limitations can make it isolating. For example, Joan Pattle noted that her inability to speak Turkish made her seven-month stint in Istanbul very lonely. "You can't really mix with the locals. . . . You can't use local transportation because you can't read any of the signs."[26]

In contrast, the *Economist* reported that just under half of employers rated language skills as important. Other reports find some but not decisive change in this view: Language competency was ranked behind job-related skills, leadership skills, and career development but ahead of motivation for working abroad, previous success abroad, and business vision in gauging the suitability of a candidate for international assignments.[27] Nonetheless, the data show that some managers believe language skills bolster international business careers;

for instance, the number of language-proficiency exams administered by companies to employees has increased 10-fold since 1989.[28] In sum, the debate suggests that, all things being equal, language skills spur career success in international business.

The question of which language to study always pops up. In loose terms, you ought to study the language you find most interesting. For many students, language training is laborious and any motivation to keep plugging is priceless. In strict terms, you ought to study the language that will give you the most valued competency, either from the perspective of where you want to target your business development or where your company is investing today for future growth. Latin may be a fascinating language, but few career paths will reward this skill. Presently, growth in expatriate positions is concentrated in Western Europe and North America. However, looking out 10 years or so, one can see the financial value of language skills that let you move into the Far East and Eastern Europe. As MNEs struggle to place expatriates in Southeast Asia, China, and Russia, for instance, proficiency in any of these languages will command salary premiums.

Inspiration and Enthusiasm

Some believe that success is 99 percent perspiration and 1 percent inspiration. Turning your interest into a thriving career in international business ultimately depends on your inspiration and enthusiasm to achieve your ambition. It helps tremendously to develop your understanding of the ethnocentric, polycentric, and geocentric mind-sets by taking courses in international business, culture, and politics (and let people know you're doing so). Also, you can wander through cyberspace and visit ministries of trade, chambers of commerce, or similar institutions in various nations to get a sense of how these nations do business. Surf the Web sites of companies from around the world to see and read what they believe is important information to share with you. Watch the international activities of entrepreneurs on any number of Internet auction sites, seeing how they define a market niche and then position, price, promote, and distribute their product in cyberspace. Tell your boss and coworkers that you want to go overseas and bring up the subject at every performance review. Keep up to date on what your company is doing abroad and where it might be going in the next decade. Get to know people on the international team, not only those who work on your floor, but also the ones visiting from foreign outposts. See if they have established a list server and, if so, whether you could add your name to it. Eventually, after seeing your enthusiasm, they may nominate you for an international job.

Expatriate Compensation

Once selected for a foreign assignment, managers negotiate with their companies to devise a compensation package that motivates superior performance. Table 14.6 shows the many contingencies of a foreign assignment that require tailoring an expatriate's compensation plan in unusual ways. Typically, expatriates negotiate their compensation package in terms of the following components:

- Base Salary: An expatriate's base salary normally falls in the same range as the base salary for the comparable job in the home country.
- Foreign-Service Premium: There are many things that expatriates must do without as well as put up with when living abroad. Consequently, MNEs

Typical First-Year Cost for a U.S. Expatriate (Married, Two Children) in Tokyo, Japan	
The cost of an expatriate to a company may be several times more than the cost of staffing the same position with a person from the local market.	
Direct compensation costs	
Base salary	$100,000
Foreign-service premium	15,000
Goods-and-services differential	73,600
Less: U.S. housing norm*	(15,400)
U.S. hypothetical taxes	(17,200)
Company-paid costs	
Schooling (two children)	15,000
Annual home leave	4,800
Housing*	150,000
Japanese income taxes†	84,000
Transfer/moving costs	38,000
Total company costs	**$447,800**

Table 14.6

* Assumes company rents housing in its name and provides to expatriate. If company pays housing allowance instead, Japanese income taxes (and total costs) will be about $65,000 higher.
† Note that Japanese income taxes will increase each year as some company reimbursements, most notably for taxes, become taxable.

source: Organization Resources Counselors, Inc.

often award expatriates foreign-service premiums for accepting a foreign assignment. Generally, most premiums range from 10 to 30 percent, after taxes, of the expatriate's base salary. Presently, foreign-service premiums are declining, especially for expatriates stationed in so-called world capitals (such as New York, London, Paris, Tokyo, and Singapore) that pose little threat or impose slight deprivation.

■ Extraordinary Allowances: Often included in an expatriate's compensation package is extra pay to cover the peculiar burdens of a foreign assignment. An expatriate earns a **hardship allowance** (sometimes called *combat pay*) when sent to a particularly difficult environment or dangerous location. A *housing allowance* ensures that expatriates will duplicate their customary quality of housing. A **cost-of-living adjustment** nullifies the risk that expatriates will suffer declines in their standard of living due to the exorbitant expense of a particular city (such as London or Tokyo) or nation (such as Switzerland). A *spouse allowance* partly funds an expatriate's spouse's effort to find work or take cross-cultural training; in some cases, it will offset the loss in income due to the spouse's forsaking a job. An *education allowance* finances the expatriate's children's access to a high-quality education. A *travel allowance* lets expatriates and their families travel home periodically or, in other cases, assists couples with a cross-national commuter marriage.

■ Fringe Benefits: Firms typically provide expatriates the same level of medical and retirement benefits abroad that they received at home rather than those customarily granted in the host country. However, most companies expand these benefits to deal with local contingencies—such as bearing the cost of transferring ill expatriates or family members to suitable medical facilities if none are available in the host country or paying the premiums on kidnapping insurance in high-risk countries.

■ Taxation: If there is no reciprocal tax treaty between the expatriate's home country and host country, then income tax may be legally owed to both governments. In such situations, the MNE ordinarily pays the expatriate's tax bill in the host country.

All things being equal, compensation can determine the success or failure of overseas work assignments. Pay inequities among home, local, and expatriate employees erode motivation. Therefore, a well-devised compensation package lets expatriates maintain their standard of living, reflects the responsibility of the foreign assignment, and ensures that after-tax income will not fall as a result of the foreign assignment.

Compensation Plans

Many MNEs, especially in the United States, apply the so-called balance sheet compensation plan to manage their expatriate accounts.[29] The balance sheet plan builds on the idea that an MNE will uphold an expatriate's standard of living throughout the foreign assignment. In principle, this plan presumes that expatriates will neither profit wildly nor suffer steep losses simply because their jobs took them abroad. In practice, though, MNEs go to great lengths to protect an expatriate from sustaining financial hardship if the cost of living in the host nation is higher than at home. Also, as with personal ownership of frequent flier miles earned during corporate travel, many companies allow an expatriate to keep the financial windfall of living in a less expensive country. There are three common methods of implementing a balance sheet compensation plan:

1. The *home-based method* bases the expatriate's compensation on the salary of a comparable job in the home city. This method, by preserving equity with home-country colleagues, treats the expatriate's compensation as if the person had never left home. This method simplifies the expatriate's eventual return. The home-based method is the most prevalent expatriate compensation plan.

2. The *headquarters-based method* sets the expatriate's salary in terms of the salary of a comparable job in the city in which the MNE has its headquarters. For example, if a Boston-headquartered MNE posted expatriates to its London, Santiago, and Indonesian offices, it would give each expatriate a salary structured in terms of Boston pay rates. This plan explicitly recognizes the disruption of a foreign assignment and goes to great lengths to make sure expatriates live much the way they did in their home country.

3. The *host-based method,* sometimes called destination pricing and localization, bases an expatriate's compensation on the prevailing pay scales in the locale of the foreign assignment. Basically, an expatriate starts with a salary equivalent to that of a local national with similar responsibilities and then adds whatever foreign-service premiums, extraordinary allowances, home-country benefits, and taxation compensation that were negotiated. This method is not as personally lucrative as the home- or headquarters-based methods. Essentially, it pays expatriates less in order to reduce tension between expatriates and their colleagues in the host country due to extreme variation in pay for similar jobs.

Complications Posed by Nationality Differences

Besides more than 1,600 expatriates stationed around the world, Unilever has 20,000 managers spread over 90 countries.[30] Figuring out how to pay each is complicated by many national factors, including legal, cultural, and competitive conditions. For example, nations with aggressive personal income tax rates spur employees to ask for pay plans that reduce taxable base salaries in favor of tax-exempt fringe benefits. The resulting variations in pay across nations are dramatic. Figure 14.7 shows that salaries for similar executive jobs vary substantially among countries, as do the relationships of salaries within the corporate hierarchy.

These sorts of differences also influence expatriate compensation. Increasingly, national attitudes regarding salary-based versus option-based compensation as the best motivator of performance explain differences in pay across nations. Long-term incentives, such as options on restricted stock, are popular in the United States but not in Germany. For example, when Daimler-Benz announced its merger with Chrysler, German newspapers were surprised by the magnitude of the stock options awarded to Chrysler's executives.[31] German companies traditionally do not award options, instead paying managers with generous housing allowances and partial payment of salary outside Germany, neither of which is taxable. Therefore, devising a single compensation

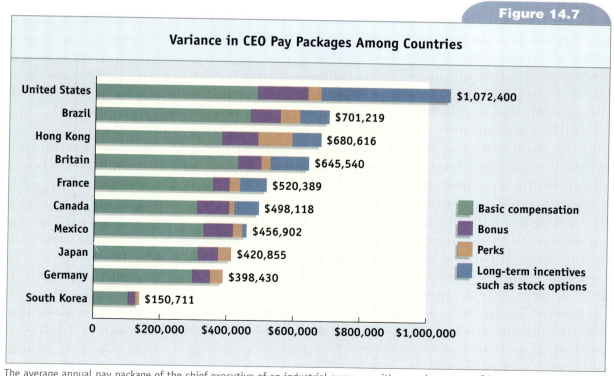

Figure 14.7

The average annual pay package of the chief executive of an industrial company with annual revenues of $250 million to $500 million in 10 countries. Figures are from April 1998 and are not weighted to compensate for different costs of living or levels of taxation.

source: *New York Times,* January 17, 1999. Reprinted by permission of NYT Pictures.

plan that motivates both expatriates and local managers, as well as addressing national differences, is unrealistic for many MNEs. Expatriates must be mindful of national contingencies when negotiating their compensation package.

Expatriate Repatriation

Returning home from a foreign assignment can be as much of a jolt as initially going overseas. Nonetheless, many MNEs worry more about preparing workers for the foreign assignment than about supporting them when they return. Consequentially, returning home can deteriorate into a dreadful part of the expatriate assignment for many managers. More precisely, a survey of repatriated executives found that 33 percent still held temporary assignments three months after returning home, more than 75 percent felt that their new job was a demotion from their foreign assignment, 61 percent felt that they did not have opportunities to transfer their international expertise to their new job, and 25 percent left their company within three months of returning home.[32] In general, repatriation strain shows up in three areas: (1) change in personal finances, (2) readjustment to the home-country corporate structure, and (3) readjustment to life at home.

Changes in personal finances can be dramatic upon return. Most expatriates enjoy abundant financial benefits during their foreign assignment. While abroad, many live in exclusive neighborhoods, send their children to prestigious schools, employ domestic help, socialize with elites, and still save much more money than they had before the move. Returning home to a reasonable compensation plan with far fewer perks, therefore, can be demotivating.

Readjustment to home-country corporate structure poses problems on several levels. Returning expatriates often find that many of their peers have been promoted above them, they now have less autonomy as they go back to being a "little fish in a big pond," and they must struggle to get back into the inner-office networking circle. For many expatriates, being out of sight overseas turns out to be truly out of mind back home. They return to a company that doesn't quite know what to do with them and, particularly in high-tech firms, sees them as having knowledge and skills that aren't quite on the cutting edge. In these situations, resentment builds within repatriated executives, who typically feel they've grown professionally during their overseas post, worked hard, and sacrificed much for the company, and hence deserve praise and promotion.

Readjusting to life at home, usually eagerly anticipated while abroad, can become surprisingly stressful. Troubles emerge as returning expatriates and their families experience "reverse culture shock." Upon return, managers and their families often find that they need to relearn much of what they once took for granted as they adapt to their "new" home. Meanwhile, children may struggle to fit into the local school system while spouses may feel isolated or out of touch with the career or friends left behind. For example, some returning U.S. expatriates who spent the late 1990s abroad regret missing the emergence of the Internet and the dot.com boom in the United States during this period.[33]

Managing Repatriation Tribulations

Companies are not blind to trials and tribulations of repatriation. Moreover, ignoring them is not an option—the greater the career difficulties that confront returning expatriates, the harder it becomes to convince others to accept foreign assignments. In recourse, MNEs experiment with a range of remedies.

Abbott Laboratories tries to keep its repatriate turnover rate less than 10 percent by focusing on career development. It also cautions workers before they leave the United States to expect the adjustment of returning home to be just as tough as going abroad and encourages them to stay in touch. Komatsu has a "return ticket policy" that pledges returning expatriates a meaningful job. Similarly, Dow Corning gives each expatriate a written guarantee of a job at the same or higher level on return. Too, Dow Corning formally assigns higher-level supervisors to serve as "godfathers" by looking after the expatriates' home-career interests. Some MNEs, such as ABB, make the manager who originally sponsored an expatriate also responsible for finding the protégé a job upon return. Motorola advises its 1,500 expatriates to maintain their home network no matter how far away they travel.

Also, some companies try to resolve the less obvious hardships of repatriation. Monsanto deals with reverse culture shock by formally addressing the social expectations of returning expatriates and giving them an opportunity to showcase their new knowledge in a debriefing session. Similarly, Viacom has set up a "comprehensive expatriate administrative tracking program" that includes specific health and retirement benefits tailored to the needs of those who have undertaken more than one consecutive overseas posting.[34]

Despite these efforts, the statistics show that many expatriates are downcast about their career when they return home. If pressed to pinpoint where repatriation begins to break down, reports suggest the principal culprit is the tough challenge of finding the right job for someone to return to. Personal career management, therefore, is vital to being selected for a foreign assignment, as well as triumphantly returning home to greater responsibilities. As we saw with Bryan Krueger in our opening discussion, expatriates cannot rely exclusively on their company to safeguard their career interests. Instead, they must navigate the repatriation process with a clear sense of its positive and negative aspects. Expatriates can boost the success of returning home by dealing with the following issues:

- Ask about the company's repatriation policy.

- If there isn't one, develop a plan. Get a clear idea of when you want to return home, how this foreign assignment helps prepare for those responsibilities, and who must do what to make it happen.

- If there is a formal policy, begin talking about your postassignment job before you even go overseas. Continue that conversation while aboard. Communicate your goals and help the company set sensible expectations.

- Stay in touch with mentors. They can pragmatically guide your repatriation planning. The same goes for top management, human resource people, and your peers.

- Ask for a formal pre-repatriation briefing and interview with the home office to share your career plans.

- Plan to visit home several times during the final stages of your foreign assignment to prepare your firm for your return.

Summary

The variety of international business careers makes it impossible to specify a 10-step program to turn a dream into a reality. Furthermore, globalization spurs career changes in ways that we do yet fully appreciate. These conditions place a higher premium on the act of positioning as a key part of your career plan. Depending on your status and long-term interests, you need to put yourself in places that will provide a path to find career opportunities in international business. Where and how you opt to position yourself begins with your outlook. Ethnocentric, polycentric, and geocentric mind-sets will, as this chapter noted, lead you to interpret the same event differently. Thus, question how you see the world, figure out what this means to a career in international business, and position yourself with people and places that value this mind-set. The transition from positioning to starting a foreign assignment creates new challenges and opportunities. Matters of compensation and repatriation, although intricate, follow sensible principles. Familiarity with these principles ensures that going overseas and coming home is a rewarding professional and personal experience.

endnotes

[1] Retrieved from eBay.com/corporatehome, January 10, 2001; ebay.com/investosrelations, January 10, 2001; Rachel Konrad, "eBay's Whitman Touts International Plans," CNET News.com, August 15, 2000; "CEO Whitman Looks Overseas, Ponders Peer-to-Peer," CNET News.com, August 17, 2000; and "eBay Faces International Checkpoints, CNET News.com, August 18, 2000.

[2] Barbara Ettorre, "A Brave New World," *Management Review,* Vol. 82, No. 4, April 1993, pp. 10–16.

[3] Melinda Ligos, "The Foreign Assignment: An Incubator, or Exile?" *New York Times,* October 22, 2000.

[4] Ibid.

[5] Sandra Jones, "Going Stateside: Once the Overseas Hitch Is Over, Homeward-Bound Expats Hit Turbulence," *Crain's Chicago Business,* July 24, 2000.

[6] "International Assignments: European Policy and Practice," Man Simpson (ed.), Pricewaterhouse-Coopers. Retrieved from www.pwcglobal.com/extweb/ncsurvres.nsf/, December 15, 2000.

[7] Linda Grant, "That Overseas Job Could Derail Your Career," *Fortune,* Vol. 135, No. 7, April 4, 1997, p. 166, Smart Managing.

[8] See, for example, "International Assignments: European Policy and Practice," "The New International Executive Business Leadership for the 21st Century," Harvard Business School and Amrop International, 1995; various reports by the Conference Board.

[9] Ettorre.

[10] Marshall Loeb, "The Real Fast Track Is Overseas." *Fortune,* Vol. 132, No. 4, August 21, 1995, p. 129, Personal Fortune.

[11] Ligos.

[12] Hugh P. Gunz, R. Michael Jalland, and Martin G. Evans, "New Strategy, Wrong Managers? What You Need to Know About Career Streams," *Academy of Management Executive,* Vol. 12, No. 2, May 1998, pp. 21–39.

[13] Tsun-Yan Hsieh, Johanne Lavoie, and Robert Samek, "Are You Taking Your Expatriate Talent Seriously?" *The McKinsey Quarterly,* No. 3, 1999, pp. 70–83.

[14] Jane Fraser and Jeremy Oppenheim, "What's New About Globalization?" *McKinsey Quarterly,* No. 2, 1997, pp. 168–179.

[15] Jeremy Kahn, "The World's Most Admired Companies," *Fortune,* Vol. 140, No. 7, October 11, 1999, p. 267.

[16] R. M. Kanter, *World Class: Thriving Locally in the Global Economy* (New York: Simon & Schuster, 1995).

[17] Leslie Holstrom and Simon Brady, "The Changing Face of Global Business: The Global Myth." Retrieved from www.204.71-242.112/fortune/sections/, November 25, 2000.

[18] Astrid Wendlandt, "The Name Game Is a Puzzle for Expats at Work," *Financial Times,* August 15, 2000, p. 3.

[19] See, for example, N. Abramson, R. Keating, and H. W. Lane, "Cross-National Cognitive Process Differences: A Comparison of Canadian, American and Japanese Managers," *Management International Review,* No. 36, 1996, pp. 123–148; P. DiMaggio, "Culture and Cognition," *Annual Review of Sociology,* No. 23, 1997, pp. 263–287; M. Hitt, T. Dacin, B. Tyler, and D. Park, "Understanding the Differences in Korean and U.S. Executives' Strategic Orientations," *Strategic Management Journal,* No. 18, 1996, pp. 159–167; and S. G. Redding, "Comparative Management Theory: Jungle, Zoo or Fossil Bed?" *Organization Studies,* No. 15, 1994, pp. 323–360.

[20] "Globesmanship," *Across the Board,* Vol. 27, Nos. 1, 2, January–February 1990, p. 26, quoting Michael Angus.

[21] Hsieh, Lavoie, and Samek.

[22] Diane E. Lewis, "Families Make, Break Overseas Moves," *Boston Globe,* October 4, 1998, p. 5D.

[23] "The New International Executive Business Leadership for the 21st Century," Harvard Business School and Amrop International, 1995. Reported in Andrew Crisp, "International Careers Made Easy," *European,* No. 254, March 24, 1995, p. 27.

[24] Hsieh, Lavoie, and Samek.

[25] Tanya Mohn, "All Aboard the Foreign Language Express," *New York Times,* October 11, 2000. Retrieved from www.nyt.com, October 11, 2000.

[26] Ligos.

[27] "International Assignments: European Policy and Practice."

[28] Mohn.

[29] Carolyn Gould, "What's the Latest in Global Compensation?" *Global Workforce,* July 1997. Retrieved from www.economist.com, December 10, 2000.

[30] Ibid.

[31] "No Man Is an Island," *Economist* (U.S.), Vol. 351, No. 8118, May 8, 1999. Retrieved from www.economist.com, December 10, 2000.

[32] J. S. Black and H. B. Gregersen, "The Right Way to Manage Expats," *Harvard Business Review,* March–April 1999, pp. 52–62.

[33] Ligos.

[34] C. Reidy, "Corporate Synergy Leads Way in Constructing Effective Retirement and Health Benefits," *IBIS Review,* January 1996, pp.16–17.

An Atlas

Satellite television transmission now makes it commonplace for us to watch events as they unfold in other countries. Transportation and communication advances and government-to-government accords have contributed to our increasing dependence on foreign goods and markets. As this dependence grows, updated maps are a valuable tool. They can show the locations of population, economic wealth, production and markets; portray certain commonalities and differences among areas; and illustrate barriers that might inhibit trade. In spite of the usefulness of maps, a substantial number of people worldwide have a poor knowledge of how to interpret information on maps and even of how to find the location of events that affect their lives.

We urge you to use the following maps to build your awareness of geography.

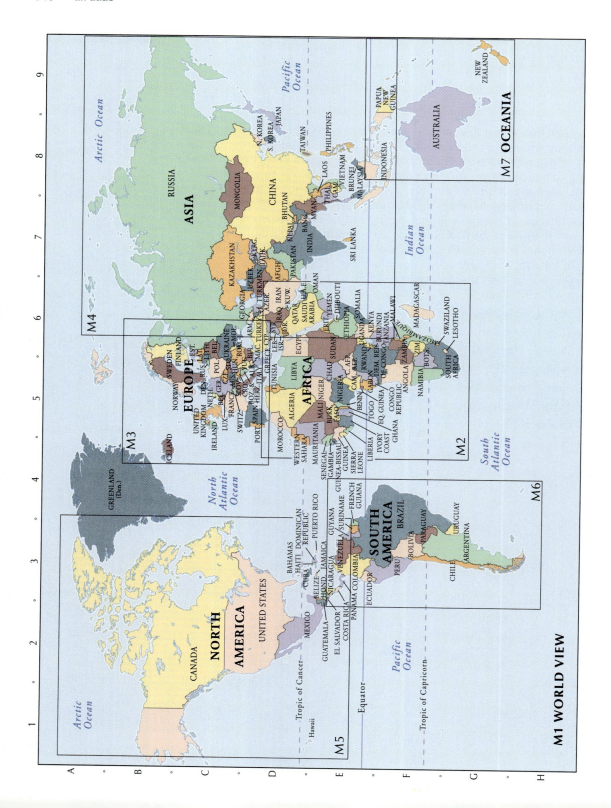

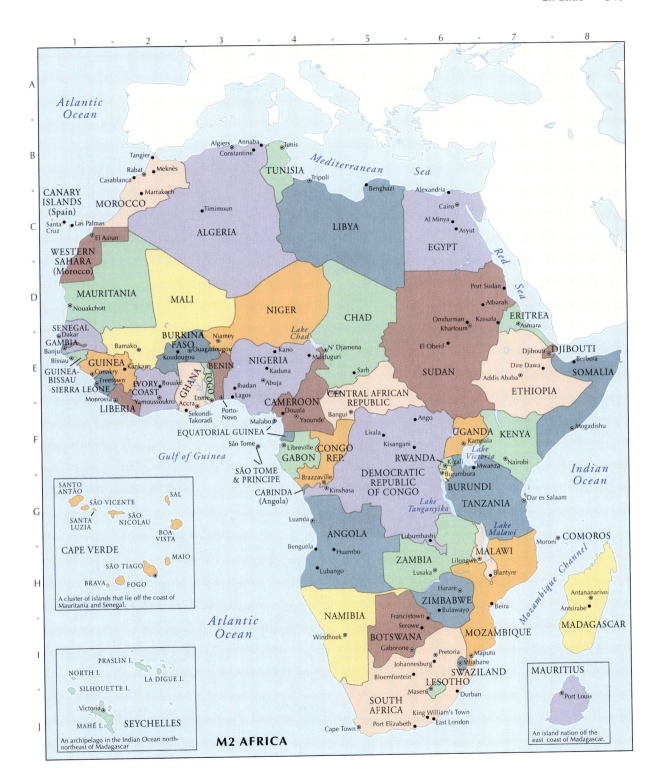

Atlantic Ocean

Algiers • Annaba • Tunis
Tangier • Constantine
Rabat • Meknès
Casablanca
CANARY
ISLANDS
(Spain)
MOROCCO • Marrakech

Mediterranean Sea

TUNISIA
Tripoli •
Benghazi • Alexandria •
Cairo ⊕
Al Minya •
Asyut •

Santa Cruz • Las Palmas
El Aaiun •
Timimoun •
ALGERIA
LIBYA
EGYPT

WESTERN SAHARA
(Morocco)

MAURITANIA
• Nouakchott
MALI
NIGER
CHAD
Port Sudan •
Atbarah •
Omdurman • Kassala
Khartoum • Asmara
ERITREA

Red Sea

SENEGAL • Dakar
GAMBIA
Banjul •
Bissau •
GUINEA-BISSAU
SIERRA LEONE
BURKINA FASO
Niamey • Bamako •
Ouagadougou •
Koudougou •
Kankan •
Conakry • Freetown
GUINEA
Bouaké •
IVORY COAST
GHANA TOGO
Kano •
Maiduguri •
N' Djamena •
NIGERIA
Kaduna •
Ibadan • Abuja
Lagos •
Sarh •
CENTRAL AFRICAN REPUBLIC
El Obeid •
SUDAN
Djibouti • DJIBOUTI
Dire Dawa •
Addis Ababa ⊕
Berbera •
SOMALIA
ETHIOPIA

Monrovia •
LIBERIA
Yamoussoukro •
Accra •
Lomé
Sekondi-Takoradi •
Porto-Novo
BENIN
CAMEROON
Douala •
Yaoundé •
Bangui •
Ango •
Lisala •
Kisangani •
UGANDA
Kampala •
Lake Victoria
KENYA
Mogadishu •

EQUATORIAL GUINEA
Malabo •
São Tomé
SÃO TOMÉ & PRINCIPE
CABINDA (Angola)
Libreville •
GABON
CONGO REP.
Brazzaville •
Kinshasa •
DEMOCRATIC REPUBLIC OF CONGO
RWANDA
Kigali •
Burumbura
BURUNDI
Mwanza •
Nairobi •
Indian Ocean

Gulf of Guinea

Luanda •
ANGOLA
Benguela •
Huambo •
Lubango •
Lubumbashi •
ZAMBIA
Lusaka •
Lake Tanganyika
TANZANIA
Dar es Salaam •
Lake Malawi
MALAWI
Lilongwe •
Blantyre •
Moroni • COMOROS

Atlantic Ocean

NAMIBIA
Windhoek •
BOTSWANA
Francistown •
Serowe •
Gaborone •
Harare •
Bulawayo •
ZIMBABWE
Beira •
MOZAMBIQUE
Maputo •
Mbabane
SWAZILAND
Antananarivo •
Antsirabe •
MADAGASCAR
Mozambique Channel

Johannesburg •
Pretoria •
Bloemfontein •
Maseru •
LESOTHO
Durban •
SOUTH AFRICA
King William's Town •
Cape Town •
Port Elizabeth •
East London •

MAURITIUS
Port Louis ⊕
An island nation off the east coast of Madagascar.

SANTO ANTÃO
SÃO VICENTE
SAL
SANTA LUZIA
SÃO NICOLAU
BOA VISTA
CAPE VERDE
MAIO
SÃO TIAGO
BRAVA • FOGO
A cluster of islands that lie off the coast of Mauritania and Senegal.

PRASLIN I.
NORTH I.
LA DIGUE I.
SILHOUETTE I.
Victoria ⊕
MAHÉ I.
SEYCHELLES
An archipelago in the Indian Ocean north-northeast of Madagascar.

M2 AFRICA

1 2 3 4 5 6 7 8

JAN MAYEN I.
(Norway)

*Arctic
Ocean*

Barents Sea

• Murmansk

Denmark Strait

ICELAND
⊛ Reykjavík

*Norwegian
Sea*

FAEROE IS.
(Den.)

SHETLAND IS.
(U.K.)

ORKNEY IS.

NORWAY

SWEDEN

FINLAND

Bergen •
Oslo ⊛

Helsinki ⊛
Stockholm ⊛

Göteborg •

*Lake
Ladoga*

RUSSIA

• St. Petersburg

• Kostroma

Tallinn ⊛
ESTONIA

• Moscow

Glasgow • • Edinburgh
*North
Sea*

DENMARK

Copenhagen ⊛
Malmö •

*Baltic
Sea*

Riga ⊛
LATVIA

LITHUANIA

RUS.
Vilnius ⊛
Kaliningrad •

• Minsk

BELARUS

Homyel' •

• Tula

• Smolensk

• Orel
• Kursk

Belfast •
**UNITED
KINGDOM**

Dublin ⊛
*Irish
Sea*

• Manchester
• Liverpool

IRELAND

Birmingham •

NETHERLANDS

Amsterdam ⊛

The Hague •

Hamburg •

Berlin ⊛

GERMANY

Essen •
Düsseldorf •

Leipzig •

Gdansk •

Bydgoszcz •

POLAND

Warsaw ⊛

Lódz •

• Kiev

UKRAINE

• Dnipropetrovsk

London ⊛
English Channel

BELGIUM
Brussels ⊛ • Liège

Le Havre •
LUXEMBOURG

*Atlantic
Ocean*

Paris ⊛
Le Mans •

Luxembourg •

Bonn •

Frankfurt •

Stuttgart •

Dresden •

Prague ⊛
**CZECH
REP.**

Brno •

Wroclaw •

Krakow •

SLOVAKIA

Vienna ⊛
Bratislava ⊛

• Lvov

Chernivtsi •

• Chisinau

MOLDOVA

• Mykolayiv

• Odesa

FRANCE

Munich •

Zurich •

Linz •
LIECHTENSTEIN

AUSTRIA

Debrecen •

HUNGARY

Budapest ⊛

Arad •

ROMANIA

*Bay of
Biscay*

SWITZERLAND
Geneva •
Bern ⊛

Lyon •

Milan •

Ljubljana ⊛
SLOVENIA

Zagreb ⊛

Timisoara •

Belgrade ⊛

• Bucharest

*Black
Sea*

Limoges •

St. Etienne •

Turin •

Padova •
Venice •

CROATIA

**BOSNIA &
HERZE-
GOVINA**

Sarajevo ⊛

YUGOSLAVIA

Bordeaux •

Genoa •

**SAN
MARINO**

BULGARIA

Sofia •

• Istanbul

• A Coruña

Toulouse •

Nîmes •

Livorno •
Florence •

• Rome

Skopje ⊛
MACEDONIA

Thessaloniki •

TURKEY

Porto •

PORTUGAL

ANDORRA

Marseille •

MONACO
CORSICA

ITALY

*Adriatic
Sea*

Tirana •

ALBANIA

Lisbon ⊛

• Madrid

SPAIN

Barcelona •

**VATICAN
CITY**

Naples •

Bari •
Taranto •

GREECE

Valencia •

SARDINIA

*Tyrrhenian
Sea*

*Ionian
Sea*

Piraïevs • ⊛ Athens

Sevilla •
Málaga •

• Granada

Cartagena •

BALEARIC IS.

Palermo •

Messina •

SICILY

*Mediterranean
Sea*

CYPRUS

CRETE

Strait of Gibraltar

Valletta ⊛

MALTA

A B C D E F G H I J

M3 EUROPE

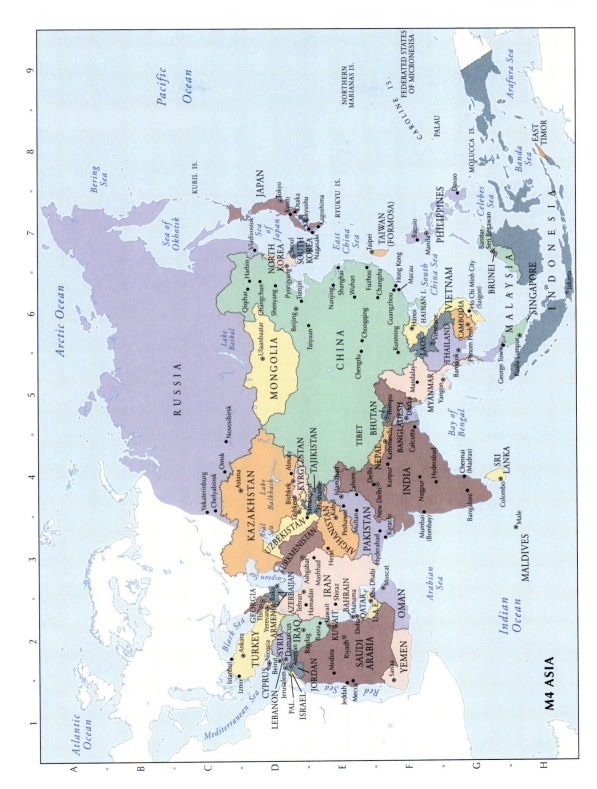

M4 ASIA

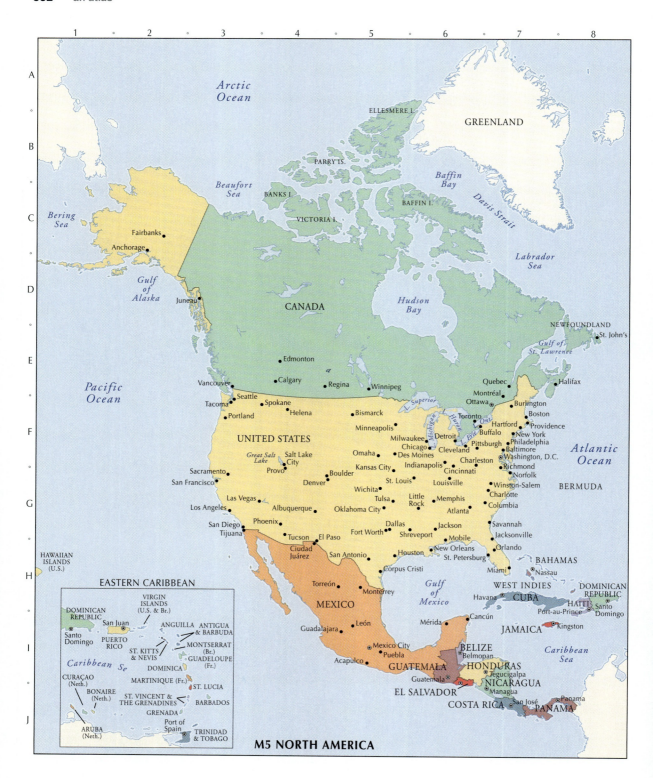

1 2 3 4 5 6 7 8

Labels on the map

Arctic Ocean
GREENLAND
ELLESMERE I.
PARRY IS.
BANKS I.
Beaufort Sea
VICTORIA I.
BAFFIN I.
Baffin Bay
Davis Strait
Bering Sea
Fairbanks
Anchorage
Gulf of Alaska
Juneau
Labrador Sea
CANADA
Hudson Bay
NEWFOUNDLAND
St. John's
Gulf of St. Lawrence
Edmonton
Calgary
Regina
Winnipeg
Quebec
Halifax
Vancouver
Montréal
Burlington
Seattle
Ottawa
Boston
Tacoma
Spokane
Helena
Toronto
Hartford
Providence
Portland
L. Superior
Buffalo
New York
Bismarck
Minneapolis
Michigan
Huron
Detroit
Pittsburgh
Philadelphia
UNITED STATES
Milwaukee
Chicago
Cleveland
Erie
Baltimore
Pacific Ocean
Great Salt Lake
Salt Lake City
Omaha
Des Moines
Indianapolis
Charleston
Washington, D.C.
Atlantic Ocean
Sacramento
Provo
Kansas City
Cincinnati
Richmond
Denver
Boulder
St. Louis
Louisville
Norfolk
San Francisco
Wichita
Winston-Salem
BERMUDA
Las Vegas
Tulsa
Memphis
Charlotte
Los Angeles
Albuquerque
Oklahoma City
Little Rock
Columbia
Phoenix
Dallas
Jackson
Atlanta
Savannah
San Diego
Fort Worth
Shreveport
Mobile
Jacksonville
Tijuana
Tucson
El Paso
Houston
New Orleans
Orlando
Ciudad Juárez
San Antonio
St. Petersburg
BAHAMAS
Corpus Cristi
Miami
Nassau
HAWAIIAN ISLANDS (U.S.)
Torreón
Monterrey
Gulf of Mexico
WEST INDIES
DOMINICAN REPUBLIC
MEXICO
León
Mérida
Cancún
Havana
CUBA
HAITI
Port-au-Prince
Santo Domingo
Guadalajara
JAMAICA
Kingston
Mexico City
Puebla
BELIZE
Caribbean Sea
Acapulco
Belmopan
GUATEMALA
HONDURAS
Tegucigalpa
Guatemala
NICARAGUA
EL SALVADOR
Managua
COSTA RICA
San José
Panama
PANAMA

EASTERN CARIBBEAN

DOMINICAN REPUBLIC
Santo Domingo
San Juan
PUERTO RICO
VIRGIN ISLANDS (U.S. & Br.)
ANGUILLA
ANTIGUA & BARBUDA
MONTSERRAT (Br.)
ST. KITTS & NEVIS
DOMINICA
GUADELOUPE (Fr.)
Caribbean Se
MARTINIQUE (Fr.)
ST. LUCIA
CURAÇAO (Neth.)
BONAIRE (Neth.)
ST. VINCENT & THE GRENADINES
BARBADOS
ARUBA (Neth.)
GRENADA
Port of Spain
TRINIDAD & TOBAGO

M5 NORTH AMERICA

M6 SOUTH AMERICA

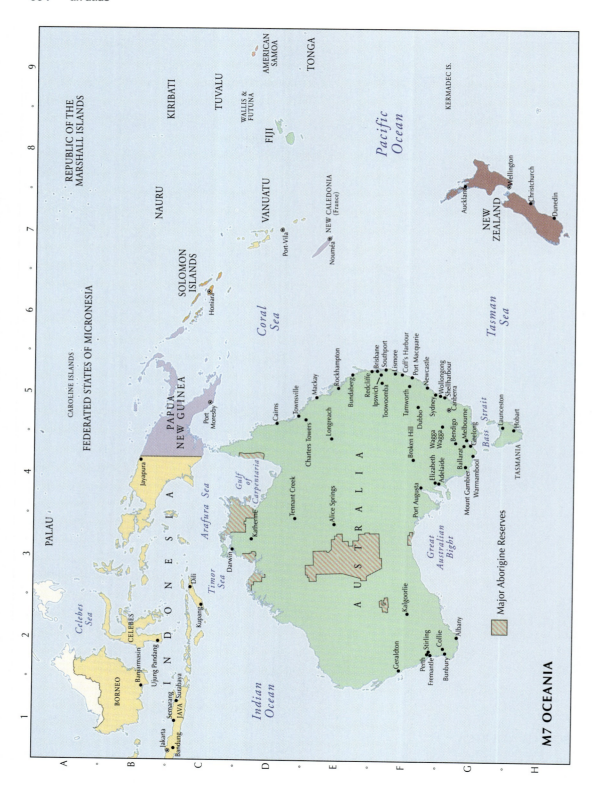

M7 OCEANIA

Maps of the World

Country and Territory	Pronunciation	Map 1	Maps 2–7
Afghanistan	af-'gan-ə-,stan	D7	Map 4, E3
Albania	al-'bā-nē-ə	C5	Map 3, I5
Algeria	al-'jir-ē-ə	D5	Map 2, C3
Andorra	an-'dòr-ə	—	Map 3, H2
Angola	an-'gō-lə	E5	Map 2, G4
Antigua & Barbuda	an-'tē-g(w)ə/bär-'büd-ə	—	Map 5, I3
Argentina	,är-jen-'tē-nə	G3	Map 6, G3
Armenia	är-'mē-nē-ə	C6	Map 4, D2
Australia	ò-'strāl-yə	G8	Map 7, E4
Austria	'ös-trē-ə	C5	Map 3, G4
Azerbaijan	,az-ər-,bī-'jän	D6	Map 4, D2
Bahamas	bə-hä'-məz	D3	Map 5, H7
Bahrain	bä-'rān	—	Map 4, E2
Bangladesh	,bäŋ-glə-'desh	D7	Map 4, F5
Barbados	bär-'bād-əs	—	Map 5, J3
Belarus	,bē-lə-'rüs	C5	Map 3, F6
Belgium	'bel-jəm	C5	Map 3, F3
Belize	bə-'lēz	D2	Map 5, I6
Benin	bə-'nin	E5	Map 2, E3
Bermuda	(,)bər-'myüd-ə	—	Map 5, G8
Bhutan	bü-'tan	D7	Map 4, F5
Bolivia	bə-'liv-ē-ə	F3	Map 6, E4
Bosnia & Herzegovina	'bäz-nē-ə/,hert-sə-gō-'vē-nə	D5	Map 3, H5
Botswana	bät-'swän-ə	F5	Map 2, I5
Brazil	brə-'zil	F3	Map 6, D6
Brunei	brōō-nī'	E8	Map 4, G7
Bulgaria	,bəl-'gar-ē-ə	D5	Map 3, H6
Burkina Faso	bùr-'kē-nə-'fä-sō	E5	Map 2, E2
Burundi	bù-rün-dē	E6	Map 2, G6
Cambodia	kam-'bd-ē-ə	E7	Map 4, G5
Cameroon	,kam-ə-'rün	E5	Map 2, F4
Canada	'kan-əd-ə	C2	Map 5, E5
Cape Verde Islands	'vard	—	Map 2, G1
Central African Rep.		E5	Map 2, E5
Chad	'chad	E5	Map 2, D5
Chile	'chil-ē	G3	Map 6, F3
China	'chī-nə	D8	Map 4, E5
Colombia	kə-'ləm-bē-ə	E3	Map 6, B3
Congo (Democratic Republic)	'käŋ(,)gō	E5	Map 2, G5
Congo Republic	'käŋ(,)gō	E5	Map 2, F4
Costa Rica	,käs-tə-'rē-kə	E2	Map 5, J7
Croatia	krō-'ā-sh(ē)ə	D5	Map 3, H5
Cuba	'kyü-bə	E3	Map 5, H7
Curaçao	'k(y)ür-ə-'sō	—	Map 5, J1
Cyprus	'sī-prəs	D6	Map 4, D2
Czech Republic	,chek	C5	Map 3, G5

Maps of the World *(continued)*

Country and Territory	Pronunciation	Map 1	Maps 2–7
Denmark	'den-ˌmärk	C5	Map 3, E4
Djibouti	jə-'büt-ē	E6	Map 2, E7
Dominica	ˌdäm-ə-'nē-kə	—	Map 5, I3
Dominican Republic	də-ˌmin-i-kən	E3	Map 5, H8
Ecuador	'ek-wə-ˌdȯ(ə)r	E3	Map 6, C2
Egypt	'ē-jəpt	D5	Map 2, C6
El Salvador	el-'sal-və-ˌdȯ(ə)r	E2	Map 5, I6
Equatorial Guinea	ē-kwə'-tȯr-ēal`gi-nē	E5	Map 2, F4
Eritrea	ˌer-ə-'trē-ə	E6	Map 2, E6
Estonia	e-'stō-nē-ə	C5	Map 3, E6
Ethiopia	ˌē-thē-'ō-pē-ə	E6	Map 2, E7
Falkland Islands	'fȯ(l)-klənd	—	Map 6, J4
Fiji	'fē-jē	—	Map 7, D8
Finland	'fin-lənd	B5	Map 3, C6
France	'fran(t)s	C5	Map 3, G3
French Guiana	gē-'an-ə	E3	Map 6, B5
Gabon	ga-'bōⁿ	E5	Map 2, F4
Gambia	'gam-bē-ə	E4	Map 2, E1
Georgia	'jȯr-jə	C6	Map 4, D2
Germany	'jerm-(ə-)nē	C5	Map 3, F4
Ghana	'gän-ə	E5	Map 2, E2
Greece	'grēs	D5	Map 3, I6
Greenland	'grēn-lənd	A4	Map 5, E7
Grenada	grə-nã'də	—	Map 5, J3
Guatemala	ˌgwät-ə-'mäl-ə	E2	Map 5, I6
Guinea	'gin-ē	E4	Map 2, E1
Guinea-Bissau	ˌgin-ē-bis-'aù	E4	Map 2, E1
Guyana	gī-'an-ə	E3	Map 6, B4
Haiti	'hāt-ē	E3	Map 5, H8
Honduras	hän-'d(y)ùr-əs	E2	Map 5, I7
Hong Kong	'häŋ-ˌkäŋ	—	Map 4, F6
Hungary	'həŋ-g(ə)rē	C5	Map 3, G5
Iceland	'ī-slənd	B4	Map 3, B1
India	'in-dē-ə	D7	Map 4, F4
Indonesia	ˌin-də-'nē-zhə	E8	Map 4, H7; Map 7, B3
Iran	i-'rän	D6	Map 4, E3
Iraq	i-'räk	D6	Map 4, D2
Ireland	'ī(ə)r-lənd	C5	Map 3, F1
Israel	'iz-rē-əl	D6	Map 4, D2
Italy	'it-ᵊl-ē	D6	Map 3, H4
Ivory Coast	ī'və-rē	E5	Map 2, E2
Jamaica	jə-'mā-kə	E3	Map 5, I7
Japan	jə-'pan	D8	Map 4, D7
Jordan	'jȯrd-ᵊn	D6	Map 4, D2
Kazakhstan	kə-ˌzak-'stan	D7	Map 4, D4
Kenya	'ken-yə	E6	Map 7, F7

Maps of the World *(continued)*

Country and Territory	Pronunciation	Map 1	Maps 2–7
Kiribati	kîr-ĭ-băs′	—	Map 7, B8
Korea, North	kə-′rē-ə	D8	Map 4, D7
Korea, South	kə-rē-ə	D8	Map 4, D7
Kuwait	kə-′wāt	D6	Map 4, E2
Kyrgyzstan	kîr-gē-stän	D7	Map 4, D4
Laos	′laủs	D7	Map 4, F5
Latvia	′lat-vē-ə	C5	Map 3, E6
Lebanon	′leb-ə-nən	D6	Map 4, D2
Lesotho	lə-′sō-(,)tō	F6	Map 2, J6
Liberia	lī-′bir-ē-ə	E5	Map 2, F2
Libya	′lib-ē-ə	D5	Map 2, C4
Liechtenstein	lĭk′tən-stīn′	—	Map 3, G4
Lithuania	,lith-(y)ə-′wā-nē-ə	C5	Map 3, E6
Luxembourg	′lək-səm-,bərg	C5	Map 3, G3
Macedonia	,mas-ə-′dō-nyə	D6	Map 3, I6
Madagascar	,mad-ə-′gas-kər	F6	Map 2, I8
Malawi	mə-′lä-wē	F6	Map 2, H6
Malaysia	mə-′lā-zh(ē-)ə	E8	Map 4, G6
Maldives	môl′dīvz	—	Map 4, H3
Mali	′mäl-ē	D5	Map 2, D2
Malta	′mȯl-tə	—	Map 3, J5
Marshall Islands	mär′shəl	—	Map 7, A8
Mauritania	,mȯr-ə-′tā-nē-ə	D5	Map 2, D1
Mauritius	mȯ-′rĭsh′əs	—	Map 2, J8
Mexico	′mek-si-,kō	D2	Map 5, I5
Micronesia	mĭ′krō-nē-′zhə	—	Map 7, A5
Moldova	mäl-′dō-və	D6	Map 3, G7
Monaco	mŏn′ə-kō	—	Map 3, H3
Mongolia	män-′gōl-yə	D8	Map 4, D5
Morocco	mə-′räk-(,)ō	D5	Map 2, B2
Mozambique	,mō-zəm-′bēk	F6	Map 2, H6
Myanmar	′myän-,mär	E7	Map 4, F5
Namibia	nə-′mib-ē-ə	F5	Map 2, I4
Naura	nä′-ü-rü	—	Map 7, B7
Nepal	nə-′pȯl	D7`	Map 4, E4
Netherlands	′neth-ər-lən(d)z	C5	Map 3, F3
New Caledonia	,kal-ə-′dō-nyə	—	Map 7, E7
New Zealand	′zē-lənd	G9	Map 7, H7
Nicaragua	,nik-ə-′räg-wə	E3	Map 5, I7
Niger	′nī-jər	E5	Map 2, D4
Nigeria	nī-′jir-ē-ə	E5	Map 2, E4
Norway	′nȯ(ə)r-,wā	C5	Map 3, D3
Oman	ō-′män	E6	Map 4, F2
Pakistan	,pak-i-′stan	D7	Map 4, E3
Palau	pä-lou′	—	Map 7, A3
Palestine	pa-lə-′stīn	—	Map 4, D1
Panama	′pan-ə-,mä	E3	Map 5, J8

Maps of the World *(continued)*

Country and Territory	Pronunciation	Map 1	Maps 2–7
Papua New Guinea	ˈpap-yə-wə	F9	Map 7, C5
Paraguay	ˈpar-ə-ˌgwī	F3	Map 6, E4
Peru	pə-ˈrü	F3	Map 6, D2
Philippines	ˌfil-ə-ˈpēnz	E8	Map 4, F7
Poland	ˈpō-lənd	D5	Map 3, F5
Portugal	ˈpōr-chi-gəl	D5	Map 3, I1
Puerto Rico	ˌpōrt-ə-ˈrē(ˌ)kō	E3	Map 5, I2
Qatar	ˈkät-ər	D6	Map 4, E2
Romania	rō-ˈmā-nē-ə	D5	Map 3, H6
Russia	ˈrəsh-ə	C7	Map 3, D7; Map 4, C5
Rwanda	rù-ˈän-də	E6	Map 2, F6
St. Kitts & Nevis	ˈkits/ˈnē-vəs	—	Map 5, I3
St. Lucia	sānt-ˈlü-shə	—	Map 5, I3
St. Vincent and the Grenadines	grĕnˈə-dēnz'	—	Map 5, J3
San Marino	săn mə-rē'nō	—	Map 3, H4
São Tomé and Príncipe	soun tōō-mĕˈprĕnˈ-sēpə	—	Map 2, F3
Saudi Arabia	ˌsaùd-ē	E6	Map 4, E2
Senegal	ˌsen-i-ˈgòl	E4	Map 2, D1
Seychelles	sā-shĕlzˈ	—	Map 2, J1
Sierra Leone	sē-ˌer-ə-lē-ˈōn	E4	Map 2, E1
Singapore	ˈsiŋ-(g)ə-ˌpō(ə)r	—	Map 4, H6
Slovakia	slō-ˈväk-ē-ə	C5	Map 3, G5
Slovenia	slō-ˈvēn-ē-ə	C5	Map 3, H5
Solomon Islands	ˈsäl-ə-mən	—	Map 7, C6
Somalia	sō-ˈmäl-ē-ə	E6	Map 2, F8
South Africa	ˈa-fri-kə	F6	Map 2, J5
Spain	ˈspān	C5	Map 3, I1
Sri Lanka	(ˈ)srē-ˈläŋ-kə	E7	Map 4, G4
Sudan	sü-ˈdan	E6	Map 2, E6
Suriname	sùr-ə-ˈnäm-ə	E3	Map 6, B5
Swaziland	ˈswäz-ē-ˌland	F6	Map 2, I6
Sweden	ˈswēd-ᵊn	B5	Map 3, C5
Switzerland	ˈswit-sər-lənd	C5	Map 3, G4
Syria	ˈsir-ē-ə	D6	Map 4, D2
Taiwan	ˈtī-ˈwän	D8	Map 4, E7
Tajikistan	tä-ˌji-ki-ˈstan	D7	Map 4, E4
Tanzania	ˌtan-zə-ˈnē-ə	F6	Map 2, G6
Thailand	ˈtī-land	E8	Map 4, F5
Togo	ˈtō(ˌ)gō	E5	Map 2, E3
Tonga	ˈtän-gə	—	Map 7, D9
Trinidad & Tobago	ˈtrin-ə-ˌdad/tə-ˈbā-(ˌ)gō	—	Map 5, J3
Tunisia	t(y)ü-ˈnē-zh(ē-)ə	D5	Map 2, B4
Turkey	ˈtər-kē	D6	Map 4, D2
Turkmenistan	tùrkˈ-men-i-stănˈ	D6	Map 4, D3

Maps of the World *(continued)*

Country and Territory	Pronunciation	Map 1	Maps 2–7
Tuvalu	tü'-vä-lü	—	Map 7, C9
Uganda	(y)ü-'gan-də	E6	Map 2, F6
Ukraine	yü-'krān	C6	Map 3, F7
United Arab Emirates	yoo-nī'tid ăr'əb i-mîr'its	D6	Map 4, E2
United Kingdom	king'dəm	C6	Map 3, F2
United States	yů-,nīt-əd-'stāts	D2	Map 5, F5
Uruguay	'(y)ůr-ə-gwī	G3	Map 6, G5
Uzbekistan	(,)ůz-,bek-i-'stan	C6	Map 4, D3
Vanuatu	van-ə-'wät-(,)ü	—	Map 7, D7
Vatican City	văt'ĭ-kən	—	Map 3, H4
Venezuela	,ven-əz(-ə)-'wā-lə	E3	Map 6, A4
Vietnam	vē-'et-'näm	E8	Map 4, G6
Western Sahara	sə-hâr'ə	D4	Map 2, C1
Yemen	'yem-ən	E6	Map 4, F2
Yugoslavia	yōō'gō-slä'vē-ə	D5	Map 3, H2
Zambia	'zam-bē-ə	F5	Map 2, H5
Zimbabwe	zim-'bäb-wē	F6	Map 2, H6

Glossary

Absolute advantage: A theory first presented by Adam Smith, which holds that because certain countries can produce some goods more efficiently than other countries can, they should specialize in and export those things they can produce more efficiently and trade for other things they need.

Acceptable quality level: A concept of quality control whereby managers are willing to accept a certain level of production defects, which are dealt with through repair facilities and service centers.

Accounting: The process of identifying, recording, and interpreting economic events.

Acquired advantage: A form of trade advantage due to technology rather than the availability of natural resources, climate, etc.

Acquired group memberships: Affiliations not determined by birth, such as religions, political affiliations, and professional and other associations.

Acquisition: The purchase of one company by another company.

Ad valorem tariff: A tariff (duty) assessed as a percentage of the value of the item.

AFTA: *See* ASEAN Free Trade Area.

ALADI: *See* Latin American Integration Association.

Andean Group (ANCOM): A South American form of economic integration involving Bolivia, Colombia, Ecuador, Peru, and Venezuela.

Appropriability theory: The theory that companies will favor foreign direct investment over such nonequity operating forms as licensing arrangements so that potential competitors will be less likely to gain access to proprietary information.

Arbitrage: The process of buying and selling foreign currency at a profit resulting from price discrepancies between or among markets.

Area division: *See* Geographic division.

Arm's-length price: A price between two companies that do not have an ownership interest in each other.

Ascribed group memberships: Affiliations determined by birth, such as those based on gender, family, age, caste, and ethnic, racial, or national origin.

ASEAN: *See* Association of South East Asian Nations.

ASEAN Free Trade Area (AFTA): A free-trade area formed by the ASEAN countries on January 1, 1993, with the goal of cutting tariffs on all intrazonal trade to a maximum of 5 percent by January 1, 2008.

Asia Pacific Economic Cooperation (APEC): A cooperation formed by 21 countries that border the Pacific Rim to promote multilateral economic cooperation in trade and investment in the Pacific Rim.

Association of South East Asian Nations (ASEAN): A free-trade area involving the Asian countries of Brunei, Indonesia, Malaysia, the Philippines, Singapore, and Thailand.

Balance of payments: Statement that summarizes all economic transactions between a country and the rest of the world during a given period of time.

Balance-of-payments deficit: An imbalance of some specific component within the balance of payments, such as merchandise trade or current account, that implies that a country is importing more than it exports.

Balance-of-payments surplus: An imbalance in the balance of payments that exists when a country exports more than it imports.

Balance of trade: The value of a country's exports less the value of its imports (*trade* can be defined as merchandise trade, services, unilateral transfers, or a combination of these).

Balance on goods and services: The value of a country's exports of merchandise trade and services minus imports.

Barter: The exchange of goods for goods instead of for money.

Base currency: The currency whose value is implicitly 1 when a quote is made between two currencies: for example, if the cruzeiro is trading at 2962.5 cruzeiros per dollar, the dollar is the base currency and the cruzeiro is the quoted currency.

Bill of exchange: *See* Commercial bill of exchange.

Bill of lading: A document that is issued to a shipper by a carrier, listing the goods received for shipment.

BIRPI: *See* International Bureau for the Protection of Industrial Property Rights.

BIS: *See* Bank for International Settlements.

Black market: The foreign exchange market that lies outside the official market.

Body language: The way people move their bodies, gesture, position themselves, etc., to convey meaning to others.

Bonded warehouse: A building or part of a building used for the storage of imported merchandise under supervision of the U.S. Customs Service and for the purpose of deferring payment of customs duties.

Branch (foreign): A foreign operation of a company that is not a separate entity from the parent that owns it.

Brand: A particular good identified with a company by means of name, logo, or other method, usually protected with a trademark registration.

Buffer-stock system: A partially managed system that utilizes stocks of commodities to regulate their prices.

CACM: *See* Central American Common Market.

Capital account: A measure of transactions involving previously existing rather than currently produced assets.

Capital market: The market for stocks and long-term debt instruments.

Capitalism: An economic system characterized by private ownership, pricing, production, and distribution of goods.

Caribbean Community and Common Market (CARICOM): A customs union in the Caribbean region.

CARICOM: *See* Caribbean Community and Common Market.

Caste: A social class separated from others by heredity.

CEFTA: *See* Central European Free Trade Association.

Central American Common Market (CACM): A customs union in Central America.

Central bank: A governmental "bank for banks," customarily responsible for a country's monetary policy.

Central European Free Trade Association (CEFTA): An association that went into effect on July 1, 1992, with an initial membership of the Czech Republic, Slovakia, Hungary, and Poland, and whose goal was to establish a free-trade area that includes the basic trade structure of the EU by the year 2000.

Centralization: The situation in which decision making is done at the home office rather than the country level.

Centrally planned economy (CPE): An economic system in which resources are allocated and controlled by government decision.

Certificate of origin: A shipping document that determines the origin of products and is usually validated by an external source, such as a chamber of commerce; it helps countries determine the specific tariff schedule for imports.

Chaebol: Korean business groups that are similar to keiretsu and also contain a trading company as part of the group.

Civil law system: A legal system based on a very detailed set of laws that are organized into a code; countries with a civil law system, also called a codified legal system, include Germany, France, and Japan.

Civil liberties: The freedom to develop one's own views and attitudes.

Code of conduct: A set of principles guiding the actions of MNEs in their contacts with societies.

Codetermination: A process by which both labor and management participate in the management of a company.

Codified legal system: *See* Civil law system.

Collaborative arrangement: A formal, long-term contractual agreement among companies.

Command economy: *See* Centrally planned economy.

Commercial bill of exchange: An instrument of payment in international business that instructs the importer to forward payment to the exporter.

Commercial invoice: A bill for goods from the buyer to the seller.

Commodities: Basic raw materials or agricultural products.

Commodity agreement: A form of economic cooperation designed to stabilize and raise the price of a commodity.

Common law system: A legal system based on tradition, precedent, and custom and usage, in which the courts interpret the law based on those conventions; found in the United Kingdom and former British colonies.

Common market: A form of regional economic integration in which countries abolish internal tariffs, use a common external tariff, and abolish restrictions on factor mobility.

Communism: A form of totalitarianism initially theorized by Karl Marx in which the political and economic systems are virtually inseparable.

Comparable access: A protectionist argument that companies and industries should have the same access to foreign markets as foreign industries and companies have to their markets.

Comparative advantage: The theory that there may still be global efficiency gains from trade if a country specializes in those products that it can produce more efficiently than other products.

Compound tariff: A tax placed on goods traded internationally, based on value plus units.

Concentration strategy: A strategy by which an international company builds up operations quickly in one or a few countries before going to another.

Confirmed letter of credit: A letter of credit to which a bank in the exporter's country adds its guarantee of payment.

Consolidation: An accounting process in which financial statements of related entities, such as a parent and its subsidiaries, are combined to yield a unified set of financial statements; in the process, transactions among the related enterprises are eliminated so that the statements reflect transactions with outside parties.

Consortium: The joining together of several entities, such as companies or governments, in order to strengthen the possibility of achieving some objective.

Consular invoice: A document that covers all the usual details of the commercial invoice and packing list, prepared in the language of the foreign country for which the goods are destined, on special forms obtainable from the consulate or authorized commercial printers.

Consumer-directed market economy: An economy in which there is minimal government participation while growth is promoted through the mobility of production factors, including high labor turnover.

Consumer price index: A measure of the cost of typical wage-earner purchases of goods and services expressed as a percentage of the cost of these same goods and services in some base period.

Consumer sovereignty: The freedom of consumers to influence production through the choices they make.

Convertibility: The ability to exchange one currency for another currency without restrictions.

Copyright: The right to reproduce, publish, and sell literary, musical, or artistic works.

Corporate culture: The common values shared by employees in a corporation, which form a control mechanism that is implicit and helps enforce other explicit control mechanisms.

Correspondent (bank): A bank in which funds are kept by another, usually foreign, bank to facilitate check clearing and other business relationships.

Cost-of-living adjustment: An increase in compensation given to an expatriate employee when foreign living costs are more expensive than those in the home country.

Countertrade: A reciprocal flow of goods or services valued and settled in monetary terms.

Country analysis: A process of examining the economic strategy of a nation-state, taking a holistic approach to understanding how a country, and in particular its government, has behaved, is behaving, and may behave.

Country-similarity theory: The theory that a producer, having developed a new product in response to observed market conditions in the home market, will turn to markets that are most similar to those at home.

Country size theory: The theory that larger countries are generally more self-sufficient than smaller countries.

Creolization: The process by which elements of an outside culture are introduced.

Cross-licensing: The exchange of technology by different companies.

Cross rate: An exchange rate between two currencies used in the spot market and computed from the exchange rate of each currency in relation to the U.S. dollar.

Cultural imperialism: Change by imposition.

Cultural relativism: The belief that behavior has meaning and can be judged only in its specific cultural context.

Culture: The specific learned norms of a society, based on attitudes, values, and beliefs.

Culture shock: A generalized trauma one experiences in a new and different culture because of having to learn and cope with a vast array of new cues and expectations.

Currency swaps: The exchange of principal and interest payments.

Current-account balance: Exports minus imports of goods, services, and unilateral transfers.

Customs duties: Taxes imposed on imported goods.

Customs union: A form of regional economic integration that eliminates tariffs among member nations and establishes common extended tariffs.

Customs valuation: The value of goods on which customs authorities charge tariffs.

Decentralization: The situation in which decisions tend to be made at lower levels in a company or at the country-operating level rather than at head-quarters.

Deferral: The postponing of taxation of foreign-source income until it is remitted to the parent company.

Demand conditions: Includes three dimensions: the composition of home demand (or the nature of buyer needs), the size and pattern of growth of home demand, and the internationalization of demand.

Democracy: A political system that relies on citizens' participation in the decision-making process.

Dependencia theory: The theory holding that emerging economies have practically no power when dealing with MNEs as host countries.

Dependency: A state in which a country is too dependent on the sale of one primary commodity and/or too dependent on one country as a customer and supplier.

Devaluation: A formal reduction in the value of a currency in relation to another currency; the foreign currency equivalent of the devalued currency falls.

Developed country: High-income country.

Developing country: A poor country, also known as an emerging country or economy.

Direct foreign investment: *See* Foreign direct investment.

Direct identification drawback: A provision that allows U.S. firms to use imported components in the manufacturing process without having to include the duty paid on the imported goods in costs and sales prices.

Direct investment: *See* Foreign direct investment.

Direct quote: A quote expressed in terms of the number of units of the domestic currency given for one unit of a foreign currency.

Direct selling: A sale of goods by an exporter directly to distributors or final consumers rather than to trading companies or other intermediaries in order to achieve greater control over the marketing function and to earn higher profits.

Disclosure: The presentation of information and discussion of results.

Discount (in foreign exchange): A situation in which the forward rate for a foreign currency is less than the spot rate, assuming that the domestic currency is quoted on a direct basis.

Distribution: The course—physical path or legal title—that goods take between production and consumption.

Distributor: A merchant in a foreign country that purchases products from the manufacturer and sells them at a profit.

Diversification: A process of becoming less dependent on one or a few customers or suppliers.

Diversification strategy: A strategy by which an international company produces or sells in many countries to avoid relying on one particular market.

Divestment: Reduction in the amount of investment.

Documentary draft: An instrument instructing the importer to pay the exporter if certain documents are presented.

Dumping: The underpricing of exports, usually below cost or below the home-country price.

Duty: A governmental tax (tariff) levied on goods shipped internationally.

Dynamic effects of integration: The overall growth in the market and the impact on a company of expanding production and achieving greater economies of scale.

E-commerce: The use of the Internet to join together suppliers with companies and companies with customers.

Economic Community of West African States (ECOWAS): A form of economic integration among certain countries in West Africa.

Economic exposure: The foreign exchange risk that international businesses face in the pricing of products, the source and cost of inputs, and the location of investments.

Economic integration: The abolition of economic discrimination between national economies, such as within the EU.

Economic system: The system concerned with the allocation of scarce resources.

Economics: A social science concerned chiefly with the description and analysis of the production, distribution, and consumption of goods and services.

Economies of scale: The lowering of cost per unit as output increases because of allocation of fixed costs over more units produced.

ECOWAS: *See* Economic Community of West African States.

ECU: *See* European Currency Unit.

EEC: *See* European Economic Community.

EEC Patent Convention: An important cross-national parent convention that involves the members of the EU.

Effective tariff: The real tariff on the manufactured portion of developing countries' exports, which is higher than indicated by the published rates because the ad valorem tariff is based on the total value of the products, which includes raw materials that would have had duty-free entry.

EFTA: *See* European Free Trade Association.

Elastic (product demand): A condition in which sales are likely to increase or decrease by a percentage that is more than the percentage change in income.

Embargo: A specific type of quota that prohibits all trade.

EMC: *See* Export management company.

Emerging economy: Low- and middle-income country; also known as developing country.

EMS: *See* European Monetary System.

Enterprise resource planning (ERP): Software that can link information flows from different parts of a business and from different geographic areas.

Entrepôt: A country that is an import/export intermediary; for example, Hong Kong is an entrepôt for trade between China and the rest of the world.

Environmental climate: The external conditions in host countries that could significantly affect the success of a foreign business enterprise.

Environmental scanning: The systematic assessment of external conditions that might affect a company's operations.

EPC: *See* European Patent Convention.

Equity alliance: A situation in which a cooperating company takes an equity position (almost always a minority) in the company with which it has a collaborative arrangement.

ERP: *See* Enterprise resource planning.

Essential-industry argument: The argument holding the certain domestic industries need protection for national security purposes.

ETC: *See* Export trading company.

Ethnocentrism: A belief that one's own group is superior to others; also used to describe a company's belief that what worked at home should work abroad.

Eurobond: A bond sold in a country other than the one in whose currency it is denominated.

Eurocredit: A loan, line of credit, or other form of medium- or long-term credit on the Eurocurrency market that has a maturity of more than one year.

Eurocurrency: Any currency that is banked outside of its country of origin.

Eurocurrency market: An international wholesale market that deals in Eurocurrencies.

Eurodollars: Dollars banked outside of the United States.

Euroequity market: The market for shares sold outside the boundaries of the issuing company's home country.

European Commission: One of the five major institutions of the EU; composed of a president, six vice presidents, and 10 other members whose allegiance is to the EU and serving as an executive branch for the EU.

European Community (EC): The predecessor of the European Union.

European Council: One of the five major institutions of the European Union; make up of the heads of state of each of the EU members.

European Currency Unit (ECU): A unit of account based on a currency basket composed of the currencies of the members of the EU.

European Economic Community (EEC): The predecessor of the European Community.

European Free Trade Association (EFTA): A free-trade area among a group of European countries that are not members of the EU.

European Monetary System (EMS): A cooperative foreign exchange agreement involving most of the members of the EU and designed to promote exchange rate stability within the EU.

European Parliament: One of the five major institutions of the EU; its representatives are elected directly in each member country.

European Patent Convention (EPC): A European agreement allowing companies to make a uniform patent search and application, which is then passed on to all signatory countries.

European terms: The practice of using the indirect quote for exchange rates.

European Union (EU): A form of regional economic integration among countries in Europe that involves a free-trade area, a customs union, and the free mobility of factors of production that is working toward political and economic union.

Exchange rate: The price of one currency in terms of another currency.

Eximbank: *See* Export–Import Bank.

Exotic currencies: The currencies of developing countries; also called *exotics.*

Expatriates: Noncitizens of the country in which they are working.

Experience curve: The relationship of production cost reductions to increases in output.

Export–Import Bank (Eximbank): A U.S. federal agency specializing in foreign lending to support exports.

Export-led development: An industrialization policy emphasizing industries that will have export capabilities.

Export license: A document that grants government permission to ship certain products to a specific country.

Export management company (EMC): A company that buys merchandise from manufacturers for international distribution or sometimes acts as an agent for manufacturers.

Export packing list: A shipping document that itemizes the material in each individual package and indicates the type of package.

Export tariff: A tax on goods leaving a country.

Export trading company (ETC): A form of trading company sanctioned by U.S. law to become involved in international commerce as independent distributors to match up foreign buyers with domestic sellers.

Exports: Goods or services leaving a country.

Exposure: A situation in which a foreign exchange account is subject to a gain or loss if the exchange rate changes.

Expropriation: The taking over of ownership of private property by a country's government.

Externalities: External economic costs related to a business activity.

Extranet: The use of the Internet to link a company with outsiders.

Extraterritoriality: The extension by a government of the application of its laws to foreign operations of companies.

Factor conditions: Inputs to the production process, such as human, physical, knowledge, and capital resources and infrastructure.

Factor mobility: The free movement of factors of production, such as labor and capital, across national borders.

Factor-proportions theory: The theory that differences in a country's proportionate holdings of factors of production (land, labor, and capital) explain differences in the costs of the factors and that export advantages lie in the production of goods that use the most abundant factors.

Favorable balance of trade: An indication that a country is exporting more than its imports.

FCPA: *See* Foreign Corrupt Practices Act.

FDI: *See* Foreign direct investment.

Fees: Payments for the performance of certain activities abroad.

First-in advantage: Any benefit gained in terms of brand recognition and lining up of the best suppliers, distributors, and local partners because of entering a market before competitors do.

First-mover advantage: A cost reduction advantage due to economies of scale attained through moving into a foreign market ahead of competitors.

Fixed price: A method of pricing in which bargaining does not take place.

Floating currency: A currency whose value responds to the supply of and demand for that currency.

Floating exchange rate: An exchange rate determined by the laws of supply and demand and with minimal governmental interference.

Foreign bond: A bond sold outside of the borrower's country but denominated in the currency of the country of issue.

Foreign Corrupt Practices Act (FCPA): A law that criminalizes certain types of payments by U.S. companies, such as bribes to foreign governmental officials.

Foreign direct investment (FDI): An investment that gives the investor a controlling interest in a foreign company.

Foreign exchange: Checks and other instruments for making payments in another country's currency.

Foreign exchange control: A requirement that an importer of a product must apply to governmental authorities for permission to buy foreign currency to pay for the product.

Foreign freight forwarder: A company that facilitates the movement of goods from one country to another.

Foreign investment: Direct or portfolio ownership of assets in another country.

Foreign trade zone (FTZ): A government-designated area in which goods can be stored, inspected, or manufactured without being subject to formal customs procedures until they leave the zone.

Forward contract: A contract between a company or individual and a bank to deliver foreign currency at a specific exchange rate on a future date.

Forward discount: *See* Discount.

Forward premium: *See* Premium.

Forward exchange rate: A contractually established exchange rate between a foreign exchange trader and the trader's client for delivery of foreign currency on a specific date.

Franchising: A specialized form of licensing in which one party (the franchisor) sells to an independent party (the franchisee) the use of a trademark that is an essential asset for the franchisee's business and also gives continual assistance in the operation of the business.

Free-trade area (FTA): A form of regional economic integration in which internal tariffs are abolished, but member countries set their own external tariffs.

Freight forwarder: *See* Foreign freight forwarder.

Fringe benefit: Any employee benefit other than salary, wages, and cash bonuses.

FTZ: *See* Foreign trade zone.

Functional division: An organizational structure in which each function in foreign countries (e.g., marketing or production) reports separately to a counterpart functional group at headquarters.

Futures contract: A foreign exchange instrument that specifics an exchange rate, an amount of currency, and a maturity date in advance of the exchange of the currency.

G-7 countries: *See* Group of 7.

GATT: *See* General Agreement on Tariffs and Trade.

General Agreement on Tariffs and Trade (GATT): A multilateral arrangement aimed at reducing barriers to trade, both tariff and nontariff ones; at the signing of the Uruguay round, the GATT was designated to become the World Trade Organization (WTO).

Generalized System of Preferences (GSP): Preferential import restrictions extended by industrial countries to developing countries.

Geocentric: Operations based on an informed knowledge of both home- and host-country needs.

Geographic division: An organizational structure in which a company's operations are separated for reporting purposes into regional areas.

Geography: A science dealing with the earth and its life, especially with the description of land, sea, air, and the distribution of plant and animal life.

Globalization: The deepening relationships and broadening interdependence among people from different countries.

Global company: A company that integrates operations located in different countries.

Go–no-go decision: A decision, such as on foreign investments, that is based on minimum threshold criteria and does not compare different opportunities.

Gray market: The handling of goods through unofficial distributors.

Gross domestic product (GDP): The total of all economic activity in a country, regardless of who owns the productive assets.

Gross national product (GNP): The total of incomes earned by residents of a country, regardless of where the productive assets are located.

Group of 7 (G-7): A group of developed countries that periodically meets to make economic decisions; this group consists of Canada, France, Germany, Italy, Japan, the United Kingdom, and the United States.

GSP: *See* Generalized System of Preferences.

Hard currency: A currency that is freely traded without many restrictions and for which there is usually strong external demand; often called a freely convertible currency.

Hardship allowance: A supplement to compensate expatriates for working in dangerous or adverse conditions.

Harvesting: Reduction in the amount of investment; also known as divestment.

Hedge: To attempt to protect foreign currency holdings against an adverse movement of an exchange rate.

Heterarchy: An organizational structure in which management of an alliance of companies is shared by so-called equals rather than being set up in a superior–subordinate relationship.

High-context culture: A culture in which most people consider that peripheral and hearsay information are necessary for decision making because they bear on the context of the situation.

Historically planned economy (HPE): The World Bank's term for Second World countries in transition to market economies.

History: A branch of knowledge that records and explains past events.

Home country: The country in which an international company is headquartered.

Home-country nationals: Expatriate employees who are citizens of the country in which the company is headquartered.

Horizontal expansion: Any foreign direct investment by which a company produces the same product it produces at home.

Host country: Any foreign country in which an international company operates.

HPE: *See* Historically planned economy.

Hyperinflation: A rapid increase (at least 1 percent per day) in general price levels for a sustained period of time.

Idealism: Trying to determine principles before settling small issues.

ILO: *See* International Labor Organization.

IMF: *See* International Monetary Fund.

Imitation lag: A strategy for exploiting temporary monopoly advantages by moving first to those countries most likely to develop local production.

Import broker: An individual who obtains various governmental permissions and other clearances before forwarding necessary paperwork to the carrier that will deliver the goods from the dock to the importer.

Import deposit requirement: Governmental requirement of a deposit prior to the release of foreign exchange.

Import licensing: A method of governmental control of the exchange rate whereby all recipients, exporters, and others who receive foreign exchange are required to sell to the central bank at the official buying rate.

Import substitution: An industrialization policy whereby new industrial development emphasizes products that would otherwise be imported.

Import tariff: A tax placed on goods entering a country.

Imports: Goods or services entering a country.

In-bond industry: Any industry that is allowed to import components free of duty, provided that the components will be reexported after processing.

Independence: An extreme situation in which a country would not rely on other countries at all.

Indigenization: The process of introducing elements of an outside culture.

Indirect selling: A sale of goods by an exporter through another domestic company as an intermediary.

Industrial country: High-income country; also known as developed country.

Industrialization argument: A rationale for protectionism that argues that the development of industrial output should come about even though domestic prices may not become competitive on the world market.

Inelastic (product demand): A condition in which sales are likely to increase or decrease by a percentage that is less than the percentage change in income.

Infant industry argument: The position that holds that an emerging industry should be guaranteed a large share of the domestic market until it becomes efficient enough to compete against imports.

Inflation: A condition where prices are going up.

Infrastructure: The underlying foundation of a society, such as roads, schools, and so forth, that allows it to function effectively.

Intangible property: *See* Intellectual property rights.

Intellectual property rights (IPRs): Ownership rights to intangible assets, such as patents, trademarks, copyrights, and know-how.

Interbank market: The market for foreign exchange transactions among commercial banks.

Interbank transactions: Foreign exchange transactions that take place between commercial banks.

Interdependence: The existence of mutually necessary economic relations among countries.

Interest arbitrage: Investing in debt instruments in different countries and earning a profit due to interest rate and exchange rate differentials.

Interest rate differential: An indicator of future changes in the spot exchange rate.

Intermodal transportation: The movement across different modes from origin to destination.

Internalization: Control through self-handling of foreign operations, primarily because it is less expensive to deal within the same corporate family than to contract with an external organization.

International Accounting Standards Committee (IASC): The international private sector organization that sets financial accounting standards for worldwide use.

International Bureau for the Protection of Industrial Property Rights (BIRPI): A multilateral agreement to protect patents, trademarks, and other property rights.

International business: All business transactions involving private companies or governments of two or more countries.

International division: An organizational structure in which virtually all foreign operations are handled within the same division.

International Labor Organization (ILO): A multilateral organization promoting the adoption of humane labor conditions.

International Monetary Fund (IMF): A multigovernmental association organized in 1945 to promote exchange-rate stability and to facilitate the international flow of currencies.

Intranet: The use of the Internet to link together the different divisions and functions inside a company.

Intrazonal trade: Trade among countries that are part of a trade agreement, such as the EU.

Invisibles: *See* Services.

Irrevocable letter of credit: A letter of credit that cannot be canceled or changed without the consent of all parties involved.

Islamic law: A system of theocratic law based on the religious teachings of Islam; also called Muslim law.

ISO 9000: A quality standard developed by the International Standards Organization in Geneva that requires companies to document their commitment to quality at all levels of the organization.

JIT: *See* Just-in-time manufacturing.

Joint venture: A direct investment of which two or more companies share the ownership.

Just-in-time (JIT) manufacturing: A system that decreases inventory costs by having components and parts delivered as they are needed in production.

Kaizen: The Japanese process of continuous improvement, the cornerstone of TQM.

Keiretsu: A corporate relationship linking certain Japanese companies, usually involving a noncontrolling interest in each other, strong high-level personal relationships among managers in the different companies, and interlocking directorships.

Key industry: Any industry that might affect a very large segment of a country's economy or population by virtue of its size or influence on other sectors.

Labor market: The mix of available workers and labor costs available to companies.

Labor union: An association of workers intended to promote and protect the welfare, interests, and rights of its members, primarily by collective bargaining.

LAFTA: *See* Latin American Free Trade Association.

Lag strategy: An operational strategy that involves delaying collection of foreign currency receivables if the currency is expected to strengthen or delaying payment of foreign currency payables when the currency is expected to weaken; the opposite of a lead strategy.

Laissez-faire: The concept of minimal governmental intervention in a society's economic activity.

Latin American Free Trade Association (LAFTA): A free-trade area formed by Mexico and the South American countries in 1960; it was replaced by ALADI in 1980.

Latin American Integration Association (ALADI): A form of regional economic integration involving most of the Latin American countries.

Law: A binding custom or practice of a community.

Lead country strategy: A strategy of introducing a product on a test basis in a small-country market that is considered representative of a region before investing to serve larger-country markets.

Lead strategy: An operational strategy that involves collecting foreign currency receivables early when the currency is expected to weaken or paying foreign currency payables early when the currency is expected to strengthen; the opposite of a lag strategy.

Lead subsidiary organization: A foreign subsidiary that has global responsibility (serves as corporate headquarters) for one of a company's products or functions.

Learning curve: A concept used to support the infant industry argument for protection; it assumes that costs will decrease as workers and managers gain more experience.

Letter of credit: A precise document by which the importer's bank extends credit to the importer and agrees to pay the exporter.

Liability of foreignness: Foreign companies' lower survival rate than local companies for many years after they begin operations.

License: Formal or legal permission to do some specified action; a governmental method of fixing the exchange rate by requiring all recipients, exporters, and others that receive foreign exchange to sell it to the central bank at the official buying rate.

Licensing agreement: Agreement whereby one company gives rights to another for the use, usually for a fee, of such assets as trademarks, patents, copyrights, or other know-how.

Licensing arrangement: A procedure that requires potential importers or exporters to secure permission from governmental authorities before they conduct trade transactions.

Lifetime employment: The Japanese custom that workers are effectively guaranteed employment with the company for their working lifetime and that workers seldom leave for employment opportunities with other companies.

Lobbyist: An individual who participates in advancing or otherwise securing passage of legislation by influencing public officials before and during the legislation process.

Local content: Costs incurred within a given country, usually as a percentage of total costs.

Locally responsive company: Synonym for *multidomestic company.*

Locals: Citizens of the country in which they are working.

Logistics: That part of the supply chain process that plans, implements, and controls the efficient, effective flow and storage of goods, services, and related information from the point of origin to the point of consumption, to meet customers' requirements; sometimes called materials management.

Low-context culture: A culture in which most people consider relevant only information that they receive firsthand and that bears very directly on the decision they need to make.

Management contract: An arrangement whereby one company provides management personnel to perform general or specialized management functions to another company for a fee.

Manufacturing interchange: A process by which various plants produce a range of components and exchange them so that all plants assemble the finished product for the local market.

Maquiladora: An industrial operation developed by the Mexican and U.S. governments in which U.S.-sourced components are shipped to Mexico duty-free, assembled into final products, and re-exported to the United States.

Marginal propensity to import: The tendency to purchase imports with incremental income.

Market capitalization: A common measure of the size of a stock market, which is computed by multiplying the total number of shares of stock listed on the exchange by the market price per share.

Market economy: An economic system in which resources are allocated and controlled by consumers who "vote" by buying goods.

Market environment: The environment that involves the interactions between households (or individuals) and companies to allocate resources, free from governmental ownership or control.

Market socialism: The state owns significant resources, but allocation comes from the market price mechanism.

Materials management: *See* Logistics.

Matrix: A method of plotting data on a set of vertical and horizontal axes, in order to compare countries in terms of risk and opportunity.

Matrix division structure: An organizational structure in which foreign units report (by product, function, or area) to more than one group, each of which shares responsibility over the foreign unit.

Mentor: A person at headquarters who looks after the interests of an expatriate employee.

Mercantilism: An economic philosophy based on the beliefs that a country's wealth is dependent on its holdings of treasure, usually in the form of gold, and that countries should export more than they import in order to increase wealth.

Merchandise exports: Goods sent out of a country.

Merchandise imports: Goods brought into a country.

Merchandise trade balance: The part of a country's current account that measures the trade deficit or surplus; its balance is the net of merchandise imports and exports.

MERCOSUR: A major subregional group established by Argentina, Brazil, Paraguay, and Uruguay, which spun off from ALADI in 1991 with the goal of setting up a customs union and common market.

Micro political risk: Negative political actions aimed at specific, rather than most, foreign investors.

Middle East: The countries on the Arabian peninsula plus those bordering the eastern end of the Mediterranean; sometimes also including other adjacent countries, particularly Jordan, Iraq, Iran, and Kuwait.

Ministry of International Trade and Industry (MITI): The Japanese governmental agency responsible for coordinating overall business direction and helping individual companies take advantage of global business opportunities.

Mission: What the company will seek to do and become over the long term.

Mission statement: A long-range strategic intent.

Mixed economy: An economic system characterized by some mixture of market and command economics and public and private ownership.

Mixed venture: A special type of joint venture in which a government is in partnership with a private company.

MNE: *See* Multinational enterprise.

Monochronic culture: A culture in which most people prefer to deal with situations sequentially (especially those involving other people), such as finishing with one customer before dealing with another.

Monopoly advantage: The perceived supremacy of foreign investors in relation to local companies, which is necessary to overcome the perceived greater risk of operating in a different environment.

Multidomestic company: A company with international operations that allows operations in one country to be relatively independent of those in other countries.

Multilateral agreement: An agreement involving more then two governments.

Multinational corporation (MNC): A synonym for *multinational enterprise.*

Multinational enterprise (MNE): A company that has an integrated global philosophy encompassing both domestic and overseas operations; sometimes used synonymously with *multinational corporation* or *transnational corporation.*

Multiple exchange rate system: A means of foreign exchange control whereby the government sets different exchange rates for different transactions.

Muslim law: *See* Islamic law.

National responsiveness: Readiness to implement operating adjustments in foreign countries in order to reach a satisfactory level of performance.

Nationalism: The feeling of pride and/or ethnocentrism focused on an individual's home country or nation.

Nationalization: The transfer of ownership to the state.

Natural advantage: Climatic conditions, access to certain natural resources, or availability of labor, which gives a country an advantage in producing some product.

Neomercantilism: The approach of countries that apparently try to run favorable balances of trade in an attempt to achieve some social or political objective.

Net capital flow: Capital inflow minus capital outflow, for other than import and export payment.

Net export effect: Export stimulus minus export reduction.

Net import change: Import displacement minus import stimulus.

Network alliance: Interdependence of countries; each company is a customer of and a supplier to other companies.

Network organization: A situation in which a group of companies is interrelated, and in which the management of the interrelation is shared among so-called equals.

Newly industrializing country (NIC): A Third World country in which the cultural and economic climate has led to a rapid rate of industrialization and growth since the 1960s.

Nonmarket economy: *See* Centrally planned economy.

Nonmarket environment: Public institutions (such as government, governmental agencies, and government-owned businesses) and nonpublic institutions (such as environmental and other special-interest groups).

Nongovernment organizations (NGO): Special-interest groups, such as environmentalists.

Nontariff barriers: Barriers to imports that are not tariffs; examples include administrative controls, "Buy America" policies, and so forth.

North American Free Trade Agreement (NAFTA): A free-trade agreement involving the United States, Canada, and Mexico that went into effect on January 1, 1994, and will be phased in over a period of 15 years.

OAU: *See* Organization of African Unity.

Objectives: Specific performance targets to fulfill a company's mission.

Obsolescing bargain (theory of): The premise that a company's bargaining strength with a host government diminishes after the company transfers assets to the host country.

OECD: *See* Organization for Economic Cooperation and Development.

Offer rate: The amount for which a foreign exchange trader is willing to sell a currency.

Official reserves: A country's holdings of monetary gold. Special Drawing Rights, and internationally acceptable currencies.

Offset: A form of barter transaction in which an export is paid for with other merchandise.

Offset trade: A form of countertrade in which an exporter sells goods for cash but then helps businesses in the importing country find opportunities to earn hard currency.

Offshore financial centers: Cities or countries that provide large amounts of funds in currencies other than their own and are used as locations in which to raise and accumulate cash.

Offshore manufacturing: Manufacturing outside the borders of a particular country.

Oligopoly: An industry in which there are few producers or sellers.

OPEC: *See* Organization of Petroleum Exporting Countries.

Open account: Conditions of sale under which the exporter extends credit directly to the importer.

OPIC: *See* Overseas Private Investment Corporation.

Opinion leader: One whose acceptance of some concept is apt to be emulated by others.

Optimum-tariff theory: The argument that a foreign producer will lower its prices if an import tax is placed on its products.

Option: A foreign exchange instrument that gives the purchaser the right, but not the obligation, to buy or sell a certain amount of foreign currency at a set exchange rate within a specified amount of time.

Organization of African Unity (OAU): An organization of African nations that is more concerned with political than economic objectives.

Organization for Economic Cooperation and Development (OECD): A multilateral organization of industrialized and semi-industrialized countries that helps formulate social and economic policies.

Organization of Petroleum Exporting Countries (OPEC): A producers' alliance among 12 petroleum-exporting countries that attempt to agree on oil production and pricing policies.

Organizational structure: The reporting relationships within an organization.

Outsourcing: The use by a domestic company of foreign suppliers for components or finished products.

Overseas Private Investment Corporation (OPIC): A U.S. government agency that provides insurance for companies involved in international business.

Over-the-counter (OTC) market: Trading in stocks, usually of smaller companies, that are not listed on one of the stock exchanges; also refers to how government and corporate bonds are traded, through dealers who quote bids and offers to buy and sell "over the counter."

Par value: The benchmark value of a currency, originally quoted in terms of gold or the U.S. dollar and now quoted in terms of Special Drawing Rights.

Parliamentary system: A form of government that involves the election of representatives to form the executive branch.

Passive income: Income from investments in tax-haven countries or sales and services income that involves buyers and sellers in other than the tax-haven country, where either the buyer or the seller must be part of the same organizational structure as the corporation that earns the income; also known as Subpart F income.

Patent: A right granted by a sovereign power or state for the protection of an invention or discovery against infringement.

Patent cooperation treaty: A multilateral agreement to protect patents.

Peg: To fix a currency's exchange rate to some benchmark, such as another currency.

Penetration strategy: A strategy of introducing a product at a low price to induce a maximum number of consumers to try it.

Piggyback exporting: Use by an exporter of another exporter as an intermediary.

Piracy: The unauthorized use of property rights that are protected by patents, trademarks, or copyrights.

Planning: The meshing of objectives with internal and external constraints in order to set means to implement, monitor, and correct operations.

Plant layout: Decisions about the physical arrangement of economic activity centers within a manufacturing facility.

PLC: *See* Product life cycle theory.

Political freedom: The right to participate freely in the political process.

Political ideology: The body of constructs (complex ideas), theories, and aims that constitute a sociopolitical program.

Political risk: Potential changes in political conditions that may cause a company's operating positions to deteriorate.

Political science: A discipline that helps explain the patterns of governments and their actions.

Political system: The system designed to integrate a society into a viable, functioning unit.

Polycentrism: Characteristic of an individual or organization that feels that differences in a foreign country, real and imaginary, great and small, need to be accounted for in management decisions.

Polychronic culture: A culture in which most people are more comfortable dealing simultaneously with all the situations facing them.

Porter diamond: A diagram showing four conditions—demand, factor endowments, related and supporting industries, and firm strategy, structure, and rivalry—that usually must all be favorable for an industry in a country to develop and sustain a global competitive advantage.

Portfolio investment: An investment in the form of either debt or equity that does not give the investor a controlling interest.

Positive-sum gain: A situation in which the sums of gains and loses, if added together among participants, is positive, especially if all parties gain from a relationship.

Power distance: A measurement of preference for consultative or autocratic styles of management.

PPP: *See* Purchasing-power parity.

Pragmatism: Settling small issues before deciding on principles.

Premium (in foreign exchange): The difference between the spot and forward exchange rates in the forward market; a foreign currency sells at a premium when the forward rate exceeds the spot rate and when the domestic currency is quoted on a direct basis.

Pressure group: A group that tries to influence legislation or practices to foster its objectives.

Price escalation: The process by which the lengthening of distribution channels increases a product's price by more than the direct added costs, such as transportation, insurance, and tariffs.

Prior informed consent (PIC): The concept of requiring each exporter of a banned or restricted chemical to obtain, through the home-country government, the expressed consent of the importing country to receive the banned or restricted substance.

Privatization: Selling of government-owned assets to private individuals or companies.

Product division: An organizational structure in which different foreign operations report to different product groups at headquarters.

Product life cycle (PLC) theory: The theory that certain kinds of products go through a cycle consisting of four stages (introduction, growth, maturity, and decline) and that the location of production will shift internationally depending on the stage of the cycle.

Production switching: The movement of production from one country to another in response to changes in cost.

Promotion: The process of presenting messages intended to help sell a product or service.

Protectionism: Governmental restrictions on imports and occasionally on exports that frequently give direct or indirect subsidies to industries to enable them to compete with foreign production either at home or abroad.

Pull: A promotion strategy that sells consumers before they reach the point of purchase, usually by relying on mass media.

Purchasing power: What a sum of money actually can buy.

Purchasing-power parity (PPP): A theory that explains exchange rate changes as being based on differences in price levels in different countries.

Push: A promotion strategy that involves direct selling techniques.

Quality: Meeting or exceeding the expectations of a customer.

Quantity controls: Government limitations on the amount of foreign currency that can be used for specific purposes.

Quota: A limit on the quantitative amount of a product allowed to be imported into or exported out of a country in a year.

Quota system: A commodity agreement whereby producing and/or consuming countries divide total output and sales in order to stabilize the price of a particular product.

Rationalization: *See* Rationalized production.

Rationalized production: The specialization of production by product or process in different parts of the world to take advantage of varying costs of labor, capital, and raw materials.

Reinvestment: The use of retained earnings to replace depreciated assets or to add to the existing stock of capital.

Renegotiation: A process by which international companies and governments decide on a change in terms for operations.

Repatriation: An expatriate's return to his or her home country.

Representative democracy: A type of government in which individual citizens elect representatives to make decisions governing the society.

Resource-based view of the firm: A perspective that holds that each company has a unique combination of competencies.

Return on investment (ROI): The amount of profit, sometimes measured before and sometimes after the payment of taxes, divided by the amount of investment.

Revaluation: A formal change in an exchange rate by which the foreign currency value of the reference currency rises, resulting in a strengthening of the reference currency.

Reverse culture shock: The encountering of culture shock when returning to one's own country because of having accepted what was encountered abroad.

Revocable letter of credit: A letter of credit that can be changed by any of the parties involved.

ROI: *See* Return on investment.

Royalties: Payments for the use of intangible assets abroad.

SADC: *See* Southern African Development Community.

SADCC: *See* Southern African Development Co-ordination Conference.

Sales representative (foreign): A representative that usually operates either exclusively or nonexclusively within an assigned market and on a commission basis, without assuming risk or responsibility.

Sales response function: The amount of sales created at different levels of marketing expenditures.

SDR: *See* Special Drawing Right.

Second-tier subsidiaries: Subsidiaries that report to a tax-haven subsidiary.

Secondary boycott: The boycotting of a company that does business with a company being boycotted.

Secrecy: A characteristic of an accounting system that implies that companies do not disclose much information about accounting practices; more common in Germanic countries.

Secular totalitarianism: A dictatorship not affiliated with any religious group or system of beliefs.

Service exports: International received earnings other than those derived from the exporting of tangible goods.

Service imports: International paid earnings other than those derived from the importing of tangible goods.

Services: International earnings other than those on goods sent to another country; also referred to as invisibles.

Services account: The part of a country's current account that measures travel and transportation, tourism, and fees and royalties.

Settlement: The actual payment of currency in a foreign exchange transaction.

Shipper's export declaration: A shipping document that controls exports and is used to compile trade statistics.

Sight draft: A commercial bill of exchange that requires payment to be made as soon as it is presented to the party obligated to pay.

Silent language: The wide variety of cues other than formal language by which messages can be sent.

Society: A broad grouping of people having common traditions, institutions, and collective activities and interests; the term *nation-state* is often used in international business to denote a society.

Soft budget: A financial condition in which an enterprise's excess of expenditures over earnings is compensated for by some other institution, typically a government or a state-controlled financial institution.

Soft currency: *See* Weak currency.

Sogo shosha: Japanese trading companies that import and export merchandise.

Sourcing strategy: The strategy that a company pursues in purchasing materials, components, and final products; sourcing can be from domestic and foreign locations and from inside and outside the company.

Southern African Development Community (SADC): An organization endeavoring to counter the economic influence of South Africa in the region by focusing on economic objectives, such as regional cooperation in attracting investment.

Sovereignty: Freedom from external control, especially when applied to a body politic.

Special Drawing Right (SDR): A unit of account issued to countries by the International Monetary Fund to expand their official reserves bases.

Specific tariff: A tariff (duty) assessed on a per-unit basis.

Speculation: The buying or selling of foreign currency with the prospect of great risk and high return.

Speculator: A person who takes positions in foreign exchange with the objective of earning a profit.

Spillover effects: Situations in which the marketing program in one country results in awareness of the product in other countries.

Spin-off organization: A company now operating almost independently of the parent because its activities do not fit easily with the parent's existing competencies.

Spot market: The market in which an asset is traded for immediate delivery, as opposed to a market for forward or future deliveries.

Spot exchange rate: An exchange rate quoted for immediate delivery of foreign currency, usually within two business days.

Spread: In the forward market, the difference between the spot rate and the forward rate; in the spot market, the difference between the bid (buy) and offer (sell) rates quoted by a foreign exchange trader.

Stakeholders: The collection of groups, including stockholders, employees, customers, and society at large, that a company must satisfy to survive.

Static effects of integration: The shifting of resources from inefficient to efficient companies as trade barriers fall.

Stereotype: A standardized and oversimplified mental picture of a group.

Strategic alliance: An agreement between companies that is of strategic importance to one or both companies' competitive viability.

Strategic intent: An objective that gives an organization cohesion over the long term while it builds global competitive viability.

Strategic plan: A long-term plan involving major commitments.

Strategy: The means companies select to achieve their objectives.

Subsidiary: A foreign operation that is legally separate from the parent company, even if wholly owned by it.

Subsidies: Direct or indirect financial assistance from governments to companies, making them more competitive.

Supply chain: The coordination of materials, information, and funds from the initial raw material supplier to the ultimate customer.

Swap: A simultaneous spot and forward foreign exchange transaction.

Syndication: Cooperation by a lead bank and several other banks to make a large loan to a public or private organization.

Tariff: A governmental tax levied on goods, usually imports, shipped internationally; the most common type of trade control.

Tax credit: A dollar-for-dollar reduction of tax liability that must coincide with the recognition of income.

Tax deferral: Income is not taxed until it is remitted to the parent company as a dividend.

Tax treaty: A treaty between two countries that generally results in the reciprocal reduction on dividend withholding taxes and the exemption of taxes or royalties and sometimes interest payments.

Tax-haven countries: Countries with low income taxes or no taxes on foreign-source income.

Tax-haven subsidiary: A subsidiary of a company established in a tax-haven country for the purpose of minimizing income tax.

Technology: The means employed to produce goods or services.

Technology absorbing capacity: The ability of the recipient to work effectively with technology, particularly in relation to the need for training and equity in the recipient in order to effect a transfer.

Temporal method: A method of translating foreign currency financial statements used when the functional currency is that of the parent company.

Terms currency: Exchange rates are quoted as the number of units of the terms currency per base currency.

Terms of trade: The quantity of imports that can be bought by a given quantity of a country's exports.

Theocratic law system: A legal system based on religious precepts.

Theocratic totalitarianism: A dictatorship led by a religious group.

Theory of country size: The theory that holds that countries with large areas are more apt to have varied climates and natural resources, and therefore, generally are more nearly self-sufficient than smaller countries.

Theory of obsolescing bargain: The erosion of bargaining strength from a group as countries gain assets from them.

Third-country nationals: Expatriate employees who are neither citizens of the country in which they are working nor citizens of the country where the company is headquartered.

Tie-in provisions: Stipulations in licensing that require the licensee to purchase or sell products from/to the licensor.

Time draft: A commercial bill of exchange calling for payment to be made at some time after delivery.

TNC: *See* Transnational company.

Total quality management (TQM): The process that a company uses to achieve quality, where the goal is elimination of all defects.

Totalitarianism: A political system characterized by the absence of widespread participation in decision making.

TQM: *See* Total quality management.

Trade creation: Production shifts to more efficient producers for reasons of comparative advantage, allowing consumers access to more goods at a lower price than would have been possible without integration.

Trade diversion: A situation in which exports shift to a less efficient producing country because of preferential trade barriers.

Trade Related Aspects of Intellectual Property Rights (TRIPS): A provision from the Uruguay round of trade negotiations requiring countries to agree to enforce procedures under their national laws to protect intellectual property rights.

Trademark: A name or logo distinguishing a company or product.

Transaction exposure: Foreign exchange risk arising because a company has outstanding accounts receivable or accounts payable that are denominated in a foreign currency.

Transfer price: A price charged for goods or services between entities that are related to each other through stock ownership, such as between a parent and its subsidiaries or between subsidiaries owned by the same parent.

Transit tariff: A tax placed on goods passing through a country.

Translation: The restatement of foreign currency financial statements into U.S. dollars.

Translation exposure: Foreign exchange risk that occurs because the parent company must translate foreign currency financial statements into the reporting currency of the parent company.

Transnational: (1) An organization in which different capabilities and contributions among different country operations are shared and integrated; (2) multinational enterprise; (3) company owned and managed by nationals from different countries.

Transnational company (TNC): A company owned and managed by nationals in different countries; also may be synonymous with *multinational enterprises.*

Transparency: A characteristic of an accounting system that implies that companies disclose a great deal of information about accounting practices; more common in Anglo-Saxon countries (United States, United Kingdom).

Triad strategy: A strategy proposing that an MNE should have a presence in Europe, the United States, and Asia (especially Japan).

TRIPS: *See* Trade Related Aspects of Intellectual Property Rights.

Turnkey operation: An operating facility that is constructed under contract and transferred to the owner when the facility is ready to begin operations.

Underemployed: Those people who are working at less than their capacity.

Unfavorable balance of trade: An indication of a trade deficit—that is, imports are greater than exports.

Unilateral transfer: A transfer of currency from one country to another for which no goods or services are received; an example is foreign aid to a country devastated by earthquake or flood.

Unit of account: A benchmark on which to base the value of payments.

United Nations (UN): An international organization of countries formed in 1945 to promote world peace and security.

United Nations Conference on Trade and Development (UNCTAD): A UN body that has been especially active in dealing with the relationships between developing and industrialized countries with respect to trade.

Universal Copyright Convention: A multilateral agreement to protect copyrights.

Unrequited transfer: *See* Unilateral transfer.

U.S.–Canada Free Trade Agreement: *See* Canada–U.S. Free Trade Agreement.

U.S. shareholder: For U.S. tax purposes, a person or company owning at least 10 percent of the voting stock of a foreign subsidiary.

U.S. terms: The practice of using the direct quote for exchange rates.

Value-added tax (VAT): A tax that is a percentage of the value added to a product at each stage of the business process.

Value chain: The collective activities that occur as a product moves from raw materials through production to final distribution.

Variable price: A method of pricing in which buyers and sellers negotiate the price.

VAT: *See* Value-added tax.

Vertical integration: The control of the different stages as a product moves from raw materials through production to final distribution.

Virtual manufacturing: Subcontracting the manufacturing process to another firm.

Visible exports: *See* Merchandise exports.

Visible imports: *See* Merchandise imports.

Weak currency: A currency that is not fully convertible.

West African Economic Community: A regional economic group involving Benin, Burkina Faso, Côte d'Ivoire, Mali, Mauritania, Niger, and Senegal.

Western Hemisphere: Literally the earth's area between the zero and 180th meridian, but usually indicates the continents of the Americas and adjacent islands, excluding Greenland.

WIPO: *See* World Intellectual Property Organization.

World Bank: A multilateral lending institution that provides investment capital to countries.

World Intellectual Property Organization (WIPO): A multilateral agreement to protect patents.

World Trade Organization (WTO): A voluntary organization through which groups of countries negotiate trading agreements and which has authority to oversee trade disputes among countries.

WTO: *See* World Trade Organization.

Zaibatsu: Large, family-owned Japanese businesses that existed before World War II and consisted of a series of financial and manufacturing companies usually held together by a large holding company.

Zero defects: The elimination of defects, which results in the reduction of manufacturing costs and an increase in consumer satisfaction.

Zero-sum game: A situation in which one party's gain equals another party's loss.

Photo Credits

Company, Trademark, and Organization Index

Name Index

Subject Index

Multilateral development banks
(MDB), 246
Multinational enterprise (MNE)
Asian financial crisis, 84
capital linkages, 110–11
consumer protection, 308–9
country-of-origin images, 194
criticism of ethical and social
behavior of, 306–7
distribution, 195–97
and foreign direct investment
(FDI), 113, 139, 140, 142
global manufacturing and supply
chain management, 150–51,
154–56
intellectual property rights
(IPR), 252
outsourcing, 169
political risks, 241–42, 244
pricing policy, 183–84
purchasing function of, 171–72
resources and contributions
of, *140*
risk management, 231
sourcing strategies, 169–70
staffing issues, 332–36
standardization and management
decision making, 280
supplier relations, 170–71
supply chain management, 160
theory of national competitive
advantage, 108

NAFTA (North American Free Trade
Agreement), 117, 119, *120,* 121,
135, 154
National competitive advantage,
theory of, 107–9
National differences facing
operations, *21,* 73–97
cultural issues, 89–96
economic issues, 74–76, 79–84
example, Gillette as, 73–74
national cultures in supply chain
management, 166–67
political issues, 74–77
population and demographics,
85–89
National economies, types of, 82–84
National-global trade-off in key
personnel development, 290
Nations. *See specific topics*
Natural advantage, 5, 105
Natural resources, availability of, 5
Network alliance, 295
Network organization, expansion
through, 294

Network plants, 154
Network sourcing strategies, 170
New venturing, 41–42
NGOs. *See* Nongovernmental
organizations (NGOs)
Noncomparative strategies, data
collection and analysis, 271–72
Nondemocratic political system, 76–78
Noneconomic objectives and trade
restrictions, 133–34
Nongovernmental organizations
(NGOs)
criticism of ethical behavior of
multinational enterprises
(MNEs), 306–7
defined, 118
improvement in stakeholder
positions, 143
poor countries vs. World Trade
Organization (WTO), 128
as stakeholders, 127
Normativism and cultural norms,
303–4
North American Free Trade
Agreement (NAFTA), 117, 119,
120, 121, 135, 154

Objectives, intent, 27
OECD (Organization for Economic
Cooperation and Development),
120, 310–11, 316
Offset of alternative financing, *215*
Oligopolistic, 40
100 people in village population
example, *85*
One price, law of, 111
OPEC (Organization of Petroleum
Exporting Countries), 233
Open account, 214
Open economies, 11
Operating-hour restrictions and
distribution systems, 199
Operating methods, preferred, and
locational considerations,
261–62
Operational forms, *21,* 48–71
about, 50–51
collaborative arrangement
motivations, 57–62
collaborative forms, 62–66
differences in, and collaborative
difficulties, 67
example, General Motors as, 48
foreign equity arrangements, 55–57
foreign production, reasons for,
53–55
imports and exports, 51–53

management of chosen operating
form, 67–39
Operational governance, *21,* 277–97
control instruments, 292–93
decision-making location in
organization, 278–84
example, Lincoln Electric as, 277
international governance
difficulties, 295
key personnel, selection and
development of, 289–91
special governance problems,
293–95
structure of organization, 284–88
supply chain management,
operational threats in, 166
Operations, choice of location. *See*
Locational considerations
Operations, national differences
facing, *21,* 73–97
cultural issues, 89–96
economic issues, 74–76, 79–84
example, Gillette as, 73–74
national cultures in supply chain
management, 166–67
political issues, 74–77
population and demographics,
85–89
OPIC (Overseas Private Investment
Corporation), 222, 246
Opportunity, risk as, 230–31
Optimum tariff, 135
Option-based vs. salary-based
expatriate compensation, 341–42
Organization for Economic
Cooperation and Development
(OECD), *120,* 310–11, 315–16
Organization of Petroleum Exporting
Countries (OPEC), 233
Outside parties and intellectual
property rights (IPR), 252
Outsourcing, 168–69
Overcapacity in value chain
integration, 37, 38–39
Overseas Private Investment
Corporation (OPIC), 222, 246

Parallel market segments, 178
Paris Convention for the Protection
of Industrial Property, 248, 251
Partnerships
differences in, and collaborative
difficulties, 67
government establishment of,
78–79
Passive exports as production
orientation, 177

Value-to-weight ratio as product
 factor, 158
Variable pricing, 187
Vertical integration as sourcing
 strategy, 169–70
Vertical linkages as collaborative
 motivation, 60
Village population example, *85*
Voluntary migrants, 115

The Wealth of Nations (Smith),
 104–5

Web sites. *See* Internet
WHO (World Health
 Organization), 309
WIPO (World Intellectual Property
 Organization), *120,* 249, 251
World Bank, 83, 86, 119, *120*
World Development Movement, 307
World Health Organization
 (WHO), 309
World Intellectual Property
 Organization (WIPO), *120,*
 249, 251

World Trade Organization (WTO)
 careers in international business, 324
 ethical behavior, 306
 intellectual property rights
  (IPR), 251
 linkages among countries, 112,
  118, 119, *120*
 poor countries vs. NGOs, 128
 pricing policy, 184
World Wide Fund for Nature, 126
WTO. *See* World Trade Organization
 (WTO)